RETHINKING NATURE

Contemporary ideas of nature were largely shaped by schools of thought from Western cultural history and philosophy until the present-day concerns with environmental change and biodiversity conservation. There are many different ways of conceptualising nature in epistemological terms, reflecting the tensions between the polarities of humans as masters or protectors of nature and as part of or outside of nature.

The book shows how nature is today the focus of numerous debates, calling for an approach which goes beyond the merely technical or scientific. It adopts a threefold – critical, historical and cross-disciplinary – approach in order to summarise the current state of knowledge. It includes contributions informed by the humanities (especially history, literature and philosophy) and social sciences, concerned with the production and circulation of knowledge about "nature" across disciplines and across national and cultural spaces. The volume also demonstrates the ongoing reconfiguration of subject disciplines, as seen in the recent emergence of new interdisciplinary approaches and the popularity of the prefix "eco-" (e.g. ecocriticism, ecospirituality, ecosophy and ecofeminism, as well as subdivisions of ecology, including urban ecology, industrial ecology and ecosystem services). Each chapter provides a concise overview of its topic which will serve as a helpful introduction to students and a source of easy reference.

This text is also valuable reading for researchers interested in philosophy, sociology, anthropology, geography, ecology, politics and all their respective environmentalist strands.

Aurélie Choné is Associate Professor in German Cultural Studies at the Faculty of World Languages and Cultures, University of Strasbourg, France.

Isabelle Hajek is Associate Professor in Sociology at the Institute for Urbanism and Regional Development, University of Strasbourg, France.

Philippe Hamman is Professor of Sociology at the Institute for Urbanism and Regional Development, University of Strasbourg, France.

Routledge Environmental Humanities
Series editors: Iain McCalman and Libby Robin

Editorial Board

Christina Alt, St Andrews University, UK
Alison Bashford, University of Cambridge, UK
Peter Coates, University of Bristol, UK
Thom van Dooren, University of New South Wales, Australia
Georgina Endfield, University of Nottingham, UK
Jodi Frawley, University of Sydney, Australia
Andrea Gaynor, The University of Western Australia, Australia
Tom Lynch, University of Nebraska, Lincoln, USA
Jennifer Newell, American Museum of Natural History, New York, USA
Simon Pooley, Imperial College London, UK
Sandra Swart, Stellenbosch University, South Africa
Ann Waltner, University of Minnesota, USA
Paul Warde, University of East Anglia, UK
Jessica Weir, University of Western Sydney, Australia

International Advisory Board

William Beinart, University of Oxford, UK
Sarah Buie, Clark University, USA
Jane Carruthers, University of South Africa, Pretoria, South Africa
Dipesh Chakrabarty, University of Chicago, USA
Paul Holm, Trinity College, Dublin, Republic of Ireland
Shen Hou, Renmin University of China, Beijing, China
Rob Nixon, Princeton University, Princeton NJ, USA
Pauline Phemister, Institute of Advanced Studies in the Humanities, University of Edinburgh, UK

Deborah Bird Rose, University of New South Wales, Sydney, Australia
Sverker Sorlin, KTH Environmental Humanities Laboratory, Royal Institute of Technology, Stockholm, Sweden
Helmuth Trischler, Deutsches Museum, Munich and Co-Director, Rachel Carson Centre, Ludwig-Maxilimilians-Universität, Germany
Mary Evelyn Tucker, Yale University, USA
Kirsten Wehner, National Museum of Australia, Canberra, Australia

The *Routledge Environmental Humanities* series is an original and inspiring venture recognising that today's world agricultural and water crises, ocean pollution and resource depletion, global warming from greenhouse gases, urban sprawl, overpopulation, food insecurity and environmental justice are all *crises of culture*.

The reality of understanding and finding adaptive solutions to our present and future environmental challenges has shifted the epicenter of environmental studies away from an exclusively scientific and technological framework to one that depends on the human-focused disciplines and ideas of the humanities and allied social sciences.

We thus welcome book proposals from all humanities and social sciences disciplines for an inclusive and interdisciplinary series. We favour manuscripts aimed at an international readership and written in a lively and accessible style. The readership comprises scholars and students from the humanities and social sciences and thoughtful readers concerned about the human dimensions of environmental change.

RETHINKING NATURE

Challenging Disciplinary Boundaries

*Edited by Aurélie Choné, Isabelle Hajek
and Philippe Hamman*

First published 2017
by Routledge
2 Park Square, Milton Park, Abingdon, Oxon OX14 4RN

and by Routledge
711 Third Avenue, New York, NY 10017

Routledge is an imprint of the Taylor & Francis Group, an informa business

© 2017 Aurélie Choné, Isabelle Hajek and Philippe Hamman

The right of the editors to be identified as the authors of the editorial material, and of the authors for their individual chapters, has been asserted in accordance with sections 77 and 78 of the Copyright, Designs and Patents Act 1988.

All rights reserved. No part of this book may be reprinted or reproduced or utilised in any form or by any electronic, mechanical, or other means, now known or hereafter invented, including photocopying and recording, or in any information storage or retrieval system, without permission in writing from the publishers.

Trademark notice: Product or corporate names may be trademarks or registered trademarks, and are used only for identification and explanation without intent to infringe.

British Library Cataloguing-in-Publication Data
A catalogue record for this book is available from the British Library

Library of Congress Cataloging-in-Publication Data
A catalog record for this book has been requested

ISBN: 978-1-138-21492-7 (hbk)
ISBN: 978-1-138-21493-4 (pbk)
ISBN: 978-1-315-44476-5 (ebk)

Typeset in Bembo
by Apex CoVantage, LLC
Printed and bound by CPI Group (UK) Ltd, Croydon, CR0 4YY

CONTENTS

List of tables   x
List of contributors   xi
Acknowledgements   xiv

Introduction: rethinking the idea of nature   1
Aurélie Choné, Isabelle Hajek and Philippe Hamman

PART I
Values and actions   11

1 Environmental ethics: respect and responsibility   15
   Catherine Larrère

2 Ecosophy: 'How deep is your ecology'?   27
   Hicham-Stéphane Afeissa

3 Ecospirituality   38
   Aurélie Choné

4 Ecopsychology: the psyche and the environment   49
   Dennis L. Merritt

PART II
Writings and representations 63

5 The aesthetics of nature 67
 Nathalie Blanc

6 Ecocriticism 75
 Emmanuelle Peraldo

7 Epistemocritical perspectives on nature: nature in culture 83
 Laurence Dahan

PART III
Movements, activism and societies 93

8 From *Lebensreform* to political ecology 97
 Catherine Repussard

9 Ecofeminism 106
 Margot Lauwers

10 From environmental sociology to ecosociologies 114
 Graham Woodgate

11 From anthropogeography to ethnoecology: is social evolutionism also natural evolutionism? 128
 Éric Navet

PART IV
Renewed ecologies 141

12 Rethinking rural nature in the era of ecocide 145
 Owain Jones

13 Urban ecology 158
 Isabelle Hajek and Jean-Pierre Lévy

14 Nature, environment and health 166
 Lionel Charles

15 Sustainable urbanism 176
 Philippe Hamman

16 Industrial ecology: between model and metaphor:
    visions of nature in industrial ecology   187
    Nicolas Buclet

17 The ecosystem services paradigm: rise, scope and limits   195
    Roldan Muradian

PART V
Human–animal   **209**

18 Ecocide, ethnocide and civilizations: multiple ways of
    destroying life   211
    Éric Navet

19 Animal studies   221
    Roland Borgards

20 Constructing an *animal* history   232
    Éric Baratay

21 Outlook: environmental humanities   243
    Sabine Wilke

    Conclusion: how nature matters   254
    Aurélie Choné, Isabelle Hajek and Philippe Hamman

Index   *259*

TABLES

10.1	Environmental sociology's paradigm shift	115
10.2	The environment in the classical sociological canon	120
10.3	Reality as stratified, rooted and emergent	123
17.1	Tentative classification of ecosystem disservices	201
17.2	Relational models between humans and ecosystems	203
17.3	Mode of influencing social decision-making	205

CONTRIBUTORS

Hicham-Stéphane Afeissa is Professor of Philosophy at Dijon and holds a PhD in philosophy and in geosciences and environment. He is a research associate at the University of Franche-Comté.

Éric Baratay is Professor of History (history of nature and animals) at the Faculty of Letters and Civilization, University Jean Moulin, Lyon 3. As a researcher he is a member of the LARHRA (Laboratoire de Recherche Historique Rhône-Alpes, UMR 5190).

Nathalie Blanc is Research Director at the CNRS and the Director of the Laboratory LADYSS (UMR 7533 CNRS) at the University Paris Diderot-Paris 7. Her research focuses on nature in urban settings and on environmental aesthetics.

Roland Borgards is Professor in German Literature at the Institute for German Philology and Director of the Graduate School for the Humanities at the University of Würzburg, Germany. His research focuses on cultural and literary animal studies, Georg Büchner and Romanticism.

Nicolas Buclet is Full Professor in Urban Planning (sustainable development, social ecology, economics of conventions) at the Urban Planning Institute of Grenoble, University of Grenoble Alpes. As a researcher he is a member of the team 'Villes et Territoires' at the PACTE Laboratory.

Lionel Charles, a philosopher, has been working as an independent social science researcher at Fractal, a private research unit located in Paris, on different environmental topics (air quality, climate change, environmental health, risk, etc.) in an historical and epistemological perspective.

Aurélie Choné is Associate Professor in German Cultural Studies (literature and history of ideas) at the Faculty of World Languages and Cultures, University of Strasbourg, France. She holds the accreditation to supervise research in German studies and is attached to the Laboratory EA 1341 German Studies. She co-edits the journal *Recherches germaniques*.

Laurence Dahan is Professor in Comparative Literature at the Faculty of Literature and Human Sciences, University of Franche-Comté, France. She is the head of the Center for Interdisciplinary and Transcultural Studies (CRIT, EA 3224), editor in chief of the online journal *Épistémocritique* and director of the website *Épistémocritique.org* which publishes electronic books on science and literature.

Isabelle Hajek is Associate Professor in Sociology of the Environment (environmental movements and urban ecology) at the Institute for Urbanism and Regional Development, University of Strasbourg, France. She is attached to the CNRS/University of Strasbourg Laboratory SAGE (Societies, Actors and Government in Europe, UMR 7363).

Philippe Hamman is Professor of Sociology (sociology of the environment and sustainability, urban sociology) at the Institute for Urbanism and Regional Development, University of Strasbourg, France. He is the Vice Dean for Research of the Faculty of Social Science and Deputy Director of the CNRS/University of Strasbourg Laboratory SAGE (Societies, Actors and Government in Europe, UMR 7363).

Owain Jones is a Professor of Environmental Humanities in the College of Liberal Arts, Bath Spa University, UK. He is currently leading a large multiuniversity project funded by the Art and Humanities Research Council on communities, water and ecological citizenship.

Catherine Larrère is Emeritus Professor at the University of Paris 1-Panthéon-Sorbonne (Centre de Philosophie Contemporaine de la Sorbonne, ISJPS, UMR 8103). Trained in moral and political philosophy, she has been working on environmental philosophy, environmental ethics and philosophy of technology since 1992.

Margot Lauwers is Adjunct Professor in American Studies and Language (cultural studies, literature, translation and language) at the Faculty of Applied Languages at the University of Perpignan, France. Her research focuses on ecofeminism in contemporary Anglophone literature. She is attached to the CRESEM Laboratory EA 7397 and is an assistant editor of *Ecozon@: European Journal of Literature, Culture and Environment*.

Jean-Pierre Lévy is Research Director (urban and social geography, habitat and urban ecology) at the CNRS. He is a member of the Laboratory LATTS (Techniques, Territories and Societies, UMR 8134) of CNRS, Marne-la-Vallée University and Ponts ParisTech School.

Contributors **xiii**

Dennis L. Merritt has a PhD in entomology from the University of California-Berkeley and is a graduate of the C. G. Jung Institute of Analytical Psychology in Zurich, Switzerland. He is a senior analyst and instructor at the C. G. Jung Institute of Chicago.

Roldan Muradian holds a PhD in ecological economics from the Autonomous University of Barcelona, Spain. He has worked for the universities of Tilburg and Nijmegen in The Netherlands. Currently he is Visiting Professor at the Faculty of Economics of the Universidade Federal Fluminense, Rio de Janeiro, Brazil. His research investigates the interface of environmental governance and economic development.

Éric Navet is Emeritus Professor of Anthropology at the University of Strasbourg (Institute of Ethnology and Laboratory SAGE Societies, Actors and Government in Europe, UMR 7363). His fields of interest are ethnoecology, 'ways of being, thinking and acting', shamanism and ethnohistory.

Emmanuelle Peraldo is an Associate Professor in British eighteenth-century literature at the University Jean Moulin, Lyon 3, and a member of the Institut d'Études Transtextuelles et Transculturelles (IETT, EA 4186). Her current research focuses on the link between geography and literature in the early modern period.

Catherine Repussard is Senior Lecturer in German Cultural Studies (literature and history of ideas) at the Faculty of World Languages and Cultures, University of Strasbourg, France. She holds the accreditation to supervise research in German studies and is attached to the Laboratory EA 1341 German Studies. She co-edits the journal *Recherches germaniques*.

Sabine Wilke is Professor of German at the University of Washington. She is also associated with the European Studies Program and teaches courses in the environmental humanities. She directs a transatlantic research network on the environmental humanities.

Graham Woodgate is Principal Teaching Fellow in Environmental Sociology at the Institute of the Americas, University College London (UCL), UK. His current research explores 'agroecology' as a science, cultural practice and social movement. He is a member of the editorial board of *Agroecology and Sustainable Food Systems*.

ACKNOWLEDGEMENTS

The editorial team would like to thank all the authors who have agreed to contribute to this collective work, thus extending scientific discussions that have been led since 2013 within the project 'Production of Knowledge about Nature: Cross-Cutting Perspectives between the Humanities, Social Science, Literary and Cultural Studies (2013–2016)' funded by the Maison Interuniversitaire des Sciences de l'Homme – Alsace (MISHA) at the University of Strasbourg. The project, directed by Aurélie Choné, Isabelle Hajek and Philippe Hamman, has been instigated by the unit 'Societies, Actors and Government in Europe' (SAGE, UMR 7363 CNRS-University of Strasbourg), in collaboration with the research teams EA 1341 'German Studies' (University of Strasbourg) and EA 4363 'Research Institute for European Languages and Literatures' (University of Haute-Alsace).

We are grateful to our research units SAGE and 'German Studies' and to the Institut d'urbanisme et d'aménagement régional (Institute of Urbanism and Regional Development) of Strasbourg for their support.

Finally we wish to thank Stéphanie Alkofer and Jean-Yves Bart, who translated most of the texts from French into English; Tim Hardwick at Routledge, for his very constructive advice; Jane Read, who proofread the manuscript; and Carole Goetz, who has helped us with the editing.

INTRODUCTION

Rethinking the idea of nature

Aurélie Choné, Isabelle Hajek and Philippe Hamman

The prospect of humankind's destruction is nowadays focusing the attention of political and economic decision makers as well as researchers in a wide range of disciplines. Rethinking the relations between nature and culture and, beyond it, the very idea of nature, has then become unavoidable. This book is revisiting the way environmental issues can be apprehended through new epistemologies and new forms of investigation. Our intention is to put emphasis on the disciplines that are emerging when connecting ecology with different specific standpoints and to highlight the circulation of knowledge across national and cultural spaces, within the Western world and through comparisons with other cultural spaces. A widely diversified range of topics is considered in order to challenge the established relations, both in representations and social practices between nature and society. With regard to environmental issues, we want to update the conversation about nature, in bringing to the fore the interconnection of knowledge produced by a series of new fields of inquiry able to redesign the traditional theoretical frames. On the one hand, the confrontation of facts and values and, on the other, the willingness to take into account the historical processes through which human activities have transformed nature and are giving rise to renewed questionings about the relationships between nature and humankind.

The crisis of the idea of nature

This book has developed out of a double insight. First, Western societies have been founded on the divide between 'nature' and 'culture'. Gaining 'mastery over nature' appears to have been a recurring preoccupation, harking back to the words of the *Holy Bible*: 'God blessed them and said to them, "Be fruitful and increase in number; fill the earth and subdue it. Rule over the fish in the sea and the birds in the sky and over every living creature that moves on the ground"' (Genesis

1:28). On the other hand, the wide-ranging environmental changes now affecting the planet, as well as the deep-seated contradictions governing the relationship between human societies and nature, are today well-established realities, drawing all the more attention as the human origin of the changes has been revealed, raising at times particularly fierce debates. Let us take climate change and its effects, from extreme weather events to ecological catastrophes, such as droughts, heat waves, floods, hurricanes, tsunamis and so on. Whereas some so-called 'climate sceptics' argue that there is nothing unusual to today's global warming when compared with previous ages, most scientists believe that the fulfilment of humans' ambition to master nature is producing dramatic changes on a global scale, even ushering in a new era, the 'Anthropocene', in which the biosphere is shaped by human activity (Lynas, 2011), and producing an 'anthropized'/artificial nature, set within a technological society. All ecosystems have been modified, and the idea that there remain places 'untouched by man' is a myth. Furthermore – and this is now a widely shared idea – some apparent wilderness areas are actually sites of former civilisations (Dudley, 2012). The nature/culture divide, often thought to be self-evident, therefore appears not to have a universal bearing (as shown by a newly evidenced 'ecology of relations': Descola, 2013 [2005]). It rather points to the effects of a culturally situated ethnocentrism: the way in which beings and things are commonly classified is but a cultural construct, which makes it impossible to truly grasp the many relations between human beings, animals, plants and minerals. We wish to disentangle this complex network of interconnections and to peer into hidden places.

Our starting point is the widely shared idea that the concept of nature is today undergoing a 'crisis', or has even now come to its 'end' (Larrère and Larrère, 2003 [1997]; Vogel, 2015); in 1989 Bill McKibben had already argued that the survival of the globe is dependent on a radical shift in the way we relate to nature. This complex and unprecedented situation in the history of humankind, and the effects of the deconstruction of the nature/culture divide, raise a few questions: How does a new perception of everything that is unthought and overlooked in this ethnocentric opposition affect the production and the global circulation of knowledge? How can we rethink nature beyond the traditional oppositions subject/object, nature/culture, and try to understand the plurality of the relations linking humans and nonhumans (Latour, 1988)?

To tackle these questions while avoiding the twin pitfalls of relativism and essentialism, we propose to rethink the idea of nature through a double comparative angle:

- First, to recognize the limitations of strictly scientific and technical approaches to nature, which rely on the guiding principles of the Enlightenment that spread throughout Europe in the eighteenth century and granted primacy to instrumental rationality, progress and development and to emphasize the importance of the symbolic, social, cultural and political dimensions of the issues raised by human societies' relationship with nature.

- Then, to build upon the polysemy of the idea of nature, as it was developed in Western cultural histories of modernity throughout the nineteenth and twentieth centuries, to show how this idea is now redefining traditional frameworks and academic disciplines and producing new fields of inquiry and new practices.

Scholars have pointed out that ecological theories are often based on the conflict between pessimism and faith in human and scientific progress, which can often be linked to a binary opposition between Romanticism and the modern conceptions brought in by the Enlightenment, or between external nature (the phenomenal world) and the internal nature of things (the thing in itself). In that respect, the present volume precisely insists on the multilayered meanings of the concept of nature by showing that these oppositions do not always stand: their polarity can indeed help us understand that what society holds as desirable merely corresponds to a to-some-degree 'artificialized' nature (Larrère and Larrère, 2003 [1997]).

Thus, if the authors pay a great deal of attention to contemporary debates on environmental issues, this book goes beyond these considerations by including diverse approaches, which, as a counterpoint to Western perspectives founded on the nature/culture divide, examine their underlying ethical, aesthetic or spiritual principles; call on the perspectives of native peoples or social activists; explore the long-ignored animal point of view; or resort to comparative approaches, analysing North and South, in their urban and rural aspects.

In each of the chapters, the authors endeavour to break down traditional barriers and to show how Western ecological theories have been appropriated and enriched through concrete examples derived from the social world. Although pointing out the tensions that can be detected in the intellectual trajectories delineated, the authors steer clear from abstract presentations by describing examples of field research and by insisting on the processual dimension of the issues at stake, without any desire to provide a rigid framework. They can thus bring out the diverse ways in which nature is imagined and used, even at times suggesting new ways of living together. Readers are thus invited to shift their perspective and open it to other, not necessarily equivalent, visions to the future (transition, sustainability, degrowth, regrowth, etc.), leading them to understand how and why the concept of nature is still a useful one.

An ongoing reconfiguration of academic fields

We have chosen to adopt a resolutely combined mode of analysis between philosophy, literature, cultural studies and social sciences, interested in the production, transfer and circulation of knowledge about 'nature' across disciplines and across national and cultural spaces. These subjects are investigated in their temporal and spatial dimensions:

- We trace the evolution of the ways of thinking about nature throughout time, up to the emergence of current new scientific debates, showing how disciplines

- have envisioned the issues at stake and, conversely, how the issues considered have given rise to new emerging perspectives.
- Our investigation is led on an international scale in order to highlight the diversity of scientific outlooks, which are informed by cultural aspects.

The goal is to trace genealogies of thinking, hinging around considerations of ecology and environmental studies as a field of investigation and investment, and to account for the ongoing reconfiguration of disciplines, as seen in the quite recent emergence of new interdisciplinary investigations (witness the popularity of the prefix 'eco-': ecocriticism, ecofeminism, ecopsychology, ecosociology, ecosophy, ecospirituality, ecotheology, ecotourism and so on), which so far have been little studied together and in their plurality. These recent perspectives are shaping the outlines of what some in the United States and in Europe refer to as 'the environmental humanities', whose guiding principle is to integrate environmental concerns to the research subject. Online journals have been developing, such as *Resilience. A Journal of the Environmental Humanities*,[1] founded in 2012 in the United States; *Environmental Humanities*, created by scholars from Canada, Australia, the United States and Sweden;[2] or the French website devoted since 2013 to environmental humanities.[3] The term, however, does not seem to have yet acquired any univocal meaning. The journal *Environmental Humanities* suggests that much when defining its area of investigation:

> The journal publishes outstanding interdisciplinary scholarship that draws humanities disciplines into conversation with each other, and with the natural and social sciences, around significant environmental issues. [. . .] Numerous groups have formed at universities around the world during the past decade under the banner of the 'environmental', 'ecological' or 'sustainable' humanities.

Some prefer to speak of *ecological humanities*, defined by a specialized website[4] in the following way, which emphasizes the dialogue between Western and non-Western perspectives:

> The ecological humanities bring together ways of knowing and interacting with the world from the sciences and the humanities, as well as from indigenous and other 'non-Western' worldviews, nourishing the connectivities and possibilities that these dialogues produce for people and the more-than-human environment.

Basing itself on this notional malleability and the underlying interdisciplinary reconfigurations, this textbook contends that, contrary to what is sometimes said, these new formulations and theorizations do not undermine the idea of nature, but rather reassert its very validity and heuristic power. Self-conscious reflections on their own thinking allow the different contributors to go beyond the now-traditional calls for systematic, complex and integrated knowledge which have been repeatedly issued since the second half of the twentieth century.

The contributions gathered in this book, all written by renowned specialists, combine theoretical analysis with empirical examples from various thematic fields and geographic locations. Case studies go beyond national cases and connect them with international debates, covering countries and regions as diverse as the UK, the United States, Germany, France and the cultural areas of the South. The types of knowledge produced about nature, their transfer and circulation within and across disciplines, are studied in relation to the representations and uses of nature, all the while keeping in mind the actual experience of human and nonhuman beings living together in an endangered world. By combining the theoretical and empirical aspects of the topic, our aim is to reflect on the way knowledge is inextricably linked to actual cases, thus making more or less irrelevant the dualistic opposition subject/object.

We are endeavouring to study the processes of redefinition at work, at different levels:

- On the one hand, existing disciplines are seen to have evolved since the rise of environmental awareness in Western societies in the 1960s: out of the field of ethics has emerged a new one focused on environmental ethics, ecosociology has risen out of sociology, ecopsychology out of psychology, animal history out of history, ecocriticism or epistemocriticism have been formed as parts of literary studies and so on. On the other hand, interdisciplinary areas of study (ecosophy, ecospirituality, ecofeminism, political ecology, urban ecology, industrial ecology, ethnoecology, sustainability studies, etc.) have been emerging and organizing, giving rise to a new way of thinking that has been fertilizing other fields. Those two processes are neither consecutive nor exclusive, one to the other, and thus cannot be studied apart.
- A second guiding thread of the book proposes to hold in balance a focus on the individual subject (moral principles, values, etc.) and a focus on the collective body (social, political and economic issues, animals and society, Western and non-Western societies and so on).

It is indeed useful to deconstruct the notion of 'subject': the initial conflict between the Enlightenment and Romanticism can be reinterpreted as an opposition between a holist conception of the social world and the desire of the individual to emancipate from the collective body – to which can be added the deconstruction of the Western imperialist subject by postcolonial studies, in particular, postcolonial ecocriticism (Tiffin and Huggan, 2010) and cultural and literary animal studies, as well as the critique of instrumental rationality through a new emphasis laid on symbolic (ecoformation, for instance) or spiritual (ecospirituality) dimensions.

As the barriers separating academic disciplines are breaking down, so the complexity of the issues related to nature and the environment can be revealed and a critical outlook is emerging, directed at the relationship between cultures and power. Ethnoecology, ecocriticism and animal studies all focus their gaze on the apprehension of invisible 'minorities' deprived of speech politically (the native peoples as well as animals or plants, etc.). The radical break they perform thus not only consists in criticizing previous scientific approaches or disciplinary configurations, but in bringing to light heretofore unquestioned assumptions, if not a whole ideology underpinning Western hegemonic discourse, as explained by Edward Said's pioneering work in postcolonial studies (Said, 1978, 1993).

A new dialogue between literature, cultural studies and social sciences

This textbook presents itself as a coherent guide aimed as much at scholars and students looking for fine analyses as at citizens, professionals and members of associations willing to know more about the issues at stake. It distinguishes itself at various levels from the existing literature. First of all, it covers environmental humanities research specifically about 'nature', identifying various and cross-disciplinary forms of knowledge production and transfer. It not only provides specific and well-founded critiques of several concepts as an end in itself, but opens up perspectives for the circulation of environmental knowledge on a world scale, even as it founds its case on specific processes and fields in order not to remain at the level of general propositions.

Perhaps the book's most challenging and innovative feature is that it reflects *ongoing controversies and dialogue* between scientists from diverse disciplinary backgrounds and locations, who are all concerned with the environmental humanities, and brings them together in a debate for the first time to overcome national boundaries about 'nature' as a research and a practical field in order to find a different way to conduct environmental studies. We have gathered together distinguished scholars in Europe and the English-speaking world to initiate such an exchange between different perspectives at a time when some may be more developed in certain national contexts than in others and when there is now intense circulation in the international academic community. Given their complementary research traditions – the United States having a lead in reflections on environmental humanities, whereas there is a long-standing tradition of studies about nature in European social sciences and philosophy – it is particularly fruitful to engage together French/European and American scholars.

A convenient and analytical reference work, this textbook is neither an anthology nor a dictionary by definition limited to short explanatory texts – like, for instance, the recent and convincing *Keywords for Environmental Studies* (Adamson et al., 2016), which presents sixty central terms currently structuring the environmental domain. Nor is it the product of a specific disciplinary investigation or of a univocal epistemological approach attempting to combine different forms of knowledge mostly by bringing them together within a historical framework.

We have rather tried to confront different outlooks on 'nature'. This distinguishes our book from the primary existing works about 'rethinking nature' which have been published over the past decade. For example, the collective book *Second Nature. Rethinking the Natural through Politics* (Archer *et al.*, 2013) is founded throughout on an approach relying on political science. Other interesting books also clearly belong to a specific disciplinary school interested in environmental philosophy (see *Rethinking Nature. Essays in Environmental Philosophy*, edited by Foltz and Frodeman, 2004; or Hailwood, 2015), or in globalization and its mechanisms from global justice or international law to ecoterrorism, etc., for example, *The Challenges of Globalization: Rethinking Nature, Culture, and Freedom* (Hicks and Shannon, 2007). Even the recent volume *Old World and New World Perspectives in Environmental Philosophy: Transatlantic Conversations* (Drenthen and Keulartz, 2014) favours an approach based on philosophy and not really on the plurality of the relationships between the humanities and social sciences.

By the same token, the present book appears innovative when compared to several handbooks flourishing since the 2000s, such as *A Companion to Environmental Philosophy* (Jamieson, 2001), *A Companion to Environmental Geography* (Castree *et al.*, 2009) or *The Routledge Handbook of Urban Ecology* (Douglas *et al.*, 2015). Indeed, among such handbooks, some volumes, written at the turn of the twenty-first century, bear the influence of the rising field of environmental studies, for example, the *Handbook of Environmental Sociology* (Dunlap and Michelson, 2002), the *Handbook of Environmental Psychology* (Bechtel and Churchman, 2003) or the more recent *Oxford Handbook of Environmental History* (Isenberg, 2014). Other handbooks adopt cross-disciplinary perspectives, but from 2010 on they have increasingly directed their attention to the forms of public action, like *The Oxford Handbook of Climate Change* (Dryzek *et al.*, 2011), which explicitly seeks to define appropriate forms of action in the face of climate change, or *The Sage Handbook of Environmental Change* (Matthews *et al.*, 2012), or the *Handbook of Global Environmental Politics* (Dauvergne, 2012), which resorts to cross-disciplinary methods in order to link global politics and environmental change. Other subjects involving theoretical and empirical cross-disciplinary research have been the focus of various handbooks: sustainable development, for instance, has inspired the *Handbook of Sustainable Development* (Atkinson *et al.*, 2007) and the *Routledge International Handbook of Sustainable Development* (Redclift and Springett, 2015). The growing interest in ecosystem services shown by many institutions, and their implications for justice and injustice, have been analysed in *The Justices and Injustices of Ecosystem Services* (Sikor, 2014) and the *Routledge Handbook of Ecosystem Services* (Potschin *et al.*, 2016), which integrates natural/social/economic sciences. The idea of 'nature', and the circulation and new configurations of knowledge around it, have, however, not been paid a lot of attention. The *Routledge International Handbook of Social and Environmental Change* (Lockie *et al.*, 2014) draws a powerful reflection on the ways to think the co-evolution of nature/society but remains confined within the limits of certain academic disciplines (sociology, political science, geography, anthropology) to the exclusion of literary and cultural studies.

There has, admittedly, been an upsurge of interest in more clearly interdisciplinary approaches, but they often take the form of collections of essays aimed at an audience already familiar with the school of thought that is at work. Books connected to ecocriticism and environmental literary criticism are cases in point, from *The Ecocriticism Reader: Landmarks in Literary Ecology* (Glotfelty and Fromm, 1996) to the more recent *Oxford Handbook of Ecocriticism* (Garrard, 2014), with, in between these two dates, such titles as *The Green Studies Reader: From Romanticism to Ecocriticism* (Coupe, 2000), *The ISLE Reader. Ecocriticism, 1993–2003* (Branch and Slovic, 2003) or *The Cambridge Companion to Literature and the Environment* (Westling, 2013). Postcolonial environmental humanities have been presented in the same way in *Global Ecologies and the Environmental Humanities: Postcolonial Approaches* (DeLoughrey et al., 2015). As a response to this, we have chosen to favour a resolutely cross-cultural and multidisciplinary approach, taking into consideration Western and non-Western paradigms, and paying attention to the perspectives of the social sciences as well as of literary and cultural studies.

This reasoning has led us to divide the book into five 'sequences', organized around couples of complementary or contending notions, whose link it is our aim to re-examine in the light of the current social situation and the state of academic studies on the subject. First are connected together 'values and actions' (Part I), then 'writings and representations' (Part II), then, with the help of the previous analyses, the book focuses more particularly on approaches interested in social movements or located at the intersection of academic criticism and social activism (Part III) and on those that challenge contemporary ecological thought by comparing different areas – urban and rural sites, in particular – and by adopting modes of analysis situated at disciplinary or thematic crossroads. These renewed perspectives are also expressed in the field of ecological economics, which the book then dwells on (Part IV) before extending the discussion to the area of human–animal interactions (Part V).

May our readers now make this textbook their own and in their turn contribute to the conversation . . .

Notes

1 www.resiliencejournal.org/ (Accessed 27/10/2016).
2 http://environmentalhumanities.org/ (Accessed 27/10/2016) and: https://www.dukeupress.edu/environmental-humanities (Accessed 27/10/2016).
3 http://humanitesenvironnementales.fr/ (Accessed 27/10/2016).
4 www.ecologicalhumanities.org/ (Accessed 27/10/2016).

Bibliography

Adamson, Joni, Gleason, William A., and Pellow, David N. (eds.) (2016), *Keywords for Environmental Studies*, New York, New York University Press.
Archer, Crina, Ephraim, Laura, and Maxwell, Lida (eds.) (2013), *Second Nature: Rethinking the Natural Through Politics*, New York, Fordham University Press.
Atkinson, Giles, Dietz, Simon, and Neumayer, Eric (eds.) (2007), *Handbook of Sustainable Development*, Cheltenham, Edward Elgar.
Bechtel, Robert B., and Churchman, Arza (eds.) (2003), *Handbook of Environmental Psychology*, New York, Wiley-Blackwell.

Branch, Michael P., and Slovic, Scott (eds.) (2003), *The ISLE Reader: Ecocriticism, 1993–2003*, Athens, GA, University of Georgia Press.
Castree, Noel, Demeritt, David, Liverman, Diana, and Rhoads, Bruce (eds.) (2009), *A Companion to Environmental Geography*, Hoboken, NJ, Wiley-Blackwell.
Coupe, Laurence (ed.) (2000), *The Green Studies Reader: From Romanticism to Ecocriticism*, London and New York, Routledge.
Dauvergne, Peter (ed.) (2012 [2005]), *Handbook of Global Environmental Politics*, Cheltenham, Edward Elgar.
DeLoughrey, Elizabeth, Didur, Jill, and Carrigan, Anthony (eds.) (2015), *Global Ecologies and the Environmental Humanities: Postcolonial Approaches*, London and New York, Routledge.
Descola, Philippe (2005), *Par-delà nature et culture*, Paris, Gallimard, translated into English by Janet Lloyd (2013) as *Beyond Nature and Culture*, Chicago, University of Chicago Press.
Douglas, Ian, Goode, David, Houck, Mike, and Wang, Rusong (eds.) (2015 [2010]), *The Routledge Handbook of Urban Ecology*, London and New York, Routledge.
Drenthen, Martin, and Keulartz, Jozef (eds.) (2014), *Old World and New World Perspectives in Environmental Philosophy: Transatlantic Conversations*, New York, Springer.
Dryzek, John S., Norgaard, Richard B., and Schlosberg, David (eds.) (2011), *The Oxford Handbook of Climate Change and Society*, Oxford, Oxford University Press.
Dudley, Nigel (ed.) (2012), *Authenticity in Nature: Making Choices about the Naturalness of Ecosystems*, London and New York, Routledge.
Dunlap, Riley E., and Michelson, William (eds.) (2002), *Handbook of Environmental Sociology*, London, Greenwood.
Foltz, Bruce V., and Frodeman, Robert (eds.) (2004), *Rethinking Nature: Essays in Environmental Philosophy*, Bloomington and Indianapolis, Indiana University Press.
Garrard, Greg (ed.) (2014), *The Oxford Handbook of Ecocriticism*, Oxford and New York, Oxford University Press.
Glotfelty, Cheryll, and Fromm, Harold (eds.) (1996), *The Ecocriticism Reader: Landmarks in Literary Ecology*, Athens, GA, and London, University of Georgia Press.
Hailwood, Simon (2015), *Alienation and Nature in Environmental Philosophy*, Liverpool, University of Liverpool.
Hicks, Steven V., and Shannon, Daniel (eds.) (2007), *The Challenges of Globalization: Rethinking Nature, Culture, and Freedom*, Hoboken, NJ, Wiley-Blackwell.
Isenberg, Andrew C. (ed.) (2014), *The Oxford Handbook of Environmental History*, Oxford, Oxford University Press.
Jamieson, Dale (ed.) (2001), *A Companion to Environmental Philosophy*, Hoboken, NJ, Wiley-Blackwell.
Larrère, Catherine, and Larrère, Raphaël (2003 [1997]), *Du bon usage de la nature*, Paris, Flammarion.
Latour, Bruno (under the pseudonym of Jim Johnson) (1988), 'Mixing Humans With Non-Humans: Sociology of a Door-Closer', *Social Problems*, 35: 298–310.
Lockie, Stewart, Sonnenfeld, David A., and Fisher, Dana R. (eds.) (2014), *Routledge International Handbook of Social and Environmental Change*, London and New York, Routledge.
Lynas, Mark (2011), *The God Species: How the Planet Can Survive the Age of Humans*, London, Harper Collins.
Matthews, John A., Bartlein, Patrick J., Briffa, Keith R., Dawson, Alastair G., De Vernal, Anne, Denham, Tim, Fritz, Sherilyn C., and Oldfield, Frank (eds.) (2012), *The Sage Handbook of Environmental Change*, London, Sage.
McKibben, Bill (1989), *The End of Nature*, New York, Anchor.
Potschin, Marion, Haines-Young, Roy, Fish, Robert, and Turner, R. Kerry (eds.) (2016), *Routledge Handbook of Ecosystem Services*, London and New York, Routledge.

Redclift, Michael, and Springett, Delyse (eds.) (2015), *Routledge International Handbook of Sustainable Development*, New York and London, Routledge.
Said, Edward W. (1978), *Orientalism*, New York, Vintage.
Said, Edward W. (1993), *Culture and Imperialism*, New York, Knopf.
Sikor, Thomas (ed.) (2014), *The Justices and Injustices of Ecosystem Services*, London and New York, Routledge.
Tiffin, Helen, and Huggan, Graham (2010), *Postcolonial Ecocriticism: Literature, Animals, Environment*, London and New York, Routledge.
Vogel, Steven (2015), *Thinking Like a Mall: Environmental Philosophy After the End of Nature*, Cambridge, MA, MIT Press.
Westling, Louise (ed.) (2013), *The Cambridge Companion to Literature and the Environment*, New York, Cambridge University Press.

PART I
Values and actions

This first part deals with values and actions. The Western worldview that arose from modernity totally swept aside any questions having to do with the 'values' contained in the idea of nature, which incidentally explains the traditional division, from an epistemological point of view, between 'facts' and 'values', between the so-called sciences of nature and the social sciences. Yet this separation is today being challenged, mainly due to the environmental crisis, the moral debates sparked by the progress of science and technology (witness the ethical issues linked to cloning and the artificialization of nature) or the debunking of the ideology of progress and of the teleological notions associated with it (development, growth and so on). The common representations of nature, on the other hand, seem to be totally impervious to such questionings: in the popular mind, the mention of 'nature' or of something 'natural' is closely associated with value judgements, conjuring up (for instance) ideas of health, strength, peace or abundance when the words are used in advertising, etc. The representation of nature as cut off from all value judgements that was shaped by modernity does not fit the conceptions of the social world, which is rife with myths, analogies and associations. The aim of this first part is to look into these values and their relevance, as well as the dangers they may lead to: the respect of a so-called 'natural order' has been shown to lead to ecofascism, whereas the desire to master nature can give rise to an overriding sense of power, with devastating consequences on the environment. Today new attention is being paid to this long-overlooked symbolical dimension, and the ethical, philosophical, spiritual and psychological aspects are being incorporated into the handling of ecological issues, leading to evolutions in existing academic disciplines and to the emergence of new, cross-disciplinary fields of inquiry. These new academic reflections are, in turn, inextricably linked to concrete actions and to the rise of a sociopolitical movement defining essential guidelines for citizens committed to the defence of the environment; for instance, guidelines for developing an educational system based on a new paradigm.

In the first chapter, on environmental ethics, Catherine Larrère demonstrates that science and technology need to be regulated by ethics. In a much-discussed 1967 article, historian of technology Lynn White Jr. called attention to the 'historical roots of our ecologic crisis'. He located the problem in the West and argued that it lay in its relationships to technology and nature. Even though philosophers could have connected the study of these two relationships, they handled them separately: North Americans focused on relationships to nature and developed an ethics of respect towards nature; Europeans investigated relationships to technology and elaborated an ethics of responsibility regarding the consequences of our technological actions. This chapter deals with the main characteristics of these two types of ethics and shows how they reflect different cultural and historical contexts. Ultimately Catherine Larrère argues that our current environmental conditions require that we combine them both.

In the second chapter, on ecosophy, Hicham-Stéphane Afeissa explores the elaboration of deep ecology, to which Norwegian philosopher Arne Naess (1912–2009) owed most of his fame. In order to explain what makes deep ecology original, this chapter compares it with other types of approaches to environmental issues and highlights their common and diverging features. Afeissa distinguishes three main ways of tackling environmental issues: the prevalent European approach, which tends to limit itself to managing the environment and quantifying natural resources, a second one which has developed in Anglo-Saxon countries under the name of environmental ethics (see Chapter 1) and, finally, deep ecology. Unlike the advocates of environmental ethics, Arne Naess believes that environmental issues should not be tackled from a moral standpoint but from an ontological perspective: human beings must first alter the metaphysical view they hold of their place in nature before their attitudes to the natural environment may evolve. Naess connects the protection of nature with self-fulfilment. This idea of self-realization is also central to ecospirituality and ecopsychology.

Aurélie Choné then argues that the common interest of the wide range of discourses that are gathered under the umbrella term of 'ecospirituality' (Chapter 3) is in showing that the current ecological crisis is an essentially spiritual crisis of values, so that answers to it should not be merely technological or material, but should be sought on a spiritual level, through an enlightened reflection on the meaning of life, the Other, the sacred. This chapter aims at better understanding the values and actions of the proponents of ecospirituality, as well as the reasons, implications and limitations of drawing a connection between ecology and spirituality. It investigates how and to what extent ecology and spirituality have been getting closer to each other since the 1980s in Europe and elsewhere in the world, through fertile intellectual exchanges (in religious circles, including new religious movements, as well as in academic circles) and through various social practices on local or global, individual or collective scales. The existential commitment entailed by such practices includes a therapeutic dimension, because healing oneself and healing the planet are considered indissociable one from the other; the links between ecospirituality and ecopsychology are strong: both can be described as examples of 'inner ecology', be it an ecology of the mind or of the psyche.

As Dennis L Merritt explains (Chapter 4), ecopsychology emerged as a new field in the mid-1990s. It can be understood as a belated response by the psychological community to the environmental crisis. It explores how our attitudes, values, perceptions and behaviour affect the environment. Religious, cultural, economic, scientific and political systems are studied for their role in generating the environmentally dysfunctional Western worldview now dominating the planet. Ecopsychology offers a radical challenge to the prevailing capitalist and corporate system based on profit, short-term gains and perpetual growth, with the environment regarded as a free resource base and waste depository. The ecology of psychology is based on the interconnectedness of interrelationships and internal relationships, the emergence and evolution of complex systems and humans as an integral part of nature experiencing its great cycles. Merritt shows that ecotherapy uses the principles of ecopsychology and incorporates nature within a therapeutic framework. The challenge is to keep the field open and interdisciplinary as it employs scientific research procedures while honouring the spiritual and transpersonal dimensions of the human experience beyond the scientific parameters.

Bibliography

White, Lynn Jr. (1967), 'The Historical Roots of Our Ecologic Crisis', *Science*, 155 (3767): 1203–1207.

1
ENVIRONMENTAL ETHICS
Respect and responsibility

Catherine Larrère

The damaging consequences of human intervention in nature – depletion of natural resources; pollution of soil, air and water; extinction of species; erosion of biodiversity; greenhouse effect; climate change; disruption of biogeophysical cycles – have worsened and become particularly sensitive issues in the second half of the twentieth century, attracting the attention of scholars, public authorities and ordinary citizens alike. These problems have been debated in various fields, and ethics is no exception. The idea is that there are good and bad ways to behave in our environment – the world in which we find ourselves, which we haven't made but alter constantly. Science and technology are ways of transforming the world, but these changes need to be regulated by ethics.

In a much-discussed 1967 article, historian of technology Lynn White Jr. called attention to the 'historical roots of our ecological crisis'. Noting that damage to the natural environment was mostly the result of the spectacular technological development that occurred in the modern era of the West, he sought to identify the roots of this unprecedented expansion. He traced them back to the biblical heritage of Christian civilization: as it claims humankind was created in God's image, the narrative of Genesis set humans apart from the rest of nature, which is perceived as merely a thing created to be at their disposal, to be used however they see fit. White explained that Northern European populations began doing just that in the Middle Ages by adopting agrarian practices that had a lasting impact on human relationships to nature: humans ceased to be part of nature and instead exploited nature to subdue and dominate it – a response to God's call to Adam.

Lynn White Jr. thus located the problem in the West and argued that it lay in relationships with technology and nature. Even though philosophers could have connected the study of these two relationships, they handled them separately: North Americans focused on relationships to nature and developed an ethic of respect towards nature; Europeans investigated relationships to technology and elaborated an ethic of responsibility regarding the consequences of our technological actions.

In the following I present the main characteristics of these two ethics and show how they reflect different cultural and historical contexts. Ultimately I argue that our current environmental conditions require that we combine these two ethics.

The ethic of respect

In the 1970s, philosophical reflection on the ethical dimension of our relationships to nature developed in Anglophone countries (particularly in the former British colonies) around two landmark papers: 'Is There a Need for a New, an Environmental Ethic'? by Australian philosopher Richard Routley (1973), and 'Is There an Ecological Ethics'? by US philosopher Holmes Rolston III (1975). In both cases, the environmental ethic (which was the name they picked) was not only going to be an ethic for the environment (applying schemes borrowed from existing moral theories to the specialized area of environmental questions), but a genuine ethic *of* the environment – determining humanity's place in nature and its resulting duties. Crucially, nature was not only the object of our technological prowess; it also required our moral consideration, which meant redefining humankind's relationship to nature morally (Light and Rolston, 2003: 1–11).

These concerns quickly coalesced into an institutionalized academic field, with peer-reviewed journals, associations, workshops and meetings making environmental ethics a recognized discipline. Yet environmental ethics also fit within a much older intellectual school of thought on conservation dating back at least to the nineteenth century, bringing together, among others, philosophers (like Henry David Thoreau and Ralph Waldo Emerson), activists (like John Muir, founder of the Sierra Club) and politicians (like Theodore Roosevelt) (Nash, 1967). These conservationists included forester Aldo Leopold, who, in the first half of the twentieth century, was in charge of wildlife management in various American states before his appointment at the University of Wisconsin in Madison. He combined scientific schooling, professional experience, activism and writing in his commitment to nature conservation. In *A Sand County Almanac* (1949), a book published shortly after his death that fell into a long line of writings on nature that began with Henry David Thoreau's *Walden* (1854), Leopold was the first to explicitly formulate an environmental ethic, called 'land ethic'.

In the book Leopold made the following statement:

> It is inconceivable to me that an ethical relation to land can exist without love, respect, and admiration for land, and a high regard for its value. By value, I of course mean something far broader than mere economic value; I mean value in the philosophical sense.
>
> *(Leopold, 1949: 188)*

In the 1970s, environmental ethicists began questioning the value of nature; like Leopold, they made sure to distinguish between the philosophical definition of value and the economic approach to value. The preamble to the Convention on Biological Diversity adopted in Rio de Janeiro (1992) recognizes both the 'intrinsic value of biological diversity' and the 'ecological, genetic, social, economic, scientific, educational, cultural, recreational and aesthetic values of biological diversity and its components': these are the two directions pursued by ethical reflection on the value of nature and its components.

Research on 'intrinsic value' received the most attention. The concept has roots in the moral philosophy of Immanuel Kant: everything that must be treated as an 'end in itself' (i.e. humanity and, more broadly, any being endowed with reason) has an intrinsic value. All the rest is considered a means, an instrumental value. Environmental ethicists called this position 'anthropocentric', as it only grants moral dignity to humans and disregards everything else, that is, nature, which is only seen as a set of resources. The ambition of environmental ethics is to show that natural entities have moral dignity, are 'intrinsic values' and, as such, are part of the sphere of morality.

The idea is that where there are means, there are necessarily ends too. All living organisms, from the most basic to the most complex, whether they are animals (even lacking sensitivity), plants or unicellular organisms, develop complex adaptive strategies to keep themselves alive and reproduce. There are therefore ends in nature. Any living being can be considered the functional equivalent of a set of intentional acts, as an 'end in itself'. The opposition between human beings and things, which is characteristic of anthropocentrism, is replaced by a range of teleonomic individualities which can all lay claim to being ends in themselves and therefore having an intrinsic value. This is the principle of 'biocentrism': every living individual is worthy of the same moral consideration as any other.

This applies to nature as a whole and to each of the entities that make up nature: they do not only exist as means at our disposal; they exist for themselves independently of us and deserve respect as such. Paul Taylor noted that intrinsic value is based on 'the belief that all organisms are teleological centers of life in the sense that each is a unique individual pursuing its own good in its own way' (Taylor, 1986: 100). The ethics of intrinsic value rests on a strong intuition: all living things exist and have value in and out of themselves, are irreplaceable and have dignity.

Following this reasoning, the value of nature is a moral value that cannot be confused with its price: it is beyond reach for the market, whose basic principles are the commensurability of uses and the exchangeability of all things. Based on a strict opposition between ends and means, the ethic of intrinsic value requires keeping nature free of human intervention. This makes for a particularly good match with a very old and very popular American variant of the idea of nature, the concept of wilderness (Nash, 1967). The 1964 Wilderness Act, which defines the legal framework for nature conservation in the United States, provides the following definition of the term:

> A wilderness, in contrast with those areas where man and his own works dominate the landscape, is hereby recognized as an area where the earth and

its community of life are untrammelled by man, where man himself is a visitor who does not remain.[1]

Respecting nature means leaving free rein to its spontaneity. The ethic of intrinsic value is an ethic of nonintervention, requiring multiple bans – on hunting, fishing, gathering; anything liable to threaten the freedom of wildlife.

Directly recognizing that nature exists in its own right and deserves our respect, intrinsic value quickly became a rallying cry for conservationists. Yet it only preached to a small choir: the idea of granting a moral value to nature is too at odds with the overwhelmingly anthropocentric-dominant ideas to be the subject of a broad consensus. Some philosophers like Bryan Norton have suggested a more pragmatic approach that consists of looking for common ground for action instead of making a vocal but little-heard metaphysical statement. This 'extended anthropocentrism' – also called 'weak anthropocentrism' – calls into question the distinction between intrinsic value and instrumental value, showing that the critique of anthropocentrism draws on a much too narrow conception of what is instrumental (Norton, 1991). We do not see that nature cannot simply be reduced to a set of resources ready to be consumed or destroyed. It is in our own interests to preserve the resources we find in nature. This is true for the services that it provides (e.g. pollination of plants, recycling of waste), for its scientific interest (naturalists should try to preserve the object of their work) and also for its aesthetic interest or religious interest. We wish to preserve the nature that we admire, that we love, that makes us feel we are better people. However, can this pragmatic stance, which rightly takes into account the diversity of uses of nature (which are far from all market based), escape economic reductionism? The evaluation of 'ecosystemic services' developed since the 2000s clearly shows that monetization can occur even in the absence of a market. Does Aldo Leopold's distinction between 'value in the philosophical sense' and 'economic value' still apply, then?

Although Aldo Leopold was a pioneer of the reflection on the value of nature, he did not himself propose an explicit conception of this value. To him, respecting nature is being aware of the connections that unite the living and the nonliving within the same community, which he calls 'biotic community' (roughly the equivalent of today's 'ecosystem'). He emphasizes the respect we owe to this community as such: 'A thing is right when it tends to preserve the integrity, stability and beauty of the biotic community; it is wrong when it tends otherwise'. One of the most famous essays in the *Almanac*, entitled 'Thinking like a Mountain', sheds light on the meaning of this maxim (Leopold, 1949: 114–118). In that essay Leopold is a hunter who comes to a realization on the need to save wolves upon hearing the howl of the wolf he has just shot. The wolf has a place in the biotic community that lives off the mountain; the long-term prosperity of herds and game depends on them. Aldo Leopold shows us the level where everyone's place is assigned: the mountain 'knows' that without the wolves, deer will proliferate, prevent forest regeneration and damage the slopes. Unlike biocentrism, which takes individualities into account, the ethic supported by Leopold takes the value of the whole into consideration. For that reason it is said to be 'ecocentric'. This approach is a better fit with nature conversation objectives, which do not target only individuals, but rather populations and their relationships to their shared environment: spaces rather than species.

The ecocentric ethics is not anthropocentric, as it does not only adopt the human point of view on the (potentially multiple) utility of things: in that sense it is not exposed to economic reductionism. It strives to decentre the human outlook by adopting the perspective of the whole, that of the mountain. Yet it does not see nature as separate from humanity; humans are an active part of the biotic community. Therefore, the ecocentric ethic does not support abstention; it seeks to gauge the impact of human action in the biotic community. In Leopold's words:

> I have read many definitions of what is a conservationist, and written not a few myself, but I suspect that the best one is written not with a pen, but with an axe. It is a matter of what a man thinks about while chopping, or while deciding what to chop. A conservationist is one who is humbly aware that with each stroke he is writing his signature on the face of his land.
> *(Leopold, 1949: 67, 'Axe-in-Hand')*

This definition requires complementing the ethic of respect (for nature) with an ethic of responsibility (regarding the consequences of our actions in nature). The latter approach has been a matter of special interest to European thinkers.

The ethic of responsibility

As Lynn White Jr. showed in his paper, the technological superiority of the West dates back to long before the Industrial Revolution in the Middle Ages. It lay in the ability of various European nations to harness energy from the natural resources available at the time (water and wind). Although there is no single European conception of nature (there is little in common between Germanic forests, English parks and French gardens), Europeans quickly rallied around the idea of a connection between technological mastery and social and political progress (Delort and Walter, 2001: 302) and found a collective identity in their shared vocation to control all natural resources and put them to use for humanity's greater good (Pagden, 2002). The development of an ecological consciousness requires reflecting on social history: in America this has focused on the relationship to nature – the concept of wilderness appeared in the United States (Nash, 1967) – whereas in Europe, as Ulrich Beck (1992 [1986]) showed, it consisted in the study of the 'risk society', highlighting the social impact of our technological hold on nature. Instead of redefining relationships to nature, this approach emphasizes the idea of regaining control over technological forces that got away from us in the course of their development and are now working against us instead of for our benefit.

Developed by sociologists (like Jacques Ellul, 1990 [1954]) and philosophers (including Martin Heidegger),[2] this idea of the autonomy of technology was addressed from a moral standpoint by Hans Jonas. In *The Imperative of Responsibility* (1984 [1979]), he expounded on the idea that technology has its own momentum and reproduces itself following its own dynamic: Jonas called this the 'cumulative' or 'compulsive' nature of technical progress. He argued that there are no purely technological solutions to the problems raised by technology. Such responses only reproduce a process of unintended consequences: because it is not likely that a technological remedy will resolve the entire issue, it will only trigger the recourse to even more technological intervention, whilst causing other nonintentional, noxious effects that will in turn require remedying. The unchecked 'automotive momentum' of technological development finds itself further accelerated.

This is why Jonas claimed that modern technology poses unprecedented moral problems. He explained that the moral evaluation of our technological actions depended on our ability to make a clear distinction between beneficial and harmful uses of our technological power:

> What becomes of the possibility of such a distinction when the action takes place in a context where any large-scale use of a capacity, despite the agents' straightforward intention, triggers a series of effects that closely relates to immediate and intentional 'beneficial' effects, [a] series which ultimately leads, at the end of a cumulative process, to nefarious consequences that sometimes go far beyond the objective pursued?
>
> (Jonas, 1997: 231)

This inability to make a distinction between positive and negative outcomes, between what is sought and what is obtained, calls into question the traditional idea that technology is neither good nor bad in itself and only its use can be (and, accordingly, the end accounting for that use). It requires us to redefine the concept of responsibility, by looking not only at intentions but also taking into account the unintentional, planned or unplanned consequences of our technological actions.

Having observed that through our unprecedentedly powerful technological actions we can seriously compromise human life on earth and cause irreversible damage to our environment, Hans Jonas called for a new conception of responsibility. Traditionally, responsibility concerns the attribution of a past action to an agent who is considered responsible for it, in that this person has to face its consequences or repair the harm done to others. Responsibility in that sense is ascribed after the fact and pertains to distinct actions. This worked for a technological age in which the main problems resulted from the failures of technological undertakings, for which someone had to take the blame. But it no longer applies in the age of technological power, as problems do not arise as a result of our failures, but instead of our successes – the successes we owe to our technological prowess, whose consequences are not entirely within our control. We are not only accountable for our failures; we must also face the long-term consequences of our technological agency. Hans Jonas's new concept of responsibility concerns the future as a whole. Being responsible means having to answer for what may happen to someone or something over the long term – if not for an unlimited future. Responsibility extends beyond present actions to include future generations: 'Act in such a way that the effects of your action are compatible with the permanence of truly human life on earth' (Jonas, 1984: 55 [1979]). Even if Hans Jonas's injunction is modelled on Immanuel Kant's moral imperative, he is not merely dictating an ethical principle that should be complied with regardless of the circumstances; on the contrary, he calls us to take into account the context of action: the moral quality of our actions will be judged in light of the consequences – or effects – of our action.

Hans Jonas's ethic is a call to master our mastery, to shift gears from technology (mastery of nature) to the nontechnological mastery of mastery, to ethics as a way to control 'human action'. This transition away from technology (which is only able to reproduce its own momentum) towards ethics (the only way of setting limits for action) is Jonas's signature contribution to the ethic of responsibility. In it we can easily detect elements of our current reflection on the environment. Sustainable development's concern for future generations, raising questions of intergenerational justice, relates to it. The adoption of the precautionary principle, which goes beyond the prevention of known risks to consider others that have not been proven yet but that threaten to cause 'serious and irreversible damage'[3] to the environment and human health, also bears the mark of Hans Jonas.

Although the ethic of respect for nature reflects a first stage in environmental ethics, emphasizing the preservation of threatened natural spaces, the ethics of responsibility characterizes a new age of political ecology, with a greater focus on the question of technology and risks. Yet this does not make the ethic of respect obsolete, especially if we look at it from a Leopoldian angle.

Combining responsibility and respect: an ethic of globality and diversity

The ethics of respect and the ethics of responsibility are not mutually exclusive. According to Hans Jonas, responsibility does not only involve a commitment towards future generations; it also means we have direct duties towards nature. Jonas recognized the latter's inherent dignity and argued that we must respect its integrity beyond utilitarian ends (Jonas, 1984 [1979]). He admired the United States's wilderness preservation policies for that reason: 'The Earth's most stunning natural parks and wildlife reserves – those of the United States – offer an example that is worth following' by all those who support a 'humanized' nature – that is, alienated, in his view (Jonas, 1984 [1979: 374]).

Yet must we necessarily see the ethics of respect and the ethics of responsibility as related to the two separate worlds of nature and technology? That natural spaces bear the traces of human history is no reason for us to abstain from protecting them as if they were worthless artefacts. In France, people mobilized in the 1990s to protect a pastoral landscape threatened with destruction by the construction of a highway. This was very much a human-made space, but one that contained a wealth of biodiversity and that could never have existed without the development of spontaneous natural processes. The transformation of the land does not mean that nature ends; in the words of Maurice Merleau-Ponty, its 'original productivity [. . .] continues under man's artificial creations' (1995: 169). Even when it has been transformed, a natural space does not cease being natural and for that reason deserves the respect that is owed to all living things. Yet transformation, especially when it is intentional, demands the responsibility of its authors. From that point of view, our duties towards human-made natural spaces are greater rather than smaller: responsibility is added to respect. Combining respect and responsibility is all the more necessary as we live in a globalized world, where the distinction between the natural and the artificial is increasingly difficult to make.

The globalization of environmental issues requires us to redefine the spatial and temporal scale of the ethics of respect for nature. Among environmental ethics specialists, John Baird Callicott (1989) set out to defend and illustrate the land ethic presented by Aldo Leopold in the final section of *A Sand County Almanac* (1949). He also sought to update it, which involves going *Beyond the Land Ethic* (Callicott, 1999), chiefly by shifting from the local to the global. Aldo Leopold's ethic was a local ethic of the mountain, with relatively short-term prospects: 'a range pulled down by too many deer may fail of replacement in [two or three] decades' (Leopold, 1949). Our current climate change perspective encompasses the entire planet and extends over dozens, if not hundreds, of thousands of years. Callicott argues that it is now important to move from the mountain to the Earth as a whole, to 'think like a planet', an idea on which he expounds in his latest book (Callicott, 2014). He embraces the Gaia hypothesis (which purports that the Earth is a living organism capable of self-regulation) and describes the Earth as the all-encompassing biotic community in relation to which our actions have relevance.

Globalizing environmental ethics in this manner means raising the question of anthropocentrism, whose criticism was an important feature of the ethic of intrinsic value, which had come to pit humanism against naturalism and consider humankind as outside nature and as a source of disruption. This isn't the case in Leopold's ethics, in which humans are part of the biotic community. Yet the latter doesn't take humans as a subject of specific moral concern. However, although they are, on the whole, responsible for climate change, they are also its victims and as such deserve the moral consideration that anti-anthropocentric ethics tend to deny them. John Baird Callicott's Earth ethic therefore takes into account the anthropocentric questions introduced by the ethic of responsibility: it takes into consideration the future generations and the associated intergenerational justice issues.

However, it also raises justice issues within the present generations. The globalization of environmental questions replaces humans within nature and highlights their diversity. The relationship between humans and nature, which environmental ethics consider globally, is not uniform between different societies or within each of them. The question of environmental justice arises from the observation of inequalities in the distribution of the environmental burden, also called ecological inequalities. According to Dale Jamieson, 'the poor suffer disproportionately from the environmental pollution produced by society at large' (Jamieson, 2002: 297). This is true both within countries and at the international level; the divide between developed and underdeveloped countries is a key area of concern for environmental justice (Jamieson, 2014). The principle of 'common but differentiated responsibilities', adopted in the Rio Conference and taken up in the following climate conventions, recognizes that although humanity as a whole can be considered responsible for environmental disruptions, the respective contributions of various populations and their means to face this challenge are unequal, which should be taken into consideration when responsibilities are assigned.

Human diversity is not only social and economic; it is also cultural, and this affects forms of conservation. At the international level, of the United Nations Environment Programme (UNEP) and of the largest environmental nongovernmental organizations (NGOs) (International Union for Conservation of Nature [IUCN], Greenpeace or World Wide Fund for Nature [WWF]), conservation objectives have been adopted with standards inspired by the ethics of intrinsic value and wilderness. They have, however, received criticism from anthropologists (Descola, 2013 [2005]), sociologists (Latour, 2004 [1999]), environmentalists from the South (Guha, 1998) and historians of the environment (Cronon, 1996). They have argued that both the concept of wilderness and the ethics organizing the protection of said wilderness reflected a binary, Western view of nature that has no equivalent in other conceptions of the world and other ontologies. Imposing the standards of wilderness in other parts of the world is not protecting nature; it means emptying spaces of their usual dwellers to turn them into amusement parks for Western tourists or areas for scientific fieldwork.

What is at stake here is not making a choice between humankind and nature, but seeking conciliation between Western environmental ethics and other cultural approaches to the life-world, which are often more respectful of the environment than their technological Western counterparts. The past years have witnessed the emergence of hybrid forms through which cultural communities and nations assert their environmental demands in a language that respects their traditions but is nevertheless compatible with that of Western environmental ethics. The Ecuadorian constitution recognizes nature as a subject of rights, and it is granted this status as Pacha Mama – Mother Earth – for indigenous peoples. Law scholar Marie-Angèle Hermitte explained that the rights of nature are not ends in themselves, but rather means to achieve *sumac quawsay*, the 'good life' in Quechuan, characterized by harmony between human and nonhuman communities (Hermitte, 2011: 211). This is a way out of the duality between the intrinsic and the instrumental and of the separation between humans and nature. The preamble to the Ecuadorian constitution states that the people of Ecuador celebrate 'nature, the Pacha Mama, of which we are a part and which is vital to our existence'.

Even if globalization requires a reassessment of environmental ethics, the latter, relying especially on Leopold's legacy, can still play their past critical role by highlighting the Western arrogance of the ethics of responsibility. Callicott makes a distinction between moral anthropocentrism, which he sees as fully justified in light of the current global situation, and a 'metaphysical' form of anthropocentrism: a philosophical and religious vision in which humans appear as the centre of creation, its final purpose, overshadowing all the other creatures, which were only designed for them (Callicott, 2014: 167–169).

Doesn't the hyperbolic responsibility that Hans Jonas attributes to man reflect such a metaphysical anthropocentrism? He calls his responsibility 'cosmic'. Due to the excess of its technological power and its potential catastrophic consequences, humankind finds itself playing

> [a] role that has been sometimes entrusted to [it] only by religion, that of a manager or guardian of creation. By increasing the power of human action to the point of threatening the general balance of things, technology broadens the responsibility of mankind to include the future of life on earth, as this life is now a defenseless subject of the excessive use of that power.
> (Jonas, 1997: 236)

Under this approach creation might not have been made for humans, but is increasingly made *by* humans, who take on full responsibility. A similar idea can be found in the concept of Anthropocene, which has become increasingly widespread to refer to a new geological era in which humans are the leading force shaping the Earth. Presenting humans as the 'heroes' of a geological era, as is the case of a book on the Anthropocene (Lorius and Carpentier, 2010), is perhaps slightly disproportionate. Callicott does not use the word Anthropocene, instead referring to the Gaia hypothesis as a means of emphasizing the dissymmetry between humans and the planet where they live: he explains that imagining that we are responsible for the whole planet as if it could not survive without us is extremely arrogant on our part (Callicott, 2014: 237). Gaia threatens us and we need her, but she doesn't need us; she doesn't care about us (Latour, 2015).

We must therefore worry about us humans, as well as all of the living species that are threatened alongside us. However, to fulfil this moral concern that goes beyond humanity, we must consider the diversity of local situations at the level where humans and nonhumans meet and combine in various forms of life. The now-global Earth ethic should not, for that matter, cease to be an ethic of the mountain, of the diversity of biotic communities, human communities and their relationships (Larrère and Larrère, 2015).

The ethic of conservation and the ethic of responsibility for the consequences of our technological actions thus converge towards a global ethic. Yet this global ethic should not be applied uniformly across the world: it must focus on combining the global and the local, not on channelling diversity into a single destructive globalization that disregards differences and neglects the past. Biological diversity and cultural diversity are mutually reinforcing.

Notes

1 *The Wilderness Act of 1964*, Public Law 88–577; 88th Congress, S. 4, 3 September 1964.
2 Particularly in *What Is a Thing* (1935), *The Question Concerning Technology* (1955) and *The Turning* (1956).
3 See the definition of the *principe de précaution* in the Barnier law (France, 1995): according to this precautionary principle, the 'lack of certainty, given current scientific and technical knowledge, should not hinder the adoption of effective and proportionate measures to prevent the risk of serious and irreversible damage to the environment, at an economically acceptable cost'.

Bibliography

Beck, Ulrich (1986), *Risikogesellschaft. Auf dem Weg in eine andere Moderne*, Frankfurt am Main, Suhrkamp, translated into English (1992) as *Risk Society: Towards a New Modernity*, London, Sage.
Callicott, John Baird (1989), *In Defense of the Land Ethic: Essays in Environmental Philosophy*, Albany, NY, State University of New York Press.
Callicott, John Baird (1999), *Beyond the Land Ethic: More Essays in Environmental Philosophy*, Albany, NY, State University of New York Press.
Callicott, John Baird (2014), *Thinking Like a Planet, the Land Ethic and the Earth Ethic*, New York, Oxford University Press.
Cronon, William (1996), 'The Trouble with Wilderness, or Getting Back to the Wrong Nature', *in:* Cronon, William (ed.), *Uncommon Ground: Rethinking the Human Place in Nature*, London, Norton: 69–90.
Delort, Robert, and Walter, François (2001), *Histoire de l'environnement européen*, Paris, Presses Universitaires de France.
Descola, Philippe (2005), *Par-delà nature et culture*, Paris, Gallimard, translated into English by Janet Lloyd (2013) as *Beyond Nature and Culture*, Chicago, University of Chicago Press.
Ellul, Jacques (1990 [1954]), *La technique ou l'enjeu du siècle*, Paris, Économica.
Guha, Ramachandra (1998), 'Radical American Environmentalism and Wilderness Preservation: A Third World Critique', *in:* Callicott, John Baird, and Nelson, Michael P. (eds.), *The Great New Wilderness Debate*, Athens, GA, University of Georgia Press: 231–245.
Hermitte, Marie-Angèle (2011), 'La nature, sujet de droit?', *Annales. Histoire, Sciences Sociales*, 66 (1): 173–212.
Jamieson, Dale (2002), 'Global Environmental Justice', *in:* Jamieson, Dale (ed.), *Morality's Progress*, Oxford, Clarendon Press: 296–307.
Jamieson, Dale (2014), *Reason in a Dark Time*, Oxford, Oxford University Press.
Jonas, Hans (1979), *Das Prinzip Verantwortung: Versuch einer Ethik für die technologische Zivilisation*, Frankfurt am Main, Suhrkamp, translated into English (1984) as *The Imperative of Responsibility: In Search of Ethics for the Technological Age*, Chicago, University of Chicago Press.
Jonas, Hans (1997), 'La technique moderne comme sujet de réflexion éthique', *in:* Neuberg, Marc (ed.), *La responsabilité. Questions philosophiques*, Paris, Presses Universitaires de France: 231–240.
Larrère, Catherine, and Larrère, Raphaël (2015), *Penser et agir avec la nature. Une enquête philosophique*, Paris, La Découverte.
Latour, Bruno (2004), *Politics of Nature: How to Bring the Sciences Into Democracy*, Cambridge, MA, Harvard University Press.

Latour, Bruno (2015), *Face à Gaïa, Huit conférences sur le nouveau régime climatique*, Paris, La Découverte.
Leopold, Aldo (1949), *A Sand County Almanac: And Sketches Here and There*, Oxford, Oxford University Press.
Light, Andrew, and Rolston, III Holmes (eds.) (2003), *Environmental Ethics, an Anthology*, Oxford, Blackwell.
Lorius, Claude, and Carpentier, Laurent (2010), *Voyage dans l'anthropocène, cette nouvelle ère dont nous sommes les héros*, Arles, Actes Sud.
Merleau-Ponty, Maurice (1995), *La nature. Cours au Collège de France*, Paris, Seuil.
Nash, Roderick F. (1967), *Wilderness and the American Mind*, New Haven, CT, Yale University Press.
Norton, Bryan G. (1991), *Toward Unity Among Environmentalists*, New York, Oxford University Press.
Pagden, Anthony (ed.) (2002), *The Idea of Europe: From Antiquity to the European Union*, Cambridge, Cambridge University Press.
Rolston, III Holmes (1975), 'Is There an Ecological Ethics?', *Ethics: An International Journal of Social, Political and Legal Philosophy*, 18 (2): 93–109.
Routley, Richard (1973), 'Is There a Need for a New, an Environmental, Ethic?', in: Bulgarian Organizing Committee (eds.), *Proceedings of the 15th World Congress of Philosophy*, vol. 1, Varna, Bulgaria, Sophia Press: 205–210.
Taylor, Paul W. (1986), *Respect for Nature: A Theory of Environmental Ethics*, Princeton, NJ, Princeton University Press.
Thoreau, Henry David (1854), *Walden; or, Life in the Woods*, Boston, Ticknor and Fields, available at: www.eldritchpress.org/walden5.pdf (Accessed 31/10/2016).
White, Lynn Jr. (1967), 'The Historical Roots of Our Ecological Crisis', *Science*, 155 (3767): 1203–1207.

2

ECOSOPHY

'How deep is your ecology'?

Hicham-Stéphane Afeissa

Ecosophy, or deep ecology, is to a large extent the brainchild of one man: Arne Naess (1912–2009). A well-known philosopher in Norway, where he pursued his entire intellectual career at the University of Oslo up to his retirement in the late 1960s, Arne Naess produced an extensive body of work, including some thirty books and hundreds of articles, which earned him international recognition and several honorary distinctions as an intellectual, a pacifist, a resistant during the Second World War and an environmental activist. The elaboration of deep ecology, to which Arne Naess owed most of his fame, was the crowning achievement of a long and fruitful intellectual life, during which the philosopher successively devoted himself to semantic empiricism; the philosophy of science, logic and the philosophy of communication; and the study of Greek sceptics, Spinoza, Gandhi and some other thinkers – a progression that Arne Naess would come to see as a coherent series of necessary stages leading him to the elaboration of his own sceptical philosophy, and without which the very meaning of ecosophy would be lost (Naess, 2005).

In Arne Naess's writings, 'deep ecology' refers both to a philosophy of the environment and to a sociopolitical movement defining essential guidelines for citizens committed to the defence of the environment. As a philosophy of the environment, deep ecology, as conceived of by Naess, is a demanding and complex theory, founded on a few metaphysical positions. Naess may have been one of our last metaphysicians, a philosopher who sought to revitalize metaphysics in the middle of the twentieth century by showing its relevance to environmental reflection. In order to try and explain in simple terms what makes deep ecology original, we shall look at deep ecology's approach together with other types of approaches to environmental issues and highlight their common and diverging features.

Roughly speaking, it is possible to distinguish three main approaches to environmental issues: the prevalent European approach, a second one which has developed in Anglo-Saxon countries under the name of 'environmental ethics' and, finally, deep ecology. We shall not present them following a chronological order but rather a pedagogical order; that is, we shall start with the best-known approach (the prevalent European conception) to move to that which remains to a large extent little known (or unknown) to the mainstream – deep ecology.

If we examine the general direction of the environmental policies that have been successively adopted in Europe, and more particularly in France, over the past three decades, two main stages or periods may be distinguished. The first period was characterized by hostility towards anything that seemed close to a philosophy of the environment, whereas conversely, during the second phase, new philosophical and ethical concerns have become integrated in environmental policies.

Until the mid-1990s, environmental issues were hardly ever considered from an ethical perspective; rather, it was largely thought that they should be solved through exclusively legal and political means, with the help of scientific expertise. The state of degradation of the planet seemed fully to justify the introduction of legal regulations, for instance, environmental laws or tax incentives in order to encourage people to change their consumption patterns or to prevent industrialists from dumping toxic waste in rivers, etc. To be effective, such initiatives required scientific expertise, and that is why it was deemed necessary to ask for impact studies or to call for scientists to find new, more efficient ways of recycling or burying nuclear waste, and so on. The very idea of formulating an environmental ethics, of determining humankind's duties to nature, of redefining humanity's relation to the natural environment as one of respect, more generally of elevating nature to an object worthy of moral consideration, was simply not judged relevant.

Even worse, not only was the idea considered pointless, it was even suspected of being dangerous, because it created rival subjects to humankind and went on balancing their claims one against the other, giving rise to such questions as whether what is good for humans is good for a river and which of those two 'subjects' should be privileged. Such questions, it was thought, could lead to terrifying deviations: prolife movements insisting that life as such should be respected and naturalistic conceptions believing in a natural norm to which humankind should be bound have always paved the way for the rise of fascist ideologies. According to the way the natural norm is defined, for instance, it is possible to say that homosexuality is unnatural, just like contraception or abortion. Once it is considered that life in itself should be protected, then the life of a baby seal will be thought to have the same worth as that of a human being. This is a very slippery slope indeed. The imperative, then, was to avoid dealing with environmental issues in terms of morality.

In the mid-1990s, this approach started to show its limitations, because it became increasingly difficult to consider that environmental issues only concerned politicians and experts, as if citizens had nothing to say, as if their opinions did not matter. Would they agree to the cultivation of genetically modified organisms (GMOs) in their fields? Would they accept that some plots of their land be turned into open-air laboratories? Would they consider that this is an acceptable social risk or not? After all, agrochemical products are grown on their territory and end up on their plates. Citizens have all the more reason to express themselves on the subject as scientists do not seem to be able to agree. Ecological issues concern us all and bring into play a general conception of society and of our common destiny. It is therefore impossible to deal with this type of issue in a purely technocratic way by permanently delegating expertise to others.

Since that time, risk assessment, the elaboration of rules for sustainable development and the invocation of the precautionary principle have become common practices, making it possible to devise ecologically and socially responsible ways of managing the economy by inserting a few ethical and political considerations into environmental decision-making.

It is clear that the insights gained during this second phase are much less hostile to the idea of an environmental ethics so that they certainly represent a form of progress. However, the continental approach to environmental issues remains distinct from environmental ethics on some essential matters.

In France, when considering environmental issues, the emphasis is usually laid on the responsibility people have to each other and on the potential dangers of technology (Afeissa, 2009a, 2009b, 2010, 2012). Such an approach exclusively focuses on interhuman relationships and on the consequences of people's actions for themselves or for future generations and never asks whether we do not have other types of duties or whether the binary opposition between humanity and nature should not be reconsidered. More serious still, there is no examination of the true nature of the current ecological crisis within this framework. What is exactly undergoing a crisis? The European approach tends to limit itself to account keeping, to listing and quantifying natural resources. Is it enough to raise the problem of the ecological crisis in the language of energy management, without ever wondering what are the *principles* and the *motivations* underlying our relationships with nature? The representations, the values that underpin humanity's relation to the natural environment, the way humans conceive of their place in nature – these questions are never raised.

Environmental ethics and deep ecology aim at examining the representations, values and ideas that have defined humankind's relation to nature, today and in the past. The concept of a *deep* ecology must be understood in this sense.[1]

'Shallow' ecological approaches are based on technological optimism (grounded on the idea that technological advance will ultimately solve all our problems) and on a quasi-religious faith in the efficiency of market mechanisms. They tend to see only the symptoms of environmental degradation, overlooking the underlying causes that environmental ethics and deep ecology are precisely endeavouring to track down. According to these two movements, examination of the cultural roots of the crisis cannot be reduced to merely challenging our free-market system – although this can certainly be part of the solution – simply because the origin of the crisis is considered to lie much deeper than the capitalistic production system or the consumption patterns of Western societies.

Such are the main common points between environmental ethics and deep ecology – maybe the only common points, as we are now going to show. The defining feature of environmental ethics, as the name indicates, is that it deals with environmental issues in terms of morality, and to this end it has developed what is probably the best-known concept of this field of research: the idea of the intrinsic value of natural entities. A rather extraordinary story reported by John Baird Callicott, one of the main theoreticians of environmental ethics, can help us understand what it means (Callicott, 1995). It is the story of an American biologist named Edwin P. Pister, who spent a good deal of his life trying to save from extinction a very rare species of fish (the Devil's Hole pupfish) living in small islands of water in the middle of the Armagosa Desert. The fish was threatened by agrobusiness agents pumping groundwater for irrigation. Edwin Pister went so far as bringing the case to the United States Supreme Court, and, incredible as it may seem, he won. He was regularly asked by his friends and family why he was spending so much energy to save such an insignificant fish, which, he had to recognize, had no particular utility (the Devil's Hole pupfish does not hold any particular scientific value, it is also too small to provide food, etc.). What good is it anyway? Why try to preserve it? Tired of searching for an answer, Edwin Pister finally responded with the question, 'What good are *you*?'

The question is interesting because it forces us to recognize that, should we even be good for nothing and deprived of any instrumental value, we would still regard ourselves as endowed with intrinsic value. Edwin Pister was urging his questioners to consider whether the intrinsic value they claimed for themselves could not be attributed to other parts of nature. Is it so absurd to believe that living beings have their own dignity, regardless of the usefulness they might have for us? The answer is to be found in respect, not in speculations about our own short- or long-term interests. If a thing has intrinsic value, it means that it is valuable independently of the use we might put it to. Humankind is not the measure of all things. We must learn to break with anthropocentric conceptions leading us to believe that only humans are endowed with intrinsic value while other beings only possess derivative value, derived from human beings' interests.

The distinction between intrinsic and instrumental value has been central to environmental ethics since its inception as a distinct area of study in philosophy, to the point that some authors believe that the search for intrinsic value in nature is the most fundamental quest of environmental ethics (Jamieson, 1983; Vilkka, 1995). In fact, this dichotomy is so fundamental that it is possible to create a taxonomy of rival schools of environmental ethics by reference to it, including those that consider the distinction and its various permutations to be less important than most others do. Although some environmental philosophers prefer the terms *inherent* to *intrinsic* and *worth* to *value*, the term *intrinsic value* has now become standard in the field.

The opposition between intrinsic and instrumental value is not an invention of environmental ethics; such a distinction has surfaced in various guises throughout the history of philosophy. Traditionally the opposition between instrumental value and intrinsic value has been posed in this form: How can means, or a sequence of means, relate to an end, to something that is not itself the means to another end (cf. Plato's *Republic*, Book 2, and Aristotle's *Nicomachean Ethics*, Book 1, for early discussions of the distinction)? If there are instrumental values that are means to ends, then there must be ends that have, by contrast, intrinsic value – ends that are not means to other ends but are ends in themselves. If an infinite regress of means is irrational, then the sequence of means must stop at some point – at the end in itself. This is the familiar, classic argument that Routley and Routley (1980) employed in some of the earliest papers in the field.

In environmental ethics, however, attributing intrinsic value to the entities of the natural world (or the discovery that these entities have such value) is a first step toward endowing them with moral status. This ethical regeneration of nature arose in the wake of the fierce denunciation of the anthropocentric nature of European and North American culture in a seminal article by Lynn White Jr. in 1967 published in *Science*. White attributed the contemporary environmental crisis to an anthropocentrism that, he argued, lies at the root of Christianity. In his view the triumph of Christianity over paganism was 'the greatest psychic revolution in the history of our culture' (White, 1967: 1204).

Two worlds were in conflict: on the one hand, there was the fundamentally animist world of Greco-Roman antiquity, in which people believed that all natural entities are guided by a tutelary deity or spirit, so that someone intending to intervene in the course of nature would need to gain the favour and win the graces of the presiding spirits; on the other hand, there was the monotheist world of Christianity, in which a de-deified nature could be exploited in indifference to the feelings of the now-exorcized natural spirits and demigods. This disenchanted world, reduced to a state of passive inertia, could be subjected to technoscientific manipulation in the service of humanity's interests. In the Christian cosmogony nature lost its intrinsic value and was reduced to pure instrumental value – a mere tool in the hands of human masters. From the perspective of modern neoclassical economics, nature is a pool of interchangeable raw materials for human use and consumption; if humans exhaust one natural resource, such as great whales, other resources can be substituted with no loss of value.

In contrast, a nonanthropocentric environmental ethic – the cornerstone of which is the theory of the intrinsic value of nature – is a radical departure from this representation of a human–nature relationship in which humans are first and everything else a bad last. Environmental philosophers initially seized on Aldo Leopold's *A Sand County Almanac* as a possible point of departure; in Leopold's words, 'men are only fellow-voyagers with other creatures in the odyssey of evolution', an implication he drew from the Darwinian worldview (Leopold, 1949: 109). A suitably modified theory of descent and the phylogenetic-tree image might undermine the prevailing anthropocentrism and foster greater receptivity to the possibility that some nonhuman natural entities and/or nature as a whole might have intrinsic value.

If humans are seen as members of a biotic community, co-evolved with other members, the boundaries of the ethical community might extend to encompass the entire biotic community. Indeed, some philosophers think that environmental ethics owes its uniqueness to its openness to the possibility that nonhuman beings and the abiotic components of the natural world have moral status (Goodpaster, 1978). One clear route to conceiving of such entities as objects of moral consideration is either to reveal that they have previously unnoticed intrinsic value or to confer intrinsic value on them as we might confer the right to vote on previously disenfranchised citizens. Encouraging environmental conservation and preservation as means to human prosperity and well-being would make environmental ethics a mere complication of human-to-human ethics. If environmental ethics is a distinct form of ethics, it demands taking the nonhuman environment into direct consideration because of an intrinsic value that, once acknowledged, places it beyond the realm of a mere natural resource for human exploitation. By analogy one might oppose slavery because it is economically backward; the prosperity and well-being of slave owners might be served by emancipation, but that is an argument based on criteria of efficiency or self-interest, not ethics. An ethical anti-slavery argument would require a recognition of the intrinsic human value of the slaves, not merely their instrumental value – or lack of it – to the slave masters.

An environmental ethic must first determine a defensible criterion for intrinsic value and then apply it in judging which natural beings possess intrinsic value and to what degree. A second task is the anchoring of moral obligations and human responsibility to the environment in a recognition of the intrinsic value in nature. Since the late 1970s three major approaches to these tasks have emerged in the work of Paul W. Taylor, Holmes Rolston III and John Baird Callicott.

According to Paul W. Taylor, all living individual (wild) organisms – whether they are animal, vegetable, or unicellular organisms – have intrinsic value because they are teleological centres of life (Taylor, 1981). In the effort to realize their shared goals of living, flourishing and reproducing, they have developed complex adaptive strategies that are the means in the service of their ends. Therefore a multitude of self-valuing, goal-seeking individuals exists in nature, independently of any human valuation of them. According to Taylor, the affirmation of an 'inherent worth' in the nonhuman world is sufficient to generate prescriptive or prohibitive norms that do not centre on human beings; among the first is the rule of noninterference, which prohibits the hindrance of the development and the prosperity of these life forms.

Holmes Rolston III (1994) agrees with Taylor's criterion for intrinsic value but harbours doubts that such a 'biocentric ethic' is suitable for developing measures to protect not just individual living organisms but also species and entire ecosystems, which include abiotic elements. As for species, they are the ends that individual organisms strive to attain. An organism's developmental trajectory ends in a fully developed specimen of its species, and what it reproduces are more specimens of that species. Ecosystems are the theatre of the evolutionary play and thus are productive of all the diverse forms of life, each of which has intrinsic value. Rolston describes with an abundance of detail the evolution of life on earth as it was made intelligible by Darwin while drawing attention to the formidable creativity of the evolutionary process so that it commands our respect and admiration. It is for this purpose that Rolston invites his readers to consider more carefully the scope and diversity of the living world and to ponder its wonders of organization, self-regulation and functional integration. Seen from this angle, asserting that a natural being possesses no value independently of human consciousness appears parochial and narcissistic because many such beings have long had their own genetically embedded agendas that they strive to realize.

But a natural being is itself only part of a whole; it is a member of a species that is adapted, through the evolutionary process, to the ecological niche that it inhabits. And the ecosystem that it inhabits is itself closely connected to a network of ecosystems hierarchically structured in successive levels of integration. That being so, although natural beings individually construct their intrinsic value, this value is transferable, passing successively from individual natural beings to the species, and from there to all the interrelated and hierarchically structured ecosystems in which the species functions.

John Baird Callicott (1986) follows another course. He attempts to construct an environmental ethic that is just as inclusive, but in the framework of a subjectivist theory of value that carefully distinguishes between the site that has a value and the source of all values. An ethic of anthropogenic values that views any valuation as the result of human conscience is not necessarily anthropocentric because it does not reduce all values – except the value of human beings – to the status of instrumental values. This theory joins forces with the Leopold land ethic. Callicott argues that *value* is first and foremost a verb and a noun only derivatively, and that *instrumental* and *intrinsic* are, therefore, adverbs, not adjectives. Something has value, in other words, only if it is valued by a conscious being capable of intentionality. There are two basic ways in which intentionally conscious beings value: instrumentally and intrinsically.

All conscious beings value aspects of their worlds instrumentally – as bats, for instance, value caves for the shelter they provide. But as Rolston effectively points out, all conscious beings value themselves intrinsically. By a kind of metaphorical extension, Rolston argues that even nonconscious organisms like plants value themselves intrinsically, to the extent that they vigorously compete with other plants for sunlight, water and nutrients. Therefore, Callicott argues, despite his protestations to the contrary, Rolston's outlook is also a subjectivist theory of intrinsic value. Organisms have intrinsic value because they value themselves. Human beings and perhaps some other robustly conscious animals are capable of ascribing intrinsic value not only to themselves but also to other entities. Although it is logically possible to value anything intrinsically, people normally do so only for good reasons. In addition to providing a cogent analysis of intrinsic value, part of the work of environmental philosophers, according to Callicott, is to provide people with good reasons to value the natural environment intrinsically. Leopold's *A Sand County Almanac* is perhaps the most effective effort so far to provide such reasons. More recent works, such as E. O. Wilson's *The Diversity of Life*, also do that kind of work well.

There is reason to wonder, however, whether the foregoing discussion is based on a misunderstanding. There are two possibilities:

(1) Environmental ethicists genuinely aim to guide policies by subjecting them to rational standards, in which case their failure to achieve this objective so far should encourage them to consider what it is in their way of expressing and dealing with problems that has prevented them from succeeding and how they can adapt their discursive strategy to the realities of politics; *or*
(2) The theorists of environmental ethics choose to indulge their metaphysical wrangles over the intrinsic value of natural entities in oblivion to the practical implications of their work.

This criticism was first formulated by Bryan G. Norton (1984, 2005) and was the starting point of what has become a dominant school of thought in environmental ethics: environmental pragmatism. Norton observes that the debate between anthropocentrists and nonanthropocentrists is futile insofar as the major concept of 'human interests' (or human utility), on which the whole discussion turns, is left undefined. In fact, Norton argues, satisfying human interests does not necessarily involve the irreversible destruction of the object of desire; he makes a distinction between a utility that is satisfied by the immediate consumption of natural goods and a utility that implies the conservation of the useful object, conservation being a prerequisite for the continued satisfaction of human interests. Norton insists that programmes for the protection of the environment are perfectly justifiable on the basis of a sufficiently broad and long-range interpretation of anthropocentric instrumental values – broad enough to transcend the traditional division of human values into only two categories: instrumental and intrinsic. That dichotomy, in his view, fails to express the whole range of values that human beings actually attribute to nature. Rather than force all the diverse values into the straitjacket of a binary theory of value, Norton proposes a plurality of human values situated on a continuum ranging from the consumptive and self-oriented to nonconsumptive concerns such as aesthetics and spirituality. He also explores a new type of value, 'transformative value': a nonconsumptive valuing of nature that can transform unself-critical preferences into expressions of higher ideals.

Some scholars dispute Norton's assumption that the idea of intrinsic value is politically ineffective. To the contrary, intrinsic value has become the war cry of many advocates of the protection of nature, including members of Greenpeace, the Wilderness Society and Earth First! Judging from the example of the preamble to the International Convention on Biological Diversity, the belief in the existence of intrinsic values in nature is playing an increasingly important role in the development of environmental attitudes and policies worldwide (Butler and Acott, 2007).

Like environmental ethics, deep ecology criticizes as shallow the type of ecology that only worries about pollution and resource depletion, but it radically breaks with environmental ethics when it comes to defining the (supposedly deeper) way in which environmental issues should be envisioned. According to Arne

Naess, these questions should not *initially* be viewed from the perspective of morality, but from that of metaphysics and ontology. Naess agrees with advocates of environmental ethics that the ecological crisis is linked to a crisis in moral values, but he considers it a mistake to believe that reforming moral systems can provide a solution. What should first be corrected is the metaphysical conception humans have of their place in nature, and then, should this be accomplished, by implication, their attitude toward their natural environment will have indirectly been modified.

Hence the close connections and the great distance between deep ecology and environmental ethics. At first reading, the books written by advocates of deep ecology (such as Arne Naess or his followers) will not demonstrate any break with environmental ethics because the words used are often the same: the proponents of deep ecology often speak of 'intrinsic value', 'biocentric egalitarianism', 'ecological holism', etc. They also make it a priority to fight against anthropocentrism. Yet some very significant terminological shifts indicate that what is at stake is different. To put it in a nutshell, the advocates of deep ecology do not adhere to the environmental ethics movement, first and foremost, for semantic reasons: because they disapprove of the term 'environment', to which they prefer 'milieu'. The word 'environment' refers to that which surrounds a subject still held as central, whereas the task should be precisely to try to envision humanity and nature as indistinct, to imagine a fundamental continuity between everything that is, a plane of radical immanence.

This last point is undoubtedly one of the key ideas of Arne Naess's deep ecology, summed up in the words 'milieu' or 'field of relations'. Originally, Naess claims, there is nothing but a field of relations. We are used to introducing distinctions, to unravelling the fabric of experience, by isolating 'objects' or 'subjects', 'living' or 'inert' beings and so on. And if we do admit that a relation can exist between a 'subject' and an 'object', between a 'subject' and another 'subject', between 'inert' and 'living' beings, then we usually consider that this relation is not very important, that it is accidental, contingent, because only separate entities can really be said to exist. On the contrary, Naess claims that things do not exist in isolation, but only by virtue of the relations they have with the milieu in which they are immersed. There is only one indivisible world, a network of relations and interacting processes, so that all the distinctions that may be introduced only falsify original experience.

Arne Naess gives an illuminating example to show that there is no difference between the world and the way we experience it (Naess, 1989: 57). Let us imagine that we are contemplating the sea during bad weather and thinking: 'The sea is grey'. The usual comment will be that, considered in itself, the sea is not grey: it is neither grey, nor green, nor blue, but colourless. What we call 'colour' does not exist in nature. What we refer to as 'colours' are only transverse electromagnetic waves which, when they strike the human eye, stimulate nerve fibres inside the eye and are finally recorded by the brain as specific colour sensations. It will also be added that a clear distinction must be made between what things are in themselves (the primary qualities of things) and what a subject experiences as their colour, heat, smell, etc. – their secondary qualities which do not really exist but depend on our perception.

Arne Naess considers that the exact opposite is true: the primary qualities of things (their shape, size, everything that can be calculated) are mere intellectual constructions, whereas secondary qualities really exist. Geometry does not belong to this world, but sensible qualities are real precisely because they are relational properties, developing from the encounter between a subject and an object. Naess also sets out to show that the same is true of the value judgments that are passed on things. The values are real because they are not independent from the object that is being appraised – they constitute a relational property. Relations and interacting processes define existence as such.

In what way can this type of speculation help elaborate a philosophy of the environment? If it can be shown that there is no rupture between our experience of the world and the world itself, then the harm done to the world is actually self-inflicted. Destroying the world means impoverishing our experience of the world, tearing asunder the very fabric of experience: if there are fewer things that we can experience in their diversity and multiple qualities, then our own life will shrink and wither, drawing back on itself like a snail in its shell because there will be no outside anymore. Naess connects the protection of nature and all its diverse parts with self-fulfilment, self-realization. Human beings will all the more fulfil their potentialities as nature will flourish in all its inexhaustible richness. The relational field of experiences must be extended, the relations must multiply, intersect, broaden, interconnect, which means that nature must be allowed to come into full bloom. That is how a metaphysical position effectively contributes to the determination of an environmental agenda.

Note

1 The distinction between 'deep ecology' and 'shallow ecology' was first outlined by Arne Naess in a 1973 article entitled 'The Shallow and the Deep, Long-Range Ecology Movement'. It has been universally adopted as a very convenient distinction.

Bibliography

Afeissa, Hicham-Stéphane (2009a), *Écosophies. La philosophie à l'épreuve de l'écologie*, Paris, Éditions MF.
Afeissa, Hicham-Stéphane (2009b), *Qu'est-ce que l'écologie?*, Paris, Vrin.
Afeissa, Hicham-Stéphane (2010), *La communauté des êtres de nature*, Paris, Éditions MF.
Afeissa, Hicham-Stéphane (2012), *Portraits de philosophes en écologistes*, Paris, Éditions Dehors.
Butler, William F., and Acott, Tim G. (2007), 'An Inquiry Concerning the Acceptance of Intrinsic Value Theories of Nature', *Environmental Values*, 16: 149–168.
Callicott, John Baird (1986), 'The Intrinsic Value of Nonhuman Species', *in:* Norton, Bryan G. (ed.), *The Preservation of Species: The Value of Biological Diversity*, Princeton, NJ, Princeton University Press.

Callicott, John Baird (1995), 'Intrinsic Value in Nature: A Metaethical Analysis', *Electronic Journal of Analytic Philosophy*, 3 (5), available at: http://ejap.louisiana.edu/EJAP/1995.spring/callicott.1995.spring.html (Accessed 07/06/2016).
Goodpaster, Kenneth E. (1978), 'On Being Morally Considerable', *Journal of Philosophy*, 75: 308–325.
Jamieson, Dale (1983), 'Values in Nature', *in:* Jamieson, Dale (ed.), *Morality's Progress: Essays on Humans, Other Animals and the Rest of Nature*, New York, Oxford University Press: 225–243.
Leopold, Aldo (1949), *A Sand County Almanac: And Sketches Here and There*, Oxford, Oxford University Press.
Naess, Arne (1973), 'The Shallow and Deep, Long-Range Ecology Movement: A Summary', *Inquiry*, 16 (1): 95–100.
Naess, Arne (1989), *Ecology, Community and Lifestyle: Outline of an Ecosophy*, Cambridge, Cambridge University Press.
Naess, Arne (2005), *The Selected Works of Arne Naess*, Dordrecht, Springer (10 vols.).
Norton, Bryan G. (1984), 'Environmental Ethics and Nonhuman Rights', *Environmental Ethics*, 6: 131–148.
Norton, Bryan G. (2005), 'Values in Nature: A Pluralistic Approach', *in:* Cohen, Andrew I., and Wellman, Christopher H. (eds.), *Contemporary Debates in Applied Ethics*, Oxford, Blackwell: 298–310.
Rolston, Holmes III (1994), 'Value in Nature and the Nature of Value', *in:* Attfield, Robin, and Belsey, Andrew (eds.), *Philosophy and Natural Environment*, Cambridge, Cambridge University Press: 13–30.
Routley, Richard, and Routley, Val (1980), 'Human Chauvinism and Environmental Ethics', *in:* Mannison, Don, McRobbie, Mike, and Routley, Richard (eds.), *Environmental Philosophy*, Canberra, Australian National University: 96–189.
Taylor, Paul (1981), 'The Ethics of Respect for Nature', *Environmental Ethics*, 3: 197–218.
Vilkka, Leena (1995), *The Varieties of Intrinsic Value in Nature: A Naturalistic Approach to Environmental Philosophy*, Helsinki, Hakapaino Oy.
White, Lynn Jr. (1967), 'The Historical Roots of Our Ecological Crisis', *Science*, 155 (3767): 1203–1207.
Wilson, Edward O. (1992), *The Diversity of Life*, Cambridge, MA, Belknap Press of Harvard University Press.

3
ECOSPIRITUALITY

Aurélie Choné

The concept of ecospirituality immediately suggests that there is a kinship between ecology and spirituality, that there is a spiritual dimension to ecology and that spirituality is indissociable from ecological concerns. Let us first take care to distinguish the spiritual from the religious. It is possible to pursue spirituality inside organized religion or out of any religious context, and even without having any faith in God. As it is founded on a personal inner experience, it is difficult to define it univocally, but it is generally associated with a quest for interiority, for self-knowledge, transcendence, wisdom, the sacred. Neither is there any simple definition of ecology, a notion which entered the mainstream in the 1970s in the wake of the first big natural disasters, but which in fact covers many different areas of interest (scientific ecology, political ecology, industrial ecology, etc.) which do not all take the same view of the preservation of nature. Spirituality and ecology seem to belong to two separate fields, because spirituality is linked to religious tradition, philosophical questionings or the quest for meaning, whereas ecology can be defined as a scientific discipline or a political movement (in a broad sense) fighting for the protection of the environment. Yet, since the 1980s, in North America, Europe and elsewhere, ecology and spirituality have been visibly drawing closer to each other through fertile intellectual exchanges (in religious circles, including new religious movements, as well as in academic circles) and through various social practices on local or global, individual or collective scales. This chapter aims at better understanding the values and actions of the proponents of ecospirituality, as well as the reasons, implications and limits of drawing such a connection.

The emergence and main ideas of ecospirituality

Ecospirituality emerged as an organized discourse around the 1980s in the context of a crisis of the environmental movement as well as of the great world religions. But it had been in the making for a long time, and its origins can be traced back at least to the seventeenth century and Spinoza's pantheistic philosophy (which assimilated nature and the divine), to the second half of the seventeenth century and Romantic *Naturphilosophie* and to the nineteenth century, more especially to the works of American thinker Henry David Thoreau (1854) and American philologist George Perkins Marsh (1864). In the early twentieth century, it was foreshadowed by some pioneering figures like Mahatma Gandhi, who popularized nonviolence in India or, in the German-speaking area, Rudolf Steiner, the founder of anthroposophy and the father of biodynamic agriculture (Pfeiffer, 2006 [1938]) and Swiss psychologist Carl Gustav Jung, who emphasized the links between nature and the psyche (see the chapter by Dennis L. Merritt in this book). In 1945, *Principles and Precepts of the Return to the Obvious* (*Éloge de la vie simple*) was published by French-speaking Italian poet Lanza del Vasto, a disciple of Gandhi who advocated a simple and vegetarian life based on agricultural work; in 1948, in France, he founded the Communities of the Ark, modelled on Gandhian ashrams, which flourished throughout the 1960s. At the same time, the French Jesuit priest Pierre Teilhard de Chardin promoted a synthesis between faith and evolution by revealing the spiritual dimension of cosmic evolution in such popular books as *The Phenomenon of Man* (*Le phénomène humain*, 1955).

The guiding principles of ecospirituality, though, were established in the 1970s, coming from a wide range of theoretical perspectives: scientific ecology and the Gaia hypothesis propounded in the 1970s by James Lovelock, a British specialist in atmospheric sciences; philosophy, with the 'deep ecology' put forward by Norwegian philosopher Arne Naess (1976) and the 'ethics for the technological age' promoted by German philosopher Hans Jonas (1979) – to name only these two thinkers; and finally, political ecology, a vast cultural movement fuelled by many diverse influences (feminism, third-worldism, degrowth, pacifism, nonviolence, etc.). All these ideas appeared at the same time as New Age, a movement encompassing very diverse spiritual practices and religious beliefs and favouring an eclectic approach to spirituality in the United States and in Europe. In the 1980s, the ecospiritual movement gained momentum in activist, intellectual, spiritual and religious circles. Before describing the ecologization of religion (in a broad sense) and the spiritualization of ecology – two complementary processes – I will first try, beyond the diversity of all these approaches, to outline their shared fundamental principles.

The proponents of ecospirituality do indeed come from very diverse backgrounds, but even if their approaches and motivations (scientific research, activism or intellectual debate) can be very different, they nevertheless share quite a number of essential values which stand in opposition to those of modern Western societies. They believe that Western societies are founded on materialism, the quest for economic profitability and technological progress, and that they are mostly responsible for today's environmental crisis. They generally take a critical view of the Enlightenment and instrumental rationality, which they consider the cause of the disconnection between nature and culture in Western societies. They advocate another, qualitative, global, symbolic and intuitive form of knowledge founded on a spiritual awakening. They insist on the absolute necessity of gaining environmental awareness in response to the North–South divide, unsustainable resources and increasingly frequent and violent disasters which have struck the Earth since the end of the twentieth century. According to them, the solution to the environmental crisis cannot be found within the framework of 'shallow ecology', which limits itself to managing the environment, but necessitates a radical shift, a profound inner change. When humankind understands that it is not separated from but part of nature and that its fate is linked to that of the biosphere or the cosmos (in the words of some environmentalists), to that of Creation or the Great Living One (to use religious or spiritual terms), it will invent a new way of inhabiting the Earth, its home, its *oikos*, which it will learn to respect in the deepest sense.

Whether they belong to a specific spiritual tradition or environmental sensibility, the advocates of ecospirituality call for a resacralization of our relations to nature and consider the Earth a living organism (Lovelock, 1995 [1988]). This intimate conviction, which most often springs from a real-life, personal, sometimes traumatic experience, entails respect for nature, especially for the sacred sites, but also the pursuit of practical wisdom and an ethical commitment to the protection of the environment and of the planet as a whole. This existential commitment includes a spiritual and therapeutic dimension, which could be referred to as 'inner ecology', because healing oneself and healing the planet are considered indissociable from one another – the links with ecopsychology are obvious; and it requires contemplation, but also practical and efficient thinking. Let us now dwell in more detail on the different characters and groups involved, beginning with those that can be associated one way or another with religion.

The ecologization of religion

At the heart of religious spirituality there lies the desire to connect (from the Latin *religare*, to connect, to bind, a possible root for the word 'religion') with God, the divine, a transcendent reality, the Other; ecospirituality posits that this also implies reconnecting with oneself and one's deep nature, with the surrounding people and nature and finally with the cosmos as a whole. Since the 1980s, institutionalized religions, especially the three monotheistic religions, have increasingly embraced ecology. Christianity has tried to counter the accusations of those who claim it has demonized nature and wanted to subjugate it: some thinkers (White, 1967) have indeed propounded the view that the roots of the current ecological crisis lie in Judeo-Christian tradition and its misinterpretation of Creation: 'Be fruitful and increase in number, fill the earth and subdue it' (Genesis 1:28).

In his message for the 2008 World Day of Peace, Pope Benedict XVI reasserted Christians' attachment to Creation and its preservation. Inside Christian churches, many theologians, be they Catholic, Protestant or Orthodox, are pushing for a more radical revolution of minds to counter the negative vision of nature promoted by the Old Testament; others interpret the incriminated verse of the

Bible as a divine promise rather than a commandment; still others emphasize the sacredness of the cosmos or look back to Saint Francis of Assisi, well known for his love of nature (especially animals and plants) which he considered the work of God (Boff, 2015). It is no coincidence that the town of Assisi has been hosting interreligious meetings between Buddhism, Christianity, Hinduism, Islam and Judaism since 1986, or that it was the location chosen by the World Wildlife Fund, the leading environmental organization, in 1986, for its twenty-fifth anniversary, to organize a debate between the representatives of the five great world religions about the religious foundations for the preservation of nature. The intense scrutiny of biblical texts encouraged by ecospirituality has thus been coupled with practical actions related to environmental activism. This is particularly clear in the American movement of 'ecotheology', represented, among others, by Catholic priest Thomas Berry (1914–2009) (Berry, 1988), activist Tom Hayden (Hayden, 1996) and ecumenical Protestant bishop Peter Kreitler, who co-founded the nonprofit environmental organization Earth Service, Inc., in 1990 and in 1996 the National Religious Partnership for the Environment.

According to Swiss sociologist and journalist Michel Maxime Egger, who is working for Swiss nongovernmental organization (NGO) Alliance Sud, the ecological crisis 'questions the very meaning of life and calls for man to act as a person, a being in quest of inner unity and of communion with God, others and the whole creation' (Egger, 2012: 22). Michel Egger finds in the panentheistic[1] beliefs of Eastern Christianity the spiritual path enabling humankind to go beyond Christian anthropocentrism and to rediscover God in the Creation. This spiritual journey will lead humans to overcome their selfish desires and change their way of life, henceforward preferring quality to quantity, simplicity, sharing and cooperation to competition, unbridled consumption and power. Similar calls for renewal, inner transformation and the redirection of human desires are being made by theologians and members of religious communities of the other great religions (Scheid, 2016).

The 'greening' of religion is also spurred on by Western esoteric movements. According to French historian of religions Antoine Faivre, one of the defining characteristics of Western esotericism is the belief in 'living Nature'. Esoterically oriented ecospirituality probably has philosophical roots in theosophy and pre-Romantic and Romantic philosophies of nature:

> From Paracelsus to Jakob Böhme [. . .], the aim was less to resign oneself to the state of man-creature than to extoll the creative mission of fallen but eternal *anthropos*; less to evoke a remote and immutable divinity than to acquire personal knowledge of a God that pervades Nature, that is linked to it, that acts through it in myriad ways.
>
> *(Faivre, 1996: 25)*

Naturphilosophen endeavoured to bridge the gap separating God from nature or humanity by underlining the identity between nature and the mind: they considered nature 'a living network of correspondences that need to be deciphered' (Faivre, 1996: 16–17) with the help of meditation, of an attentive, respectful and self-conscious immersion in the great Book of Nature.

Esotericism has integrated the whole of nature, visible and invisible, into its spiritual praxis and has developed very concrete practices such as divination (astrology, fortune-telling, etc.), alchemy and magic in its various guises. These different branches of Western occultism all try to grasp the hidden, occult aspects of nature through the detection of correspondences and cosmic analogies. According to Austrian esotericist Rudolf Steiner, the apprehension of nature thus rests on a true 'science of the occult' able to reveal correspondences between plants, the human body, the planets and so on. Anthroposophy is best known today for its practical applications in the field of biodynamic agriculture (Demeter certification). Theorized by Steiner in 1924, biodynamics relies on a qualitative and global approach to nature (Pfeiffer, 2006 [1938]). Biodynamic practitioners replace chemical pesticides with organic preparations (made from nettles, ferns, etc.) and pay particular attention to the cycles of the moon and the planets (as gardening calendars show).

Inside the new religious movements which have been forming a loose mystical-esoteric and New Age network since the end of the 1960s, discussions are centred around criticism of Christianity's approach to nature and the need to incorporate the insights of Eastern doctrines, in which nature and culture are not separated one from the other. The upsurge of interest in Eastern religions and practices – Buddhism, yoga and Hinduism, Taoism, feng shui, Chinese medicine, shiatsu – springs from their vision of the human as a whole, body, mind and soul. The New Age movement can be referred to as a form of 'ecologic religion', founded not on the idea of a transcendent God, exterior to nature, but on nature itself seen as a creative principle. It is a 'nature religion' or a 'mystique of nature' calling for a *unio mystica* with the divine, understood as universal cosmic energy. This syncretic and holistic religion, founded on a form of immanent transcendence, has not only been fed by Eastern doctrines, but also by earth religions and ancient, especially matriarchal, mythologies, such as the cult of Earth goddess Gaia.

The craze for pagan cults can be linked to the fascination inspired by native peoples' relation to nature, because in the West they are largely believed to have been able to preserve a symbiotic relation to nature (Barbadoro and Nattero, 2004). The Ecospirituality Foundation was thus founded in 2000 as a nonprofit organization to protect 'the various cultural heritages of native, or natural peoples and ethnic minorities around the world, in so far as they may be able to make a contribution to the experiential and spiritual heritage of the whole of Humanity'.[2] One of the first actions of the foundation, led in cooperation with the United Nations Human Rights Commission, concerned Mount Graham, the sacred mountain of the Apaches. In this context, the religions of native peoples, like shamanism or animism – which generally feature pantheistic beliefs and worship of the Earth – are attracting increasing interest among New Age circles and giving rise to new types of 'earth religions' such as neodruidism or neoshamanism.

The spiritualization of ecology

In parallel to the move toward a 'greener' religion, ecology has become increasingly 'spiritual' since the 1980s. Environmentalists are now challenging the binary opposition nature/culture and fighting against the conception of nature as an object, as a resource and against prevalent anthropocentric views. Nature is thus endowed with an intrinsic value and with rights, becoming a subject in itself. As they are inviting humans to reconnect with their nonhuman environment and to inhabit the Earth in a spirit of communion rather than opposition, it seems that quite a number of intellectuals and environmental activists are now opening ecology to a spiritual dimension.

The Gaia hypothesis, which proposes that the Earth is a living being, a vast, self-regulated, dynamic natural system, including the biosphere which makes life possible, testifies to the influence of earth religions, as is made clear by the reference to Gaia, the goddess of the Earth in Greek mythology. Several scholars have pointed out the religious purport of this theory. According to some, James Lovelock's conception of nature (which has been criticized on the scientific level) expresses a desire for a mystical reunion with Mother Earth (Primavesi, 2003). For others, the Gaia theories are close to paganism, one of its defining features being the belief in pantheism, that is, the idea of communion with nature, and the conception of the Earth as a spiritual entity (Ruse, 2013).

Ecospirituality also permeates the academic field of environmental ethics, which was born in the United States at the beginning of the 1970s and is nowadays well established (Rozzi et al., 2015). Because it grants intrinsic or moral value to nature, some have wondered whether it does not contribute to sacralizing it. Environmental ethics is in any case searching for a form of wisdom, of ecosophy, and as a lived ethics, it raises for each person the question of their intimate relationship to the world. It would thus probably be incomplete without a spiritual dimension. According to American philosopher Holmes Rolston, the sight of the Earth from space delivers an ethical imperative and can be assimilated to an epiphanic experience, an awe-inspiring revelation of a superior creative power, enveloping us and assigning to us a specific position in Creation. This revelation 'triggers a movement of inner conversion whereby, in Saint Paul's words, we "put off the old man" (the figure of a master and owner) and "put on the new man" (a protector and guardian of Creation)' (Afeissa, 2009: 19).

As distinct from environmental ethics, the 'deep ecology' promoted by Norwegian Arne Naess is a holistic and biocentric ecosophy that developed at the end of the 1970s and was particularly influenced by Spinozian ethics and Gandhi's principle of nonviolence (*ahimsa*): it posits that all species are endowed with an equal right to live and that the existence of each species is an end in itself: 'The well-being and flourishing of human and nonhuman life on Earth have value in themselves. These values are independent of the usefulness of the nonhuman world for human purposes'. Deep ecology has been studied in relation to world religions (Landis Barnhill and Gottlieb, 2001) and has even been assimilated to religion because it is founded on 'the cult of life' and 'comes to consider the biosphere as a quasi-divine entity, infinitely more elevated than any individual reality, human or nonhuman' (Ferry, 1995: 79). It has been considered a gnosis, celebrating 'self-realization' and imbued with esoteric references to the sacred (Lamb Lash, 2006), and even described as a form of ecopaganism founded on the sacralization of nature (Taylor, 2005: 191).

Nature should also become a subject, and even a legal subject, according to French philosopher Michel Serres, who considers that a universal declaration of the rights of nature is needed (Serres, 1992). The Earth needs the wisdom of man, and in the face of the collective threat of death, it is urgent for man to sign a tacit contract with all inert things and living beings (in short, with nature), based on the model of the social contract, and declare them legal subjects. Only then will it be possible to dispense justice to nature. Indeed, the Earth, bounded and vulnerable, constitutes a common horizon for all human beings: it is what unites them. This search for an unprecedented symbiotic relationship between men and the planet Earth does indeed smack of spirituality.

Ten years later, a French philosopher of science, Jean-Pierre Dupuy, observes that we are unable to think of the disaster to come and exposes the belief in optimal risk management as a delusion. Basing his ideas both on French philosopher René Girard's mimetic theory and on German philosopher Hans Jonas's ethics of responsibility, which states that only ascetic principles of life may enable humans to ward off the environmental disasters made possible by technology (Jonas, 1979), Jean-Pierre Dupuy deems it necessary for human societies to anticipate future disasters and to set limits to their behaviour coming from beyond themselves by exerting their capacity for 'self-transcendence'. The sacred – although it is repressed by our modern societies – is thus a necessary, unquestionable reference, because it lies beyond the social realm (Dupuy, 2013).

Spiritual issues do not only concern intellectual circles, but also field activists: many environmentalists thus imbue their militant practices with a spiritual dimension. For instance, Algerian-born French philosopher Pierre Rabhi engaged in biodynamic agriculture in Ardèche since the 1960s before becoming involved with the degrowth movement and creating in 2007 Colibris, an association encouraging people to change their lifestyles in various ways (food, habitation, travel, etc.) by promoting spiritual values such as 'happy sobriety' (Rabhi, 2010), sharing and mutual help. These values are also fundamental to Incredible Edible, a citizen movement coming from the north of England that has now reached a global scale and aims at 'transforming towns into giant kitchen gardens' and making them 'self-sufficient in food', particularly through neighbourhood initiatives.[3] Let us finally mention José Bové, a French politician, agricultural unionist and alterglobalization activist, whose main references are Gandhi, Lanza del Vasto, Martin Luther King and Henry David Thoreau, all key representatives of the principles of nonviolence and voluntary simplicity (Comte-Sponville et al., 2006 [2002]: 67–71).

Critical views on ecospirituality

We will finally dwell on the criticisms that such attempts at drawing together ecology and spirituality have attracted. Although the Catholic Church is convinced of the endless interdependence between humanity and nature, it has always rejected biocentrism. According to Pope John Paul II, 'placing human well-being at the centre of concern for the environment is actually the surest way of safeguarding creation; this in fact stimulates the responsibility of the individual with regard to natural resources and their judicious use' (message for the celebration of the World Day of Peace, 1 January 1999). Ten years later, Pope Benedict XVI advocates

> the adoption of a model of development based on the centrality of the human person, on the promotion and sharing of the common good, on responsibility, on a realization of our need for a changed life-style, and on prudence, the virtue which tells us what needs to be done today in view of what might happen tomorrow.

According to him, technology 'is a response to God's command to till and keep the land (*cf.* Gen 2:15)' (message for the celebration of the World Day of Peace, 1 January 2010). This is far removed indeed from deep ecology, which has always been critical of the Catholic Church's anthropocentric views.

Rationalists profoundly distrust deep ecology and ecospirituality. They point out that both dangerously move away from the spirit of the Enlightenment and scientific objectivity and risk sinking back into religious obscurantism and its attendant feelings of guilt and fear. Due to its rejection of Western instrumental modernity, ecology has often been considered the heir of Romanticism rather than of the Enlightenment, and its inextricable links with politics, religion and esotericism have been underlined. Rationalists have called its romantic ideas of communion with origins 'the illusion of a return to the state of nature' (a fantasy derived from Rousseau) and have criticized the image of a virgin and pure nature – for instance, the representations of the forest as a beautiful harmonious community that can be found in Germanic mythology or in the works of German romantic poets like Joseph von Eichendorff (1788–1857). These representations have been shown to have been hijacked by nationalist, reactionary, if not racist, ideologies (Lekan, 2004).

The deep regional and local roots of rural communities; the importance of conservative values extolling family, blood and soil; the belief in the naturality of social order, have raised suspicion because of their possible drift into xenophobia and communalism in times of identitarian closure. More generally, ecospirituality has been attacked for sliding into ecofascism and far-right ideologies. French philosopher Luc Ferry assimilated modern ecological thought, and more particularly deep ecology, to an anti-humanist doctrine 'guided by a hatred of modernity'

(Ferry, 1995: 89), which he compared to Romanticism and to the Nazi conception of nature:

> [T]he same obsession with putting an end to humanism is being asserted in at times schizophrenic fashion, to the point that one can say that some of deep ecology's roots lie in Nazism [. . .] the philosophical underpinnings of Nazi legislation often overlap with those developed by deep ecology [. . .]: in both cases, we are dealing with a same *romantic and/or sentimental* representation of the relationship between nature and culture, combined with a shared revalorization of the *primitive* state against that of (alleged) civilization.
> *(Ferry, 1995: 90–93, my italics)*

The sectarian drift of this 'ecologic-religious mysticism' has also been denounced. Starting in the 1970s, several more or less sectarian groups[4] have been constituted within the New Age movement, offering their members to engage in a wide array of practices, such as working the Earth, participating in the cult of Gaia, communicating with the spirits of plants, learning feng shui or neoshamanic rites and so on. These groups have been amply criticized for their ideological mix of esotericism, occultism and ecology. Since the 1990s, criticism has come from left-leaning environmental activists like Jutta Ditfurth[5] – who cofounded the German party *Die Grünen* – and from intellectuals who consider that such esoteric biases lead the way to 'ecofascism' (Biehl and Staudenmaier, 1995) and try to demonstrate their closeness to racist and conservative ideologies.

Conclusion

The concept of ecospirituality thus refers to a wide range of discourses, whose common interest is in showing that the current ecological crisis is an essentially spiritual crisis of values, so that answers to it should not be merely technological or material but should be sought on a spiritual level, through the foundation of an 'inner ecology' and an enlightened reflection about the meaning of life, the Other, the sacred. Whatever the forms taken by this 'greener spirituality' – ecologic Christianity, ecopagan religions or the simple need to reconnect to one's self, the others, nature and the cosmos – and by this 'spiritual ecology' – the Gaia theories, the commitment to a natural contract or deep ecology – all share the same environmental awareness founded on the sacralization of the relationships between humanity and nature and the belief in a cosmic link uniting them. Although this approach has attracted criticism among religious communities – who blame it for favouring nature over man – as well as among scientific circles – who accuse it of anti-humanism, irrationalism and obscurantism and fear its possible ideological, totalitarian or sectarian drift – it is today increasingly popular, probably due to our need, in times of globalization, secularization, environmental threats and the eclipse of social utopias, to re-enchant the world.

Notes

1 Panentheism is a semi-gnostic belief system, holding that the universe is part of God and emanates from the Creator. Michel Egger points to 'the subtle line separating pantheism (this tree *is* God) from orthodox panentheism (God is *in* this tree)' (Egger, 2012: 115).
2 Available at: www.eco-spirituality.org (Accessed 05/10/2016).
3 Available at: www.incredible-edible-todmorden.co.uk (Accessed 05/10/2016).
4 Let us mention two groups standing at opposite poles: Ecoovie is an ecologic sect and cooperative founded in 1978 by 'Piel', a Canadian who is known to unashamedly exploit his followers. On the other hand, the Findhorn Foundation is a respectable community, inspired by anthroposophy, which was created in Scotland by Peter and Eileen Caddy and Dorothy MacLean, officially registered as an association in 1972 and recognized as an NGO in 1997. The foundation presents itself on its website as 'a spiritual community, eco-village and an international centre for holistic education, helping to unfold a new human consciousness and create a positive and sustainable future' (www.findhorn.org. Accessed 05/10/2016).
5 Jutta Ditfurth levels the charge of 'ecofascism' at anthroposophy and at various other communities promoting an alternative lifestyle based on the preservation of the environment, such as the *Zentrum für experimentelle Gesellschaftsordnung* (Centre for an Experimental Social Order) founded in 1991 by German psychologist Dieter Duhm.

Bibliography

Afeissa, Hicham Stéphane (2009), *Écosophies. La philosophie à l'épreuve de l'écologie*, Paris, Éditions MF.
Barbadoro, Giancarlo, and Nattero, Rosalba (2004), *Natural Peoples and Ecospirituality*, Turin, Triskel.
Berry, Thomas (1988), *The Dream of the Earth*, San Francisco, Sierra Club.
Biehl, Janet, and Staudenmaier, Peter (1995), *Ecofascism: Lessons From the German Experience*, Edinburgh, AK Press.
Boff, Leonardo (2015), *Toward an Eco-Spirituality*, New York, Church at the Crossroad.
Comte-Sponville, André, Jacquard, Albert, Monod, Théodore, Pelt, Jean-Marie, Rabhi, Pierre, and De Souzenelle, Annick (2006 [2002]), *Écologie et spiritualité*, Paris, Albin Michel.
Del Vasto, Lanza (1945), *Éloge de la vie simple*, Paris, Denoël, translated into English (1974) as *Principles and Precepts of the Return to the Obvious*, New York, Schocken Books.
Dupuy, Jean-Pierre (2008), *La marque du sacré*, Paris, Carnets Nord, translated into English (2013) as *The Mark of the Sacred*, Stanford, CA, Stanford University Press.
Egger, Michel Maxime (2012), *La terre comme soi-même. Repères pour une écospiritualité*, Genève, Labor et Fides.
Faivre, Antoine (1996), *Philosophie de la Nature. Physique sacrée (XVIIIe–XIXe siècles)*, Paris, Albin Michel.
Ferry, Luc (1992), *Le nouvel ordre écologique. L'arbre, l'animal et l'homme*, Paris, Grasset, translated into English (1995) as *The New Ecological Order*, Chicago, University of Chicago Press.
Hayden, Tom (1996), *The Lost Gospel of the Earth*, San Francisco, Sierra Club.
Jonas, Hans (1979), *Das Prinzip Verantwortung. Versuch einer Ethik für die technologische Zivilisation*, Frankfurt am Main, Suhrkamp, translated into English (1984) as *The Imperative of Responsibility: In Search of Ethics for the Technological Age*, Chicago, University of Chicago Press.
Lamb Lash, John (2006), *Not in His Image: Gnostic Vision, Sacred Ecology, and the Future of Belief*, Vermont, Chelsea Green.

Landis Barnhill, David, and Gottlieb, Roger S. (eds.) (2001), *Deep Ecology and World Religions: New Essays on Sacred Ground*, Albany, NY, SUNY Press.
Lekan, Thomas M. (2004), *Imagining the Nation in Nature: Landscape Preservation and German Identity, 1885–1945*, Cambridge, MA, Harvard University Press.
Lovelock, James (1995 [1988]), *The Ages of Gaia: A Biography of Our Living Earth*, New York, Norton.
Marsh, George Perkins (1864), *Man and Nature, Physical Geography as Modified by Human Action*, New York, C. Scribner.
Naess, Arne (1989 [1976]), *Ecology, Community, and Lifestyle*, Cambridge, Cambridge University Press.
Pfeiffer, Ehrenfried (2006 [1938]), *Soil Fertility, Renewal and Preservation: Bio-Dynamic Farming and Gardening*, Delhi, Asiatic Publishing House.
Primavesi, Anne (2003), *Gaia's Gift: Earth, Ourselves, and God After Copernicus*, London and New York, Routledge.
Rabhi, Pierre (2010), *Vers la sobriété heureuse*, Arles, Actes Sud.
Rozzi, Ricardo, and Chapin III, F. Stuart, Callicott, John Baird, Pickett, Steward T. A., Power, Mary E., Armesto, Juan J., and May Jr., Roy H. (eds.) (2015), *Earth Stewardship: Linking Ecology and Ethics in Theory and Practice*, New York, Springer.
Ruse, Michael (2013), *The Gaia Hypothesis: Science on a Pagan Planet*, Chicago, University of Chicago Press.
Scheid, Daniel P. (2016), *The Cosmic Common Good: Religious Grounds for Ecological Ethics*, New York, Oxford University Press.
Serres, Michel (1992 [1990]), *Le contrat naturel*, Paris, Flammarion, translated into English (1995) as *The Natural Contract*, Chicago, University of Chicago Press.
Taylor, Bron (2005), 'Bioregionalism and the North American Bioregional Congress', in: Taylor, Bron (ed.), *Encyclopedia of Religion and Nature*, New York, Thoemmes Continuum, 190–192.
Teilhard de Chardin, Pierre (1955), *Le phénomène humain*, Paris, Seuil, translated into English (2008) as *The Phenomenon of Man*, New York, Harper Perennial Modern Classics.
Thoreau, Henry David (1854), *Walden, or Life in the Woods*, Boston, Ticknor and Fields, available at: www.eldritchpress.org/walden5.pdf (Accessed 05/10/2016).
White, Lynn Jr. (1967), 'The Historical Roots of Our Ecologic Crisis', *Science*, 155 (3767): 1203–1207.

4
ECOPSYCHOLOGY
The psyche and the environment

Dennis L. Merritt

Ecopsychology emerged in the 1990s as a belated response from the psychological community to the environmental crisis. It was not a psychologist but the American social historian Theodore Roszak who coined the term in 1992 and began to develop a conceptual system in his book, *The Voice of the Earth* (Roszak, 1992). This book and *Ecopsychology*, a primer Roszak co-edited, plus Deborah Du Nann Winter's *Ecological Psychology* established a framework for the field (Roszak *et al.*, 1995; Winter, 1996). Ecopsychology is at the centre of a multidisciplinary approach to radically restructure our social, economic and cultural systems in order to live ecologically and sustainably (Fisher, 2013). It examines how our values, attitudes, perceptions and behaviours affect the environment. Ecopsychology is about the movement of energy in relational processes that extends from within the psyche to social interactions and the environment. These processes occurring across all levels can be conceived of as the interactions of organisms within organisms and described mathematically. The descriptions are put into imaginal forms and psychological concepts by Swiss psychiatrist Carl Jung's holistic and syncretic system that offers an ecological perspective for exploring the relationship between psyche and the environment. Jung emphasized that everything we know comes out of or through the human psyche – mathematics, the arts, sciences, humanities, myths and religions – so psychology, the science of the psyche, the soul, is the foundation for understanding how we developed our dysfunctional relationship with the environment and what we can do to change it (Shamdasani, 2003: 15–22). Every branch of psychology has important contributions to make in this endeavour.

The mathematics of the organism and the self as the archetype of God

Ecopsychology suggests that a basic problem is that modern humans do not perceive themselves as being part of nature. Connecting people more deeply to nature is an important aspect of ecopsychology because it is seen as a means of creating a natural desire to protect the environment (Chalquist, 2010). The scientific principles of ecology and systems theory address this issue from a rational perspective. Ecology is based on the interrelationships of all elements in the environment, organic and inorganic, and cycles of change in varying time frames. The central concept is that of an organism. An organism has an irrepressible tendency at all levels of organization of any system to develop and maintain an organized whole. Humans experience these tendencies as purpose, direction and meaning (Ho, 1998: 50–52).

Quantum mechanics and the revolutionary mathematics of complexity theory, which began to emerge in the 1960s, explain the underlying dynamics of organisms. Complexity theory describes fluctuations within set parameters and the generation and evolution of complex systems, even from within relatively simple systems, when stress or energy is increased. All elements in organisms are in immediate relationship with all other elements, and no part can be separated from the whole. A mathematically described, self-organizing principle is found at all levels of organization and among activities ranging from the subatomic to the galactic. Organisms nested within larger organisms extend from the smallest to the largest of these systems. An organism is dynamic, evolving and heterogeneous. It is creative; has nonlinear, multidimensional space-time; and is participatory – the observer affects what is being observed (Ho, 1998: 52–55). When one considers that the dreaming brain functions within a symbolic realm and operates on the principles of complexity theory, we can say that humans experience the basic dynamics of the universe in a developmental, emotional, artistic, bodily and symbolic manner (Merritt, 2012b: 87–127).

The human psychic experience of the integral organism is conveyed by Jung's concept of the archetype of the Self – Jung's most ecological (relational) concept. Archetypes are recurring themes found in all cultures across all time frames, like the archetype of the hero. The Self is defined as the archetype of wholeness and totality whose processes, mathematically described as self-organizing principles, keep all aspects of the psyche in relationship, like consciousness to the unconscious, and body and instincts to spirit and mind. Relationship within the psyche is maintained through such means as symbols, dreams, bodily reactions and symptoms. The Self as the archetype of the organism is experienced in such ways as God within or as Atman (Hindu) and projected or experienced without as God, Allah and *Wakantanka* (Sioux) to name a few (Merritt, 2012a: 35–54).

An ecology of the psyche

The concept of the organism begins in humans at the intrapsychic level with an 'ecology of the psyche'. The human psyche has an innate ability to personify the elements of an inner jungle of conflicting drives, interests, memories and instincts (limited in our species) and turn them into images, metaphors, narratives and symbols. This is easily seen with the people in our dreams. Jung emphasized the importance of being in relationship to the 'little people' within – an ecological concept because of the emphasis on interrelatedness and the absence of a dominant position (Jung, 1969: 100). That which is denigrated and ignored turns against us or gets projected onto our perceived enemies, other races and religions, people of different sexual orientation, etc. Compassion for our inner people is an aspect of compassion for ourselves and makes it less likely we will demonize our opponents, a process that contributes to the polarizations now crippling our systems.

Intrapsychic dynamics also seen at the societal level include psychoanalytic descriptions of primitive responses to conflicts using violence and aggression, splitting objects into good and evil aspects and projecting the evil or idealized goodness onto others. The first challenge is to become aware of these processes and provide an analysis of them to the individual and to the culture that shapes the individual. This is done through therapy and self-reflection and commentary on our systems and art forms like film.[1] The Freudian Oedipal conflict can be described as a powerful desire to remain a child forever as the centre of love and attention where all needs are immediately gratified. Idealizations and the inability to face reality lead to a host of irrational activities in an attempt to maintain our illusions. Narcissism in the individual and in our culture is fed by advertising that drives consumerism. 'You deserve it – now!' is the mantra (Weintrobe, 2013: 146–148, 152, 205, 206).

Many group activities and therapies deal effectively with conflicts and consciousness raising, such as the nonviolent communication techniques that can be learned in groups. Joanna Macy, an American ecophilosopher, lifelong activist and Buddhist and systems theory scholar, has developed an impressive array of group processes to deal with conflict and raise awareness of the suffering within ourselves, others and the environment. She emphasizes the importance of being able to acknowledge the reality of the damage we have done to the environment and to face and embrace the deep grief that accompanies that awareness (Macy and Brown, 2014).

An ecology of psychological approaches

Ecopsychology incorporates important contributions from every psychological system, with each system having the properties of an organism, to create an ecology, a symbiotic relationship, between the systems as they address environmental problems. Freud, the father of *psychoanalysis*, focused on the individual's struggles against what he described as an inner core (*id*) that was weak, selfish, irrational and rigidly determined.[2] The *ego*'s personal struggle against these forces is mirrored by the principal task of civilization, as Freud saw it, to struggle *against* nature whose destructive powers can only be temporarily and anxiously warded off. We consider ourselves to be intelligent and rational, but our instincts for pleasure and aggression drive us towards overconsumption and the destruction of the environment. Freudians suggest that we become as aware as possible of our unconscious drives and defences so we can more effectively deal with them, recognize our defences against disturbing information and face our despair over environmental problems, and find alternatives to consumerism to express our unconscious needs for a personal identity and for fulfilment (Winter, 1996: 112–134, 144–152).

Jung was the second psychoanalyst to leave Freud's inner circle in 1913, believing that not all psychic energy (libido) was sexual and that spirituality was not simply repressed sexuality used as a defence against the harsh realities of life. Much of what was in the unconscious, Jung maintained, was not of personal conscious origin but of a universal, collective nature: the collective unconscious. His main discovery was the central archetype in the collective unconscious, the Self, a self-organizing principle that moves an individual and a culture towards wholeness, including wholeness as being a part of nature. Alchemy became Jung's main symbolic system and model for psychoanalysis after 1930 when he realized the alchemists were symbolically attempting to integrate into Christianity the elements it had rejected and demonized with its propensity to perceive the world in terms of good and evil – the feminine, sexuality and sensuality, the pagan world, animals and nature (Merritt, 2012a: 58–61, 196–207). For Jung, who died in 1961, the goal of individuals was to fully realize through a process of individuation what universal motifs (archetypes) of the collective unconscious they were embodying, thereby connecting them not only to the human collective but to all life forms and the basic patterns of the universe.

German-born Jewish Kurt Lewin became the most important founder of *social psychology* after immigrating to America in 1933 to escape Hitler's Germany. Attempts to understand the Nazi phenomenon stimulated the development of social psychology as the study of the effects of social and cultural influences on the individual. In relation to environmental issues it calls for participation in environmentally responsible groups, developing transitional communities and ecovillages, and creating more norms, roles and social influence mechanisms that encourage environmentally friendly behaviours (Hopkins, 2008). Psychologist B. F. Skinner, an environmentalist, was instrumental in developing *behavioural psychology* in America. It eclipsed Freud by the late 1950s by ignoring the nebulous symbolic and unconscious realms and focusing on outward, observable behaviours that could be measured. The aim is to change behaviours by changing the stimuli for behaviours and rewarding good behaviours and/or punishing the bad. Environmentally appropriate behaviour can be reinforced by giving tax breaks for conservation behaviour and punishing inappropriate behaviour by adding taxes for polluting behaviour. *Cognitive psychology* strengthened in the 1980s and pushed aside the dominant behaviourism school by the early 1990s because of a return to an interest in the activities of the mind. This interest arose from such developments as Swiss psychologist Jean Piaget's influential theory of cognitive development in children and from a comparison of the mind's activities to computer operations and the growing interest in artificial intelligence in the 1970s. Cognitive psychology focuses on how the mind processes information, observing that we can often correct erroneous beliefs and attitudes when we become aware of our errors, ignorance and misunderstandings. We must be reminded how easily we are distracted by irrelevant information and our tendency to look for examples that confirm our viewpoint rather than actively seeking counterexamples that could uncover the correct rule (Winter, 1996: 62–111, 153–227).

Gestalt and *transpersonal psychology*, which include Jungian psychology, emphasize the experience of relationship, wholeness and embeddedness in the larger world, countering the Western worldview of ourselves as segmented and autonomous beings acting in our own self-interest. *Gestalt psychology* is based on the holistic nature of perception that creates meaning by seeing the form or pattern that exists between separate elements. The three founders of gestalt psychology were the Jewish Austro-Hungarian psychologist Max Wertheimer who fled Hitler for America in 1933, the German Jewish psychologist Wolfgang Kohler who left for America in 1935 and German psychologist Kurt Koffka who began teaching in America in 1924. Another German Jew, psychiatrist Frederich (Fritz) Perls, popularized *gestalt therapy* in America in the 1960s and 1970s. Perls left Germany in 1933 and incorporated neo-Freudian, Zen and social psychology concepts into *gestalt theory* to develop *gestalt therapy*. It emphasizes that our full integrity exists only in a full sensory experience of the present. *Humanistic psychology* emerged in the 1960s and 1970s as a study of the positive, loving aspects of being human. American psychologist Abraham Maslow, a father of humanistic psychology, noted that the most fully functioning individuals are in search of intrinsic 'being' values such as truth, beauty, goodness and simplicity. *Transpersonal psychology* soon evolved out of humanistic psychology as the study of the spiritual and mystical dimensions of human experience, including shamanism, that transcends our sense of being a unique and separate self. The transpersonal self has similarities to Plato's *anima mundi*, the cosmos as a great organism with feeling and intelligence. A related form is the Gaia theory of a symbiotic relationship between the organic and inorganic realms that function as a single huge organism. *Transpersonal ecology* seeks to extend our connection beyond human identification, optimally to a mystical identification with everything (Winter, 1996: 228–269).

More attainable than mystic identity is an expanded identity arising from an appreciation of evolution. All living forms are related if one goes back far enough in time, with evolutionary lines differentiating as they branch off from common ancestors and the evolutionary tree of life unfolds. A concept in *deep ecology* is that 'all things in the biosphere have an equal right to live and blossom and to reach their own individual forms of unfolding and self-realization within the larger Self-realization' (Devall and Sessions, 1985: 67). The nonhuman world should be considered valuable *in and of itself* and not simply for its human-use value. Norwegian philosopher Arne Naess coined the term and developed many of the concepts of deep ecology in 1973, advocating the deepest possible exploration of the many dimensions of our dysfunctional relationship with the environment and that we learn how to live in harmony with nature (Devall and Sessions, 1985: 65–77).

The various psychological approaches can be combined to create an acknowledgement of the complex web of human interdependence with all life forms, developing what Aldo Leopold called a 'land ethic' and an 'ecological conscience'

(Leopold, 1949: 201–226). What American psychologist Deborah Du Nann Winter calls the 'ecological self' retains the sense of a separate physical self as it integrates the larger self that identifies with the ecosphere. From an ecological, evolutionary perspective, entities have some degree of independent existence *and* are part of a web of interrelationships that intimately link them to others. Interrelationships are also internal relationships that transcend dualism in that all things imply or contain one another in their very being. Any deep inquiry into a system, Winter notes, 'demonstrates our interdependence and embeddedness within a larger social and ecological system', and our sense of self changes 'when we experience [embeddedness] in an emotionally meaningful way' (Winter, 1996: 248–249).

The experience of embeddedness is supported by the nondualistic philosophy of the French phenomenologist Maurice Merleau-Ponty, who has been influential in encouraging a noncognitive, direct, sensual experiencing of nature (Abram, 1996). We can expand activities like going for walks; gardening; and taking time to appreciate clouds, smells, rainstorms, sunrises, etc. Outward Bound and 'rewilding' activities immerse people in nature in solo and group experiences with minimal or no modern amenities (Kahn and Hashbach, 2013). Other activities include full moon, equinox and solstice celebrations and symbolic appreciation and expression of the 'natural bases' of the holidays (Merritt, 2013: 29–57). Artists and writers can evoke a sense of reverence and respect for the natural world. Meditation and practising silence in nature help clear our minds and sharpen our senses so we can appreciate the subtleties and complexities of the natural world.

The collective unconscious and our (dis-)connection with nature

Jung's concept of consciousness in relation to the layers of the collective unconscious is useful for analyzing the many dimensions of our dysfunctional relationship to the environment. All layers are to be thought of as continually interactive and informing each other as they affect how we perceive and respond to the inner and outer environment. At the *personal* intrapsychic level, our relationship with the unconscious and the 'little people' within sets the pattern for our relationship with others and with nature. Our *family*, especially attachment issues with the mothering figure, can generate anxiety, emptiness and a narcissism that consumerism and fundamentalist religions prey upon (Weintrobe, 2013: 41, 43, 127–128, 145–146). The *national* myths in America around the cowboy and conquering the Wild West engender a hyperindependence, a conquering attitude towards nature and a belief in progress.

Western *culture* is strongly influenced by two mythical/religious traditions. The Oedipal complex of human intelligence trumping the Great Goddess of life and nature, imaged as the Sphinx in the Greek myth of Oedipus, is poised to inflict the plagues of Thebes upon the entire planet. The Judaeo-Christian religion established core values in Western culture that have little connection with nature, the body, sensuality and sexuality. Ecotheologian Thomas Berry described the myth of the West, the doctrine of progress, as originating in John's Book of Revelation, the last book in the Bible. A thousand years of abundance and human perfections were supposed to precede the end of the created world. Humans decided to manifest the myth themselves when it did not occur by divine grace by 'trying to bring about this promised state through their own efforts by exploiting the resources of the earth' (Riley, 1998: 207–208).

The Cartesian-Newtonian worldview that began to emerge in the West in the seventeenth century, coupled with the rise of capitalism, industrialization and the modern corporation, were other major factors in the development of our dysfunctional relationship with nature. The belief is that humans are separate from an environment that is dead and inert, nature can and should be controlled, individuals have a right to maximize economic gain and progress equals growth (Scott et al., 2016: 31–41).

The *primeval ancestors* at the clan and tribal level of human relationships experienced an animated cosmos, a sense that survives in our dreams. Their belief in spirit animals as healing guides of the soul illustrates how close they were to the *animal ancestor* foundation of the psyche, which survives as our emotional connection to other species (Scott et al., 2016: 272–275). The deepest disturbance in our collective unconscious is at the animal soul level, because for the first time in the history of life on earth, one species will be responsible for eliminating 30 to 50 per cent of the other species. And through the consequences of climate change we will decimate the basic requirements for *our* life as an animal: food, water, shelter and a relatively stable climate.

The importance of establishing a sense of the sacred in humans and in nature

The primeval ancestors of all cultures had a sense of the sacred in nature that informed their morality and guided their lives in relation to each other and to the environment. In 1992 the American astrophysicist Carl Sagan as co-chair of *A Joint Appeal by Science and Religion for the Environment* presented a petition stating that unless we can establish a sense of the sacred about the environment, it will be ruined because the forces arrayed against it are too powerful (Sagan, 1992). Jung maintained that a culture will not have a holistic base unless it honours a sense of the numinous, the sacred. The spiritual dimension of human experience is revealed through such means as near-death experiences, 'big dreams' with numinous imagery and symbols and visions that are either spontaneous or 'induced' by vision quests or intensive meditation.

Modern medicine has made it possible to hear many direct accounts of near-death *experiences*, not *beliefs*. American anthropologist John Robinson had such an experience that included a scene where this nonbeliever sat at a table with a being emanating divine love. In that presence Robinson reviewed his whole life, *feeling* the consequences of the sins of commission and omission – the ultimate last judgement (personal communication). His experience illustrates the transcendent, transpersonal dimension of the psyche.

Self-images like Robinson's divine being occur more often in archetypal situations like illness and death when the psyche is *in extremis*. The increase in psychic energy pushes an experience from the personal into the transpersonal realm in a manner that can be described by the transitional state in complexity theory working within the symbolic dimension of human experience. Initiations and intensive rituals are deliberate attempts to push the psyche into hopefully producing a numinous unitary image. These can be images of plants, animals, rocks, the wind and sacred landscapes that can establish a new foundation in the psyche and provide a natural avenue for developing a deep connection with nature (Merritt, 2008).

Robinson's experience illustrates the importance of love as a container necessary for an individual and for a culture in facing unpleasant realities within and without, including grief. Religious practices, rituals and group activities like Joanna Macy's have been designed to help humans support one other and cultivate compassion for ourselves, others and the natural environment – and give us hope (Macy and Brown, 2014).

The myths and numinous experiences that emerge out of or through the psyche form the base of religions, the foundation of our moral and ethical systems and the types of relationships we have with each other and with the environment. Dogmatic, God-on-our-side, good-versus-evil religious positions cripple social and political discourse, making it difficult to reach consensus and take action. Whatever is considered to be of ultimate value is part of a belief system, and *beliefs* in free market capitalism and the unseen hand of the market have powerful effects on economic, political and environmental behaviours.

Modern society needs both science and a sense of the sacred in science

Sagan's petition also stated that many scientists 'have had a profound experience of awe and reverence before the universe' (Sagan, 1992). Indeed, it was the processes in nature, not we humans, that generated a species able to make matter conscious of itself and have spiritual experiences. Ecotheologians like Thomas Berry and Matthew Fox, both inspired by the French Jesuit Teilhard de Chardin, call for a new universe story, with the Big Bang and evolutionary history providing a narrative in many ways more awesome than the creation stories in sacred literatures (Ryley, 1998: 237–272). Science can also help establish a sense of place, an important aspect of ecopsychology, by revealing the fascinating geological and natural history of a local place and region (Merritt, 2013).

Rationality and the scientific process have proven their power and usefulness, but they crimp the psyche when they stifle the spiritual and irrational dimensions of human experience and ignore, even denigrate, anything not amenable to measurable, replicable results. The archetype of the provider side of the Great Mother, with her desire for stability and security, has captivated our species, aided by the wonders of science and technology to give us an abundance of food, clothing, shelter, cheap energy and good health. Science itself is not the problem, but how it is used in the service of the archetypal Great Mother within the dominant worldview exercised by unfettered capitalism and the reigning corporate mentality. These systems are designed by humans and can be changed by humans. With climate change, for example, greater political and economic support is needed to create technological advances in all forms of alternative energy sources and employ those already available that could replace fossil fuels if adapted on a wide scale (Flannery, 2015).

Science itself has a mythic foundation in Western culture under the guise of the Greek god Apollo who personifies in a sacred way a purity of thought, rationality and far-sightedness. The Greek pantheon was an ecology of mythic relationships with no god or goddess dominating. It included Hermes, who complements Apollo's attributes. Hermes personifies what we now call complexity theory by being the god of exchanges and transitions, and as the progenitor of gods and myths, he is the god of the emergence of new phenomena and stable attractors (archetypal patterns) (Merritt, 2012b: 128–132). Hermes rules over liminal and transitional experiences like birth, journeys and initiations where shocks and surprises can emerge from the unknown. He leads the way or leads astray. As god of business, psychology, rhetoric and advertising, he drives consumerism and is behind the deliberate *1984*-style misinformation put forth by the fossil fuel industry to create doubt in the public's mind about the human element in climate change (Klein, 2014).

The science of the psyche, psych-ology and the practice of psychotherapy are in need of a thorough revisioning. American archetypal psychologist James Hillman championed the idea of getting the psyche/soul out of the therapist's office and into the world with the neoplatonic concept of the Greek goddess Aphrodite, goddess of sensuality and sexuality, as the Soul of the World (Hillman, 1992: 91–130). Even the physical elements can be related to in a poetic, I–Thou, subject-to-subject manner where each element has an interiority with depth, mystery and intentions that elicits our imagination (Fisher, 2013: 9–10, 51–89). Ecotherapy begins with an ecological concept of the psyche and the interconnectedness of all things. Dreams about nature, especially numinous dreams, can be used to entice the client into learning about and connecting with that sacred dream animal, plant or landscape (Merritt, 2012a: 3–4, 112–113, 109–117, 2013). Therapy sessions can be done in natural environments and clients encouraged to spend time in nature, including specific elements in nature, depending on their psychological condition (Buzzell and Chalquist, 2009).

Moving forward

Huge challenges face our species in relation to each other and to nature. Most people now live in urban areas quite removed from a natural environment, whereas research has shown the benefits of extended periods of unstructured time in nature for children's development and their physical, emotional, cognitive and psychological well-being (Scott *et al.*, 2016: 285–292). It is shocking that American preteens and teens spend nine hours a day in front of screens playing video games, being on Facebook, etc.[3] On the positive side, research is investigating the use of technology like live broadcasts of natural settings to reduce stress in the workspace. Peter Kahn, the American editor of an online ecopsychology journal, is encouraging more scientific rigour in the exploration of the human connection with nature, statistically proving what approaches work best for education and experiences of nature (Kahn and Hasbach, 2012: 8–11).

Jung said the major challenge for modern men and women was to unite our cultured side, which would include science, with 'the two million-year-old man within'. That person has also been called 'the indigenous one within' and the 'totemic self' from our Palaeolithic years marked by totems expressing kinship with the greater-than-human world (Kahn and Hasbach, 2012: 11–12). American biologist Edward O. Wilson coined the term 'biophilia' for our innate emotional connection to nature, and Theodore Roszak spoke of an 'ecological unconscious' functioning by the principles in the biosphere. Ecopsychologists admire the indigenous experience of a sacred relationship with nature, their practice of reciprocity with each other and with nature, living in small groups with a democratic process and rootedness to place (topophilia) (Sampson, 2012). All indigenous cultures believe in synchronicity, and Jung said no worldview is complete without it (Jung, 1969: 512–519).

Ecopsychology will play a major role in the necessary move to a 'green' steady-state global economy. The *industrial growth society* (Macy and Brown, 2014) is premised on perpetual growth while it treats the environment as an endless resource base and waste dump. The very concept of the corporation is unecological, a model based solely on profits without regard for people or the environment. The steady-state model requires global population numbers be reduced and labour better distributed with fewer hours worked per person (Dietz and O'Neill, 2013). Consumption rates of Westerners have to be lowered, requiring positive human values to be encouraged. Research has shown that people would prefer to work fewer hours and spend more time with family and friends, engage in community activities and work on personally fulfilling projects. Winter notes that fulfilment comes with simplicity, quiet awareness, 'practising the principle and value of sufficiency' and 'rejoic[ing] in the incredible beauty of the ecosystem and our role in it' (Winter, 1996: 268–269).

The principle of interconnection applies to the need for a fairer distribution of income and improving the basics for all humans – food, water, health care, shelter and education. Equal rights and women's rights are integral to the process (Winter, 1996: 80–104; Dietz and O'Neill, 2013: 87–97). Regional planning to concentrate human populations and preserve open spaces and natural areas will be essential to respect the rights of both humans and animals. Buildings and city designs can bring people to nature and nature to people, including in the inner city (Scott *et al.*, 2016: 267–271).

An integrated vision is needed for people to be able to confront the immense entrenched political, economic and religious powers. The ecopsychological concepts presented here can help frame that vision and provide the guidelines for developing an educational system based on a new paradigm. This is a paradigm that integrates the sciences, mathematics and the arts; educates about environmental problems at the scientific and mythic levels as it connects us deeply to our local habitat; and brings together the spiritual and the rational[4] (Merritt, 2012a: 117–124). It will be a system that cultivates relationships, activism and compassion for self, others and the environment. A holistic overview of Western culture and history will be necessary, including an understanding of the evolution of its main symbolic forms expressed in its religions and in its compensatory symbolic systems like alchemy (Tarnas, 1991).

Winter calls for ecopsychologists to develop a strong background in the natural sciences, humanities and social sciences as they work at several different levels in an interdisciplinary and integrative manner (Winter, 1996: 297–298). A leading figure in the integration of science, the humanities and the depth psychologies of Carl Jung and James Hillman has been Lori Pye, who founded the Viridis Graduate Institute of Ecopsychology and Environmental Humanities. Winter summarized the challenges to ecopsychology, what she calls ecological psychology:

> [Ecological psychology] should be pluralistic in its methodology and creative in its conduct. Sophisticated about the limits of objective knowledge, ecological psychologists will need to be rigorously attuned to the distorting effects of their own political, emotional, and intellectual blinders. As we become more conscious of our limitations, so will we become more empowered to transcend them.
>
> *(Winter, 1996: 298)*

The field must, of necessity, be bold and open to every possible avenue for investigation and change. We are at the beginning of what Joanna Macy named 'The Great Turning' and what Jung called a 'New Age'. Our species is being pushed to consciously develop an ecological worldview, or it will be forced upon us after much destruction. The pathologies in the environment are compelling people to become aware that they are indeed part of nature. It is an exciting time, and much is at stake.

Notes

1 For an example of the psychoanalysis of a film, Google 'Jungian Ecopsychology and Hunger Games': www.jungianecopsychology.com/2012/04/hunger-games-jungpoliticsand.html (Accessed 26/10/2016).
2 In Freud's system the reality-oriented *ego* as the centre of consciousness has to struggle to maintain its integrity against the powerful unconscious instinctual forces (the *id*) and the equally powerful unconscious forces of the *superego*, the internalized moral principles from one's parents and society.
3 www.forbes.com/sites/jordanshapiro/2015/11/03/teenagers-in-the-u-s-spend-about-nine-hours-a-day-in-front-of-a-screen/2/ (Accessed 26/10/2016).
4 Teaching environmentally focused psychology is the theme of the *Ecopsychology* online journal, 4 (2): http://online.liebertpub.com/toc/eco/4/2 (Accessed 26/10/2016).

Bibliography

Abram, David (1996), *The Spell of the Sensuous: Perception and Language in a More-Than-Human World*, New York, Vintage.

Buzzell, Linda, and Chalquist, Craig (eds.) (2009), *Ecotherapy: Healing with Nature in Mind*, San Francisco, Sierra Club Books.

Chalquist, Craig (2010), 'Earth Is Not My Mother – Towards Contemporary Styles of Earthly Discourse', *ReVision – A Journal of Consciousness and Transformation*, 31 (3–4): 7–12.

Devall, Bill, and Sessions, George (1985), *Deep Ecology*, Salt Lake City, UT, Gibbs Smith.

Dietz, Ron, and O'Neill, Dan (2013), *Enough Is Enough – Building a Sustainable Economy in a World of Finite Resources*, San Francisco, Berrett-Koehler.

Fisher, Andy (2013 [2002]), *Radical Ecopsychology – Psychology in the Service of Life*, Albany, NY, SUNY Press.

Flannery, Tim (2015), *Atmosphere of Hope: Searching for Solutions to the Climate Crisis*, New York, Atlantic Monthly Press.

Hillman, James (1992), *The Thought of the Heart and the Soul of the World*, Woodstock, CT, Spring Publications.

Ho, Mae-Wan (1998), 'Organism and Psyche in a Participatory Universe', *in:* Loye, David (ed.), *The Evolutionary Outrider: The Impact of the Human Agent on Evolution*, Essays in Honour of Ervin Laszlo, Westport, CT, Praeger: 49–65.

Hopkins, Robert (2008), *The Transition Handbook: From Oil Dependency to Local Resilience*, White River Junction, VT, Chelsea Green.

Jung, Carl (1969 [1960]), *The Structure and Dynamics of the Psyche*, vol. 8 of *The Collected Works of C. G. Jung*, edited by Read, Herbert, Fordham, Michael, Adler, Gerhard, and McGuire, William, and translated by Hull, R. F. C., Princeton, NJ, Princeton University Press.

Kahn Jr., Peter, and Hashbach, Patricia (eds.) (2012), *Ecopsychology – Science, Totems, and the Technological Species*, Cambridge, MA, MIT Press.

Kahn Jr., Peter, and Hashbach, Patricia (eds.) (2013), *The Rediscovery of the Wild*, Cambridge, MA, MIT Press.

Klein, Naomi (2014), *This Changes Everything: Capitalism vs. the Climate*, New York, Simon and Schuster.

Leopold, Aldo (1949), *A Sand County Almanac: And Sketches Here and There*, Oxford, Oxford University Press.

Macy, Joanna, and Brown, Molly (2014), *Coming Back to Life*, Gabriola Island, British Columbia, New Society.

Merritt, Dennis (2008), 'Sacred Landscapes, Sacred Seasons: A Jungian Ecopsychological Perspective', *in:* Nash, George, and Children, George (eds.), *The Archaeology of Semiotics and the Social Order of Things*, Oxford, Archaeopress: 153–170.

Merritt, Dennis (2012a), *The Dairy Farmer's Guide to the Universe: Jung, Hermes, and Ecopsychology*, vol. 1, *Jung and Ecopsychology*, Carmel, CA, Fisher King.

Merritt, Dennis (2012b), *The Dairy Farmer's Guide to the Universe: Jung, Hermes, and Ecopsychology*, vol. 3, *Hermes, Ecopsychology, and Complexity Theory*, Carmel, CA, Fisher King.

Merritt, Dennis (2013), *The Dairy Farmer's Guide to the Universe: Jung, Hermes, and Ecopsychology*, vol. 4, *Land, Weather, Seasons, Insects: An Archetypal View*, Carmel, CA, Fisher King.

Roszak, Theodore (1992), *The Voice of the Earth*, New York, Simon and Schuster.

Roszak, Theodore, Gomes, Mary, and Kanner, Allen (eds.) (1995), *Ecopsychology – Restoring the Earth, Healing the Mind*, San Francisco, Sierra Club Books.

Ryley, Nancy (1998), *The Forsaken Garden: Four Conversations on the Deep Meaning of Environmental Illness*, Wheaton, IL, Quest Books.
Sagan, Carl (1992), 'To Avert a Common Danger', *Parade Magazine*, March: 10–12.
Sampson, Scott (2012), 'The Topophilia Hypothesis: Ecopsychology Meets Evolutionary Psychology', *in:* Kahn Jr., Peter, and Hashbach, Patricia (eds.), *Ecopsychology – Science, Totems, and the Technological Species*, Cambridge, MA, MIT Press: 23–53.
Scott, Britain, Amel, Elise, Koger, Susan, and Manning, Christie (2016), *Psychology for Sustainability*, 4th ed., New York and London, Routledge.
Shamdasani, Sonu (2003), *Jung and the Making of Modern Psychology*, Cambridge, Cambridge University Press.
Tarnas, Richard (1991), *The Passion of the Western Mind: Understanding the Ideas That Have Shaped Our World View*, New York, Harmony.
Weintrobe, Sally (ed.) (2013), *Engaging With Climate Change: Psychoanalytic and Interdisciplinary Perspectives*, London and New York, Routledge.
Winter, Deborah Du Nann (1996), *Ecological Psychology: Healing the Split Between Planet and Self*, New York, Harper Collins.

PART II
Writings and representations

Nature is first and foremost a human construct, a representation. How do we write about the natural world, and how do we represent it? These questions, which lie at the centre of this second part of the book, need to be investigated before any real change in our understanding of, and behaviour toward, nature may arise. In opposition to the 'Promethean attitude' (prevalent in the scientific and technological approaches to nature), which consists in tearing nature's secrets away from her, the 'Orphic attitude' seeks to discover the mysteries of nature through art, poetry and theoretical reflection, to take up Pierre Hadot's words: 'Man should always remember that he is a natural being himself, and that nature, in its diverse expressions, suggests the outlines of what would seem to us properly artistic processes, that there is therefore a profound continuity between nature and art' (Hadot, 2004: 285 [extract translated by Stéphanie Alkofer]). These ideas can be found in the writings of many poets, from Goethe to Baudelaire. The latter thus claimed in 1859: 'I believe that Art is, and cannot be other than, the exact reproduction of Nature' (Baudelaire, 1955). Since the beginnings of the current environmental crisis, ecology has given rise to new aesthetic forms, inspiring artists as well as urban planners to produce physical works in the shape of greenways, or ephemeral installations made of natural materials, and so on. A true aesthetics of nature has thus been born, through developments linked to the fields of knowledge, technology or urban planning (Kagan, 2013). In the field of literary studies, directions have been taken since the 1990s to bridge the gap between art and science. Literature and art (which are traditionally connected with fiction) have indeed developed as distinct from science (usually connected with facts). In reaction to this, ecocriticism (defined as the study of the relationship between humans and their physical environment in literary texts) and epistemocriticism (the study of the interactions between sciences and literature) have been founded on the premise that there is no watertight separation between literary studies and the sciences of nature.

In Chapter 5, Nathalie Blanc looks beyond the natural environment towards built environments and contends that the aesthetics of nature is not environmental aesthetics. It is one component therein, or vice versa. The author nevertheless insists on the fact that we must not see nature only as a component that is external to our societies; rather, it is a part of our social life and politics, in the sense of what constitutes the future of socially involved individuals. For some inhabitants, feeling connected to nature has become a factor in their personal well-being beyond the affirmation of social status; greenways and blueways are part of this push for a more popular and egalitarian access to nature in its ecological forms via biodiversity. And yet, we must not forget that such nature is the product of specific planning. Moreover, it also depends on the aesthetic and ethical criteria that express different sensibilities from living beings. For Blanc, re-examining the place of nature in our cultures does not simply involve adding a new actor or group of actors to the running of our democracies; rather, it involves a deeper modification of democratic processes: citizens have become inhabitants.

In Chapter 6, Emmanuelle Peraldo explores the origins and meanings of ecocriticism. She points out that ecocriticism is both a critical method of inquiry and an ethical discourse. It has been defined as the interdisciplinary association of literary and environmental studies and as a re-evaluation of literary criticism from an ecocentric perspective. As Peraldo shows, its aim is to analyze some literary genres, like the travel narrative or the road novel, as vehicles for an ecological, and thereby ethical, reflection. Even if ecocriticism is commonly associated with the study of nature and its role in literary works, the urban environment is also of major interest to this new critical and theoretical movement that has developed in opposition to postmodernism and poststructuralism and has run in parallel directions to postcolonialism. Just as there is no single ecocritical approach restricted to one discipline, ecocritical analysis does not apply only to our times and the current environmental crisis. A diachronic perspective shows that ecocriticism is an evolving method, which can be brought to bear on different geographical areas or time periods. The chapter also presents the limits of ecocriticism and the main reproaches that have been directed at it.

Like ecocriticism, epistemocriticism crosses the boundaries of disciplines and opens up a dialogue between natural science and cultural studies. Chapter 7 considers epistemocriticism as a new branch of literary studies interested in finding the traces of a general negotiation between the sciences and literature in literary texts. Epistemocritics observe that, through the process of circulation of knowledge, our representations (of time, space, nature and man) inform both science and literature in comparable yet different ways. When applied to nature, the aim of epistemocriticism is not to study nature itself, but the different kinds of knowledge about nature, which are not first-hand knowledge but have been constituted through a double process of cultural and textual formation. It is difficult to strike a balance between the idea of a wholly cultural nature and that of a wholly natural culture, as the history of the notions of nature and culture has shown. Literature has also expressed this precarious balance through various tropes, as Laurence

Dahan reveals in this chapter through the analysis of selected literary texts that question the separation between culture and nature.

Bibliography

Baudelaire, Charles (1955 [1859]), 'On Photography', *in:* Mayne, Jonathan (ed.), *Charles Baudelaire: The Mirror of Art*, London, Phaidon: 230–231.

Hadot, Pierre (2004), *Le voile d'Isis. Essai sur l'histoire de l'idée de Nature*, Paris, Gallimard.

Kagan, Sacha (2013 [2011]), *Art and Sustainability, Connecting Patterns for a Culture of Complexity*, Bielefeld, Transcript.

5

THE AESTHETICS OF NATURE

Nathalie Blanc

Philosopher Immanuel Kant (1724–1804) first mentioned the aesthetics of nature in the eighteenth century. In his *Observations on the Feeling of the Beautiful and Sublime* (1764) and *Critique of the Power of Judgement* (1790), Kant outlined a subjective approach to aesthetic satisfaction as a free process of the faculties and an opportunity for learning together; he saw this as a new way to look at nature. He was interested in sensory appreciation devoid of dogmatism in the creation of subjectivity. During the nineteenth century, a new way to describe nature developed and flourished, particularly in the United States; it conferred autonomy on nature and was open to the possibility of an interface with humans. This approach was inspired by American transcendentalist writing, like Ralph Waldo Emerson's *Nature* (1836) and *Walden; Or Life in the Woods*, Henry David Thoreau's (1817–1862) seminal work and the foundation stone of nature writing (1854) in which Thoreau chose to spend two years living in a cabin on the edge of Walden Pond (1845–1847). It was greatly influenced by the realization that nature was being damaged by nineteenth-century urban and industrial development – as visible in George Perkins Marsh's *Man and Nature* (1864) and John Muir's *A Near View of the High Sierra* (1894). It was not until the 1960s and 1970s, however, that philosophers of aesthetics really took an interest in nature. Ronald Hepburn's seminal 1966 article 'Contemporary Aesthetics and the Neglect of Natural Beauty' called for aesthetic thinking to be enhanced by looking to the natural world, largely ignored by aesthetic theory at the time. This opened the door to studying other topics and contexts such as landscape, the environment, the city and everyday life. The goal was to look beyond the natural environment towards built environments and even to think about nature like a heritage. Caution is needed, however, with this assimilation of nature and the environment under the terminology of the natural environment.

Distinguishing between environment and nature

We need to distinguish between the concepts of environment and nature. Nature is such for those who objectify it. The world can exist as nature only for someone who is no longer a part of it, someone with an outsider's perspective – similar to a detached scientist – a person who can observe from such a safe distance that it is easy to accept the illusion that nature is not affected by their presence. Nature is seen as external, not only to humanity but also to history. The natural world is the unchanging backdrop – both spatial and temporal – upon which human activities are played out. As Maurice Merleau-Ponty has argued, nature is our soil:

> Nature is an enigmatic object, an object that is not an object at all; it is not really set out in front of us. It is our soil [*sol*] – not what is in front of us, facing us, but rather, that which carries us.
> *(Merleau-Ponty, 1995: 19)*

Merleau-Ponty nonetheless defined nature before pursuing his lecture:

> There is nature wherever there is a life that has meaning, but where, however, there is not thought; hence the kinship with the vegetative. Nature is what has a meaning, without this meaning being posited by thought: it is the autoproduction of a meaning. Nature is thus different from a simple thing. It has an interior, is determined from within; hence the opposition of 'natural' to 'accidental'. Yet nature is different from man: it is not instituted by him and is opposed to custom, to discourse. Nature is the primordial – that is, the nonconstructed, the noninstituted; hence the idea of an eternity of nature (the eternal return), of a solidity.
> *(Merleau-Ponty, 1995: 19)*

To carry on in this vein, we can add that talking about nature refers to the soil, but also to its history and to natural cycles at the scale of geological time.

Recent research into the Anthropocene has popularized the idea that the eighteenth century and James Watt's 1785 invention of the steam engine ushered in a new geological era; an era which made humans the main source of transformation on planet Earth. The term was popularized by Paul Crutzen, winner of the 1995 Nobel Prize for chemistry. Others disagree and date the Anthropocene era to earlier, notably to a time in history when humans affected forested areas and caused the extinction of large herbivores, thus eliminating a major source of methane gas production. The Anthropocene approach is interesting for two reasons: it points up the role of human activity in large-scale environmental transformation at the planetary scale, and it underscores the importance of interdisciplinary crossover between the social sciences and humanities and the life sciences and provides keys to better understanding these phenomena.

From this perspective, nature is a story: the story of its evolution. It therefore becomes great Nature. Increasingly, the human footprint on nature is measured more on a temporal scale than in spatial terms. Nature as such is offset against human history. Talking about the aesthetics of Nature is in this respect very different from addressing the issue of the aesthetics of natural and built environments. Nature evokes the theatrical backdrop of the history of human destruction, whereas the natural environment involves taking into account the share of naturality (i.e. the portion of spontaneous processes) in an environment. Given this, which aesthetics of Nature should be singled out? And how do environmental aesthetics differ from it?

Within the aesthetics of Nature it is necessary to consider the appreciation of nature – that is, the appreciation of spontaneous processes and their role in society. When assessing our environments, it is indeed important to estimate the importance placed on the soil that supports us, on the living matter that gives meaning, without this meaning having been established by thought (Merleau-Ponty, 1995). Further, it is just as important to verify the relationship between appreciation for nature and the recognized quality of environments, as well as phenomena related to health and well-being. This complex approach begs us to look at nature independently from culture, to objectify it in such a way that we step back and observe it from a distance. Such interpretation of the term Nature reproduces a split between objects produced culturally and naturally. It points towards accepting the path of naturalism without interiority (Descola, 2013 [2005]).

Forms and environments

The goal is to move from the perception of nature and the built environment towards the process of thinking about or practically creating natural and built environments. Why? It is important not to separate environments from the individuals or groups at their origin. This needs to be emphasized (Demos, 2015). Natural and built environments are involved in the construction of individuals and groups. It is not as though they are external to them, objectively placed, while such individuals or groups would be just as happy with an aesthetic interpretation or representation. The environment is an important element in the construction of self in the world. Two authors have explained this in different terms. Pragmatic American philosopher Arnold Berleant (2013) has argued that the work of creating an environment is a way of being together. In his critique of the separation of nature and culture, Tim Ingold (2013) has argued that multiple environmental forms are the result of the dynamic working of development systems created by the action of humans in their environments. In sum, we need to define the types of activities that create different environmental spheres, both in the biological and cultural sense. We need to return the environmentalization process to the forefront; we need to move away from a specific definition of humanity that ontologically separates it from other living beings and creates an opposition between nature and culture. The environmentalization process (i.e. that of creating environments) involves a formative activity that is accomplished through constantly renewed variations across space and time. We need to emphasize the need for all living creatures to develop in time and in space, with and within the environment. Trees, landscapes, blue skies or red or orange skies from countless shared sunsets are all forms which, when recognized, define what makes it possible to be together. We thus refer to the new speculative field called New Materialisms (Dolphijn and Tuin, 2012).

The ecological emergency

In this sense, rethinking the separation between the aesthetics of nature, on the one hand, and the aesthetics of the environment, on the other, and the aesthetics of natural and built environments is a new way of looking at nature as a 'constructed' framework, or one that is at least dependent on human activity. It makes possible the sensory appreciation of different types of environments and forces us to think about what makes an environment. How far does it stretch from what is close, from what our eyes can see – the share of space in which we habitually move about – all the way to our understanding of an environment as a world system that is currently disrupted by imbalances caused by human activity? What does it make of the body's relationship with a given space, to the language spoken there, the ties created with other living beings, other groups and with the practices that develop over time?

The definition of the sphere of the 'environment' by this branch of aesthetics is therefore obviously greater than an understanding based purely on the scope of the objects within it: for example, when assessing biodiversity, gardening in urban areas or the quality of a habitat, taking a complex approach that considers both scientific knowledge about a milieu and the social ties and cultural uses within a given space. Environmental aesthetics does not in this sense simply involve drawing attention to a set of previously ignored facts. It aims to point up a new means of expressing the ecological emergency: it is a form of aesthetics that extends beyond art. This type of aesthetics involves an experience of ordinary phenomena and cannot be contained in a museum. This type of aesthetics is also concerned with environmental forms and the processes behind them. Philosopher John Dewey (2005 [1934]) was among the first to call for an extension of the aesthetic experience into ordinary life. He saw in this a way of improving political life and making it less elitist. Let us take this a step further and examine the forms involved.

Forms, but which ones?

Since 2007 in France, and particularly following the 'Grenelle 2 de l'Environnement' Conference, greenways and blueways have met with growing success.[1] Created to preserve biodiversity, these planning tools combine vegetative spaces and aquatic spaces in such a manner as to link up a territory; they are a product of the booming field of landscape ecology. Reproducing biodiversity – that is, plant and animal species, the genetic resources they embody and the varied ecosystems they help define – is indeed one role of greenways and a component in their planning. More specifically, blueways and greenways are represented on diagrams that have green spots of various sizes labelled 'natural green space', which are interconnected by linear green spaces also known as corridors. Greenways and blueways apply to all spatial scales, from regional ecological coherence plans (*Schémas régionaux de cohérence écologique* – SRCE) to local planning documents (*Plans locaux d'urbanisme* – PLU), and they can be implemented in different types of environments (e.g. forest, heath, prairie or marsh subzones). They are synonymous with broadened thinking about the ecosystem services provided by nature (producing, regulating or cultural and recreational).

Many questions exist:

- What is the relationship between a planning pattern – most often graphically represented as a green network that connects lines and spots – and the actual way these greenways and blueways are experienced? Such questioning inevitably refers back to the relationship between the aesthetics of nearby nature and an aesthetic that is more formal and abstract, schematically mapped.
- What is the relationship between the representation of a network and the landscape? If by 'landscape' we mean a specific aesthetic form which helps enhance the relationship with nature, the hypothesis is that the spatial layout of greenway and blueway planning creates landscapes, particularly given that they affect the ecology of the landscape.
- And what do these types of landscape tell us? Can we really believe that they are a metaphor for a social turn towards widespread connectivity?

A recent interdisciplinary conference (March 2013) entitled 'Greenways: The Interconnected Pathways of Communication and the Environment' at the University of Tennessee-Knoxville invited planners, writers, ecologists and many others to think about greenways as metaphors for broad-scale connectivity, in connection with ecological thinking:

> Following the natural contours of the landscape, greenways are man-made paths that work to link human communities to the surrounding environment. In the same way, this conference seeks to promote connectivity between various disciplines and their approaches to the environment.[2]

Several elements as such indicate that the idea of greenways and blueways is sign of a true shift towards broad-scale connectivity. The first is that the planning of greenways and blueways promotes a type of landscape ecology that underpins a landscape-based vision of biodiversity. The second is that greenways and blueways play on the natural connection that appears to exist between human communities across space and time through the protection of nature. The third harnesses the power of visually imposing cartography at different scales as a means of representing (in political terms) relationships that ignore administrative divisions and national borders.

This perspective concerns landscapes in a way that goes beyond the fact that greenways and blueways are connected to landscape ecology at the disciplinary level. Formal approaches to landscape go against the idea that a landscape is simply a territory with aesthetic criteria (Pitte, 2012 [1983]) or that it is the product of a process of 'artialization' in the sense of a backdrop with aesthetic value. The notion of 'artialization' (that Alain Roger borrowed from Montaigne) establishes the idea of an 'artistically mediated' look at landscape and renews with the principle of separating nature and culture (Roger, 1997). Landscape is no longer a perceived space, whose analysis is reduced to phenomenology. Moreover, the fact that a given culture has a term to describe its landscape is not enough (Berque, 2000; Berque *et al.*, 1994). Form-based approaches to landscape see forms as socionaturally produced activities that function by structuring the parts and the whole; that structure a specific spatial framework that includes nature; and that transform territories into thoughts and practices, codifying the latter, and condensing together functions and services across an area. Taken together, this makes sense and is seen by all as the abstract representation of a new sociopolitical approach. Rooted as such in the local, regional, national and international territory, landscapes require natural connectivity in order to generate biodiversity.

Lastly, when it comes to people's lived experience, it is important to note that the way they project themselves in an environment, feel connected to it and the aesthetic perception of such biologically diverse areas only very rarely take into account the connectivity of greenways and blueways. And yet greenways are nonetheless 'vegetative' spaces that strive to reunify and create a shared territory for animals, plants and humans. In Strasbourg, France, where greenways are already broadly implemented and are an example of shared mobility, the discourse is clear:

> Nature is greenery, but it's also animals. It's everything I see when I'm on my bicycle, on my way to work and going home. To me, being on my bicycle and surrounded by such nature, a swan, a duck, I don't know, birds and all that, for me, it's a breath of fresh air for my mind. I feel good, I feel really good. So yeah. Because I think to myself: 'There are things living here.' I observe them. And it makes me feel good, personally.
> *(pericentral Strasbourg environmentalist, quoted in: Blanc, 2015: 155)*

Conclusion

The aesthetics of nature is not environmental aesthetics. It is one component therein, or vice versa. But it is important not to forget that we must not see nature only as a component that is external to our societies; rather, it is a part of our societies and politics, in the sense of what constitutes the future of socially involved individuals. Philosopher Emily Brady (2003, 2007: 64, translated here) has written in Kantian terms about environmental aesthetics:

> [This new field] recognises that natural environments are not only experienced as landscapes, but also as environments in which the aesthetic

subject appreciates nature as dynamic, changing, and evolving. It takes an aesthetic approach which, depending on its different forms, draws on ecological knowledge, imagination, emotion, and a new understanding of nature as a bearer of its own narrative.

For some inhabitants, feeling connected to nature has become a factor in their personal well-being beyond the affirmation of social status; greenways and blueways (alongside other things like shared gardens and urban agriculture) are part of this push for more popular and egalitarian access to nature in its ecological forms via biodiversity. And yet, we must not forget that such nature is the product of specific planning. The conditions under which living matter and its place are defined hinge on the social compromise and territorial conflicts that such planning involves. Moreover, it also depends on the aesthetic and ethical criteria that express different sensibilities from living beings. Broadly speaking, the idea of greenways is to connect city dwellers to nature. They point up the spatial and temporal connections between humans and other living beings. The presence or absence of animals is a test of the success of such planning which uses plants when such spaces are created. Re-examining the place of nature, of natures, in our cultures does not simply involve adding a new actor or group of actors into the running of our democracies; rather, it involves a deeper modification of the nature of democratic processes. Citizens have become inhabitants. Given that, and given the difficulties of local democracy, how should the importance of taking into consideration territorial ties be expressed? Changes in the ties between nature and artifice no longer challenge the hybrid nature of species and spaces and require a new form of environmental art.

Notes

1 The so-called 'Grenelle 2 Law' on the 'National Commitment for the Environment (ENE)' was passed on 12 July 2010. It was a practical application of some of the commitments taken during the Grenelle environmental conference and promoted the idea of greenways. Numerous researchers have adopted the term 'greenway', both in the United States and Europe (e.g. in the UK, Italy and Portugal). The term 'greenway' is occasionally used in connection with other terms such as 'ecological networks' and 'green infrastructure'. Planners generally agree on green networks and the structure of such networks, but they rarely agree on the planning methods, the outcome of such planning or the related environmental, socioeconomic and/or cultural goals.
2 Call for papers for the 'Greenways: The Interconnected Pathways of Communication and the Environment. A NEXUS Interdisciplinary Conference', available at: https://call-for-papers.sas.upenn.edu/node/53352 (Accessed 14/05/2016).

Bibliography

Berleant, Arnold (2013), 'What Is Aesthetic Engagement?', *Contemporary Aesthetics*, 11, available at: www.contempaesthetics.org/newvolume/pages/article.php?articleID=684 (Accessed 05/10/2016).
Berque, Augustin (2000 [1990]), *Médiance, de milieux en paysages*, Paris, Belin-Reclus.
Berque, Augustin, Conan, Michel, Donadieu, Pierre, Lassus, Bernard, and Roger, Alain (1994), *Cinq propositions pour une théorie du paysage*, Seyssel, Champ Vallon.

Blanc, Nathalie (2015), 'Shared Animal/Human Mobility', *in:* Mackenzie, Louisa, and Posthumus, Stéphanie (eds.), *Through the Cultural Prism: Thinking about Animals from a French and Francophone Perspective*, Ann Arbour, MI, University of Michigan Press: 149–162.

Brady, Emily (2003), *Aesthetics of the Natural Environment*, Edinburgh, Edinburgh University Press.

Brady, Emily (2007), 'Vers une véritable esthétique de l'environnement', *Cosmopolitiques*, 15: 61–73 (special issue: Lolive, Jacques, and Blanc, Nathalie (eds.), 'Esthétique et espace public').

Demos, T. J. (2015), 'Rights of Nature: The Art and Politics of Earth Jurisprudence', *in:* Demos, T. J. (ed.), *Rights of Nature: Art and Ecology in the Americas*, n.p., Nottingham Contemporary: 1–15.

Descola, Philippe (2005), *Par-delà nature et culture*, Paris, Gallimard, translated into English by Janet Lloyd (2013) as *Beyond Nature and Culture*, Chicago, University of Chicago Press.

Dewey, John (2005 [1934]), *L'art comme expérience. Œuvres philosophiques III*, translated by Jean-Pierre Cometti, Christophe Domino, Fabienne Gaspari, Catherine Mari, Nancy Murzilli, Claude Pichevin, Jean Piwnica and Gilles A. Tiberghien, Pau, Publications de l'Université de Pau-Éditions Farrago.

Dolphijn, Rick, and Tuin, Iris (van der) (eds.) (2012), *New Materialism: Interviews and Cartographies*, n.p., Michigan Publishing.

Emerson, Ralph Waldo (1836), *Nature*, Boston, James Munroe and Company, available at: https://archive.org/details/naturemunroe00emerrich (Accessed 05/10/2016).

Hepburn, Ronald W. (1966), 'Contemporary Aesthetics and the Neglect of Natural Beauty', *in:* Williams, Bernard, and Montefiore, Alan (eds.), *British Analytical Philosophy*, London, Routledge and Kegan Paul: 285–310.

Ingold, Tim (2013), *Marcher avec les dragons*, Paris, Éditions Zones sensibles.

Kant, Immanuel (1992 [1764]), *Observations sur le sentiment du beau et du sublime*, Paris, Vrin, series Bibliothèque des textes philosophiques, translated by Roger Kempf.

Kant, Immanuel (2000 [1790]), *Critique de la faculté de juger*, Paris, Flammarion, translated by Alain Renaut.

Marsh, George Perkins (1864), *Man and Nature*, New York, C. Scribner.

Merleau-Ponty, Maurice (1995), *La nature, notes, cours du Collège de France*, edited by Dominique Séglard, Paris, Seuil, series Traces écrites.

Muir, John (1894), 'A Near View of the High Sierra', *in:* Muir, John (ed.), *The Mountains of California*, New York, Century: 26–39.

Pitte, Jean-Robert (2012 [1983]), *Histoire du paysage français. De la préhistoire à nos jours*, 5th ed., Paris, Tallandier, series Texto.

Roger, Alain (1997), *Court traité du paysage*, Paris, Gallimard.

Thoreau, Henry David (1854), *Walden; or, Life in the Woods*, Boston, Ticknor and Fields, available at: www.eldritchpress.org/walden5.pdf (Accessed 05/10/2016).

6
ECOCRITICISM

Emmanuelle Peraldo

The origins and meanings of ecocriticism

Although the environmental movement is usually considered to have begun in the 1960s, ecocriticism only developed in the early 1990s as an emerging field in literary and cultural studies. The word 'ecocriticism', however, seems to have first been used in an essay by William Rueckert published in 1978 entitled 'Literature and Ecology: An Experiment in Ecocriticism', and proto-ecocritical insights can be found in *The Country and the City* (1973), a famous survey of English literature in terms of changing attitudes towards two geographical and social spaces (the country and the city) by Raymond Williams, or in the even earlier *Nature in American Literature* (1923) by Norman Foerster. Nature is indeed at the core of the preoccupations of ecocritics, especially nowadays, in an era dominated by technologies and technological progress that tend to alter the natural sphere.

Ecocriticism is both a critical method of inquiry and an ethical discourse and aims at bridging the gap between the arts and science. It can be defined as the study of 'the relationship between environmental awareness and literary aesthetics' (Blanc et al., 2008), of the way literature and the arts connect with an examination of the relationship between humankind and its environment (Buell, 1995, 2005), including studies of the species, biodiversity and the wilderness. Its aim is to analyze some literary genres, like the travel narrative or the road novel, as vehicles for an ecological, and thereby ethical, reflection. Even if ecocriticism is commonly associated with the study of nature and its role in literary works, the urban environment is also of major interest to this new critical and theoretical movement.

Ecocriticism has emerged as a reaction to postmodern[1] and poststructural[2] approaches, in which nature and the environment had lost all importance. Ecocritics have attacked postmodernism for discarding the concept of 'nature' in order to focus too exclusively on humans. As a result, many of them have deemed it necessary to redirect their attention to nonhuman life in order to repair the harm done by centuries of anthropocentrism (Drew and Sitter, 2011). Postmodern approaches consider that we live in a virtual world, and this may lead us to close our eyes to the impact of human activity on ecosystems (Bayer, 2009), whereas ecocritics argue that nature only exists in its authentic state where there is no human presence, that is to say in the wilderness (Garrard, 2011 [2004]). Similarly, ecocritics claim that Derrida's concept of '*différance*'[3] and his vision of a constantly 'deferred', irremediably elusive and virtual reality, as well as the poststructuralists' refusal to acknowledge any stable reality outside the text, have obscured the importance of the natural environment. As a reaction, ecocritics insist on physical reality and on the (mostly negative) influence of human activities on the environment. Ecocritical texts are pervaded by a quasi-apocalyptic rhetoric, warning the reader against the threats faced by the environment and reminding him or her of the bucolic state of nature before humans' destructive action, as shown by the repeated use of pastoral imagery.

Whereas ecocriticism has developed in opposition to postmodernism and poststructuralism, it has run in parallel directions to postcolonialism, as Robert P. Marzec underlines in *An Ecological and Postcolonial Study of Literature. From Daniel Defoe to Salman Rushdie* (2007). As the title of the first chapter of Marzec's book suggests ('Enclosures, Colonization, and the Robinson Crusoe Syndrome: Notes toward an Ontology of Land'), Daniel Defoe illustrates in his treatment of space and environment in his texts the two historical developments of his time, that is, 'the rise of the British Empire, and the land-reformation phenomenon known as the Enclosure Movement' (Marzec, 2007: 1). These two areas of research – ecocriticism and postcolonialism – indeed overlap in many ways, as they shed light on the different perceptions of nature across cultures, and especially as they emphasize the way in which Western attitudes to nature have fed the colonialist project of domination and exploitation (Bayer, 2009). Originally more interested in humans than in nature, postcolonialism has undergone an ecocritical turn and redirected its attention to the impact of colonialism on the environment.

Lawrence Buell's book *Writing for an Endangered World* (2001) can be considered seminal for ecocritical studies. In it, he defines ecocriticism as the interdisciplinary association of literary and environmental studies. *The Environmental Imagination* (2005) further develops his analyses. In *The ISLE Reader*, Michael Bennett underlines Lawrence Buell's contribution to the field, which was to

> reevaluate many of the fundamental concepts of literary criticism from an ecocentric perspective. He goes to the root terms of literary analysis – representation, reference, metaphor, setting, characterization, *personae*, and canonicity – to suggest that all these elements are dramatically transformed by an environmental perspective.
>
> (Bennett, in: Branch and Slovic, 2003: 308)

These studies have striven to define their position on the critical map. They focus on the link between environmental awareness and literary aesthetics, between creative imagination and political action in their study of the relationship of the human and the nonhuman. Greg Garrard also underlines the political dimension of this approach when he says that 'ecocriticism is an avowedly political mode of analysis, as the comparison with Feminism and Marxism suggests. Ecocritics generally tie their cultural analyses explicitly to a "green" moral and political agenda' (Garrard, 2011 [2004]: 3).

Other theoreticians of ecocriticism include Cheryll Glotfelty, who defines it as the study of the relationship between literature and the physical environment: '[ecocriticism] takes as its subject the interconnections between nature and culture, specifically the cultural artifacts of language and literature' (Glotfelty and Fromm, 1996: xix). In her programmatic introduction to the first highly visible textbook of this new field, *The Ecocriticism Reader*, Cheryll Glotfelty asked: '[I]n addition to race, class and gender, should place become a new critical category?', and she seemed to answer her own question by saying that 'as a critical stance, ecocriticism has one foot in literature and the other on land' (Glotfelty and Fromm, 1996: xix). This in-betweenness suggested by Glotfelty in this metaphor is one of the biggest assets of the ecocritical approach: it uses objects and methods that it borrows from different disciplines, opening new horizons for literary criticism. It brings together the natural sciences and the humanities, thus helping to 'bridg[e] the gap between scientific and literary fields' (Bayer, 2009).

Nowadays, the world is facing a major environmental crisis visible through air pollution, deforestation, the destruction of the ozone layer and the potential exhaustion of some of our natural resources, among others. In this context, Richard Kerridge and Neil Sammells (1998: 5) write that 'ecocriticism seeks to evaluate texts and ideas in terms of their coherence and usefulness as responses to environmental crisis'. In the introduction, Richard Kerridge associates the writing of the environment not with the rhapsodic celebration of beautiful, bountiful nature, but with the more bitter genre of the Jeremiad, as he underlines in a quasi-biblical tone that ecological disasters are signs of divine retribution for humans' excessive exploitation of natural resources (Kerridge and Sammells, 1998: 3) and for their alienation from nature.

Stories of apocalypse, of the Earth rebelling against human pollution, of humans going into space because the Earth has become uninhabitable, have taken an important place in science fiction (SF) stories. Buell concedes that 'no genre potentially matches up with a planetary level of thinking "environment" better than science-fiction does', and he adds that 'for half a century science fiction has taken a keen, if not consistent interest in ecology, in planetary endangerment, in environmental ethics, in humankind's relation to the nonhuman world' (Buell, 2005: 57). One type of SF that particularly exemplifies the osmosis between the environment and literature is dystopian novels. The terrible experience of the environment in these novels makes readers aware of the role they have to play in the preservation of their world. In 1980, Carolyn Merchant had already used a sensational title for her book, *The Death of Nature*. In *Practical Ecocriticism* (2003), Glen Love exhorts human beings to gain stronger awareness of their place within this threatened environment.

Ecocriticism is thus shaped by a variety of theoretical approaches and disciplinary influences, all founded on a common concern about humanity's ethical relationship to nature.

What are the goals and ambitions of ecocriticism?

The aforementioned approaches all share the same desire: to draw the readers' attention to the role of nature (i.e. the material world, which may or may not include human beings) and the environment (strictly defined as 'the space surrounding man'),[4] particularly through the analysis of literary texts, for instance, by conjuring the evocative power of images (whether pastoral or apocalyptic) in order to make readers feel connected to the space, the places and elements surrounding them. Greg Garrard defines ecocriticism as 'a truly transformative discourse' (Garrard, 2011 [2004]: 4), suggesting that there is potential for action in this discourse.

Literary analysis is not the only means through which ecocritics attempt to re-evaluate nature: ecocriticism crosses the boundaries of disciplines and opens up a dialogue between natural sciences and cultural disciplines, which accounts for its hybridity. Ecocritical concerns are thus voiced through the study of cinema, human geography, the urban environment, pictorial art and especially land art, exemplified (among others) by walking artist Hamish Fulton who says that '[t]he only thing one should make with a landscape is photographs. The only things one should leave on a landscape are one's footprints'.[5] The ASLE (Association for the Study of Literature and Environment) is an interdisciplinary association created in 1992 in the United States, and different disciplinary perspectives are reflected in its journal, the *ISLE (Interdisciplinary Studies in Literature and Environment)*. Its British counterpart, *Green Letters*, also publishes a wide range of contributions to ecocritical discourse by artists, teachers and activists, and not only literary scholars, and has recently published a special issue on 'Literature and Sustainability' (Squire and Jarvis, 2015).

A diachronic perspective on ecocriticism's objects of study

Just as there is no single ecocritical approach restricted to one discipline, ecocritical analysis does not apply only to our times and the current environmental crisis. A diachronic perspective shows that ecocriticism is an evolving method, which can be brought to bear on different geographical areas or time periods. What's more, as Glen Love says, 'an important function of ecocriticism is to reexamine and reinterpret the depictions of nature in the canonical works of the past' (Love, 2003: 34).

In its beginnings, ecocriticism exclusively focused on the literature of the American West and on the representation of American nature in nonfictional texts dealing with the wild. The canonical writers for the first generation of ecocritics were the transcendentalist Henry D. Thoreau (*Walden*, 1854), Mary Austin (*The Land of Little Rain*, 1903) and Ralph W. Emerson (*Nature*, 1836), the advocates of new models of ethical relationships between humans and the space they are immersed in. One of the most studied works was *Silent Spring* (1962) by American biologist and zoologist Rachel Carson, a work whose impact on public policies was moreover quite significant. In this book dealing with pollution, Rachel Carson established a connection between the chemical pesticides used in agriculture and the death of birds, emphasizing through the use of pastoral nostalgia and apocalyptic rhetoric the mythical scale of the ecological disaster wrought by man. Ecocritical theories have then been extended to the British context[6] and to earlier texts, less obviously suited to ecocritical readings.

In *Romantic Ecology* (1991), Jonathan Bate nostalgically looks back on William Wordsworth as a 'poet of nature' (Garrard, 2011 [2004]: 42) and dwells on those times when humans lived in harmony with nature, when there was as yet no over-consumption of natural resources and when nature stood as the emblem of permanence compared to the fleeting quality of human life. Wordsworth's experience of crossing the Alps or the rustic way of life of Thomas Hardy's characters are celebrated by Jonathan Bate, who, quoting from the eighth book of William Wordsworth's *Prelude*, reminds us that 'Love of Nature [leads] to love of mankind'. Yet this nostalgic conception of a pastoral and bucolic past in which man was interconnected with nature has been challenged, because some ecocritics like Greg Garrard argue that the nature extolled by William Wordsworth has nothing to do with the nature today's environmentalists are trying to protect and was never really threatened in the first place.

Still, this use of a modern concept as a tool to read earlier texts has become more and more widespread. Basil Willey had already examined the practice in 1939 in *The Eighteenth-Century Background Studies on the Idea of Nature in the Thought of the Period*. More recently, Erin Drew and John Sitter (2011), who apply ecocritical methods to eighteenth-century texts, find it a promising way of studying and teaching that period, which saw the development of our modern attitudes to nature. This is also pointed out by Christopher Hitt, who thinks that an ecocritical approach may lead students to understand that the eighteenth-century texts they are asked to read are connected to their present life (Hitt, 2004: 125).

Such an approach may nevertheless run the risk of anachronism by projecting modern ideas onto the literature of the Enlightenment. According to Erin Drew and John Sitter, 'much of 18th-century writing not only deals with the natural world but does so in ways arguably more ecocentric and less egocentric in orientation than much Romantic writing' (Drew and Sitter, 2011: 227). It is indeed possible to detect in some eighteenth-century texts traces of a proto-environmental awareness, of a sensibility to nature that then faded with the Romantics, who were much more interested in their own feelings in response to nature than in nature itself.

James Thomson's poem *The Seasons* (1726), which details the relationship between nature and the poet's imagination, particularly rewards an ecocritical reading. In this nature poem, Thomson repeatedly expresses his concern for the environment, as when he denounces the killing of animals for food (*Spring*: 336–373), when he attacks hunting (*Autumn*: 360–457) or when he opposes the caging of birds (*Spring*: 1172–1207).

In my recent work, I have applied ecocritical theories to Daniel Defoe's texts, more precisely to *Robinson Crusoe* (1719). My initial question was to determine whether it was possible to trace signs of a proto-environmental awareness and sensibility to nature in the works of Daniel Defoe, a pragmatist who envisioned nature, above all, as an instrument for the economic and political development of Great Britain. Indeed, he wrote a detailed account of Great Britain's natural resources in *A Tour Thro' the Whole Island of Great Britain* (1724–1726). I chose to study the role played by the environment in early eighteenth-century novels, focusing especially on Robinson Crusoe's island (Peraldo, 2012). In one of the novel's key passages, Robinson discovers a footprint in the sand, an ambivalent motif symbolizing humankind's will to imprint itself on nature in order to control and exploit it, but also hinting at the continuity between humans and their environment. An ecocritical reading of this episode can show the attempt to warn humans what Kerridge was talking about (Kerridge and Sammells, 1998: 5). The print of a naked human foot that Robinson finds one day in the sand of his desert island surprises and terrifies him. It can be seen as the epitome of the contact between humankind and nature. Robinson first imagines it is the Devil's before concluding that 'it must be some more dangerous creature' (Defoe, 1975: 154): by this expression he means a savage, but, of course, one could also read in it the danger of the action of a human being that leaves a trace, like a scar, on the pristine sand of the island. This footprint may also symbolize Robinson's transformation of the land, and because he attributes it to the Devil, it could be seen as a sign of divine punishment for tampering with nature. The space in which Robinson finds himself transforms him: Daniel Defoe thus endows the island with a capacity to act that turns it into an actant. The island is raised to the status of a subject, on the same level as Robinson. The use of many hypallages – the island, at the beginning, is a 'desolate place' (Defoe, 1975: 51), but then it turns into Robinson's 'happy desert' or 'beloved island' (Defoe, 1975: 110) – along with the personification of the island, show that, whereas eighteenth-century urban and industrial developments might lead us to think that nature was considered simply an instrument, there was then a real sense of the interconnectedness and continuity between humans and nature.

Today, critics tend to point to the limits of ecocriticism, viewing it from outside the North American context in which it emerged. In *Littérature et environnement. Pour une écocritique comparée* (2012), Alain Suberchicot judges that the kind of environmental literature written by Edward Abbey or Annie Dillard is 'too "easy", too lyrical, too far removed from social questions'. Other critics also question the idealized, excessively romanticized, if not dehumanized, vision of nature often conveyed by ecocriticism. Some now prefer to turn to geocriticism (Westphal, 2007, 2016; Tally, 2011), which is more interested in the relationship between literature and space but also tackles the themes of landscape, nature and the environment in a less politically biased way. But ecocriticism and geocriticism are quite close, as suggested in Tally and Battista's recent interdisciplinary volume entitled *Ecocriticism and Geocriticism. Overlapping Territories in Environmental and Spatial Literary Studies* (2016). This volume focuses on the common emphasis that both schools of thought lay on the lived environment through social or natural spaces. The subtitle of the book, *Overlapping Territories*, shows the intrinsic connectedness between these two fields. Finally, ecocriticism may run the risk of forcing an anachronistic reading strategy onto earlier texts, and care must be taken not to distort the meaning of early modern texts by trying to force an ecocritical reading grid onto them.

Human attitudes to nature, both in terms of theory and practice, evolved during the eighteenth century and the Romantic period, which emphasized the notions of sympathy and compassion towards animals and the environment. Since then, they have undergone ever-deeper transformations, especially in a context in which new technologies are now reshaping or even defacing nature. Yet whatever the period, the texts associating literature and the environment are characterized by the same underlying tension between activism and aesthetics.

Notes

1 Postmodernism is characterized by temporal and spatial dislocation.
2 Poststructuralism is a philosophical movement, represented by Michel Foucault and Jacques Derrida, calling for a decentring of the subject as well as a deconstruction of texts.
3 For a definition of this key term coined by Derrida, see web.stanford.edu/class/history34q/readings/Derrida/Differance.html (Accessed 31/10/2016).
4 For a precise definition and distinction of the concepts of 'nature' and 'the environment', see the glossary in Buell (2005: 140–143).
5 Translation is mine. Original quotation reads: '*La seule chose que l'on devrait faire avec un paysage, ce sont des photographies. Les seules choses que l'on doit y laisser, ce sont les traces de ses pas*' (White, 1994: 114).
6 Ecocriticism has also spread throughout other countries, like France. Alain Suberchicot, in his desire to write a 'comparative ecocritical study' (2012), sets out to compare French, English and Chinese ecocritical texts, as well as texts belonging to different genre categories.

Bibliography

Austin, Mary Hunter (1903), *The Land of Little Rain*, Boston, MA, Houghton Mifflin.
Bate, Jonathan (1991), *Romantic Ecology: Wordsworth and the Environmental Tradition*, London and New York, Routledge.
Bayer, Gerd (2009), 'Ecocriticism', in: *The Literary Encyclopedia*, available at: www.litencyc.com/php/stopics.php?rec=true&UID=307 (Accessed 31/10/2016).
Blanc, Nathalie, Pughe, Thomas, and Chartier, Denis (2008), 'Littérature et écologie: vers une écopoétique', *Écologie et politique*, 36: 1–12.
Branch, Michael P., and Slovic, Scott (eds.) (2003), *The ISLE Reader: Ecocriticism, 1993–2003*, Athens, GA and London, University of Georgia Press.
Buell, Lawrence (1995), *The Environmental Imagination: Thoreau, Nature Writing, and the Formation of American Culture*, Cambridge, MA and London, Harvard University Press.
Buell, Lawrence (2001), *Writing for an Endangered World: Literature, Culture and Environment in the United States and Beyond*, Cambridge, MA and London, Harvard University Press.

Buell, Lawrence (2005), *The Future of Environmental Criticism: Environmental Crisis and Literary Imagination*, Malden, MA, Blackwell.
Carson, Rachel (2002 [1962]), *Silent Spring*, New York, Mariner Books.
Defoe, Daniel (1975 [1719]), *Robinson Crusoe*, New York and London, Norton.
Drew, Erin, and Sitter, John (2011), 'Ecocriticism and Eighteenth-Century Studies', *Literature Compass*, 8 (5): 227–239.
Emerson, Ralph Waldo (2003 [1836]), *Nature*, Harmondsworth, Penguin Classics.
Foerster, Norman (1923), *Nature in American Literature*, New York, Macmillan.
Garrard, Greg (2011 [2004]), *Ecocriticism: The New Critical Idiom*, London and New York, Routledge.
Glotfelty, Cheryll, and Fromm, Harold (eds.) (1996), *The Ecocriticism Reader: Landmarks in Literary Ecology*, Athens, GA and London, University of Georgia Press.
Hitt, Christopher (2004), 'Ecocriticism and the Long Eighteenth Century', *College Literature*, 31 (3): 123–147.
Kerridge, Richard, and Sammells, Neil (eds.) (1998), *Writing the Environment: Ecocriticism and Literature*, London and New York, Zed Books.
Love, Glen A. (2003), *Practical Ecocriticism: Literature, Biology, and the Environment*, Charlottesville, VA and London, University of Virginia Press.
Marzec, Robert P. (2007), *An Ecological and Postcolonial Study of Literature: From Daniel Defoe to Salman Rushdie*, New York and Basingstoke, Palgrave Macmillan.
Merchant, Carolyn (1980), *The Death of Nature: Women, Ecology, and the Scientific Revolution*, San Francisco, HarperCollins.
Peraldo, Emmanuelle (2012), 'Two Broad Shining Eyes: Optic Impressions, Natural Imprints, and Landscape in Robinson Crusoe', *Digital Defoe: Studies in Defoe and His Contemporaries*, 4 (1): 17–30.
Rueckert, William (1978), 'Literature and Ecology: An Experiment in Ecocriticism', *Iowa Review*, 9 (1): 71–86.
Squire, Louise, and Jarvis, Matthew (eds.) (2015), *Green Letters: Studies on Ecocriticism*, 19 (1), special issue on 'Literature and Sustainability': 1–7.
Suberchicot, Alain (2012), *Littérature et environnement. Pour une écocritique comparée*, Paris, Honoré Champion, series Unichamp-Essentiel.
Tally, Robert T. Jr. (ed.) (2011), *Geocritical Explorations: Space, Place, and Mapping in Literary and Cultural Studies*, New York, Palgrave Macmillan.
Tally, Robert T. Jr., and Battista, Christine (eds.) (2016), *Ecocriticism and Geocriticism: Overlapping Territories in Environmental and Spatial Literary Studies*, New York, Palgrave Macmillan.
Thomson, James (1970 [1726]), *The Seasons*, Folcroft, Folcroft Library Editions.
Thoreau, Henry David (1854), *Walden; or, Life in the Woods*, Boston, Ticknor and Fields, available at: www.eldritchpress.org/walden5.pdf (Accessed 31/10/2016).
Westphal, Bertrand (2007), *La géocritique. Réel, fiction, espace*, Paris, Minuit.
Westphal, Bertrand (2016), *La cage des méridiens. La littérature et l'art contemporain face à la globalisation*, Paris, Minuit.
White, Kenneth (1994), *Le plateau de l'albatros. Introduction à la géopoétique*, Paris, Grasset and Fasquelle.
Willey, Basil (1939), *The Eighteenth-Century Background: Studies on the Idea of Nature in the Thought of the Period*, London, Chatto and Windus.
Williams, Raymond (1973), *The Country and the City*, London, Chatto and Windus.

7

EPISTEMOCRITICAL PERSPECTIVES ON NATURE

Nature in culture

Laurence Dahan

Epistemocriticism

Over the centuries science and literature have drifted ever further apart and have been constructed as separate academic fields of knowledge, yet they have always been linked by secret connections. Literature has never totally severed its links from science; on the contrary, it has always been fed by scientific discoveries, thus showing that knowledge can adopt various forms according to the needs and the circumstances (Safir, 2015). New awareness of these interactions and the need to map them out have given rise to epistemocriticism, a new branch of literary studies interested in finding the traces of this general negotiation between the sciences and literature in literary texts. Epistemocritics observe that through the process of circulation of knowledge, our representations (of time, space, nature and man) inform both science and literature in comparable, yet different, ways. The aim of epistemocriticism is not to study nature itself, but the different kinds of knowledge about nature, which are not first-hand knowledge but have been constituted through a double process of *cultural* and *textual* formation. On the one hand, they have already been disseminated throughout society; they have been translated, transformed, distorted, vulgarized; on the other hand, they have been manipulated by writers, ever free to select only the features most relevant to their aims and to use them in original contexts.

Knowledge as expressed in literature is thus distinct from scientific knowledge: it is the result of a double process of imaginary and rational construction, which can help us grasp the notion of 'nature' in all its complex and multiple meanings: indeed, 'nature' ambiguously refers 'both to the objects governed by physical laws and to the principle that is acting throughout everything as well as within each individual, throughout the whole of creation as well as within each creature' (*Dix-huitième siècle*, 2013: back cover). The notion has been used in many varied ways, in the fields of physics and aesthetics, biology, geology and ecology, as well as metaphysics, theology, moral and political philosophy – and literature and the arts. Since it was rediscovered in the eighteenth century, the notion of nature has been at the heart of a series of debates reflecting the profound shifts in modern intellectual history and the gradual dissociation of two main ways of conceiving nature: one being promoted by science, in particular, by biology and physics, whereas the other is represented by literature and painting.

Because it focuses on points of intersection between these two fields, epistemocriticism can yield original insights on the notion of 'nature': as it does not dissociate knowledge from the culture in which it is disseminated and from the discourse through which it is expressed, it is able to reveal the ways in which several epistemological, aesthetic, moral, philosophical or ideological competing conceptions overlapped or succeeded each other over time, causing interference or interbreeding. It can thus remind us that nature does not exist independently from culture, but is constructed by cultural determinants and that its historical and cultural variations need to be explored (Gerrard, 2012; Goodboy and Rigby, 2011).

Most disciplines have now dismissed essentialist conceptions of nature to acknowledge the fact that we have no access to it other than through historical and cultural modes of perceiving, knowing and transforming it. Nature can only be grasped through a whole system of symbolic forms, practices, modes of production, perception and action, which turn it into a social space, itself interpreted, transformed, shaped and preserved by technology, knowledge systems, rituals and social rules generating cultural values. Yet at the same time, nature also refers to physical phenomena and to the space of our experience: it is not only an object of discourse, it is also the place where we live, work, play – a place that preexisted all cultures and constituted the frame within which cultures have developed while making it evolve. It is difficult to strike a balance between the idea of a wholly cultural nature and that of a wholly natural culture, as the history of the notions of nature and culture shows. Literature has also expressed this precarious balance through various tropes, as I aim to show through the analysis of a few literary texts that question the separation between culture and nature. Indeed, nature can best be grasped through traditional binary oppositions, such as nature/culture, natural/artificial, nature/social norm, nature/the city and so on.

The naturalization of social relations: Goethe's *Elective Affinities*

The eighteenth century was a crucial stage in the process of the rediscovery of nature, marked by decisive epistemological debates and ideological conflicts. As Colas Duflo has reminded us, the notion of nature was then invested with multiple values and meanings and was often invoked as a source of norms, as the notion was used to express 'both facts and laws, the positive and the normative'. At the same time, the notion was associated with 'principles of constancy, regularity, rationality, which could apply both to material phenomena and to human history' (Duflo, 2013: 10). Thus developed a powerful impulse to 'naturalize' – that is, to refer back to the idea of nature or to ground in nature – the order of the world, morals, religion, etc. The understanding of 'nature' was most profoundly renewed in the field of natural science: whereas life sciences opposed mechanistic and vitalistic conceptions, 'the emergence of chemistry [. . .] led to the revision of models derived from Cartesian physics and emphasized a principle of immanence, on both methodological and metaphysical planes, which stated that nature is its own explanation' (Duflo, 2013: 12). At the time appeared the notion of 'elective affinity' in order to solve the questions raised by chemical reactions during which certain substances bind together while others separate. In 1775, Torbern Bergman proposed the notion of 'elective attraction', derived from the Newtonian theory of gravitation, to explain why certain chemical substances separate to create new compounds with elements to which they are bound by stronger 'affinities'.

Goethe's plot for *Elective Affinities*, which opposes the fateful force of passion to the quiet legality of marriage, famously rests on the idea of 'chemical attraction'. The chemical metaphors are used to structure the relationships between the characters, which are governed by the dynamics of 'attraction' and 'repulsion'. Goethe considered this exploration of human relationships through the concepts of natural science relevant because the language of chemistry was alone able to describe the polarity animating vital processes, in the natural as well as in the human world. To justify the legitimacy of such a metaphorical transfer, Goethe indeed invoked nature as the explanatory principle for human behaviour:

> [T]here is ultimately only one nature everywhere, and even the realm of serene freedom of reason is ceaselessly permeated with the traces of dark, passionate necessity that are only extinguishable by a higher power and perhaps also not in this life.
>
> *(Goethe, 1809)*[1]

At a time when 'the humanities have no more effect on the mind of the one who studies them' (Goethe, 1808), chemistry represented a modern mode of investigation, enabling Goethe to formulate a new anthropology, between idealism and materialism, and to show that the social world could not be grounded in nature. In the novel, the characters are subjugated by the natural laws of elective affinities, which are stronger than their 'freedom of reason' and indicate the force of 'dark, passionate necessity'. Elective affinity thus challenges reason and suggests less the need to rationalize human relations than the impossibility of naturalizing social law (the laws of divorce and marriage): nature cannot take the place of the law dictating social norms, lest it should deprive it of its symbolic force and make the social collapse back into the realm of the mythical, ruled by the cosmic game of the one and indivisible nature, as it once was by the whims of the gods.

This challenge to reason also raises an epistemological issue: far from trying to align chemistry with the models derived from celestial mechanics, Goethe considered it as exemplifying another type of science, 'imposed by chemical activity, by the affinities and passions of matter', which could not be accounted for by the laws of physics but only by effective experience (Stengers, 1997: 461). Goethe opposed the realm of laws, in which effects are predictable and constant, to chemical activity, inaccessible to rational prediction, and characterized chemistry as the 'art' of understanding 'circumstances' rather than a 'science' aimed at defining 'laws' (Stengers, 1997: 460). He thus ran counter to the evolution of chemistry itself, during the eighteenth and nineteenth centuries, from a branch of natural philosophy (*Naturphilosophie*) to the epitome of positive science, before it was finally downgraded to a 'subscience' subordinated to physics and biology. The evolution of chemistry from 'speculative' in the eighteenth century to 'positive' in the early nineteenth century also ran parallel to its shift from a 'science of experience' to 'a science of experimentation,' no longer predicated upon the multiple and unpredictable movements of nature, but capable of mastering its processes (Stengers, 1997: 478). In the novel, this paradigm shift is also documented through the motif of the garden, an ancient literary *topos* granting access to the world of humanized nature, the interface 'between science and meditation, between the act of reshaping nature and the regenerative contemplation of landscape, between the art of cultivation and the cultivation of the self' (Haberl, 2010: 243).

Nature humanized: gardens and grafting

Elective Affinities takes place in a garden set apart from the world, a kind of *hortus conclusus* in which the cultivated society is free to pursue self-cultivation while its constituent characters cultivate their garden. In this space are manifested the signs of an ongoing paradigm shift, as the numerous elements referring to an eighteenth-century context show, such as the park, the castle, the hut, but more particularly the reflections of the 'old gardener' responsible for taking care of the vegetation, which contain explicit allusions to classical paradigms and hint at their inadequacy for a truly scientific approach to nature.

The old gardener indeed laments the advent of a modern generation of dilettantes, who are subordinating taste to fashion, commercializing the art of gardening and importing costly new species. While acknowledging the changes brought about by the development of trade, he is refusing to change his methods and nostalgically clings to traditional practices, preferring to deal only with a limited number of well-known species within a well-defined context. The gardener applies the same 'method' to all plants, whether familiar or foreign, keeping knowledge within the confines of experience and merely observing superficial features, before classifying them with the help of catalogues in which they are listed under 'foreign names'. The old gardener's practice explicitly echoes Linnaeus's descriptive and taxonomic approach, whereby plants and animal species were classified and ordered on the basis of their external features and with the help of a precise terminology. But, as Goethe suggests, however perfect a 'nomenclature' may be, it cannot account for a natural phenomenon, because it is limited to mere exterior details and thus cannot express the true nature of things. Discarding such a taxonomic analysis, Goethe thus moved beyond the classical *episteme* favoured by the old gardener, sketching the outlines of a 'phenomenological approach of nature' which would not simply consider 'external forms' but would push for an investigation of the inside. Rather than artificially applying the same method to all natural objects (whether plants, rocks or animals), it would deduce the adequate method from the object itself and develop a qualitative approach, sensitive to the morphogenetic processes in which the forms and colours of nature originate. As it thus combined several approaches – poetry's sensitive approach, scientific analysis and philosophical speculation – Goethe's method stood at the opposite pole of physics and mathematics and shared with *Naturphilosophie* the same ambition of reaching a global and unified conception of nature (Mauch, 2004).

However, this did not keep Goethe from transcribing the epistemological shifts occurring in his times of accelerating change, when experimental science and utilitarianism were on the verge of imposing their laws and were feeding man's ambition to dominate disenchanted nature. In the novel, the image of the garden thus reverses its meanings and is imperceptibly transformed from an idyllic setting into a 'bourgeois principle of utility', as the effects of agricultural development are seen to encroach on it (Niedermeier, 1992: 193). In this perspective, one should pay attention to grafting as a central epistemic image, symbolizing man's desire to dominate nature (Haberl, 2010: 251–257). It appears at the very outset of the novel, when Edouard is shown inserting grafts onto seedlings in his nursery, whereas the incipit has guided the reader through a domesticated and supposedly idyllic natural setting, like a painted landscape framed and dominated by the gaze of the painter/viewer. But the image of grafting soon reveals what this utopia of a new arcadia conceals; that is, the emergence of agrarian capitalism (Weber et al., 2011: 236). Grafting is an experimental technique aimed at improving 'nature' in qualitative and quantitative ways, that is, in artificially 'ennobling' a plant through a process of asexual hybridization. As such, it can be considered an allegory of the new times, dominated by instrumental rationality, a materialistic and utilitarian corruption of Enlightened Reason and its emancipatory force, a Promethean ambition to use technology to dominate nature. Grafting thus serves to foreground the themes of change and modernization, seen in their scientific, social and epistemological dimensions, in the context of a general reflection on human knowledge and its relation to nature.

When Flaubert took up the literary motifs of the garden and of grafting in *Bouvard and Pécuchet* at the end of the nineteenth century (the initial plan for the novel dates back to 1872 but the novel was left incomplete after the death of Flaubert in 1881), arboriculture had become 'a beautiful industry' and the nomenclature of botany still appealed to writers' imaginations. Bouvard and Pécuchet order young plants whose names 'sound wonderful to them' and introduce them into their landscape garden, taking care to follow all the rules and going as far as mimicking the posture of the gardeners shown in their reference books – which does not keep them from failing with their grafts. Like Goethe, Flaubert undermines his characters' private utopia and brings down their ambition to master nature, which is expressed in three different forms in the course of the novel: through the analytical study of nature (taxonomy), the transformation of nature in order to make it yield an economic profit (agriculture and arboriculture) and aesthetic contemplation (the creation of a picturesque garden) (Weber et al., 2011: 245). But these three strategies all lead to a dead end. The attempt to create a landscape garden, for instance, only leads to the construction of a mean, heterogeneous space, a caricature of romantic gardens, showing the conflicting combination of nature and culture and the fragmentation of nature as a whole into a sum of disparate curiosities, exemplifying 'a style Flaubert here denounces as rococo' (Weber et al., 2011: 250). The copy clerks' failure both to master nature and to turn it into a space of aesthetic experience can be set down to social changes (the rise of the bourgeoisie and of utilitarianism, etc.), but it also springs from an epistemological crisis because the current modes of knowing do not seem to yield the 'truth' of nature anymore: Linnaeus's classification system contains more exceptions than rules, the most sophisticated technology cannot fight weather and science can but give in to the mystery of nature. If humankind sometimes manages to force an order onto nature, it is always a short-lived achievement. Even a garden cannot be successfully controlled through botany, the science of gardening. Instead of presenting botany and natural history as truths, Flaubert emphasized the historicity of human fabrications and the precariousness of our knowledge, which is always dependent on a specific point of view and moment. Time, its hazards and changes inexorably subvert the order established by humans, reminding them of the transience of all human creations, or even knowledge. Roland Recht reminds us that landscape gardens have always incorporated a strong sense of time and of the fleetingness of things: 'Their aim was to produce a condensed image of the world and its history and to put it on display' (Recht, 1989: 152). The action of time is manifested in *Bouvard and Pécuchet* in the collapse of ancient knowledge, which opens the space of the garden to conflicts and disasters. This garden is indeed very far removed from the Garden of Eden, the garden of knowledge, which the Encyclopaedists envisioned as the emblem of the organic, natural and ordered development of knowledge (Haberl, 2010: 271).

Through the alliance of realism and allegory, Goethe and Flaubert used the strategic setting of the garden to expose the precariousness of all knowledge about nature and of all order imposed by human technology. They reversed the traditional meanings associated with the garden and transformed it from the symbol of a harmonious whole into a site revealing the signs of new emerging epistemic and social configurations.

Beyond nature and culture: the posthuman paradigm

The idea that nature tends to maintain itself in a state of predetermined harmony has been amply challenged (Buell, 2005; Scheffer, 2009). The metaphor of nature as a harmonious and stable machine was at the heart of ecology when it emerged at the beginning of the nineteenth century and permeated the rhetoric of environmental movements even as scientists were viewing the concept of a 'balance of nature' with increasing scepticism. Their rhetoric, based on outdated and often misapplied scientific models, posited that, free from human 'interference', nature was characterized by stability and harmony. But it has now become clear that 'nature undisturbed is not constant in form, structure, or proportion, but changes at every scale of time and space' (Botkin, 1992: 62). The idea of a highly structured, ordered and regulated natural world is now giving way to more dynamic conceptions emphasizing the fact that states of imbalance, instability or disorder also belong to the normal functioning of the natural world.

Writers have not ignored this epistemic shift: repudiating the ideal of a redemptive virgin nature, considered an antidote to the disenchantment caused by industrialization, they are now interested in the 'nonplaces' of modern urban space, like city outskirts, industrial zones, dump sites, wastelands, occupying a kind of no-man's land between nature and culture. They are advocating an integrative view in which humanity and its creations (technology, industry, knowledge) are considered the result of a process whereby they have become fully part of the natural world (Armbruster and Wallace, 2001; Gersdorf and Mayer, 2006). Nature is a gift made to humankind, but it has also been reshaped by it.

Besides urban spaces, literature also resorts to other symbols in order to subvert the nature/culture opposition, among which the image of the cyborg holds a pride of place, as, according to Donna Haraway, it challenges many binary divisions: animal/human, organism/machine, male/female, physical/nonphysical, etc. What is more, the cyborg associates microelectronics and biology at a time when computers have started to imitate and incorporate biological processes, so that the science of living organisms has become 'a powerful engineering science for redesigning materials and processes' (Haraway, 1991). The cyborg can be coupled with another borderline figure, that of the genetically engineered organism. Together these two figures testify to the emergence of a new cultural concept, the posthuman, questioning the relationships between humanity and its technological environment at a time when humans have become able to redesign themselves and go beyond their own limitations, using artificial devices such as prostheses, implants, genetic engineering or performance-enhancing drugs (Alaimo, 2010). Darwin had already challenged the idea of a metaphysical difference between humans and animals by insisting on the natural continuum linking them, but today it is the very distinction between what is human and what is nonhuman (nature, animals or machines) that is being radically questioned (Besnier, 2009: 20; Michaud, 2002). The very notion of human nature and of the boundaries that define it are today the focus of intense philosophical, ethical and scientific debates, which have been relayed by writers.

Maurice Dantec is thus predicting the advent of a posthuman era, which will only come to pass if humans stop considering themselves as 'the endpoint of the natural and/or historical process' to admit that they are 'a *crisis*, a critical commentary on nature' and that they hold within themselves the tools of their own 'metanatural' evolution (Dantec, 2001: 18, original emphasis). This is also the path traced by Michel Houellebecq in *Les particules élementaires* (*Atomised*). He observes that humankind is on the verge of being surpassed by its own creations: science has produced the conditions for a fundamental mutation by making humans 'the first species in the universe which had developed the conditions for its successor' (Houellebecq, 2001: 378). In the novel, two key ideas embody the switch from the human to the posthuman: procreation dissociated from sex, and a new interpretation of biology in the light of quantum theory. Reducing love to sex and sex to a mere biological function, Houellebecq attacks nature itself: characterized by the struggle for domination and the survival of the fittest, nature is presented as an inherently evil, blind force that human history should not depend on anymore. Natural selection indeed promotes a hierarchy and leads to the destruction of the weak. The solution should therefore lie in supplementing the idea of natural history with that of a 'metanatural history' in which science and technology would be major factors of evolution. In other words, science should be naturalized, become 'a second nature', by contrast with 'original nature' or 'natural nature', which never exceeds its own limitations, whereas the very point of posthumanism should be to raise the question of a new humanism (Sloterdijk, 2010: 30).

These themes are also tackled by Richard Powers in *Generosity*, which more particularly dwells on genetic engineering. In the novel, a brilliant geneticist thinks he has managed to find the 'happiness' gene in a young woman who has been particularly battered by life and hopes that his work will benefit humanity. Geneticists aim at transforming human nature and, because it is summed up in the genome of an individual, at modifying and improving genomes. This new eugenic approach does not consider improving the race, but 'enhancing' humans, and freeing them from the hazards of nature or education, eliminating the defects occasioned by natural birth and enabling them to overcome the natural limitations that hamper self-fulfilment. From an epistemological point of view, genetic 'enhancement' raises the issue of the relationships between innate and acquired features, in other words, between nature and culture. However, since geneticists have become interested in genomics, they have learned not to consider 'heredity *against* the environment' but to understand 'heredity *through* the environment' (Powers in Artus, 2011, original italics). Biologists have indeed discovered the influence of the environment on ontogeny and that of epigenesis on gene expression, thus demonstrating that genes are the products of a history that is not only natural but also cultural. The logical implications then are that nature and culture should not be pitted against each other as mutually exclusive totalities but should be considered, 'beyond nature and culture' (Descola, 2005), as two intimately interconnected levels of organization and complexity.

In a sense, fictions of the posthuman merely push modern thought – which considers that humanity only exists as radically distinct from nature – to its extreme consequences. But when

> the idea of Nature (as an opposite, an alien reality calling for respect owing to its irreducible alterity) is discarded and it is viewed as senseless matter – that

can be grasped and humanized – then transgression is no longer possible and all realities are leveled down, creating a general sense of disenchantment.

(Besnier, 2009: 98)

Here is modernity's so-called achievement, which the posthuman might well force us to stare in the face, while making us recognize that 'there is no other Nature for us but that which offers itself in excess, diverse and unmastered, and that is why the progress of our sciences and technology must be encouraged and led on by ethics' (Besnier, 2009: 103). The myth of a culture/nature divide should then be exploded, and we should finally recognize the interweaving of nature and culture, which has always framed and made our actions possible. This also entails challenging the separation between the sciences and the humanities: if nature is nothing more than 'an ontological tool of a particular kind' designed to establish 'on the one hand, a world of things endowed with an intrinsic factuality and, on the other, a world of human beings governed by arbitrary meanings', then the opposition between the sciences and the humanities collapses as much as that between nature and culture (Descola, 2005: 62–63). The dismantling of such oppositions is precisely the aim of epistemocriticism: challenging the preconstructed separation between the 'two cultures', which it views merely as the contingent expression of Western representations at a specific moment of time, it makes literature more fully intelligible within cultural evolution, for which it is both a cause and an effect.

Note

1 See Goethe Johannes Wolfgang (von) (1809), *Selbstanzeige im 'Morgenblatt für gebildete Stände' vom 4 September 1809*, HA 6, p. 639, quoted by Clemens Pornschlegel, 'Goethe et la critique conservatrice du monde techno-scientifique. Remarques sur la fonction mythologique de la science chez Goethe', available at: www.goethezeitportal.de/db/wiss/goethe/pornschlegel_critique.pdf (Accessed 05/10/2016).

Bibliography

Alaimo, Stacy (2010), *Bodily Natures: Science, Environment, and the Material Self*, Bloomington, Indiana University Press.
Armbruster, Karla, and Wallace, Kathleen (eds.) (2001), *Beyond Nature Writing: Expanding the Boundaries of Ecocriticism*, Charlottesville, University of Virginia Press.
Artus, Hubert, interview with Richard Powers (2011), ' "Générosité" de Richard Powers: la littérature des gènes', *Le Nouvel Observateur*, available at: http://blogs.rue89.com/cabinet-de-lecture/2011/03/24/generosite-de-richard-powers-la-litterature-des-genes-196670 (Accessed 05/10/2016).
Besnier, Jean-Michel (2009), *Demain les posthumains. Le futur a-t-il encore besoin de nous?*, Paris, Fayard.
Botkin, Daniel (1992), *Discordant Harmonies: A New Ecology for the Twenty-First Century*, New York, Oxford University Press.
Buell, Laurence (2005), *The Future of Environmental Criticism: Environmental Crisis and the Literary Imagination*, Oxford, Blackwell.

Dantec, Maurice (2001), *Le théâtre des opérations 2000–2001. Laboratoire de catastrophe générale*, Paris, Gallimard.

Descola, Philippe (2005), *Par-delà nature et culture*, Paris, Gallimard, translated into English by Janet Lloyd (2013) as *Beyond Nature and Culture*, Chicago, University of Chicago Press.

Dix-huitième siècle (2013), special issue 'La nature', 45.

Duflo, Colas (2013), 'Introduction', *Dix-huitième siècle*, 45: 7–15.

Flaubert, Gustave (1980 [1881]), *Bouvard et Pécuchet*, Paris, Folio-Gallimard.

Gerrard, Greg (2012), *Ecocriticism*, London and New York, Routledge.

Gersdorf, Catrin, and Mayer, Sylvia (eds.) (2006), *Nature in Literary and Cultural Studies: Transatlantic Conversations of Ecocriticism*, Amsterdam, Rodopi.

Goethe, Johann Wolfgang (von), letter dated 25 November 1808, *Briefe 1786–1814*, in: Goethe, Johann Wolfgang von, *Werke. Kommentar. Register*, 1993, Hamburger Ausgabe, edited by Erich Trunz, Munich, C. H. Beck.

Goethe, Johann Wolfgang (von) (1978 [1809]), *Elective Affinities*, London, Penguin Classics.

Goodboy, Axel, and Rigby, Kate (eds.) (2011), *Ecocritical Theory: New European Approaches*, Charlottesville, University of Virginia Press.

Haberl, Hildegard (2010), 'Ecriture encyclopédique – écriture romanesque. Représentations et critique du savoir dans le roman allemand et français de Goethe à Flaubert', PhD. Dissertation, EHESS-University of Vienna.

Haraway, Donna (1991), 'A Cyborg Manifesto: Science, Technology and Socialist-Feminism in the Late Twentieth Century', available at: http://faculty.georgetown.edu/irvinem/theory/Haraway-CyborgManifesto-1.pdf (Accessed 05/10/2016).

Houellebecq, Michel (1998), *Les particules élémentaires*, Paris, Flammarion, translated into English (2001) as *Atomised*, London, Vintage.

Mauch, Christof (ed.) (2004), *Nature in German History*, New York, Berghahn.

Michaud, Yves (2002), *Humain, Inhumain, Trop Humain*, Paris, Flammarion.

Niedermeier, Michael (1992), *Das Ende der Idylle*, Bern and New York, Peter Lang.

Recht, Roland (1989), *La lettre de Humboldt: du jardin paysager au daguerréotype*, Paris, Christian Bourgois.

Safir, Margery Arent (ed.) (2015), *Storytelling in Science and Literature*, Lewisburg, PA, Bucknell University Press.

Scheffer, Marten (2009), *Critical Transitions in Nature and Society*, Princeton, NJ, Princeton University Press.

Sloterdijk, Peter (2010), *Essai d'intoxication volontaire*, suivi de *L'heure du crime et le temps de l'œuvre d'art*, Paris, Hachette.

Stengers, Isabelle (1997), 'L'affinité ambiguë: le rêve newtonien de la chimie du 17e siècle', in: Serres, Michel (ed.), *Éléments d'histoire des sciences*, Paris, Larousse: 445–478.

Weber, Anne-Gaëlle, Barel-Moisan, Claire, Giboux, Audrey, and McIntosh, Fiona (2011), *Fictions du savoir, savoirs de la fiction*, Paris, Atlande.

PART III
Movements, activism and societies

Rethinking nature is a process performed by committed individuals and collective groups, by movements that emerge and define themselves around some specific objectives in relation to what has constituted itself as 'society' as compared to nature. Environmentalism, which some see as a school of thought and others as a political movement, has known three main forms according to Joan Martinez-Alier: wilderness, ecoefficiency and environmental justice (2016: 97). These different stances are inherently political and not just naturalistic, economic or social stances. This may be examined through a consideration of values and actions, as in the first part of this book, or through the analysis of writings and representations, as in the second part. Thus emerge common points as well as substantial divergences between the different positions. This third part is based on the rise of new, various forms of critical awareness of the way in which our connection with nature, and more precisely our capacity to know nature, is inextricably bound up with the relationships between cultures and power. In order to fully grasp the complexity of these issues, the contributors of this volume have adopted reflexive and cross-disciplinary perspectives.

This critical inquiry first examines the scientific modes of apprehension and their links with social practices, as well as political, economic, social or academic calls to action, echoing the tension between distantiation and involvement that characterizes the researcher's work and can sometimes lead him or her to open up unexpected new questionings. Disciplines from the social sciences have, even more largely, undergone evolutions in their paradigms, subjects and methods that have provided glimpses into their close links with the social world. Noel Castree is right to point out that, historically, reflections on nature, more than on any other issue, have demonstrated that 'scientists change our *actualité* not only through their technological inventions but also through the vocabularies and methods they employ to persuade those outside science to pay attention' (Castree, 2016: 151).

The reverse – the fact that scientific references have been used to legitimate social movements as well as the priorities of public action – is also true.

Two linked questions therefore need to be examined: the aim is to understand first how some specific disciplinary fields have defined themselves around an issue as fraught as that of nature, and more particularly, how ecosociology has risen out of sociology, a discipline seemingly devoted to the analysis of the 'social', not the 'natural', world; second, how cross-disciplinary fields of inquiry have emerged, such as political ecology, ecofeminism or ethnoecology, rejecting the separation between theory and practice. Let us only remind the reader that the ecofeminist praxis associated with the work of Rachel Carson was generated from the observation of an unusual phenomenon of environmental health: mass bird deaths (Carson, 1962).

Both cases underline the permanent tension between essentialism and relativism and challenge the idea that there should be anything 'natural' to nature. This is also plainly revealed by the various approaches that focus on 'minorities' and on all the groups that may consider themselves cast out, socially or spatially (political ecology, ecofeminism), erased or silenced, like the native peoples (ethnoecology).

Catherine Repussard argues (Chapter 8) that political ecology has been generated by a 'heuristic of fear' (in the sense given to it by Hans Jonas, 1979) and the attending claim of the necessity of protecting the environment defended by local, national and international institutions (earth summits, climate change conferences, etc.). As such, political ecology blends science and activism and expresses itself on the level of intellectual debate, like the *Lebensreform* movements born at the turn of the twentieth century, as well as on an individual and social level. It is thus far different from the kind of 'politicking' ecological parties engage in. The author underlines the fact that political ecology is today taking two opposite directions: some of its proponents advocate adapting economy to nature and call for a new form of 'green capitalism'; others question the Western model of development and favour economic degrowth, with the twin aim of teaching respect of nature and setting up an 'economics of happiness', thus looking back to the belief in a redemptive antimodernism.

Margot Lauwers (Chapter 9) then explains the way in which ecofeminism, which was born around the 1970s, sees the oppression of women and nature as being linked by a conceptual logic of domination common to all forms of oppression (sexism, speciesism, racism, etc.), that is, the intersectionality of power relations. However, ecofeminism has had to cope with a lot of criticism often based on misconceptions. Accordingly, this chapter deals with some of ecofeminism's major challenges, for example, moving past the essentialism debate and the eurocentrism of some of its thinkers, as well as gaining recognition for some of the interdisciplinary configurations which it helped create. Lauwers also addresses the subdiscipline of feminist ecocriticism which emerged directly from ecofeminist thinking and has helped it attract more academic attention, especially from European academic circles.

The history of sociology also abounds with examples of misconception. The discipline has not embraced 'the environment' with ease, in large part due to its historical mission to avoid any form of biological or environmental determinism. Graham Woodgate's contribution (Chapter 10) interestingly traces the evolutions from a sociology of the environment to different forms of 'ecosociology' in Anglo-Saxon thought: How does the consideration of nature affect the evolution of the discipline, from its founding fathers to contemporary sociology? The chapter charts the history of environmental sociology, between theories of environmental degradation and ecological reform, and suggests an integrating framework for ecosociologies that is able to propose alternatives to the increasing encroachment of modern industrial society. As Woodgate concludes, 'the role of ecosociologies in the Anthropocene then becomes the analysis of alternative socio-ecological discourses and practices in terms of their capacity to heal the planetary metabolic rift, address the intra- and intergenerational dimensions of ecological debt and promote environmental justice'.

Éric Navet (Chapter 11) similarly advocates an ethnoecological approach. After explaining the way in which Christian philosophy established a break between man and nature, through the belief that the 'savage' part of humanity had to be subdued and nature in the common sense 'domesticated', he shows that ethnology, itself conditioned by the same preconceptions and the colonial context, has only recently integrated the philosophy of native peoples, who consider that human beings are part of a 'nature' that they must accept and to which they must adapt to survive in this world. Authors like Philippe Descola, Jared Diamond or Tim Ingold are called upon in order to emphasize that we should not take into consideration human societies independently from the environments where they develop and that any ethnology or anthropology cannot be anything but a *human ecology*.

Bibliography

Carson, Rachel (2002 [1962]), *Silent Spring*, New York, Mariner Books.
Castree, Noel (2016), 'Nature', *in:* Adamson, Joni, Gleason, William A., and Pellow, David N. (eds.), *Keywords for Environmental Studies*, New York, New York University Press: 151–156.
Jonas, Hans (1979), *Das Prinzip Verantwortung. Versuch einer Ethik für die technologische Zivilisation*, Frankfurt am Main, Suhrkamp, translated into English (1984) as *The Imperative of Responsibility: In Search of Ethics for the Technological Age*, Chicago, University of Chicago Press.
Martinez-Alier, Joan (2016), 'Environmentalism(s)', *in:* Adamson, Joni, Gleason, William A., and Pellow, David N. (eds.), *Keywords for Environmental Studies*, New York, New York University Press: 97–100.

8
FROM *LEBENSREFORM* TO POLITICAL ECOLOGY

Catherine Repussard

Political ecology strives to interweave ecological concerns and political action while rethinking socioeconomic organization. Yet it remains a somewhat elusive, shape-shifting concept, between political imaginary, scientific discourse and economic beliefs. Political ecology relates both to power and counterpowers. The intertwining of political ecology and power, particularly in its institutional form, was evidenced in the 1970s by the foundation of green parties in the wake of *Die Grünen* (the Greens) in the Federal Republic of Germany and by the development of national and transnational institutions dedicated to environmental protection. Political ecology's role in the crystallization of counterpowers has been demonstrated by the engagement of civil society actors in promoting an alternative form of development, making political ecology a nexus of resistance to modernity.

The development of political ecology also remains closely linked to what Hans Jonas called the 'heuristics of fear' in his book *The Imperative of Responsibility* (1979), which he believed allows us to better anticipate and know the threat, while pointing us towards a new environmental ethic in the making. Since the 1980s, indeed, ecological discourses – although varied and manifold – have become increasingly alarmist and pessimistic, eliciting political responses not only at the international and national levels, but also on local and individual scales. These range from the approaches to nature as sanctuary that started to be developed in the late nineteenth century to the development of alternative models embedded in sustainability, perceived as a guarantee of respect for the natural environment. The most radical theses question the very ideas of indefinite growth and development that emerged with the industrial revolution and propose to bid 'farewell to growth', which they believe is the only way to save our planet. In this sense, political ecology is not a recent phenomenon.

Early centres and thinkers of 'ecologism'

In the second half of the nineteenth century, the aspiration to fundamentally rethink humankind's relationship to its natural and social environmental already had deep roots in the German-speaking world but also beyond, characterized by an eagerness to 'reform' – to repair the damages caused by modernity. This concern was shared by the first ecologists, such as the American geographer George Perkins Marsh (1801–1882), who penned one of the monuments of ecological and geographical thought, *Man and Nature or Physical Geography as Modified by Human Action* (1864). At a time when modernity was consolidating, the ideological foundations for moving beyond it were being laid, for instance, with the geographer and prominent anarchist Élisée Reclus (1830–1905), who authored the hefty *The Earth and Its Inhabitants* (published in six volumes between 1905 and 1908), in which he argues that all human action must comply with social, aesthetic and moral criteria. In the German-speaking world, however, these ideas had a greater sociopolitical impact than elsewhere. They were defended by alternative ecological groups then generally lumped together under the term 'life reform movements' (*Lebensreform*) (Cluet and Repussard, 2014), in the wake of Goethe's *Naturphilosophie* and an approach to political romanticism chiefly concerned with rethinking the relations between individuality and collectivity. Politically, this movement ran counter to rationalism and the idea of universalism, and explicitly opposed the discourse of the Enlightenment and the French Revolution asserting the autonomy of the individual, which had given birth to political modernity. Structurally the life reform movement can be described as a 'movement of movements' that emerged out of civil society around 1900 as a response to the powerlessness, if not the inanity, of the leading elites. It can also be seen as an attempt of the 'cultural bourgeoisie' (*Bildungsbürgertum*), as it moved away from Wilhelminian ideals to find a way out of its political, economic, social and societal 'class malaise'. This bourgeoisie strongly asserted its reformist intentions. They had no Marxist revolutionary ideas about changing the world; rather they sought to change life, in the sense of changing individuals' lifestyles as they interacted with their natural and social environment. This was meant to foster a bond between humans and their environment, but also to promote a life that fitted their own nature. The life reform movement intended to reform the entire social body in the name of a 'natural' order. Its ambitions of integration were reflected in a culture of the oxymoron, an effort to reconcile contradictory aspirations. This 'alternative conservatism' aimed at linking individuals and groups, socialism and capitalism, nature and culture. The movement's vocation is to promote what some consider 'another modernity', based on the refusal of duality (between humankind and nature in particular) and an effort to create harmony, a key value for all *Lebensreform*-related thought. In the face of political and civilizational choices believed to be harmful, this intellectual current elicited the development of alternative communities. In these enclaves respect for nature was combined with a remodelled economic order emphasizing concepts of sharing, equity and justice. Their founders hoped these ideas would catch on in larger political spaces and ultimately bring all humankind together. Thus this movement, which aspired to give meaning and sustainability to humankind's relations to its environment, arguably pioneered the ecological perception of politics and the political perception of ecology that would later expand within the German-speaking world and beyond.

Furthermore, as a response to the will to subdue and therefore exploit nature, the romantics had revived the idea that humans are inevitably a part of their natural environment and that it was necessary to comply with a natural order they viewed as primordial, designed to be unalterable due to its beauty and harmony. Immersion into the wild became one of their ideals, and one that had a lasting influence on the trailblazers of ecological thought worldwide. A famous example is the remarkable *Walden* (1854), in which Henry D. Thoreau (1817–1862) relates life in a cabin he had built in Concord (Massachusetts) to live alone in the woods. We may think also of the monistic approaches developed in Germany by the 'founder of ecology' Ernst Haeckel (1834–1919). In 1866, Haeckel defined ecology as 'the whole science of the relations of the organism to its surrounding outside world, [. . .] in a broader sense [. . .] all conditions of existence' (Haeckel, 1866: 286). He believed living beings and the physical world were made up of the same matter. This inclusive approach, which linked humanity to all other living beings, was also conceived as a model for human societies. As he emphasized the connections between the biological and political environment, which he viewed as applied biology, Haeckel gave a bio-political dimension to his thought that would have a lasting impact on a number of political ideologies throughout the twentieth century, including ecofascism.[1] The immersion into the wild was an important part of the meditations of the American forester and ecologist Aldo Leopold (1887–1948) recorded in *A Sand County Almanac* (1949), which inspired philosopher John Baird Callicott (born 1941), a pioneer of the environmental ethic who wanted the power of human consciousness to serve the natural world, understood as living forms and landscapes in their diversity. It is also a core feature of the contemporary deep ecology movement as it was conceived by Norwegian philosopher Arne Naess (1912–2009). Naess's thought (1989, 2008) built on monism, in the sense that he placed nature and not humanity in the centre and gave no priority to humankind in his defence of the rights of living spaces, all the while expanding on the concept of the 'heuristics of fear'.

The 'heuristics of fear' (Hans Jonas)

This first era of ecologism, centred in the German-speaking world, related to the development of alternative philosophical and political thoughts, but also to individual and social practices concerned with environmental protection. It was followed by a period of decline until a resurgence in the 1960s, which was particularly intense across the industrialized world. This new wave of ecologism was heralded by such whistleblowers as the American biologist Rachel Carson (1907–1964).

Her book *Silent Spring* (1962), in which she describes pesticides as biocides, raised unprecedented awareness among American opinion, leading to a ban on some products (including DDT) and to the creation of the Environmental Protection Agency. The need to find 'another way' became the universal motto of increasingly numerous groups, initially active in Western countries. Additionally, *Silent Spring*, as it denounced the harmful effects of intensive farming on humanity, also called into question the political and industrial choices of the then so-called developed nations. A long series of ecological disasters, from oil spills – starting in 1967 with the wreck of the *Torrey Canyon* – to nuclear accidents – such as Three Mile Island (1979) in the United States, Chernobyl (1986) in Ukraine and Fukushima (2011) in Japan – heightened the sense of insecurity. Talk of the prospect of the destruction of nature, as well as of the end of civilization or even of humanity as a whole, inevitably increased fear. Books including those of French agronomist René Dumont (1904–2005), *L'utopie ou la mort!* [*Utopia or Death*] (1973), or more recently biologist Jared Diamond's *Collapse: How Societies Choose to Fail or Succeed* (2005), are perfect illustrations of this attitude. Despite the stances taken by such climate change deniers as Richard Lindzen (born 1940), a researcher at the prestigious Massachusetts Institute of Technology and a member of the IPCC (see *infra*), or Bjorn Lomborg (born 1965), the author of the bestseller *The Skeptical Environmentalist* (1998), the Anthropocene[2] (Hamilton, 2015; Bonneuil, 2016) and global warming are almost unanimously perceived as the warning signs of a planetary disaster. This disaster would cause major national and international political crises, especially due to the dozens of millions of expected climate refugees (Welzer, 2015; Hirsch, 2016).

In the face of perils such as the human and social 'denaturation' that caused so much concern around 1900 or the collective threat questioning the very survival of humankind as a whole a century later, a number of responses have been put forward.

First, the idea of preservation prevailed, implying the creation of protected spaces, conceived as resistance enclaves – a response observed around 2000 as well as a hundred years before. This was a fundamental idea of the emerging ecological thought in Europe, with the creation of protected natural spaces in Germany, but also in the United States, where preserved areas were introduced in the late nineteenth century to provide sanctuaries for a wilderness threatened by progress. The oldest such protected area is Yellowstone National Park (1872), the first in a long line of areas protected to varying extents by national and then international organizations, ultimately leading to UNESCO's concept of 'world heritage' (1972). Although these initial steps towards the protection of certain spaces reflected growing awareness of human-made damage to nature on the global scale, it did not trigger a fundamental change of general approach, instead partaking in a logic that essentially consisted of turning wild natural areas into museums.

Subsequently, responses were devised by national political institutions, in which the foundation of green parties only had a limited impact. The green parties that have secured representation in coalition governments (in Italy, France and Germany) have influenced a few governmental choices without fundamentally changing policy. The international and transnational organizations that have accompanied the rise of expertise have probably had a greater impact. The Intergovernmental Panel on Climate Change (IPCC), for instance, was established in 1988 (GIEC) on the recommendation of the G7 by the World Meteorological Organization and the United Nations. It was tasked with synthetizing research conducted in laboratories across the world regarding human influence on the climate. IPCC reports are supposed to steer political decision-making at the international level. At the European level, DG Environment is one of the European Commission's forty directorates-general. Recently, US President Barack Obama put together a 'green dream team' composed of Steven Chu, Carol Browner, John Holdren and Jane Lubchenco, experts in charge of developing green technologies to put the United States on the path towards energy independence and control pollution by introducing strict checks meant to limit environmental damage.

This attention to the environment has also been reflected by the organization of world climate summits. Although the 2009 Copenhagen Conference was a failure, the 2010 edition held in Cancun was relatively successful in comparison. Earth Summits are decennial meetings of world leaders organized by the UN since 1972, aiming to define means of stimulating sustainable development at the global level. The first summit took place in Stockholm (Sweden) in 1972, the second in Nairobi (Kenya) in 1982 and the third in Rio de Janeiro (Brazil) in 1992. The latest Earth Summit, the so-called Rio+20, also took place in Rio in 2012. The 178 participating nations set collective objectives for the reduction of greenhouse gas emissions, including a countdown, and committed to dividing emissions by two in order to ensure climate stability.

These international summits attest to the fact that the only solution is global. They are conceived as an international institutional effort to favour a scientific response to the damage caused by science itself, with an emphasis on developing 'green technologies' (Sachs and Ki-moon, 2015; Carius, 2016). The adaptation of the capitalist model to ecology is supposed to bring about sustainable development and an energy transition expected to create millions of green jobs. This option refuses to give up Western lifestyles, although they are responsible for the degradation of the environment. It is characterized by policies promoting growth and progress – a 'green capitalism' that carries hope only to some degree. Indeed, many civil society actors have expressed scepticism about the agreements signed at world summits (Rio+20, COP 21 held in Paris in December 2015, etc.) (Chichilnisky and Bal, 2017), whose impact on the deterioration of the environment seems small in the face of unchecked market-led globalization. They seek to open other political avenues, generally at a different level. Admittedly, transnational associations like Greenpeace attempt to act globally, but civil society mostly operates at the local level through ecological activism, with the targeted actions of ecowarriors (Scarce and Brower, 2016) and the work of associations and politicians at the level of regions and cities to anticipate the demands of sustainable development, for instance, in experimental neighbourhoods called 'eco-districts'.

Market ecology vs. growth objectors

In its first report, *The Limits to Growth* (1972), the Club of Rome, a think tank bringing together scientists, economists, national and international civil servants and industrialists, had denounced the search for unlimited exploitation of a world with limited resources (Meadows and Randers, 2004). This idea was taken up by many thinkers, combining environmentalism with a radical critique of the modern world, as well as of the latter's dominant mode of capitalist production. Ivan Illich (1926–2002), for instance, evidenced the counterproductivity of the productive model. His book *Energy and Equity* (1974) documents the harmful effects of development. Beyond a certain threshold, the ever-increasing production of goods and services becomes a source of alienation, at odds with the concept of conviviality as a basis for harmonious human relationships, as explored in his *Tools for Conviviality* (2001 [1973]). In his books, including *Toward an Ecological Society* (1980), Murray Bookchin (1921–2006) promotes a libertarian municipalism that theorizes political decentralization as the conditions of an ecological society or social ecology. In *Ecology as Politics* (1975), André Gorz (1923–2007), one of the pioneers of political ecology in France and Europe, pinpointed the intertwining of the devastations of the Earth and the destruction of humanity's natural bases as the consequences of the capitalist mode of production, criticizing the techniques embodying the domination of humans over nature. Having researched with Bernard Charbonneau the growing standardization of humanity under the grip of technology, Jacques Ellul (1912–1994) defended 'voluntary simplicity' as a path towards liberation in an abundant body of work (Charbonneau and Ellul, 2014). A few decades later, his approach would inspire many alternative thinkers embracing a change of lifestyle following a model of 'serene' degrowth described by Serge Latouche (born 1940), who is pursuing the 'gamble of de-growth' (the title of his 2006 book) or Paul Ariès (born 1956) in his book *La simplicité volontaire contre le mythe de l'abondance* (2010). Highly critical of market-led globalization, these thinkers have also connected with alter-globalization movements since the turn of the twenty-first century (Juris, 2008; Holloway and Grubacic, 2016). These promoters of another globalization are now active globally. They defend local economies and favour use over ownership, sharing and mutual aid; they seek to be rather than to have and revive the dream of a new, convivial, solidary Arcadia by proposing an 'economics of happiness' where GDP would no longer be the yardstick for measuring the health of an economy – an approach condensed in the slogan 'More fun, less stuff'. Their goal is to reorganize civil society at the global level to compensate for the powerlessness of political institutions. The engagement of the Indian ecologist and feminist Vandana Shiva, the director of the Research Foundation for Science, Technology and Ecology, exemplifies this change of scale (Shiva, 2015). These thinkers raise the question of the relation between ecology and democracy with a new urgency. In their view, the alternative will come from a remodelled political ecology, emphasizing participatory and deliberative democracy to renew and enrich a discredited representative democracy whose members will be better armed to face environmental challenges. This involves, for instance, organizing citizens' conferences on the international level.

These movements unanimously reject political parties that call themselves 'green'. The 1980s was marked by the creation of green parties in many countries, aiming to influence political choices from within the system. Yet their success remained limited, due to the so-called 'greening' of the other parties, albeit sometimes very superficial, in a bid to attract environmentally conscious voters. Facing the failure of the green parties, the civil society movements inspired by ecology tend to strongly assert the primacy of individual engagement and action, based on the idea that collective change will only happen through the addition of 'ego-ecological' behaviours (Zavalloni, 2007). Ecological behaviours are approached as the outcomes of individual and personal choices designed to change everyday individual behaviours relating, for instance, to food, the quality of clothing, means of transportation, waste management, etc. This 'new way' of inscribing ecology in everyday life is reminiscent of the ideals of the life reform movements discussed earlier in this chapter. They envision political ecology as part of a reform of the self (*Selbstreform*), understood as everyday individual behaviour, just as the other path traced by today's political ecologists is heavily reliant on the sum of individual engagements across the world, an idea that alternative communities picked up and expanded upon in the 1970s. Their representation of political change clearly resonates with life reform movements, even if time may have somewhat altered the echo – individual behaviours in the name of ecology relate to the customs of their respective eras. Regardless, the two undoubtedly share the promotion of a life of harmony, combining respect for nature and the 'economics of happiness' (Steedman *et al.*, 2010), in which conviviality and voluntary simplicity prevail over greed, in an update of the idea of a life-saving anti-modernity.

Overall, the current ecologist engagements centred on individual choices or limited to small organized groups, at the neighbourhood or village level, for instance, with a view to changing ways of life and adapting them to the constraints resulting from a succession of ecological crises, do not have the same momentum as those of the 1970s. The emphasis on the individual sphere, which can be considered a sort of 'backyard ecology', has certain limitations, attested by the emergence of NIMBYists (meaning 'not in my backyard'),[3] for whom not being close to any form of pollution, which they otherwise accept, is of paramount importance. When combined with the NIMEY discourse ('not in my election year') of candidates looking for voters, they create a real obstacle to significant change. The convergence of local or personal interests with the detriment of a global vision of ecology is certainly an important factor in the lack of real effort to turn ecology into a political priority implying brave choices.

Notes

1 The Finnish philosopher and writer Pentti Linkola (born 1932) is presented as one of the current representatives of 'ecofascism', defined as ecological radicalism. Linkola advocates the rapid decline of the human population and deindustrialization and sees the market economy and economic growth as deadly threats.

2 This term was popularized in the late twentieth century by meteorologist and atmospheric chemist Paul Crutzen. It refers to the period during which humans' influence on the biosphere has reached such a degree that it has become a major 'geological force'.
3 The NIMBY syndrome refers in particular to the attitude of people who are eager to benefit from technological advances, but refuse to suffer from the harmful consequences of the infrastructure they require in their immediate surroundings.

Bibliography

Ariès, Paul (2010), *La simplicité volontaire contre le mythe de l'abondance*, Paris, La Découverte.
Bonneuil, Christophe (2016), *The Shock of the Anthropocene: The Earth, History and Us*, London and New York, Verso.
Bookchin, Murray (1980), *Toward an Ecological Society*, Montreal, Black Rose.
Carius, Alexander (2016), *Towards a Green Economy in Emerging and Rapidly Growing Countries: The Way Forward After Rio+20*, Munich, Œkom.
Carson, Rachel (2002 [1962]), *Silent Spring*, New York, Mariner Books.
Charbonneau, Bernard, and Ellul, Jacques (2014), *Nous sommes des révolutionnaires malgré nous. Textes pionniers de l'écologie politique*, Paris, Seuil.
Chichilnisky, Graciela, and Bal, Peter (2017), *The Carbon Market: The Conference of the Parties for Combating Climate Change (COP 21), Solutions and Implementation*, Singapore, World Scientific Publishing.
Cluet, Marc, and Repussard, Catherine (eds.) (2014), *La Lebensreform ou la dynamique sociale de l'impuissance politique*, Tübingen, Francke.
Diamond, Jared (2005), *Collapse: How Societies Choose to Fail or Succeed*, London, Penguin.
Dumont, René (1973), *L'utopie ou la mort!*, Paris, Seuil.
Gorz, André (1975), *Écologie et politique*, Paris, Galilée.
Haeckel, Ernst (1866), *Generelle Morphologie der Organismen*, vol. 2, Berlin, Reimer.
Hamilton, Clive (2015), *The Anthropocene and the Global Environmental Crisis: Rethinking Modernity in a New Epoch*, London and New York, Routledge.
Hirsch, Rebecca E. (2016), *Climate Migrants: On the Move in a Warming World*, Washington, DC, Twenty-First Century.
Holloway, John, and Grubacic, Andrej (2016), *In, Against, and Beyond Capitalism: The San Francisco Lectures*, Oakland, CA, PM Press.
Illich, Ivan (1974), *Energy and Equity*, New York, Harper and Row.
Illich, Ivan (2001 [1973]), *Tools for Conviviality*, London, Marion Boyars Editions.
Jonas, Hans (1979), *Das Prinzip Verantwortung. Versuch einer Ethik für die technologische Zivilisation*, Frankfurt am Main, Suhrkamp, translated into English (1984) as *The Imperative of Responsibility: In Search of Ethics for the Technological Age*, Chicago, University of Chicago Press.
Juris, Jeffrey S. (2008), *Networking Futures: The Movements Against Corporate Globalization*, Durham, NC, Duke University Press.
Latouche, Serge (2006), *Le pari de la décroissance*, Paris, Fayard.
Leopold, Aldo (1949), *A Sand County Almanac: And Sketches Here and There*, Oxford, Oxford University Press.
Lomborg, Bjorn (1998), *The Skeptical Environmentalist*, Cambridge, Cambridge University Press.
Marsh, George Perkins (1864), *Man and Nature or Physical Geography as Modified by Human Action*, New York, C. Scribner and Co.
Meadows, Donella H., and Randers, Jorgen (2004), *Limits to Growth*, White River Junction, VT, Chelsea Green.

Naess, Arne (1989), *Ecology, Community and Lifestyle: Outline of an Ecosophy*, Cambridge, Cambridge University Press.
Naess, Arne (2008), *Life's Philosophy: Reason and Feeling in a Deeper World*, Athens, GA, University of Georgia Press.
Reclus, Élisée, (1905), *L'homme et la terre*, Paris, Librairie Universelle (6 vol.).
Sachs, Jeffrey D., and Ki-moon, Ban (2015), *The Age of Sustainable Development*, New York, Columbia University Press.
Scarce, Rik, and Brower, David (2016), *Eco-Warriors: Understanding the Radical Environmental Movement*, London and New York, Routledge.
Shiva, Vandana (2015), *Earth Democracy: Justice, Sustainability, and Peace*, Berkeley, CA, North Atlantic.
Steedman, Ian, Atherton, John R., and Graham, Elaine (eds.) (2010), *The Practices of Happiness: Political Economy, Religion and Wellbeing*, London and New York, Routledge.
Thoreau, Henry D. (1854), *Walden, or the Life in the Woods*, Boston, MA, Ticknor and Fields.
Welzer, Harald (2015), *Climate Wars: What People Will Be Killed for in the 21st Century*, Cambridge, Polity.
Zavalloni, Marisa (2007), *Ego-écologie et identité: une approche naturaliste*, Paris, Presses Universitaires de France.

9
ECOFEMINISM

Margot Lauwers

Born worldwide around the 1970s, ecofeminism sees the subjugation of women and nature as being linked by a conceptual logic of domination common to all forms of oppression (sexism, speciesism, racism, etc.). Few standpoint theory movements have gone as far down the road as ecofeminism when it comes to recognizing the intersectionality of power relations (Stephens, 2015). However, ecofeminism has had to – and still does – cope with a lot of critique often based on misconceptions and misunderstandings. Accordingly, this chapter deals with some of ecofeminism's major challenges, for example, moving past the essentialism debate and the eurocentrism of some of its thinkers, as well as gaining recognition for the interdisciplinary configurations which it helped create. We will also address the subdiscipline of feminist ecocriticism, which emerged directly from ecofeminist thinking while positively influencing it by granting it more academic attention, especially from European academic circles.

Introduction

The ecofeminist movement is based on the idea that the domination of women by men and the exploitation of nature by humanity have the same conceptual basis. It is considered both an alternative to feminism and environmental ethics. Although the term 'ecofeminism' was coined for the first time by the French radical feminist Françoise d'Eaubonne in her 1974 book *Feminism or Death* (*Le féminisme ou la mort*), the movement and ideology itself have their roots planted on the Australian, African and American continents with writings and grassroots actions alike (Diamond and Orenstein, 1990).

Some of the most notable books that were produced on ecofeminism during the 1970s include *Woman and Nature: The Roaring Inside Her* by Susan Griffin (1978) and Caroline Merchant's *Death of Nature: Women, Ecology and the Scientific*

Revolution (1980). Although both authors base their work on elaborate academic research, Merchant writes in a seemingly conventional style. Griffin, on the other hand, breaks away from conventional academic essay writing by producing a passionate prosaic poem in which she exposes the hypocrisy of Western thought regarding women and the environment. She does this by thoroughly mixing and paraphrasing texts of different origins. The result is a powerful denunciation of the idea perpetuated through age-old Western culture according to which women would be closer to nature and thus, like nature itself, subjected to man's dominion.

The decade following the publishing of these three books saw a flourishing of activist ecofeminism: various conferences and political and cultural actions celebrated the ideas developed by Merchant and Griffin. But it is only during the second half of the 1980s that the theory around ecofeminist thinking began to take a literary and academic stand, transforming it into a more coherent ideology. Two papers showed a change in the perception of ecofeminism: the first one is a 1984 paper by Australian sociologist Ariel Salleh and, in 1987, an article by American critic Karen Warren, both on the necessity of making connections between feminism and ecology. Thanks to these texts, 'the logic of domination' and the links between environmental degradation and the oppression due to gender, class or sexual orientation became more obvious. And, more importantly, their publishing signed the start of a new – albeit reluctant – acceptance of the nascent ideas into academic circles.

Ecofeminism and the intersectionality of power relations

As previously stated, ecofeminism sees oppressive structures such as racism, speciesism, sexism, ageism, etc., as stemming from a unique logic of domination. The various links existing between the subordinate position of women in patriarchal societies and of nature within the world, as conceptualized by human beings, might have proven helpful in recognizing these structures as oppressive.

According to Françoise D'Eaubonne (1974) and Ariel Salleh (1984), the ecological crisis is in fact the predictable result of patriarchal culture. According to some ecofeminists such as Spretnak, it is possible to trace the prototypical patterns of the 'logic of domination' as far back as the first Indo-European invasions before the Common Era. Others, such as Griffin or Plumwood (1993), claim that its roots would reside in seventeenth-century rationalism and the conceptual dichotomies put forth by the Ancient Greek philosophers. Merchant (1980) and Mies and Shiva (1993) believe that the scientific revolution and the associated cultural and scientific changes allowed the establishment of the natural world's exploitation for unlimited industrial and commercial purposes as well as a more pronounced domination of women. Moreover, the need for the recognition of an empirical link between feminism and the environment was highlighted. Some authors like Léonie Caldecott and Stéphanie Leland (1983) have put forth the increased health risks for women and children such as radiations, pesticides and other toxic waste. For others (Mies, Salleh, Shiva, Gaard), the empirical link would have been made visible by the economic and postcolonial behaviour of industrialized countries, which might directly affect the economic difficulties experienced mostly by women in developing countries. Similarly, industrial patriarchal behavioural practices have also been criticized regarding eating habits (excessive meat consumption), hunting, livestock farming and animal testing: scholars such as Carol Adams (2014) and Marti Kheel (2008) see these practices as a means of reinforcing dichotomous patriarchal conceptualizations, especially with regard to the way feminized beings (also called Feminized Others) are thought of within these societies.

On the one hand, it appears that in much of the world, women suffer more from environmental degradation due to the gendered division of labour, common to a large number of societies that impose the role of family caretaker to women. The fact that these women are in charge of gathering wood, of fetching water and of collecting food, for example, places them in a position in which they more easily feel the restraints linked to environmental change (i.e. having to walk farther and farther to collect wood).

The other relationship between women and nature resides on a conceptual level. This connection is structured in different ways, which is why it is more difficult to explain in its entirety. The core of the issue lies in the hierarchical mode and binary thinking applied in Western societies or societies under Western influence. These dualistic conceptual structures affect the way the world is perceived and organized. It is this binary structure that is at the origin of such dualities as reason/emotion, culture/nature, sky/earth, body/mind and man/woman. Ecofeminists claim that through this compartmentalization, the feminine gender would be conceptually identified as relating to the body, the earth, sexuality, the carnal and the emotional, inasmuch as the masculine gender would be identified as relating to the cerebral, the intellectual, reason and power. These implicit associations appear to be justified, and even natural, whereas a re-evaluation of the philosophical and conceptual perception allows for, according to ecofeminists, a better understanding of the way they were socially and culturally constructed, as well as a mutual reinforcement.

Beyond essentialism and eurocentrism

Numerous different critics have addressed the ways in which ecofeminism has been misunderstood. The idea that ecofeminism fosters the presupposition that women are closer to nature, more caring and nurturing about living things is a misconception, as well as the idea that ecofeminism claims women have an inner sensitivity men lack toward everything that concerns living beings. Ecofeminism, on the contrary, rejects these ideas and tries to explain why this train of thought is a cultural construct. Ecofeminism is the denunciation of a presupposed relationship between women and nature, as well as a movement which promotes a better understanding and respect for living things.

The diversity in positions makes ecofeminism into an ideology that has to be approached as a whole, but this also discouraged scholars who had initially showed an interest. The handful of people who advocated cultural ecofeminist positions[1] put the entire movement in the shade by representing it as an essentialist celebration of a natural link between women and nature:

> Focusing on the celebration of goddess spirituality and the critique of patriarchy advanced in cultural ecofeminism, post-structuralist and other third-wave feminisms portrayed all ecofeminisms as an exclusively essentialist equation of women with nature, discrediting ecofeminism's diversity of arguments and standpoints.
>
> *(Gaard, 2011: 32)*

Although it has been asserted that essentialist theories within academic ecofeminism are rare, the charges of essentialism are a still widely used argument to try to undermine the theory and practice of this ideology (Carlassare, 1994). Some writers even put forward the theory according to which this argument is used to silence ecofeminists (Gaard, 1992). Furthermore, some writers – often seen as acquainted with ecofeminism – have added to this essentialist critique by misunderstanding the movement itself and thus conveying an erroneous idea within their own writings (for example, Clarissa Pinkola Estes's, 1992 *Women Who Run with Wolves*).

However, for the same reasons that the entirety of the feminist movements cannot be discarded just because some of its advocates claim that biological determinism is a reality, one cannot discard ecofeminism as a whole because of loose cannons in its midst. In the light of the present-day Anthropocene era, it might seem important to bear in mind that a purely socialist or feminist analysis might prove to be reductionist (because it will only address one side of the problem); we are in a position in which we have to ask ourselves if the essentialist/constructionist dichotomy remains legitimate as a general approach to the ecofeminist movement. This question was raised in 1990 by Diana Fuss in her book *Essentially Speaking: Feminism, Nature and Difference*, but the relevance of Fuss's ideas was muted by the climate of fear created by the term 'essentialist' that enveloped the ecofeminist movement. Fuss advocates drawing away from the opposition between essentialism and constructivism, as negative reactions opposed to feminisms and ecofeminisms these last decades would largely originate from it: '[. . .] it can also be maintained that this same dispute has created the current impasse in feminism, an impasse predicated on the difficulty of theorizing the social in relation to the natural, or the theoretical in relation to the political' (Fuss, 1990: 1).

As with its feminist counterparts, ecofeminism has experienced a backlash at the turn of the century. This is partly due to the sterile debate around the alleged essentialism of some but also, and probably more importantly so, due to the eurocentrism of its worldview. This eurocentrism is exactly what made the ideas of scholars such as Maria Mies and Vandana Shiva (Mies and Shiva, 1993) so difficult to accept for other academics working within a eurocentric Western framework. Maria Mies's work received much critique before Chandra Mohanty presented it as valid and Ariel Salleh praised it as stemming 'from hands-on womanist and ecological praxis' (Salleh, 2004: 202). In her 1998 article 'Under Western Eyes', Mohanty addresses most feminist movements' eurocentric worldviews and the way this prevented ecofeminism from being truly all-encompassing. The critiques that this eurocentrism have been raising all acknowledge the fact that ecological feminism cannot be understood as meaning the same for someone living in the United States or in India, for example. This is what Ariel Salleh refers to in her article 'Global Alternatives and the Meta-Industrial Class' when she explains that 'the current global crisis is exacerbated by the abstract, disembodied, and inaccurate knowledge base of white masculine middle-class decision makers' (Salleh, 2004: 210). Salleh and others contend that the often-patronizing stance Euro-American research may put forth has been problematic in challenging postcolonial discourses.

It has to be conceded that the field has, up until recently, remained largely dominated by US scholars. The hypervisibility of US scholarship is by no means proof that the United States is more active on a research level, but it does constitute evidence of its dominating the field so strongly as to make research from other countries less noticeable at first glance. However, these past five years have witnessed the sprouting of a whole new variety of French, Italian, German (in short, European) and Indian research on the subject of ecofeminism. Attesting to that, 120 participants have taken part in the international conference in June 2016 in Perpignan, they were coming from over twenty different countries. All the more important is the most recent publishing data which show a thorough increase in contemporary European works on the subject of ecofeminism.[2]

Ecofeminism's rhizomatic developments

The variety within ecofeminism reinforced itself and made it more complicated for traditional dualistic academic thinking to take ecofeminism seriously. Indeed, the intertwining of social, philosophical and spiritual writings turned it into a difficult-to-grasp movement, and certain critics, at first interested by its possibilities, backed away, repelled by the apparent intricacy of the ideas.

The flourishing of writings continued after the turn of the century and the years after 2000 were, again, a prolific period for ecofeminism. A notable difference, however, is the urge with which writers have emphasized the need to come up with a new nondualistic way of apprehending our environment and our relationships to other living beings (human or nonhuman). Ecofeminism grew stronger in spite of the criticisms it received, and the plurality of the movement, instead of remaining a point of weakness, started to appear as a clear characteristic.

And indeed, during the past two decades, ecofeminist thinking has gained in academic importance. This may be due to exactly the variety that most critics have attacked: indeed, the last twenty years have seen the evolution of ecofeminist literary criticism with writers such as Patrick D. Murphy and Greta Gaard showing how the analyses of texts identifying women with nature and vice versa, as well as texts denouncing exactly that literary identification, can help to broaden our critical minds in order to move away from the dualisms upholding these ideas. Feminist ecocriticism, the term newly associated with ecofeminist literary criticism, has allowed for a better understanding of ecofeminist ideas.

Whereas a growing number of intellectuals seemed to turn away from the ecofeminist movement, or at the very least avoided the use of the term so as not to be discredited, a new application of ecofeminist theories gradually gave way to their return to favour. Instead of resulting in what some had predicted as the end of ecofeminism, the great variety of ways in which the ecofeminist movement could be used was once more recycled – if so to speak – into an as-yet-unexplored manner.

Despite the dissent with which it has been faced, ecofeminism has been able to remove a number of barriers surrounding the difficulty of introducing a new way of conceiving the relationships (Iovino and Oppermann, 2015; Oppermann, 2017) that human beings maintain not only amongst each other, but also – and more importantly so – with their environment (Brereton, 2015; Murphy, 2015: 1). Although it is during the 1990s that the all-encompassing aspect of ecofeminism has proved prejudicial, it is also during this period that the use of ecofeminist theories articulated itself in such a way as to enrich the landscape of literary criticism and thus, by extension, of ecofeminism itself. If the universality introduced by ecological feminism hampered its actual recognition as a global social critical theory, it was not because the arguments put forth were not valid, but rather because the 'formatting' of our minds did not enable the acquisition of the analytical tools necessary to the overall understanding of the movement.

Attesting to that, Greta Gaard adduces the fact that expanding contemporary critical theories such as ecocriticism, ecopoetics and critical animal studies seem to 'discover', as if innovative, analyses and interdependencies that ecofeminism has highlighted over three decades ago. These observations are clearly illustrated in the article 'Ecofeminism Revisited' (Gaard, 2011), as well as in the introduction of *International Perspectives in Feminist Ecocriticism* (Gaard et al., 2013). These analyses demonstrate that the linearity of masculinist, white, male eurocentrism failed to enable the adherence to ideas brought forth by the ecofeminist movement (it rather provoked its discrediting through accusations of essentialism), while one may have witnessed, this last decade, a revival of these very ideas and their 'rediscovery' by thought patterns of which ecofeminism had already exposed the androcentric and Eurocentric nature: '[. . .], current developments in allegedly new fields such as animal studies and naturalized epistemology are "discovering" theoretical perspectives on interspecies relations and standpoint theory that were developed by feminists and ecofeminists decades ago' (Gaard, 2011: 26).

Conclusion

As Richard Twine explains: 'Dualism provides an unconscious frame of reference in our typical self-constitutions. We tend to regard, for example, our bodies and minds as separate, despite evidence to the contrary' (Twine, 2001: 10–11). This is also applicable to ecofeminism as a whole: what needed to evolve for a better understanding of the global variety of the ideology is the manner in which it was looked upon. Ecofeminism has already overcome a great number of obstacles surrounding the difficulty of introducing a new way of conceiving human relationships between one another and their surrounding environment. Rethinking nature in a way that does not conceptually separate it from culture will need time, although signs are encouraging (Murphy, 2015: xiii–1). Ecofeminism now needs to push analysis one step further by designing a new way of addressing theories, philosophies, artistic creations and spiritualities alike. In order to do this, the first shift needed is one in the global way in which we imagine and analyze the world surrounding us, by turning from a dichotomized eye on things to a gaze conscious of the many ties hidden behind all things natural, humans and their evolution included.

This global shift seems well under way within French academe. What we now refer to as the 'environmental humanities' have been on the crest of a wave for the past year or two, as is evidenced by the number of articles and books published or conferences held on these subjects. Endeavours such as the newest collection *Witches* (*Sorcières*) of the Parisian publisher Cambourakis – which published a long-awaited anthology of French translations of ecofeminist literature extracts – tend to demonstrate that ecofeminism is finally being taken seriously by academic circles.

Notes

1 This strain of thought belongs to the spiritual branch of the movement. The term 'cultural ecofeminism' refers directly to its feminist counterpart, cultural feminism, also known as differentialist feminism, and advocates feminine and masculine essences or biologically determined characteristics (as opposed to socially constructed ones).
2 Such as *Contemporary Perspectives on Ecofeminism* by Mary Phillips and Nick Rumens, published in 2016 by Routledge, which presents works by a majority of European (British, Dutch, etc.) contributors.

Bibliography

Adams, Carol, and Gruen, Lori (2014), *Ecofeminism: Feminist Intersections With Other Animals and the Earth*, New York, Bloomsbury Academic.
Brereton, Pat (2015), *Environmental Ethics and Film*, London and New York, Routledge (Kindle Edition).
Caldecott, Leonie, and Leland, Stephanie (eds.) (1983), *Reclaim the Earth: Women Speak Out for Life on Earth*, London, Women's Press.
Carlassare, Elizabeth (1994), 'Essentialism in Ecofeminist Discourse', *in:* Merchant, Carolyn (ed.), *Ecology: Key Concepts in Critical Theory*, Amherst, NY, Humanity Books: 220–234.
Cook, Julie (1998), 'The Philosophical Colonization of Ecofeminism', *Environmental Ethics*, 20 (3): 227–246.
D'Eaubonne, Françoise (1974), *Le féminisme ou la mort*, Paris, Pierre Horay.
Diamond, Irene, and Orenstein, Gloria (eds.) (1990), *Reweaving the World: The Emergence of Ecofeminism*, San Francisco, Sierra Club Books.
Fuss, Diana (1990), *Essentially Speaking: Feminism, Nature and Difference*, London and New York, Routledge.

Gaard, Greta (1992), 'Misunderstanding Ecofeminism', *Z Papers*, 3 (1): 20–24.
Gaard, Greta (2011), 'Ecofeminism Revisited: Rejecting Essentialism and Re-Placing Species in a Material Feminist Environmentalism', *Feminist Formations*, 23 (2): 26–53.
Gaard, Greta, Estok, Simon, and Oppermann, Serpil (eds.) (2013), *International Perspectives in Feminist Ecocriticism*, London and New York, Routledge.
Griffin, Susan (2000 [1978]), *Woman and Nature: The Roaring Inside Her*, London, Women's Press.
Iovino, Serenella, and Oppermann, Serpil (eds.) (2015), *Material Ecocriticism*, Bloomington, IN, Indiana University Press.
Kheel, Marti (2008), *Nature Ethics: An Ecofeminist Perspective*, Lanham, MD, Rowman and Littlefield.
Merchant, Carolyn (1980), *The Death of Nature: Women, Ecology and the Scientific Revolution*, San Francisco, HarperCollins.
Mies, Maria, and Shiva, Vandana (1993), *Ecofeminism*, London, Zed Press.
Mohanty, Chandra Talpede (1988), 'Under Western Eyes: Feminist Scholarship and Colonial Discourses', *Feminist Review*, 30 (1): 61–88.
Murphy, Patrick D. (2015), *Persuasive Aesthetic Ecocritical Praxis: Climate Change, Subsistence and Questionable Futures*, Lanham, MD, Lexington Books.
Oppermann, Serpil (2017), ' "Storied Matter" and "Ecomaterialism" ', *in:* Braidotti, Rosi, and Hlavajova, Maria (eds.), *Posthuman Glossary*, London, Bloomsbury.
Phillips, Mary, and Rumens, Nick (eds.) (2016), *Contemporary Perspectives on Ecofeminism*, London and New York, Routledge.
Pinkola Estes, Clarissa (1992), *Women Who Run With Wolves*, New York, Ballantine.
Plumwood, Val (1993), *Feminism and the Mastery of Nature*, London and New York, Routledge.
Salleh, Ariel (1984), 'Deeper Than Deep Ecology: The Eco-Feminist Connection', *Environmental Ethics*, 6 (1): 339–345.
Salleh, Ariel (2004), 'Global Alternatives and the Meta-Industrial Class', *in:* Albritton, Robert, Shannon Bell, John Bell, and Richard Westra (eds.), *New Socialisms: Futures Beyond Globalization*, London and New York, Routledge: 201–211.
Stephens, Anne (2015), *Ecofeminism and Systems Thinking*, London and New York, Routledge.
Twine, Richard (2001), 'Ecofeminisms in Process', available at: http://richardtwine.com/ecofem/ecofem2001.pdf (Accessed 31/10/2016).
Warren, Karen (1987), 'Feminism and Ecology: Making Connections', *Environmental Ethics*, 9 (1): 3–20.

10
FROM ENVIRONMENTAL SOCIOLOGY TO ECOSOCIOLOGIES

Graham Woodgate

Sociological engagement with the material bases of social life has a long, but intermittent and sometimes overlooked, genealogy. The emergence of the modern environmental movement in the 1960s and events like the first 'Earth Day' in 1970, followed soon after by the postulation of material 'limits to growth', although generating significant sociological interest, also revealed the inadequacy of then-dominant forms of sociological enquiry. Entrenched anthropocentrism, born from engagement with the 'exuberant expansion' of Western civilization in a context of abundant natural resources, limited sociology's ability to shed light on the societal relevance of changing ecological circumstances. At a time when heavyweight US sociologists such as Talcott Parsons were still focusing their attention on functional societal evolution and Daniel Bell was deriding the concerns of the ecology movement as 'apocalyptic hysteria', Catton and Dunlap (1978, 1980) called for sociology to reject what they termed the 'human exceptionalist paradigm' (HEP), which they associated with the dominant US sociological canon, and adopt a 'new ecological paradigm' (NEP) for a 'postexuberant' sociology.

The following pages will sketch out some key contributions to the construction of a new ecological paradigm of what is now widely referred to as 'environmental sociology'. These include not only recent conceptual developments and theories of environmental degradation and ecological reform, but also reappraisals of the ecological dimensions of the work of sociology's founding scholars.[1] The chapter will also highlight important cleavages within environmental sociology and the enduring controversies that these have produced. It will close by supporting the idea that critical realist philosophy might provide a framework for the integration of a variety of ecosociological approaches that acknowledge the importance of both social and material influences in the character and dynamics of socioenvironmental relations.

Theories of environmental degradation and ecological reform

In their seminal paper 'Environmental Sociology: A New Paradigm', Catton and Dunlap criticized contemporary sociology as deeply anthropocentric and incapable of illuminating the societal relevance of environmental change, proposing their NEP as a corrective (see Table 10.1). The central focus of environmental sociology, they declared, should be *'interaction between the environment and society'* (Catton and Dunlap, 1978: 44, emphasis in original), including the impacts of environment on society, as well as those of society on the environment. These interactions imply ecological relations (flows of energy and materials) and social relations (of production and consumption), both of which occur across space and time. Emerging in the context of growing societal concern about resource scarcity and ecological decline, research and scholarship initially sought to explain the social causes of these phenomena.

Ecological explanations were informed by human ecology, the basic tenets of which are reflected in the assumptions of the NEP. According to Catton and Dunlap (1980: 34), environmental degradation is produced by the failure of the dominant Western worldview to recognize and acknowledge the ecological embeddedness and interdependence of society, and the HEP of conventional sociology made it blind to the social and political dimensions of environmental change. For Catton and Dunlap, the solution to continuing environmental decline resided in the spread of values associated with the NEP among mass publics and the institutionalization of ecological behavioural norms. Research in this branch of environmental sociology includes large-scale surveys to measure public endorsement of the NEP (Dunlap *et al.*, 2000) and statistical analyses of interrelationships between variables in the ecological complex such as population, affluence, social organization and technology. Of particular note is Dietz and Rosa's (1994)

TABLE 10.1 Environmental sociology's paradigm shift

Human exceptionalist paradigm (HEP)	*New ecological paradigm (NEP)*
Our culture makes us exceptional.	Humans are one species among many.
Past experience of 'abundance' makes 'scarcity' difficult to comprehend.	The world is finite, so there are potent physical and biological limits constraining economic growth and social progress.
Focus on 'social environment' and functional evolution of society led to neglect of material circumstances/ ecological embeddedness.	Intricate linkages of cause, effect and feedback in the web of nature produce many unintended consequences from purposive human action.
Cultural accumulation means that progress can continue without limit, making all social problems ultimately soluble: society is *exempt* from 'natural laws'.	Although human inventiveness may appear to extend global carrying capacity, our exceptional status does not exempt us from the laws of nature.

Source: adapted from Catton and Dunlap (1978, 1980)

stochastic reformulation of the simple I = PAT[2] ecological model of environmental impact, which has allowed them and their colleagues to generate more sociologically nuanced, comparative analyses of societies' environmental impacts. As we shall see later, their STIRPAT[3] model has also been employed to test empirical support for environmental social theory.

In contrast, early work by Schnaiberg (1975, 1980) turned to political economy and dialectical reasoning to explore the role of capitalist relations and modern state institutions in the genesis of environmental degradation. His 1975 paper, 'Social Syntheses of the Societal-Environmental Dialectic', posited that economic growth requires increased environmental extraction, leading to ecological disruption and resource depletion, which further threaten economic expansion. He identified three possible syntheses for the dialectic: the 'economic synthesis' – involving minimal or no response to degradation but the acceleration of economic expansion; the planned scarcity synthesis – where science and regulatory policy address only the most serious resource constraints and ecological problems; and the ecological synthesis – where ecological disruption is subject to detailed analysis and economic growth is restricted, with the aim of moving towards a steady-state economy. The distributional effects (regressive, neutral or progressive) of policies associated with each synthesis would affect social stratification and prompt political mobilization.

Schnaiberg further developed this approach in his 1980 book *The Environment*, where he introduced the concept of 'the treadmill of production' into his explanatory model of environmental decline. The concept is closely associated with the growing ecological crisis, because accumulation requires the extraction of ever more resources and produces increasing levels of pollution. At the same time, as suggested by the societal-environmental dialectic, declining resource availability and increasing ecological degradation engender both political mobilization and state regulation.

In the 1970s and 1980s, efforts to incorporate nature into the explanatory framework of political economy and to address the absence of 'power' in human and cultural ecology resulted in the emergence of 'political ecology' as an approach to struggles over the environment in less industrialized countries. At the same time, the birth of the modern environmental movement in the advanced capitalist countries was accompanied by the formation of green political parties and the emergence of what has been termed the 'environmental state' (Mol and Buttel, 2002), as governments established environment ministries and enacted environmental legislation aimed at addressing the most significant ecological problems associated with industrial development. Since the 1980s, however, neoliberal demands for 'smaller states' and deregulation aimed at stimulating economic growth have coincided with the establishment of political programmes of 'ecological modernization' at national, regional and global scales. This trend was accompanied by the development of ecological modernization as a social theory (EMT) of environmental reform (Mol, 1997). In contrast to treadmill theory and political ecology, EMT emphasizes the importance of market dynamics in ecological reform, identifying green entrepreneurs and environmentally aware consumers as social carriers of ecological restructuring. Similarly, rather than viewing science and technology as perpetrators of ecological and social disruption, EMT casts them as key institutions of ecological reform. In line with neoliberal thinking, EMT maintains that state interventions in the economy should be limited and focused on promoting sustainability through decentralized, participatory policymaking, thus engaging environmental social movements as they transition from critical commentators on development to critical participants in ecological reform (Mol, 1997: 140–142). Thus, in stark contrast to treadmill theory, ecological modernization focuses on social processes that delink economic growth from its environmental impacts, through gains in production efficiency and demands for more environmentally friendly goods and services from ecologically aware consumers, facilitated by the environmental state.

This shift in focus also reflects a notable, although not rigid, distinction between North American and European approaches and subject matter.[4] US scholars have tended to focus on the social causes and consequences of environmental degradation and have embraced what Schnaiberg (1980) termed 'impact science' as a source of empirical evidence of ecological decline. Their European colleagues, meanwhile, have been more inclined to engage with social responses to *perceived* environmental change and institutional processes of environmental reform, often maintaining a strong commitment to conventional sociological approaches and integrating insights from emergent sociological framings. In particular, the postmodern turn in European sociology took up a critical position vis-à-vis environmental knowledge claims (Macnaghten and Urry, 1995) and argued vociferously against the sociologically naïve incorporation of environmental science in public policy (Shackley and Wynne, 1996). There followed intense and sometimes heated debate between realists and constructivists.[5]

In a 2003 paper, York, Rosa and Dietz employed their realist, human ecology-inspired STIRPAT model to interrogate the empirical validity of the assumptions underlying human ecology, political economy and EMT theoretical constructs. Using ecological footprint data to operationalize the dependent variable 'environmental impact', their analysis sustained the claims of human ecology, as well as some of those suggested by political economy models such as the treadmill of production. However, the analysis offered no support for the delinking of economic growth from environment impact (the Environmental Kuznets Curve); found a positive link between urbanization and environmental decline; and revealed no clear mitigation effects of policy, political rights, civil liberties, service-sector development or market liberalization on environmental impact, thus completely undermining EMT. More recently, Foster (2012) has launched a withering attack on EMT, which he brands the 'new human exemptionalism', for its lack of attention to the material outcome of political programmes of ecological modernization. Mol and colleagues have responded to this critique by analysing differences between the North American and European traditions in terms of the contexts in which they developed and the distinct cultures of environmental sociology that these have spawned. North American environmental sociology has focused predominantly on resource scarcity and environmental degradation and developed in response to the perceived inadequacies of classical sociological theory. As a result,

US environmental sociologists have re-examined classical theory and developed a view of the environment 'as partly constituted by biophysical realities independent of social practices'. In contrast, European environmental sociology has engaged more with contemporary sociological theory and focused on processes of environmental reform, taking up the position that although the biophysical world is undeniably real, it is 'always and only actualised through social practices and interpretative processes' (Lidskog et al., 2015: 351).

For Lidskog et al. (2015), the differences between US and European environmental sociologies have become more entrenched in recent years, although in some ways the gulf between realists and constructivists has narrowed. Realists have deconstructed and debunked climate change denial (McCright and Dunlap, 2010) and generally taken up a more critical position with regard to environmental knowledges. Constructivists, on the other hand, have demonstrated convincingly that sophisticated computer models are just as likely to underestimate as to overestimate the climatic impacts of global warming, clearly accepting climate change as empirically verifiable, even if its complex causes, feedback loops and precise dimensions are only relevant in terms of the knowledge claims and policy prescriptions that are made in relation to them. Constructivists have also criticized attempts to translate science directly into public policy (Wynne, 2010), set within the disempowering neoliberal framing of the green consumer (Redclift and Woodgate, 2014). Such critiques arguably reinforce rather than undermine ecological reform as an intellectual mission. Nonetheless, Dunlap (2010: 28) is in agreement with Lidskog and colleagues, in detecting a broader cleavage between what he terms '"environmental agnosticism" (a sceptical attitude towards evidence about environmental conditions)', which he associates mostly with European environmental sociologies and '"environmental pragmatism" (an emphasis on measuring and investigating rather than problematizing such conditions)', which continues to characterize most North American contributions.

In setting out their original critique of the HEP, Catton and Dunlap (1978, 1980) made reference to Durkheim's declaration that social facts were reducible neither to biology nor psychology, but could only be explained in reference to other social facts. Although Dunlap has since argued that their intention was simply to point out that over the course of the twentieth century Durkheim's dictum had become institutionalized within sociology, it nonetheless prompted a number of scholars, particularly in North America, to return to the discipline's classic texts and reveal their ecological underpinnings.

Revisiting sociology's foundational works

In their contribution to a symposium celebrating Catton and Dunlap's foundational work in establishing the NEP, Rosa and Richter (2008) challenged the idea that Durkheim should be seen as the original source of the HEP. They did this on three grounds. First, they questioned the pervasiveness of the notion that social facts are exclusively self-referential in the classical sociological canon. Second, they referred to Durkheim's 1893 work *The Division of Labour in Society*, pointing out his explicit recognition of the links between people, nature and society and that his model of social evolution resulting in the division of labour was driven by population growth and the attendant competition for natural resources. Finally, they examined Durkheim's 1887 inaugural lecture as the world's first professor of sociology to elucidate precisely what Durkheim meant by the term 'social fact'. The key point of this lecture was to establish sociology as a science of social action. In doing so, Durkheim acknowledged the work of zoologists researching animal social behaviour in establishing a basis for sociological method. More importantly, they claimed, his notion that societies are greater than the sum of their parts suggests the principle of 'emergence': a concept that resides at the heart of systems biology and is a key element of recent critical realist proposals for an ecologically embedded sociology.

The possibility that Marx's thought might contribute useful concepts to an emergent ecological paradigm is far less problematic, as for him it was the continuous struggle to extract from nature the material means of social reproduction that led to the discovery of increasingly advanced forces of production. Foster (2000) has provided significant new insight into the centrality of ecology to Marx's conception of the nature–society nexus, pointing out that Marx conceived of nature as our external or 'inorganic' body and claimed that, in order to flourish as human beings, we must maintain an intimate and ongoing 'dialogue' with nature, a dialogue that is systematically denied by the alienating structures of capitalism. Our material exchanges with nature Marx characterized as 'socio-ecological metabolism', and he described the rupturing of this metabolic relationship that accompanied the development of capitalism in the nineteenth century, as European populations migrated from the countryside to find industrial work in cities (Foster, 2000: 141–177).

Together with Hannah Holleman, Foster has also revisited the sociology of Max Weber (Foster and Holleman, 2012). Weber dismissed the idea that we can know directly what he referred to as 'first nature', insisting that nature only becomes part of society through cultural representation (second nature). However, although there is a clear rejection of simple environmental determinism, Weber's sophisticated interpretive/causal-analytic position clearly acknowledges how the values and meanings attached to environmental conditions and events provide cause for social change, resulting in historically significant (socioecological) consequences. The most significant consequence of Weber's environmental analysis, suggest Foster and Holleman, is the extent to which it informed his critique of the 'origins, development and (perhaps) decline' of 'modern, rational-inorganic capitalism'. Weber's understanding of the impacts of agricultural industrialization on the soil reflects Marx's notion of the 'metabolic rift', whereas his characterization of capitalism as destroying everything that might restrict its progress bears a clear resemblance to Schnaiberg's model of the 'treadmill of production'. Foster and Holleman conclude that Weber's 'refracted materiality' can assist in the task of bringing nature back in and 'constructing a sociology fully equipped to address the human-environmental challenges of the 21st century' (2012: 1666–1667).

TABLE 10.2 The environment in the classical sociological canon

Durkheim (Rosa and Richter, 2008)	Marx (Foster, 2000)	Weber (Foster and Holleman, 2012)
Social facts are not exclusively self-referential. Division of labour driven by population growth and competition for natural resources.	Nature as man's (*sic*) inorganic body. To survive and thrive as human beings, we must maintain a close and continuing 'dialogue' with nature. *Stoffwechsel* socioecological metabolism.	'Refracted materiality'. Values and meanings attached to nature provide cause for social change with historically significant consequences. Modern, rational-inorganic capitalism.
That societies are greater than the sum of their parts suggests the principle of 'emergence'. 'Emergence' is a key concept in systems biology [and critical realism].	Capitalist agriculture provokes 'an irreparable rift in the interdependent process of socioecological metabolism.'	Development limited by finite nature of resources, especially fossil fuels (coal/coke).

Table 10.2 summarizes the environmental foundations of classical sociological thinking uncovered by recent scholarship. The final section of this chapter takes key elements from the preceding discussions and sets them within a critical realist ontology that might serve as an integrating framework for emerging ecosociologies.

Towards an integrating framework for ecosociologies

The preceding brief genealogy of sociological engagement with the material bases of social life reveals two broad epistemological approaches to incorporating nature into sociological analyses, either directly as biophysical explanatory variables or indirectly as culturally mediated social constructs. As Freudenberg et al. pointed out in 1995, most environmental sociology at the time maintained a clear distinction between the physical and the social dimensions of reality, such that even where analytic balance was attempted, the nature–society dualism carried the inherent risk of analytic primacy being afforded to one or the other. In order to overcome this, Freudenberg and colleagues offered the notion of 'conjoint constitution', which highlights how 'what have commonly been taken to be "physical facts" [. . .] have been shaped [. . .] by social construction processes, while [. . .] what appear to be "strictly social" phenomena [. . .] have been shaped by the fact that social behaviors often respond to stimuli and constraints from the biophysical world' (Freudenburg et al., 1995: 366). The idea that society shapes nature and nature shapes society over time is encapsulated within the notion of 'coevolution' (Norgaard, 1994; Woodgate and Redclift, 1998). Borrowing the term from evolutionary ecology, Norgaard suggests that human values, knowledge, institutions and technology all coevolve with the environment. As Manuel-Navarrete and Buzinde (2010) indicate, however, both conjoint constitution and co-evolution are underlain by systemic or structuralist reasoning, which obscures 'agents' motivations and actual potential (e.g. introspective or reflexive power) to enact transformations or sustain reproductions, other than saying that these are determined culturally and historically' (Manuel-Navarrete and Buzinde, 2010: 140). If addressing the global environmental crisis requires a radical transformation of the structures of modernity that created the crisis, Manuel-Navarrete and Buzinde ask how such a transformation can occur if human agency is so strongly conditioned by these same structures. Their answer is that the coproduction of socioenvironmental structures must be 'mediated by a self-reflexive, or transcendental, form of agency enacted by individuals in their interaction with not only society and the environment, but also with themselves: with their inner worlds', what they term 'socioecological agency' (Manuel-Navarrete and Buzinde, 2010: 140).

Conjoint constitution and co-evolution are clearly helpful models for the study of nature–society interaction, and socioecological agency provides the possibility of the material and social inventiveness required to imagine and create alternative socioecological realities. For Carolan (2005: 394–395), however, constructs such as conjoint constitution, co-evolution and socioecological agency are problematic on a number of counts. To begin with, they do not explain the ontological asymmetry between nature and society – that without nature there can be no humans or human society. Carolan also claims that such concepts lack the capacity to speak of causal tendencies and objects that cannot be easily observed. He goes on to insist that because all sociobiophysical phenomena are seen as equally 'impure', the constructs lack the analytic power to distinguish between different types of hybridity. As a result, Carolan argues, the theoretical possibility of socioecologically reflexive agents developing ecological ethics to guide us out of our current environmental predicament is sacrificed. These criticisms are not, however, fatal. Carolan uses them to support his argument that before we can bring nature back into sociological discourse and practice, we must first clarify what nature is.

Carolan proposes that nature be 'collapsed' into 'three open, embedded, and emergent strata': Nature, nature, and 'nature'. This, he claims, creates space for 'both dynamism and temporality to enter into our understanding of societal-biophysical interaction' and provides a 'pragmatic guide to more fully explore the diverse causal interactions that make up social life' (Carolan, 2005: 399). Nature (capitalized) refers to phenomena of materiality and physical causality that underlie the other two strata, whereas nature (lowercase) is 'the environment': the conjointly constituted, co-evolving sociobiophysical world in which we participate. Finally, 'nature' (in inverted commas) is 'the "nature" of discourse, power/knowledge, cultural violence, and discursive subjugation' (Carolan, 2005: 401). Table 10.3 sets out this ontological scheme and furnishes it with some of the concepts and theories already discussed, together with others that are briefly introduced in this section.

Nature, nature and 'nature' are porous strata: higher-level phenomena (nature and 'nature') are rooted in and emerge from lower-level phenomena. This proposition resonates with the Durkheimian notions that social facts are emergent properties and that the division of labour is driven by population growth and competition for resources. Causal tendencies do not reside in Nature alone, however. They are multidirectional: our discourses of 'nature' affect our material transactions within nature. Consequently, the stratified ontology also provides room for Weberian refracted materiality and the idea that cultural constructions ('nature') produce historically significant consequences. Thus the door is left open for methodological pluralism.

Marx's concept of socioecological metabolism is a phenomenon of nature (lowercase): an emergent property of the causal tendencies of Nature – the 'laws of thermodynamics' and the biochemical structure of metabolic pathways. At the same time, socioecological metabolism is shaped by human values, knowledge and organization ('nature'), and technology (nature/artefacts), as suggested by the co-evolutionary model of the nature–society interaction. In her exploration of the origins of the concept of metabolism in the natural and social sciences, Fischer-Kowalski (1997: 119) describes social metabolism as 'the flow of materials and energy in [. . .] society through the chain of extraction, production, consumption and disposal'. It is composed of endosomatic metabolism within the body to sustain physiological activity and exosomatic metabolism outside the body to enhance the

TABLE 10.3 Reality as stratified, rooted and emergent

Real objects and causal tendencies existing in a state of permanence with flux	Actual environmental conditions and flow of events in space-time sociobiophysical phenomena/hybrids	Empirical observations and social constructions refracted materiality
Nature	nature (Weber's first nature)	'nature' (Weber's second nature)
	↕ emergence ↕	
	multidirectional causal tendencies	
Unobserved/unobservable objects and causal tendencies. Thermodynamics. Gravity. Atmospheric physics. Metabolic pathways. Nutrient cycles: carbon, nitrogen, phosphorus, etc. Ecological processes and causal tendencies.	Human populations: biologically embodied and ecologically embedded, socioecologically structured. Environmental social movements, environmental states. Cultural practice, direct experience, socioecological agency, cultural landscapes. Artefacts, technology, industry. Ecosystem/agroecosystems/urban ecosystems, biological diversity, genomes. Socioecological metabolism: endosomatic and exosomatic flows of energy and materials. Carbon in lithosphere, hydrosphere and biosphere.	'Global warming and climate change'. 'Ecological modernization, sustainable consumption, efficiency and sufficiency, sustainable intensification, genetic engineering, food security, carbon capture and storage'. 'Knowledge rifts and epistemic ruptures'. 'Coevolution, conjoint constitution, metabolic rifts, ecological debt, ecological footprints/biocapacity, environmental justice, postdevelopment discourses, food sovereignty, degrowth'.

productivity of labour through the development and operation of technology. She suggests that the 'study of the social (i.e. economic, technological and cultural) regulation of society's metabolism [should] become a genuine sociological task of highly practical value in view of the ecological problems' that confront us today. Fischer-Kowalski's proposal echoes Marx's claim that addressing the metabolic rift between town and country required the (ecologically) rational regulation of the metabolic relation between human beings and the earth (Foster, 2000).

The concept of metabolic rift has been developed considerably since Foster brought it to the attention of the social sciences. In his critique of EMT (Foster, 2012), he talks of a 'planetary rift' that goes well beyond the disruption of soil nutrient cycles to encompass climate change, biodiversity depletion, desertification, declining water resources, chemical pollution and a host of other ecological issues, many of which 'are approaching points of irreversibility and cumulative, catastrophic change' (Foster, 2012: 211). From the critical realist position, although it may be possible to establish the validity of claims about material circumstances, their ultimate veracity remains unknowable, and it is more important to understand where such claims originate, how they are sustained and contested and how they serve particular political interests. What becomes apparent from such analyses is that some environmental claims are more powerful and violent than others and that they support the interests of some social groups over those of others (Forsyth, 2003).

In a very interesting and helpful contribution to contemporary discussions of the metabolic rift, Schneider and McMichael (2010) extend its social conceptualization to include the practice as well as the organization of labour and, in doing so, embed it more firmly in nature (lowercase). Their wider conceptualization of the social dimensions of metabolism leads them to identify another rift: 'the capitalist division of labour creates a rift in the production and reproduction of embodied knowledge of local ecosystems and potentially sustainable [. . .] [labour] practices'. This 'knowledge rift', a rift between nature and 'nature', is compounded and deepened by what Schneider and McMichael term 'a further layer of violence', that of abstraction and scientific reductionism. 'Not only is the metabolic rift a material transformation of production, with spatial and ecological consequences, but also it involves an epistemological break [. . .] [it] conditions social thought' (Schneider and McMichael, 2010: 477–478). In other words, the exosomatic metabolism of industrial capitalism threatens the basic endosomatic metabolism that sustains all life, and knowledge and epistemic rifts undermine human agency and society's ability to address the deepening metabolic rift.

The widening and deepening of the metabolic rift in ecological terms has produced what is now widely referred to as 'ecological debt': the debt accumulated by the global North at the expense of the global South through the export of natural resources at prices that take no account of the degradation caused by their extraction, processing and distribution, nor the occupation of environmental space through the dumping of production wastes. In a recent article, Warleniusa et al. (2015) examine the relevance of ecological debt to the goal of environmental justice. Ecological debt implies biophysical measures, such as 'ecological footprint';

legal instruments, such as those encompassed within multilateral environmental agreements; and the distributional principle that equality should be restored between those that overconsume and pollute and those that underconsume and suffer from pollution. Thus, 'ecological debt' can be used to analyze environmental injustices within countries, between genders, classes, races and ethnic groups, as well as between nations, in order to inform and monitor the impact of policies aimed at restoring environmental justice and bringing global social metabolism back to a level at which a liveable nature (lowercase) can be sustained.

Schneider and McMichael (2010) argue that a reunification of the social and the ecological in historical thought and practice will be indispensable to repairing the metabolic rift, both conceptually and practically. The framework proposed by Carolan (2005) and similar efforts by Forsyth (2003) and York and Mancus (2009) towards critical human and political ecologies are significant efforts in this direction. Establishing reality as an open, ontologically stratified whole allows us to perceive the actual environments (natures) we experience, as spatially and temporally dynamic, co-evolving flows of conjointly constituted sociobiophysical events rooted in an underlying domain of real objects and causal tendencies existing in a state of permanence-with-flux (Nature), but varyingly coconstructed and contested by different social groups. That is to say, the environment of human action is continually remade through socioecological agency.

Social facts may indeed reside in a distinct domain of reality ('nature'), but they are embedded in and emerge from lower-level strata (Nature and nature) and are continually reproduced and refashioned through the intended and unintended consequences of the actions of socioecological agents. Thus, the 'reunification of the social and the ecological, in historical thought and practice' demanded by Schneider and McMichael must have its starting point within the individual, as a new form of socioecological agency characterized by reflexivity and an awareness of the interconnected character of individual, social and material forms of agency. The role of ecosociologies in the Anthropocene, then, becomes the analysis of alternative socioecological discourses and practices in terms of their capacity to heal the planetary metabolic rift, address the intra- and intergenerational dimensions of ecological debt and promote environmental justice.

Notes

1 There is not room here for a full account of these developments, and so readers are also referred to some of the many assessments of environmental sociology's recent genealogy (see, *inter alia*, Buttel 1987; Dunlap, 2010; Hannigan, 2014: 18–49; Redclift and Woodgate, 2014; Lidskog *et al.*, 2015).
2 Impact = Population × Affluence × Technology.
3 STochastic Impacts by Regression on Population, Affluence and Technology.
4 It is also important to note significant contributions to environmental sociology from scholars outside Europe and North America in countries such as China, Japan, South Korea, Argentina, Brazil and Chile (see Dunlap, 2010; Lidskog *et al.*, 2015).
5 This debate has been reviewed by scholars from both camps (see, *inter alia*, Dunlap, 2010; Lidskog *et al.*, 2015).

Bibliography

Buttel, Frederick H. (1987), 'New Directions in Environmental Sociology', *Annual Review of Sociology*, 13: 465–488.
Carolan, Michael S. (2005), 'Society, Biology, and Ecology: Bringing Nature Back into Sociology's Disciplinary Narrative through Critical Realism', *Organization and Environment*, 18 (4): 393–421.
Catton, William R. Jr., and Dunlap, Riley E. (1978), 'Environmental Sociology: A New Paradigm', *The American Sociologist*, 13: 41–49.
Catton, William R. Jr., and Dunlap, Riley E. (1980), 'A New Ecological Paradigm for Post-Exuberant Sociology', *American Behavioral Scientist*, 25: 15–47.
Dietz, Thomas, and Rosa, Eugene A. (1994), 'Rethinking the Environmental Impacts of Population, Affluence and Technology', *Human Ecology Review*, 1: 277–300.
Dunlap, Riley E. (2010 [1997]), 'The Maturation and Diversification of Environmental Sociology: From Constructivism and Realism to Agnosticism and Pragmatism', *in:* Redclift, Michael, and Woodgate, Graham (eds.), *The International Handbook of Environmental Sociology*, Cheltenham, UK and Northampton, MA, Edward Elgar: 15–32.
Dunlap, Riley E., Van Liere, Kent D., Mertig, Angela G., and Jones, Robert E. (2000), 'Measuring Endorsement of the New Ecological Paradigm: A Revised NEP Scale', *Journal of Social Issues*, 56 (3): 425–442.
Fischer-Kowalski, Marina (1997), 'Society's Metabolism', *in:* Redclift, Michael, and Woodgate, Graham (eds.), *The International Handbook of Environmental Sociology*, Cheltenham, UK and Northampton, MA, Edward Elgar: 119–137.
Forsyth, Tim (2003), *Critical Political Ecology*, London and New York, Routledge.
Foster, John B. (2000), *Marx's Ecology: Materialism and Nature*, New York, Monthly Review Press.
Foster, John B. (2012), 'The Planetary Rift and the New Human Exemptionalism', *Organization and Environment*, 25 (3): 211–237.
Foster, John B., and Holleman, Hannah (2012), 'Weber and the Environment: Classical Foundations for a Postexemptionalist Sociology', *American Journal of Sociology*, 117: 1625–1673.
Freudenburg, William R., Frickel, Scott, and Gramling, Robert (1995), 'Beyond the Nature/Society Divide: Learning to Think About a Mountain', *Sociological Forum*, 10: 361–392.
Hannigan, John (2014 [1995]), *Environmental Sociology*, London and New York, Routledge.
Lidskog, Rolf, Mol, Arthur, and Oosterveer, Peter (2015), 'Towards a Global Environmental Sociology? Legacies, Trends and Future Directions', *Current Sociology*, 63 (3): 339–368.
McCright, Aaron, and Dunlap, Riley (2010), 'Anti-Reflexivity: The American Conservative Movement's Success in Undermining Climate Science and Policy', *Theory, Culture and Society*, 27 (2–3): 100–133.
Macnaghten, Philip, and Urry, John (1995), 'Towards a Sociology of Nature', *Sociology*, 29 (2): 203–220.
Manuel Navarrete, David, and Buzinde, Christine N. (2010), 'Socio-Ecological Agency: From "Human Exceptionalism" to Coping with Exceptional Environmental Change', *in:* Redclift, Michael, and Woodgate, Graham (eds.), *The International Handbook of Environmental Sociology*, 2nd ed., Cheltenham, UK and Northampton, MA, Edward Elgar: 136–149.
Mol, Arthur P. J. (1997), 'Ecological Modernization: Industrial Transformations and Environmental Reform', *in:* Redclift, Michael, and Woodgate, Graham (eds.), *The International Handbook of Environmental Sociology*, Cheltenham, UK and Northampton, MA, Edward Elgar: 138–149.

Mol, Arthur P. J., and Buttel, Frederick H. (eds.) (2002), *The Environmental State Under Pressure*, Oxford, Elsevier: 149–169.

Norgaard, Richard B. (1994), *Development Betrayed: The End of Progress and a Co-Evolutionary Revisioning of the Future*, London and New York, Routledge.

Redclift, Michael, and Woodgate, Graham (2014), 'The European Contribution to Environmental Sociology', *in:* Koniordos, Sokratis, and Kyrtsis, Alexandros-Andreas (eds.), *Routledge Handbook of European Sociology*, London and New York, Routledge: 225–237.

Rosa, Eugene A., and Richter, Lauren (2008), 'Durkheim on the Environment: Ex Libris or Ex Cathedra? Introduction to Inaugural Lecture to a Course in Social Science, 1887–1888', *Organization and Environment*, 21 (2): 182–187.

Schnaiberg, Allan (1975), 'Social Syntheses of the Societal Environmental Dialectic: The Role of Distributional Impacts', *Social Science Quarterly*, 56: 5–20.

Schnaiberg, Allan (1980), *The Environment: From Surplus to Scarcity*, New York, Oxford University Press.

Schneider, Mindi, and McMichael, Philip (2010), 'Deepening, and Repairing, the Metabolic Rift', *Journal of Peasant Studies*, 37 (3): 461–484.

Shackley, Simon, and Wynne, Brian (1996), 'Representing Uncertainty in Global Climate Change and Policy', *Science, Technology and Human Values*, 21: 275–302.

Warleniusa, Rikard, Piercea, Gregory, and Ramasarb, Vasna (2015), 'Reversing the Arrow of Arrears: The Concept of "Ecological Debt" and its Value for Environmental Justice', *Global Environmental Change*, 30: 21–30.

Woodgate, Graham, and Redclift, Michael (1998), 'From a "Sociology of Nature" to Environmental Sociology: Beyond Social Construction', *Environmental Values*, 7: 3–24.

Wynne, Brian (2010), 'Strange Weather, Again: Climate Science as Political Art', *Theory, Culture and Society*, 27 (2–3): 289–305.

York, Richard, and Mancus, Philip (2009), 'Critical Human Ecology: Historical Materialism and Natural Laws', *Sociological Theory*, 27 (2): 122–149.

York, Richard, Rosa, Eugene A., and Dietz, Thomas (2003), 'Footprints on the Earth: The Environmental Consequences of Modernity', *American Sociological Review*, 68: 279–300.

11

FROM ANTHROPOGEOGRAPHY TO ETHNOECOLOGY

Is social evolutionism also natural evolutionism?

Éric Navet

The explorer and the geographer's view

In his *Anthropogeography* (Ratzel, 1909), whose publication began in 1882, German geographer Friedrich Ratzel (1844–1904) introduced the eponymous concept in a bid to reconcile earth science with the humanities. He faulted the ethnographers of his day for not taking enough interest in the geographic conditions in which human societies and cultures thrive; he argued that geographers, on the other hand, had never ceased placing their discipline within a specifically human framework and perspective. But how did – and do – they consider human beings' relationships with their environments? Although this is not the place to retrace the history of the disciplines that founded this interdisciplinary approach, an epistemological investigation will be used to shed light on the historical and ideological conditions for the emergence of a genuine 'human ecology'.

It should be first noted that the schism between earth science and the humanities is a recent development. Over a century ago, Ratzel was reacting against what he saw as a negative trend in Western sciences: their fragmentation into many different schools. It is worth remembering that all of these sciences, including geography and ethnography, have a shared root: philosophy – the reflection of man on himself, the world and his relation to the world.

Geography, which is literally the graphical description and representation of the Earth, bears witness to the spontaneous curiosity of human beings towards the world (or worlds, we should say) that surround(s) them. This interest naturally extends to the peoples who inhabit that world. The first travellers who left us written reports on their explorations – whether they wrote it themselves or had their scribes do it for them – were therefore the forebears of both geography and ethnography. In early *in situ* and *in vivo* observations, countries and humans were considered as a whole in which each element occupied a place assigned by divine order. Many ancient narratives exemplify that approach quite eloquently, for instance, that of the Carthaginian Hannon, who towards 500 BCE travelled along the Gulf of Guinea, possibly to Gabon; or Pytheas, who during the fourth century BCE reached an island beyond the British Isles where the day lasts 24 hours – he called it Thule.

Many historians of science consider Herodotus (c. 484–420 BCE) the founder of the social, geographical and historical sciences. For many reasons he may also well have been the first anthropogeographer. Of course, like his peers, he worked in the field, but he thought it important to conduct genuine investigations – he called his work *inquiries*[1] – by combining observations and interviews as modern ethnologists do. Furthermore, he never discussed any of the peoples he encountered (Persians, Egyptians, Libyans, etc.) without including a wealth of detail on the geography of the places where he travelled (rivers, mountains, climates, natural resources, etc.).

Yet it is not so much his geographical value that made Herodotus so remarkable as the fact that he conducted his 'inquiries' with no other concerns than discovery and knowledge. Other explorers had commercial or colonial motives: Hannon and Alexander the Great (356–323 BCE) took scholars along on their travels, but mostly they led abundant groups of expatriates who took residence in the lands they discovered or conquered.

This connection between knowledge and power (of the colonial enterprise) was not only seen in Greek and Roman culture; in what later became Western culture, the most famous explorers were sometimes brilliant ethnographers and geographers, but also often the agents of colonization. In New France, Jacques Cartier (mid-sixteenth century) and Samuel de Champlain (early seventeenth century) represented the interests of trading companies; Nicolas Perrot and Baron de La Hontan (late seventeenth century) served the interests of the homeland and of foreign powers, respectively. Outside of France, Marco Polo, who would make the Europeans discover the East, was chiefly a 'merchant traveller' working on behalf of the Republic of Venice in the thirteenth century. Likewise, at the turn of the eighteenth century to the nineteenth, the German Alexander von Humboldt not only made valuable scientific observations in fields such as botany, geography, astronomy and ethnology; he also gave an account of the political and economic state of affairs in Spain's New World possessions (Humboldt, 1970).

To varying degrees, all of these observers, explorers and cartographers were vessels and actors of an ideology specific to the so-called revealed religions (Christianity, Judaism and Islam) and their underlying civilizations, according to which nature was created by God for humankind, who have a duty to become its master. In the West, for instance, the ethnocentrism that characterizes all human societies was confused with a basic form of anthropocentrism. Humankind are only human if they show themselves able to rule over their environment and tame their own nature; here nature is opposed to culture. This very clear-cut opposition is displayed both in cartographical representations and in the first narratives of geographers and scholars. Ancient maps display the 'natives' alongside the features deemed most characteristic of their environment. But it was logically assumed that these 'natural' peoples were too much part of nature to be considered humans. The West projected in them everything it repressed in itself; the first anthropo-geographical documents are often of a teratological nature: the 'savages' bore the stigmata of an unknown, undifferentiated, dark and scary world – the world of nature itself and of animal nature.

As Western peoples progressively asserted their claim to the world by simultaneously committing *ethnocide* (destruction of indigenous people, eradication of everything 'primitive' in us and outside of us) and *ecocide* (destruction of natural and supernatural environments), they developed a form of knowledge that would become curiously known as 'naturalistic', aimed at acquiring an intellectual – and not only physical – command of things, marked by a concern for dissecting, analyzing in order to understand. In the nineteenth century in particular, this rationalized scientific approach progressively replaced the prevailing immediate, intuitive approach that had dominated until then.

The initial roadmap laid out in the holy writings of the Christian West was evolutionist from the start. The history of human beings as a species, it was thought, followed a line that was to lead them from a savage and uncultured state to the civilized state. But it was soon clear that the search for causes – which constituted the beginning of science – and the implementation of ideas of 'progress' and 'development' (also founding ideas in science) did not enlighten humans about the world, but instead created a hiatus between the two.

Scientific and economic development required a solution that involved continuity between humanity, as a species and an individual, and the world. Early geography and ethnography bore the hallmarks of this shift; in the same way that states in the making and their colonial extensions marked the divorce between 'civilized' humans and the natural environment, the so-called 'natural' sciences split from the humanities. This resulted in the creation of multiple disciplines: in its early stages, geography was more historical than history and ethnography were geographic. Humankind in its evolution, humankind dominating nature and exploiting it for its own benefit, was to be the starting and end point of geography. Arguably, contemporary geography is not radically different in its approach.

An early twentieth-century primary school geography manual presented the different stages of evolution as follows: (1) Civilization: 'Since the primitive man, who was miserable, lived in caverns and was constantly tormented by hunger, human civilization, particularly in the past century, has made extraordinary progress'. (2) Degrees of civilization: 'Nowadays, a distinction still applies between several degrees of civilization where human existence is more and more secure and easy'.

1   *Primitive peoples* can only fish or hunt – example: the *Australian savages*
2   *Pastoral peoples* make their living from breeding and are *nomadic* – example: the Arabs
3   *Farming people* know how to reap *regular harvests* from the soil and are sedentary – example: the Chinese

4   Lastly, *high civilization* is that of our societies, who not only have perfected breeding and farming, but have also developed a prodigiously active mechanical industry and exchange their products all over the world (Kaeppelin, n.d.: 12).

More recently, in a 1977 book on 'new geography', Paul Claval classified human societies according to their degree of technical mastery of space. He identified three main levels:

> Archaic societies can only hunt, fish and gather; they do not have efficient means of transportation and lack knowledge of distant communication: their dominant characteristics are their imperfect mastery of their environment and the difficulty of relationships.
>
> Historical or intermediate societies have efficient farming and breeding if results are measured in terms of yield, but low labor productivity. These civilizations have writing; however, their transportation technologies are often mediocre, as are their skills in crafting nonfood consumer goods, equipment and tools.
>
> After the great transition that has seen the shift from traditional society to advanced society (which began with the industrial revolution; we are probably experiencing its end), the mastery of ecological pyramids no longer requires much work; transformation technologies have endlessly diversified; transport has become fast and cheap; the transmission of news happens instantaneously.
>
> *(Claval, 1977: 72–73)*

It is difficult to see how exactly this geography could be called 'new'. Both in spirit and in form, this typology of human societies reflects the old evolutionist pattern typically outlined by Lewis H. Morgan (1877): savagery, barbarism, civilization. History is considered as one and unilinear: it presents the human species as evolving through the growing mastery of its environment from the 'archaic' to the 'advanced' stage. The universality of this development is not called into question, and judgements on primitive societies are based not on any real knowledge of the functioning and principles of these cultures, but on widespread Western prejudice. These societies are defined negatively by lack or inability. Yet where lies the efficiency of a technology – like the means of transportation discussed by Paul Claval – if not in its ability to fulfil the objectives assigned to it? How can one claim that traditional peoples have an 'imperfect' mastery of their environment on the basis of aspirations of profit and yield that are not theirs?

In such an approach, social evolutionism comes hand in hand with natural evolutionism – a nature that changes not in function of natural (biological, ecological, etc.) laws, but of the sole will of human beings.

Nothing is more difficult to eradicate than prejudice. Indeed, such perversion of discourses on the Other is not an isolated occurrence for traditional or 'new' geographers. In a paper on the relationships between human geography and ethnology,

Mariel Jean-Brunhes Delamarre shows that despite commendable attempts at reconciliation, positions still diverge between geographers and ethnologists:

> Rather than primitive societies (which can have a derogatory sense and cause confusion, as ethnology has taught us that most of these societies had very sophisticated technologies and a highly complex parental and social organization), some ethnologists have accustomed us to the term 'traditional societies', or better yet, 'pre-industrial societies'.
> (Jean-Brunhes Delamarre, 1968: 1471–1472)

Even if some ethnologists still have some lingering evolutionist nostalgia, few of them dare to use a term such as 'preindustrial' to refer to traditional societies, which assumes that all of our planet's traditional societies (comprising 300 to 400 million individuals) are destined (doomed?) to become industrial societies, thereby losing their specificity.

The aforementioned excerpt also shows that when geography 'humanizes' itself, it is chiefly to look into the multiple ways in which humans change and transform their environment, to study how they *anthropize* the natural environment:

> To simplify in the extreme, one might say that the human geographer, the 'geo-humanist' first looks at the 'landscaped works' (Deffontaines) of man, those that are set in the landscape for a certain amount of time and using a certain amount of space. To him, human groups are geographical agents who alter aspects of the Earth, just as water which carves out the land, or alluvium that makes up the soil [. . .] Men alter space in order to find shelter, feed, clothe or entertain themselves. This involves *increasingly complex* [emphasis mine] actions and interactions between physical environment and human environment – environments and relationships being themselves transformed over the years by a variety of agents – physical and mechanical, chemical and biological, etc.
> (Jean-Brunhes Delamarre, 1968: 1466)

No ethnologist would be naïve enough to argue that humanity has no bearing on its environment, as every living thing (stone, animal, vegetal element, etc.) influences and is influenced by all the others. The ethnologist's concern is to know whether, as the geographer claims, 'actions and interactions' are 'increasingly complex'. This simple question, which arose from knowledge of other cultures, places the disciplines of geography and ethnology in different approaches, depending on whether scholars consider it under debate or settled. For some geographers – and a few ethnologists – this is a nonexistent issue, as all societies are thought to aspire to the single model of industrial society or to be condemned to it by some hypothetical historical law that escapes human will:

> The 'before' and 'after' of the industrial revolution evoke diverse situations and relationships between human groups and within them – human groups

which are still today at very different *development stages*; the most pre-industrial and the least industrialized are often privileged centers of study offered to the converging or diverging beams of the observation and reflection of geographers and ethnologists.

(Jean-Brunhes Delamarre, 1968: 1472)

The 'primitive' and the ethnologist's views

The Ojibwa, whose lands extend from the south of the Great Lakes to the confines of the Canadian taiga,[2] make up the third-largest Native American population in North America (in Canada and the United States, where they are generally called Chippewa).[3] They believe that the Great Spirit, *Gitche Manitou*, received the vision of a 'beautiful, orderly and harmonic' world and that he 'felt the urge' to project his vision and shape – or give life – to the 'world without evil' of his dreams. Nobody knows how the world came to be, let alone why, and Ojibwa philosophy offers a common-sense explanation, or at least an ethic that is fundamentally life oriented. Human beings were created after celestial bodies, the elements, plants and the other animals, and they were not placed on the Earth to rule and assert their power over the other creatures; rather, they are adrift in a world of which they have lost the keys, and their only path towards survival consists in following the same natural laws observed by the other creatures (Navet, 2007).

Native Americans do not locate the origin of the world in a distant past, as they see Creation as a permanent act, the actualization of an inner vision with no beginning or end. This cyclical, nonlinear concept of time also comes with a sanctification of the world. The geographer and ethnologist Jean Malaurie discussed the latter phenomenon in the Inuit whom he extensively observed on the western coast of Greenland:

> When [ethnology] bases its research on hunting peoples [. . .] how could it minimize the man/nature dialectic? [. . .] Their environment – fauna and flora – , their land in its physical texture, their sensory and oracular understanding of stones, plants, the air, their vertical perception of space, their cosmic vision [. . .] creates a sacred geography.
>
> (Malaurie, 1985: 151)

The Teko (formerly known as 'Émerillons') of French Guiana share with the Ojibwa and with traditional peoples in general the same ideal of a 'land without evil' where all things are harmony, order and beauty. The Tupi-Guarani spoke of a 'land without evil' (*iwimalã e'i*); the Émerillons named it *Alapukup*. As for the Ojibwa, the founding and (in)formative myth demonstrates that this ideal is incompatible with life; the vision remains a vision – a hope, a deep aspiration – and life is essentially not about conflict as it is fashionable to claim (particularly among sociologists), but about the duality and the complementarity of qualities and feelings. If there is beauty, there is ugliness; if there is hot, there is cold; if there are liquids, there are solids; if there is good, there is evil, etc. Ultimately we may define traditional societies as moved by the constant concern to maintain a threefold balance at all cultural levels:

1. the balance of the relationships, individual or collective (as members of communities, humans are gregarious by nature), of human beings with their non-human environments, visible and invisible, past and present;
2. the balance of the relationships of human beings, as individuals or members of groups, with other human beings, in each local group and between local groups;
3. the individual's inner balance between the *id* (in Freudian terms), the source of urges and anxieties, and the *super-ego*, which is not repressive but organizes social life and life in this world.

The Inuit, Native Americans and men and women in traditional societies in general do not seek to harness nature and use it to serve their needs, as they believe that the Earth will survive humanity anyway. The Earth, which is impregnated by the sun, gives its bounty to all creatures and makes plants grow that large herbivores eat (caribou, moose, bison); in turn the latter are eaten by predators. Humans are one of these predators, but like the others, they depend on the preservation of 'chains of life' for their survival; if these chains break at any point, the world's balance and order are threatened. If an animal or vegetal species disappears, the circle, which is a symbol of life, is broken.

In the introduction to his classic book *The Perception of the Environment* (2000), Tim Ingold writes that he owes his vocation as an anthropologist to his feeling that the gap needed to be filled between natural sciences and what was then called the 'humanities'. His entire work grew out of this necessity and demonstrated that 'the critical task for anthropology [. . .] was to understand the reciprocal interplay between the two kinds of system, social and ecological' (Ingold, 2000: 3).

This was not a necessity 'on principle', but rather one inferred from ethnographic observation. Ingold himself drew on his experience with the reindeer hunting and herding of circumpolar peoples:

> My concern is to find a way of comprehending how human beings relate to their environment in the tasks of making a living, that does not set up a polarity between the ecological domain of the relations with non-human 'nature' and the cognitive domain of its cultural construct.
>
> *(Ingold, 2000: 5)*

The concept of 'environment' therefore encapsulates the human environment – the societies that make it up – and visible *as well as invisible* nonhuman environments. This was already noted in the early 1930s by Diamond Jenness, a Canadian anthropologist of New Zealand origin, regarding the Ojibwa in Parry Island, Ontario:

> It is impossible to comprehend the daily life of the Parry Island Ojibwa (or indeed of any people) without some knowledge of their religious beliefs, and

their religious beliefs are unintelligible without an understanding of their interpretation of what they saw around them. They lived much nearer to nature than most white men, and they looked with a different eye on the trees and the rocks, the water and the sky. One is almost tempted to say that they were less materialistic, more spiritually minded than Europeans, for they did not picture any great chasm separating mankind from the rest of creation, but interpreted everything around them in much the same terms as they interpreted their own selves.

(Jenness, 1935: 18)

It follows from these observations, and this has major implications, that traditional peoples do not follow the so-called 'revealed' religions in making a distinction between a *profane* and a *religious* world.

In his book *Beyond Nature and Culture* (2013 [2005]), the French ethnologist Philippe Descola, drawing on his knowledge of the culture of the Achuar people in the Western Amazonian (Ecuador and Peru) and on a wide body of ethnographic literature, reached a similar conclusion: traditional peoples do not perceive a discontinuity between human worlds and the worlds that surround them: 'In the Far North, as in South America, nature is not opposed to culture but is an extension of it and enriches it in a cosmos in which everything is organized according to the criteria of human beings'. Later, he adds:

In Siberia, as in America, then, many peoples seem resistant to the idea of a clear separation between their physical environment and their social environment. For them, these two domains that we normally distinguish are facets that are hardly contrasted within a continuum of interactions between human and nonhuman persons.

(Descola, 2013 [2005]: 14, 21)

Accounting for native knowledge

In the footsteps of Franz Boas (1858–1942), Julian H. Steward (1902–1972), who invented the concept of 'cultural ecology' (Steward, 1972), and Leslie A. White (1900–1975) were among the forerunners of ethnoecology (White, 1949). Yet its founding act was the publication of Harold C. Conklin's book *The Relation of the Hanunoo Culture to the Plant World* (1954) – the author himself referred to his approach as 'ethnoecological'. The first tenet consisted of taking into consideration 'indigenous knowledge' – most specifically the ways in which local populations perceive, conceptualize, classify and deal with the components (animals, plants, minerals, etc.) of the environments or biotopes *where* they live and *off which* they live. *Traditional ecological knowledge* (TEK) used to be treated with indifference, if not contempt, as it was thought to be obsolete. Now, in the face of the failures of the dominant model of the industrial, technocratic, market-based civilization, they appear to be possible bases for solving current human and ecological problems and ensure a sustainable development. For anthropologists, this requires working in close collaboration with those who possess such knowledge, particularly the elders, who are the guardians of oral tradition and its associated human, ecological and spiritual values.

In North America, many universities and scientific institutions have developed research programmes of applied, engaged anthropology in a variety of regions of the world: Fikret Berkes (University of Manitoba) (1998) works with subarctic natives (Ojibwa, Cree, etc.); Julie Cruikshank (University of British Columbia) (2005) with the Athapaskan in Yukon and the Tlingit; Michael Dove (Yale University) (2012) in Southeastern Asia; Virginia Nazarea (University of Georgia) (1999) in the Philippines and Ecuador, etc.

Witnessing the emergence of 'development' projects endangering both the environments (biodiversity) and the lifestyle of indigenous communities (see the chapter on ethnocide in this book), many anthropologists become closer to the 'political ecology' movement: for instance, anthropologist and biologist Darell A. Posey (1947–2001) spent a long time fighting for the right of the Brazilian native populations he researched (Posey, 2004; Posey and Balick, 2006).

In the wake of the pioneering works of Marcel Mauss (1950), many authors, including (in France) Claude Lévi-Strauss (1962), Pierre Grenand (1980), Serge Bahuchet (1985), Jean Malaurie (1985), Pierre Robbe (1994), Alain Testart (2012), Philippe Descola (2013), etc.,[4] elaborated on this demonstration: in traditional societies, the human and nonhuman, visible and invisible, past and present worlds constitute a continuum in which each component is necessary and ensures the cohesion and sustenance of the whole. These societies of small numbers can be termed communitarian-ecological; nowadays any form of ethnology must be (regardless of whether it identifies as such) an *ethnoecology* or a *human ecology*.

Not making a distinction between relationships among human beings and their relationships with other living beings is also, for instance, the position defended by Serge Bahuchet (1985), an ethnologist specializing in the Aka Pygmy people of Central Africa and one of the forerunners of the ethnoecological approach. His teaching at the Parisian Muséum National d'Histoire Naturelle was based on the two key concepts of *subsistence strategy* and *social space*. Here, there is nothing pejorative about the word 'subsistence', which relates to an economy in the broader sense that is neither aimed at productivity or yield, nor at some domination over beings and things. English-language authors such as Marshall Sahlins (1972) have demonstrated that a subsistence economy does not result in shortages and poverty – far from it.

Anthropology must now decentre its approach and situate human beings and the communities they form on a horizontal plane; humanity must step down from the throne where it has been arbitrarily placed and deprived of its title as 'king of the universe'. In the words of Tim Ingold:

> There can, then, be no radical break between social and ecological relations; rather, the former constitute a *subset* of the latter [. . .] The first step in the establishment of this ecological anthropology would be to recognize that

the relations with which it deals, between human beings and their environments, are not confined to a domain of 'nature', separate from, and given independently of, the domain in which they lead their lives as persons. For hunter-gatherers, as for the rest of us, life is given in engagement, not in disengagement, and in that very engagement the real world at once ceases to be 'nature' and is revealed to us as an environment for people. Environments are constituted in life, not just in thought, and it is only because we live in an environment that we can think at all.

(Ingold, 2000: 60, my emphasis)

Does the future belong to small groups?[5]

The very concept of 'race', which was popular in the nineteenth and twentieth centuries, has been scientifically invalidated. Not more than there are 'races' or 'superior' or 'inferior' peoples, the idea that the societies studied by ethnologists must ultimately become 'industrial', 'state-led', etc., negates conscious choices expressed and implemented on a daily basis. Evolutionist fatalism is magical thinking that isn't supported by any facts.

In his book *Collapse: How Societies Choose to Fail or Succeed* (2005), the American biologist and geographer Jared Diamond demonstrates that there is no such fatality: although the influence of geological and climate conditions is undeniable, human beings have always had some responsibility in the demise of the civilizations they built. In a more recent book, *The World until Yesterday: What We Can Learn from Traditional Societies* (2012), Diamond calls us to take into consideration the knowledge, technologies and strategies developed by traditional societies in order to find solutions to the multiple problems raised by 'modernity'.

The main challenge at stake is now to get those who believe themselves immune to them to stop defying 'natural laws' and to rebuild a connection that is the only guarantee of survival on this Earth, according to the Canadian Mohawks, for instance:

> We do not consider that we dominate and can egoistically exploit other living beings; on the contrary, we see ourselves as part and parcel of Creation. Our essential goal is to strive for living in peace, in harmony and balance with all the living beings of the Earth.
>
> *(Akwesasne Notes)*[6]

Notes

1 The title of Herodotus' work is generally translated as *Histories* in several languages, which according to Hellenistic scholar Jacques Lacarrière (1986) does not reflect the meaning intended by the author.
2 'Taiga' refers to the forested area that still covers vast swathes of Canadian land.
3 The first and second largest are the Navajo, in the American Southwest, and the Cree, who live in a large area of the Canadian North, close to the Inuit.

4 This entry focuses on the English- and French-speaking worlds for space reasons, but this ethnoecological approach to the humanities has obviously also been pursued in other countries.
5 In his book *Utopies réalisables* (*Achievable Utopias*, 1975: 10), Yona Friedman suggests that 'today's marginal movements might represent the solutions of the future'.
6 *Akwesasne Notes* is a magazine published by the Mohawk community of Kanesatake, Canada.

Bibliography

Akwesasne Notes, An International Paper for Native and Natural Peoples, Rooseveltown, NY, Mohawk Nation.
Bahuchet, Serge (1985), *Les pygmées Aka et la forêt centrafricaine. Ethnologie écologique*, Paris, Société d'études linguistiques et anthropologiques de France and CNRS.
Berkes, Fikret (1998), 'Exploring the Basic Ecological Unit: Ecosystem-Like Concepts in Traditional Societies', *Ecosystems*, 1 (4): 409–415.
Claval, Paul (1977), *La nouvelle géographie*, Paris, Presses Universitaires de France, series Que sais-je?
Conklin, Harold C. (1954), 'The Relation of Hanunóo Culture to the Plant World', Doctoral dissertation, Yale University.
Cruikshank, Julie (2005), *Do Glaciers Listen? Local Knowledge, Colonial Encounters and Social Imagination*, Vancouver and Seattle, UBC Press and University of Washington Press.
Descola, Philippe (2005), *Par-delà nature et culture*, Paris, Gallimard, translated into English by Janet Lloyd (2013) as *Beyond Nature and Culture*, Chicago, University of Chicago Press.
Diamond, Jared (2005), *Collapse: How Societies Chose to Fail or Succeed*, New York, Viking Penguin.
Diamond, Jared (2012), *The World Until Yesterday: What We Can Learn from Traditional Societies*, New York, Viking Penguin.
Dove, Michael R. (2012), *The Banana Tree at the Gate: The History of Marginal Peoples and Global Markets in Borneo*, Singapore, National University of Singapore Press.
Friedman, Yona (1975), *Utopies réalisables*, Paris, Union Générale d'Éditions.
Grenand, Pierre (1980), *Introduction à l'étude de l'univers wayãpi: ethnoécologie des Indiens du Haut-Oyapock (Guyane française)*, Paris, SELAF.
Humboldt, Alexandre (von) (1970 [1814–25]), *Relation historique du voyage aux régions équinoxiales du Nouveau Continent*, Stuttgart, F. A. Brockhaus.
Ingold, Tim (2000), *The Perception of the Environment: Essays on Livelihood, Dwelling and Skill*, London and New York, Routledge.
Jean-Brunhes Delamarre, Mariel (1968), 'Géographie humaine et ethnologie', *in*: Poirier, Jean (ed.), *Ethnologie générale*, Paris, Gallimard, series Encyclopédie de la Pléiade: 1465–1503.
Jenness, Diamond (1935), *The Ojibwa Indians of Parry Island, Their Social and Religious Life*, Ottawa, Canada Department of Mines, National Museum of Canada, Bulletin 78, Anthropological Series 17.
Kaeppelin, Paul (n.d.), *Géographie. Cours moyen*, Paris, Hatier.
Lacarrière, Jacques (1986 [1981]), *En cheminant avec Hérodote*, Paris, Pluriel.
Lévi-Strauss, Claude (1962), *La pensée sauvage*, Paris, Plon.
Malaurie, Jean (1985), 'Dramatique de civilisations: le tiers-monde boréal', *Hérodote*, 39: 145–169.
Mauss, Marcel (1950), *Sociologie et anthropologie*, Paris, Presses Universitaires de France.

Morgan, Lewis H. (1877), *Ancient Society, or Researches in the Line of Human Progress from Savagery, Through Barbarism to Civilization*, London, Macmillan.
Navet, Éric (2007), *L'Occident barbare et la philosophie sauvage: Essai sur le mode d'être et de penser des Indiens Ojibwé*, Paris, Homnisphères.
Nazarea, Virginia D. (ed.) (1999), *Ethnoecology: Situated Knowledge/Located Lives*, Tucson, University of Arizona Press.
Posey, Darrell A. (2004), *Indigenous Knowledge and Ethics: A Darrell Posey Reader*, London and New York, Routledge.
Posey, Darrell A., and Balick, Michael J. (eds.) (2006), *Human Impacts on Amazonia: The Role of Traditional Ecological Knowledge in Conservation and Development*, New York, Columbia University Press.
Ratzel, Friedrich (1909), *Anthropogeographie*, Stuttgart, J. Engelhorn.
Robbe, Pierre (1994), *Les Inuit d'Ammasalik, chasseurs de l'Arctique*, Paris, Éditions du Muséum National d'Histoire Naturelle, vol. 159.
Sahlins, Marshall (1972), *Stone Age Economics*, Piscataway, NJ, Transaction.
Steward, Julian H. (1972), *Theory of Culture Change: The Methodology of Multilinear Evolution*, Chicago, University of Illinois Press.
Testart, Alain (2012), *Avant l'histoire. L'évolution des sociétés, de Lascaux à Carnac*, Paris, Gallimard.
White, Leslie A. (1949), *The Science of Culture*, New York, Farrar, Straus and Co.

PART IV
Renewed ecologies

The links between the notions of 'nature' and 'the city' or 'urban' and 'rural' are particularly complex and fraught with tensions, partly overlapping the division between 'nature' and 'culture'. Ever since the classical era in Europe, indeed, the city has appeared as the site of 'culture', according to associations suggesting that 'civility and civilization, urbanity and urban are kin terms; they are opposed to rusticity' (Roncayolo, 1990: 73). This constitutes a reversal of the meaning of 'culture', which henceforth has referred to the realities of the mind and intelligence, whereas in its original Roman sense it related to 'the intercourse of man with nature' characterized by an attitude of loving care (Arendt, 1977). In our presently massively urbanized Western societies, these distinctions tend to become more and more blurred: 'rural' does not refer only to the main alternative form of space to '(sub)urban', and 'the city' and 'nature' are set less into a strict opposition than thought of as more or less embedded one within the other; similarly, the notion of 'nature' appears very reductive when trying to grasp in their holistic dimension the plurality of the interactions between humankind, their 'modes of inhabiting' (Mathieu, 2014) and their 'environment'. This new crisis in the very idea of 'nature', which would seem to follow after the crisis of the 'city' and of the 'rural' world, while making their regeneration possible, calls for a thorough re-examination of their links.

Paying attention to the diversity of the spaces and actors of the living world and of societies also entails taking into account the important role of economic issues, and especially recognizing and holding in balance the embeddedness of the economy not only in society (Polanyi, 2001 [1944]) but in nature too. This appears plainly necessary when one considers long-term processes and the studies already initiated in that direction by most of the 'founding fathers' of the social sciences (see Woodgate's chapter on ecosociologies). In his critique of political economy, Karl Marx, in particular, underlined the key issue of the collective relationships to nature, suggesting that the social world was essentially shaped through institutions devoted to the management of these relationships (Charbonnier, 2015: 227–230).

According to Marx, capitalism broke the original unity between man and nature and led to the exploitation he denounced: 'All progress in increasing the fertility of the soil for a given time, is a progress towards ruining the lasting sources of that fertility' (1867: 330). Other authors, in their critical analysis of the market and of the depletion of natural resources caused by growth, have been led to redefine what 'economics' should be, giving rise to 'ecological economics', that is, the bringing together of what is desirable with what is sustainable in our finite world (Costanza, 1991). Nicholas Georgescu-Roegen (1971), for instance, proposed a new take on the idea of double-embeddedness by analyzing the laws of thermodynamics and arguing that economic growth cannot go on indefinitely in a world in which energy and raw materials are limited. Some have interpreted this as the premises of the movement of degrowth, others as an attempt at formulating a system of global ecological economics, whose most concrete developments are to be found in the field of industrial ecology as a response, limited though it is, to entropy. These ongoing debates are today reshaping disciplinary configurations around the apprehension of nature and the environment, at the same time as new forms of actions are rising, premised on the aforementioned double-embeddedness of the economy. The use of the notion of 'ecosystem services' in socioeconomic analyses and in public policies clearly points to the various interconnections between biodiversity and society, as shown by the recognition of the intrinsic value of threatened species.

Owain Jones (Chapter 12) observes that in developing countries where large tracts of apparent wilderness remain, the distinction between 'nature' and 'rural space' is more complex because the major steps in the development of human society have, in a way, played out within this spatial framework. This chapter thus explores the past, present and future overlayings of ideas of 'nature' onto the 'rural' and seeks to challenge them: from the move from hunter-gatherer to agrarian cultures; then the industrial revolution and the acceleration of urbanism; to today's predominantly urban world (in terms of economy, consumption and population) where more than half of the world's vastly increased population lives in cities. In a globalized, topological world of networks and flows, does the rural/urban divide have any analytical and governance purchase? Is ecocide more at play in rural or urban space? (See also Chapter 18) Where can biodiversity best flourish?

With the same aim of questioning the hardened dichotomies between 'nature' and 'rural', Isabelle Hajek and Jean-Pierre Lévy (Chapter 13) investigate how, for a few years, there has been a new rapprochement between city and 'nature' under the combined influence of new social expectations and advances in an ecology of landscape, along with the manner in which sustainable development has prompted certain cities to reinterpret the question of nature. In this context, they show how the very idea of urban ecology fits into a long-standing conceptual framework opposing city and 'nature' that would subsequently come to include a concern with the ecological impact of cities and a first generation of research on urban ecology. Then they examine the adjustments made to this approach by a second generation of research, which led to considerable disciplinary diversification in the definition of urban ecology, part of a 'paradigm shift', the elaboration of a new concept in thinking about the city and 'nature' in their reciprocal relations.

All these transformations in the relations between 'nature' and social spaces have led to a renewed understanding of man's 'modes of inhabiting'. In this context one must take into account the emerging and newly recognized notion of 'environmental health', as well as that of 'sustainable urbanism'. According to Lionel Charles (Chapter 14), the notion of 'environmental health' introduced a new and particularly innovative definition of health, emphasizing its composite, altogether subjective, medical and social character. This definition sheds light on the limited resources the idea of nature offers for the development of a relevant sanitary dynamic. In a world increasingly affected by human activities, the term 'environment', with its double heuristic and pragmatic-contextual dimension, seems much more appropriate to account for the relative, dynamic, multidimensional and indeed relational character of health. This also fits with historical developments, testifying to a strong continuity between Hippocratic medicine in its empirical and environmental dimensions and its rediscovery, with the renewal of empiricism initiated by British and European modernity. It sets the foundations of modern epidemiology and of the widened approach to health summarized in the World Health Organization definition in a deeply renewed scientific and social context. This contribution, rejected in France in the nineteenth century, remains only very partially and belatedly apprehended, as shown by the slow development of 'environmental health'.

The notion of 'sustainable urbanism' has enjoyed quick fame since the 1990s among urban decision-makers and planners. This is the subject of the chapter written by Philippe Hamman (Chapter 15), who investigates how and to what extent the repertoire of 'sustainable development' is applied to the urban environment, using a knowledge-based approach, and looking at sustainability as both a rhetorical corpus and a principle of action, in order to better understand how sustainability brought about transformations in urban development. He shows how the overarching incentive to take 'sustainability' into account now informs what has become both a field of knowledge and a field of practices and how this has found an echo in urban theories. The presence of these two dimensions explains the coexistence of a literature with operational purposes – concerned with what to do – and research applying the concept of 'sustainable development' to urban planning with cognitive or critical purposes. 'Sustainable urbanism' is a recent and evolving reference in Europe, diverging partly from 'sustainable development' in its conceptual and historical dimensions: more than simply serving as a global or alternative motto, it is embodied by interacting networks of cities and professional interests. It now faces competition from other notions and other approaches to gaining knowledge on nature, as, for instance, resilience and transition.

'Ecological economics' is first practised in the field of industrial ecology, as analyzed by Nicolas Buclet (Chapter 16), a field whose principles can be traced back to the nineteenth century but which has grown quickly over recent years. Taking into consideration the metabolism of human activities – especially economic ones – alongside the metabolism of human organisms in order to account for the interactions between the economy and its environment reflects an attempt to reconcile man and nature, especially with a view towards achieving a loop of material and energy flows. After outlining the principles of industrial ecology, this chapter investigates the superficial ties between ecology and industrial ecology and goes on to evidence their contradictions, basing itself on the case of Kalundborg (Denmark). As a matter of conclusion, Nicolas Buclet discusses the perspectives of a genuine interchange between these two disciplinary fields.

In the same way, since the publication of the Millennium Ecosystem Assessment in 2005, the idea that nature provides services to people has served as the foundation stone for a type of approach centred on the role that biodiverse ecosystems play in the environment and their benefits for humankind. This approach is popular among environmental managers and institutions in an operational way, which should encourage us to some critical distance. In this context, Roldan Muradian (Chapter 17) undertakes to assess to what extent this particular way of looking at human–nature relations is providing new analytical tools that can actually advance our understanding of the drivers of socioenvironmental transformations and is increasing the chances of changing the value system of contemporary societies that is ultimately responsible for the widespread degradation of ecosystems. According to the author, the ecosystem services paradigm has been definitively successful in renovating the discourse of environmentalism, mobilizing new resources and creating channels of dialogue with the private sector and between different academic fields. This has allowed environmental issues to regain an important position in the global policy agenda. However, due to internal inconsistencies in the definition and classification of services and an unjustified neglect of ecosystem disservices, despite its great communication power, the ecosystem services framework can be deemed analytically problematic. That is why the chapter also discusses and elaborates briefly on some alternatives.

Bibliography

Arendt, Hannah (1977), 'The Crisis in Culture', *in:* Arendt Hannah, *Between Past and Future*, New York, Penguin (reprinted from Viking, 1961).

Charbonnier, Pierre (2015), *La fin d'un grand partage. Nature et société, de Durkheim à Descola*, Paris, CNRS Éditions.

Costanza, Robert (ed.) (1991), *Ecological Economics: The Science and Management of Sustainability*, New York, Columbia University Press.

Georgescu-Roegen, Nicholas (1971), *The Entropy Law and the Economic Process*, Cambridge, MA, Harvard University Press.

Marx, Karl (2015 [1867]), *Capital, Vol. I: A Critique of Political Economy*, available at: www.marxists.org/archive/marx/works/download/pdf/Capital-Volume-I.pdf (Accessed 29/10/2016).

Mathieu, Nicole (2014), 'Mode d'habiter: un concept à l'essai pour penser les interactions hommes-milieux', *in:* Chenorkian, Robert, and Robert, Samuel (eds.), *Les interactions hommes-milieux. Questions et pratiques de la recherche en environnement*, Versailles, Quae: 97–130.

Polanyi, Karl (2001 [1944]), *The Great Transformation: The Political and Economic Origins of Our Time*, Boston, Beacon.

Roncayolo, Marcel (1990), *La ville et ses territoires*, Paris, Gallimard.

12
RETHINKING RURAL NATURE IN THE ERA OF ECOCIDE

Owain Jones

Introduction

Tim Ingold writes: 'No-one yet has made the crossing from nature to society, or vice versa, and no-one ever will. There is no such boundary to be crossed' (Ingold, 2005: 508). The logics behind this statement made by this celebrated anthropologist are compelling and critical in today's era of ecological crisis (as discussed later). But perhaps, when the need to care for nature and the environment has never seemed more pressing and critical to all life on earth, it seems perverse to be seeking to dissolve nature as a concept at the same time. But, as also discussed later, Ingold and related thinkers consider that the ways 'nature' and the environment have been constructed by modernity underpin much of the ecological crisis in the first place.

We need to dissolve the idea of nature in order to save nature. Put simply, nature – as it stands – is 'outside' modern politics, culture and economy in key ways of value (political, ethical, spiritual). This means it is not protected from the ways *it is in modernity* as realms of resources and commons to be enclosed, exploited, despoiled and exhausted by extraction and discharge. The approach of eco-system services (Bouma and van Beukering, 2015) to development decision-making is one procedure that has recently emerged as an attempt to change this relationship. Nature is brought more fully into modernity by recognizing hitherto disregarded services it provides to society – the same goes for the related approaches of environmental and ecological economics. These new economic-based approaches, however, do not venture to challenge the *culture*/nature divide in terms of ethics and visions of what humans are and how they are 'in ecology', as do (say) deep ecology, ecofeminism and related 'ecological self' approaches. That is their fatal flaw.

This chapter seeks to explore the key *culture*/nature architecture of modernity and its ecological crisis in relation to rural space. To leave a densely built-up city by train, bus or car and ride out into the countryside and then maybe go on to remoter, wilder areas is to feel like moving from one kind of space to another. The same goes for taking off from a vast international hub airport (the ultimate in modern space?) and then fly out over rural hinterlands, then maybe oceans and the vastnesses of, say, Greenland and northern Canada. As the view through the window changes from concrete, glass, technologies of communication and transport, images and practices of consumption, to fields, trees, hills, mountains, streams – or from dense, complex and dazzling patterns of fixed and moving lights to deep darkness – it is difficult not to think that a move from 'culture' to 'nature' is being made.

Indeed, trips to the countryside (rural or wild lands) are commonly constructed, and marketed, as trips into nature, as retreats and escapes. Of course, this was one of the hallmarks of the Transcendental and Romantic movements in the United States and Europe which did so much to shape modern understandings of nature and its relationships to the urban and to the industrial (Bate, 1991). Conversely, trips and migrations the other way, such as from remoter rural areas to the 'city', are often constructed as trips to culture and to 'civilization'. Of course, there are marked national variations in these rural/urban dynamics. For example, there is the notion of the 'rural idyll' – a valorization of the rural over the urban in a number of ways which is a powerful construct in Britain and parts of America and Europe, but which is absent in other national cultures. In Australia, notions of rural idyll are largely absent in the dominant settler cultures. This is related to the recent colonial history where European settlers found the 'outback' more hostile in climatic and other conditions than those from whence they came. Also the farming methods imported soon revealed a set of much less 'harmonious' relationships with local conditions (soil, water resources, indigenous flora and fauna). Farming and rural life was much more of a 'battle against hostile elements'. Also the deep traditions of paganism and early Christianity which were so bound up with rural and national culture in the UK/Europe through land and nature were absent in Australia where, instead, there was a deep rupture between settler cultures and aboriginal spirituality and culture (which, of course, did *not* see the land as hostile: see Robin, 2007, for an account of this history).

But what happens to the rural/urban divide and its foundation of 'nature' once the very idea of nature – in the Enlightenment/modern worldview – is lost? What does this 'do' to rurality, and what does it do to nature and to urban space? The 'greening' of modern cities has been a movement based upon bringing tree cover and regenerated waterways, habitats and species into urban space. Often this is summarized as bringing 'nature' to the city (Benton-Short and Short, 2008). If the *culture*/nature divide of modernity needs to be dissolved to save nature – and that means, more or less, preventing the ongoing steep decline in types and extent of habitats, ecosystems and the biodiversity therein – does the *urban*/rural divide need to be dissolved too? Is it the case that new flourishing forms of eco-social ecology are forming in some cities while the overall pressure from cities in terms of economy and culture is driving an ecocide (Guattari, 2000) that is playing out most violently in what appears to be rural space?

Do the very alarming, existential threats stemming from the current spatial and ontological settlements of modernity challenge us to really 'start again' in our understanding of how the world is created in ongoing relational practices? And, if so, what kind of spatial and processual analytical units do we need to be using?

Losing nature, losing the world

Nature is being lost in two conflicting senses. First, in the notion of the 'end of nature' as famously set out by Bill McKibben (1990): nature exists only as a separate realm from culture, and once culture has permeated everywhere (e.g. traces of pollution throughout the atmosphere and in the remotest polar ice sheets) nature is no more – all is culture. This notion is challenged by the second sense of losing nature – that it never really existed as the West imagined it (and implicit in McKibben's analysis) in the first place, as is discussed later. But this first sense remains an important idea which is bound up with the eras of the Anthropocene and Ecocide (defined later).

It is quite clear that nature in terms of the biosphere and the communities of life it consists of is being radically altered and degraded – altered and degraded in relative terms, that is. The planet and its biosphere, some other form of Gaia (i.e. the current 'settled' condition of the biosphere), will, of course, persist despite all human activity and beyond it. But the nature of that settlement – the biodiversity embedded in habitats and ecosystems – is being drastically diminished.

The WWF *Living Planet Report 2014* contains a stark summary:

> This latest edition of the *Living Planet Report* is not for the faint-hearted. One key point that jumps out and captures the overall picture is that the Living Planet Index (LPI), which measures more than 10,000 representative populations of mammals, birds, reptiles, amphibians and fish, has declined by 52 per cent since 1970.
>
> *(WWF, 2014: 4)*

This is a shocking and sobering situation. Even if the science can be questioned, it surely cannot be wrong to such an extent as to make his warning irrelevant. It must be recognized that although climate change is seen as *the* greatest, and existential, threat in environmental terms, the biodiversity extinction crisis is of equal severity, and, of course, the two are linked and likely to feed one another in a spiral. The WWF go on to point this out:

> Put another way, in less than two human generations, population sizes of vertebrate species have dropped by half. These are the living forms that constitute the fabric of the ecosystems which sustain life on Earth – and the barometer of what we are doing to our own planet, our only home. We ignore their decline at our peril.
>
> *(WWF, 2014: 4)*

Nature, or at least much of the biodiverse life of this planet, is being lost. The mapping of this would show the vast majority of this happening, in terrestrial terms, in rural or wildlands space, driven largely by the ongoing conversion of wildland habitats to economically 'productive' lands; the spread of modernist agriculture replacing traditional farming methods (reduction in domestic plant and animal species); the impact of modern agriculture on the diversity of wildlife that can share space with it; and the degradation of soil and water systems through extraction, transformation and pollution.

The second way in which nature is 'lost', as articulated by writers such as Bruno Latour (1993), William Cronon (1996) and Tim Ingold (2005, 2011), is that 'nature' never really existed as a separate realm in the first place. It was and is a construction of certain modern (Western) ideologies and philosophies which have been developed and applied in the service of all manner of dubious political and economic enterprises such as colonialization, industrialization and globalization.

The idea of nature as a 'pure' nonhuman realm that recedes with the 'touch' of man has been roundly interrogated by accounts of how non-Western/nonmodern human societies co-evolved with richly biodiverse ecosystems, which, following colonial invasion, became seen as first wilderness, then wilderness to be exploited and settled and then, after despoliation, wilderness to be 'saved' by projects such as national parks.

The toxic mega-edifice that is human exceptionalism – conjured up and supported by a range of theological, pre-Enlightenment and Enlightenment ideological trajectories – and the challenge thereof, is key in both these senses of losing nature. Not only do we need to be rethinking what nature and culture are and what rural/urban means, but we also need to define the human/nonhuman relationship.

But where does all this leave that feeling, when one travels out of a city into rural spaces, that one is going from culture to nature? What do both senses of losing nature say to us about what we think of as rural space? Is this partly the difference between levels of phenomenological experience and systems-level analysis? To move from a place dominated by other humans and things of human construction to spaces with a richer diversity of nonhumans with varying levels of free-living agency is to be resituated in a more-than-human world, even if bears the trace of human influence at varying scales of (in)visibility.

Nature(s) and rurality(ies)

The associations between nature and rural space in Western political, economic and cultural discourses are powerful and persistent. As Raymond Williams puts it in *The Country and The City*, constructions of the country (rurality) come from a contrast to the city – 'here nature, there worldliness [culture]' (1985: 46). And as Lisa Benton-Short and John R. Short observe, 'cities provide an inevitable contrast to the "natural"' (2008: 3). A consistent strand of thought has sought to place the city as a human invention in opposition to the 'natural', the 'pristine' and the 'wilderness'. These associations between rurality and nature have deep roots stretching back as far as Ancient Greek thinking, but they came more fully into form through the eras of the Enlightenment, industrialization and rapid, unregulated urbanization.

Despite so much obvious evidence that many flows of process such as food chains, energy chains, water catchments and waste disposal systems weave the rural and urban into powerfully seamless systems, the idea of distinctive rural/natural space remains deep and intuitive and is played out not only in culture but also in political and economic structures.

Culturally, economically and politically rural areas can still have very different 'identities' operating at the individual and collective community levels which distinguish them from the power bases of urban areas. Consider, for example, the political atmosphere of the American Midwest, the ongoing political force of the Countryside Alliance in the UK, the very distinctive and assertive agri-rural politics of some areas of France and the overwhelmingly urban balance of modern Australia where the rural is the 'outback' with little charm and, instead, much danger and a dark history. But through all these differing constructions of rural space run some or other idea of 'nature' and economic, cultural and political relationships to it held by those in rural space *and* those, including political and economic elites, in urban centres.

The rural/urban divide is present in just about all national (i.e. nation-state) politics and cultures. Indeed, there are approaches seeking to analyze the notion of 'global rurality' in the era of globalization (Woods, 2016). As the relationships between the country and the city change into the twenty-first century they retain shifting political and cultural purchase. Most modern states still have administrative departments and agencies dedicated to the strategic management of 'rural space' for a range of purposes, such as effective social provision away from large population centres, the provision of agriculture, landscape conservation, ecological conservation, water catchment management, forest cover management and so on. These shape not only the rural and nature in imagination and material practice, but also the urban in a complex web of dualized interplays.

Scholars of the history of rural studies will know that the subject has waxed and waned as an area of study, and throughout there has been debate on what the rural is and whether it is a legitimate concept of space in the first place. Eminent scholars such as Mormont (1987) have questioned the rural as a category, given the degrees of social and political diversity found in rural areas within national settings – let alone between them. In their argument for 'postrural' studies, Murdoch and Pratt (1993) draw back from the universal concepts of 'urban' and 'rural', prioritizing instead the exploration of local variants of these concepts using the tools of social science.

In popular culture in the UK many national television and radio programmes retain a persistent focus upon rural landscape and lifestyle. They do so in ways in which nature is to the fore as a context, as an asset and sometimes as a challenge. Many accounts and images of rural lifestyles offer affective, emotionally expressive accounts of how individual and collective identities are performed in relation to a rich mix of nature (landscape), animals (domestic and wild) and agriculture crystallized in political movements such as the Countryside Alliance (Jones, 2013).

The shape and feel of history in rural/urban space

The rural/urban divide, although differently articulated culturally and politically in differing national contexts, seems to remain one of the main de facto divisions of terrestrial space, particularly so in those societies where all nonurban land has been very obviously modified by land use over many centuries, as in the UK and many European countries. Here the rural provides the main 'alternative' form of space to the urban and suburban and thus also the spaces of nature (as in national parks, nature reserves and other landscape designations). In some other countries, both developed and developing, where large tracts of apparent wilderness remain, the distinction is yet more complex with a wilderness–rural–suburban–urban spectrum in play. Here nature in terms of the rural stands against the wilder regions.

The major steps in the development of modern Western human societies can be seen to be played out within and through these spatial frameworks. The move from hunter-gatherer to agrarian cultures (which had a series of epochs) and the industrial revolution with its consumerism, globalization and the acceleration of urbanism, to today's predominantly urban world (in terms of settlement, economy, consumption and population) are great movements in the fundamental relationships between humans, land and natures as articulated in wilderness–rural–urban–suburban space. Of course, in other continents beyond the initial reach of the West this history is very different. It could be argued that in places like Australia and the United States, once colonization occurred a kind of speeded-up version of this history unfolded that exposed the true violence of it.

Human societies have gone through radical changes in terms of what humans are and how they 'see' their place in the cosmos and in nature. Robert P. Harrison (1992) suggests civilizations (cities) began – quite literally – as clearings in the primordial forest which grew and connected over time. Rosalind Williams (2008) points out that shifts from hunter-gatherer to pastoral, agricultural and industrial civilizations provoked cultural and spiritual upheavals and breakdowns which resonated for thousands of years. This model now colonizes the majority of the world's lands, and Williams suggests we are now embarked on yet another period of cultural upheaval and mourning as we enter the 'postnatural era' where globalized society is increasingly urbanized and evermore removed from obvious manifestations of 'nature'. As Tim Ingold puts it, even if the nature/culture divide is an illusion, modern society can become separated from the textures, qualities and rhythms of natural phenomena, such as the earth, as soil – the medium of life – itself (Ingold, 2011: 124). Obviously this plays out in some sense at least in aspects of rural and urban space.

Clearly all humans are embedded in nature in terms of food and energy chains, the atmosphere, climate and so on. But it is possible to become increasingly removed from many textures of the nonhuman even if not the fundamentals of nature itself. Russell Hitchings (2010) conducted studies revealing that certain London workers lived in highly 'artificial' indoor environments making up their work, travel, home and recreation spaces for the vast majority of their waking day. Contact with 'nature' in terms of space – even a city park – was fleeting.

Deep questions about biophilia (affective bonds between humans and natural systems: Wilson, 1984), human health and well-being (and nonhuman health and well-being) crowd around this. For example, there is the issue of 'nature deficit' disorder in modern children. This can apply to children in both rural and urban locations as safety fears and the lure of the screen keep them indoors. Children have long been seen to be 'at home' in rural areas because they are 'in nature' (Jones, 2002; Cloke and Jones, 2005). However, the geographies of the rural and urban child still have distinctive characteristics in relationship to space and nature (Ward, 1978, 1990). Key scholars such as Raymond Williams, in his seminal *The Country and the City* (1985), have discussed how the loss of the rural and nature, and the longing for them, as in the poems of the celebrated pastoral poet John Claire, is a complex retrospective construction, as much wrapped up in the challenges of time and the self (changing from child, to youth, to young adult, to older adult). Of course, Claire was mourning for the loss of the preenclosure rural landscape of his youth and early adulthood, but, as his many poems dedicated to the creatures of that land show, forms of nature were integral to that.

In a world of lost nature – in both senses – and in a globalized, hyperconnected, topological world of networks and flows, does the rural/urban divide have any analytical and governance purchase? Is ecocide more at play in rural or urban space? Where is the greatest biodiversity, and where can it best flourish?

'The city is everywhere and in everything'

In their book on cities, Ash Amin and Nigel Thrift (2002: 1) assert that 'the city is everywhere and in everything'. This is not really so much about the oft-quoted fact that at least half the world's greatly expanded human population now live in urban rather than rural areas; it is more about the extent to which the cultural, economic, political and bio/material power emanating from urban centres pervades the whole of global society and the planetary biosphere. Put another way, the effects of the global urban in terms of input (energy, water, food, raw materials) and output (waste of various kinds, products, services) pervade the entire planet.

The city is in the fields of all rural areas, for example, through long, complex food chains and/or the shaping of commodity prices. The city is in all wilder landscapes as conservation measures and tourist pressures shape how rural and wilderness landscapes are valued and managed. The water, energy and waste disposal needs of cities all utterly penetrate rural areas. Beyond these there are the more systemic issues of climate change, pollution, and so on, where the global atmospheric/water cycles are transformed and tainted. Clearly these do not, in any way, heed the rural/urban divide in spatial terms, yet political and policy responses still seek to discuss rural sustainability and urban sustainability as if somehow one could, for example, protect the atmosphere – the sky – over rural areas alone.

This is essentially a topological view of the world where connections and flows between points and processes construct the fabric of space. It sits in some tension with more topographical views of space where the rural and the urban could still be said to exist in terms of material and visual form, culture and legislation. The question – or challenge – could be this. Which view should shape our understanding of and management of the rural? And of the rural/urban divide? And of nature? Could it be that dualistic views of this kind are zero-sum games in conceptual thinking? In answer I suggest that both these views have purchase. Their consequences might well play out differently in rural/urban terms. For example, in the UK, recent formulations for flood prevention expenditure rest on numbers of household defended per pound sterling. Therefore, those in remote, thinly populated areas are likely to have less money spent on their behalf than those living in larger settlements. Thus, in some ways the rural persists, or emerges, as a challenge even if, in other ways, it dissolves. The challenge is how to effectively enfold topological and topographical approaches through which we can begin to deal with the shifting complexities of rural/urban space and nature.

The rural/urban dimensions of ecocide

Nature – and the biosphere as configured in the current 'settlement' of Gaia – seems to be crashing around disastrously in waves of 'slow violence' made up of climate change, pollution, species extinctions and so on. Donna Haraway sums up the crisis:

> It's more than climate change; it's also extraordinary burdens of toxic chemistry, mining, depletion of lakes and rivers under and above ground, ecosystem simplification, vast genocides of people and other critters, etc., etc., in systemically linked patterns that threaten major system collapse after major system collapse after major system collapse.
>
> *(Haraway, 2015: 159)*

This is the era of ecocide (Guattari, 2000). As the powerful (urban) cultural and political elites, which include academic scholars in the developed world, 'look down' on the spectacle, the implications are grim, not only for the biosphere but for us as individuals and collectives. Isabelle Stengers writes:

> We do, however, know one thing: even if it is a matter of the death of what we have called a civilization, there are many manners of dying, some being more ugly than others. I belong to a generation that will perhaps be the most hated in human memory, the generation that 'knew' but did nothing or did too little (changing our lightbulbs, sorting our rubbish, riding bicycles . . .).

But it is also a generation that will avoid the worst – we will already be dead. I would add that this is the generation that, thirty years ago, participated in, or impotently witnessed, the failure of the encounter between two movements that could, together, perhaps have created the political intelligence necessary to the development of an efficacious culture of struggle – those who denounced the ravaging of nature and those who combated the exploitation of humans.

(Stengers, 2015: 10–11)

Does ecocide have a rural/urban dimension and/or speak to how we might continue to understand and practise rural space?

It is not hard to point to 'rural' located acts of ecocide: the use of 'remote' Australian aboriginal lands for nuclear testing by the British government between 1952 and 1957; the ploughing of prairie grasslands in the United States in the 1920s, rendering ancient and rich ecosystems to dust in a matter of years; the clearing of Indian lowland forests for railway sleepers in the nineteenth century – all the ecology, the elephant herds gone. The same story repeats and repeats and repeats: the digging out of sand banks on Indian rivers for building and subsequent loss of nest sites for the river-dwelling gharial crocodiles. For those in the UK and Europe where there are seemingly more 'settled' pastoral, picturesque forms of rural landscape/nature, these seem like faraway stories. But here, too, a 'soft ecocide' is unfolding with many common species of plants and animals in decline.

Here I will set out how ecocide is being defined. We are using Felix Guattari's term (first published in French in 1989) where he claims that ecocide is devastating three sorts of ecology on a planetary scale. These three are as follows: (1) ecology as in biodiversity of habitats, species, etc.; (2) ecology as in cultural diversity of languages, customs, nonmodern cultures; and (3) ecology as in individual psychic diversity, which becomes eroded by the onslaught of ideologies of consumerism, liberalism and the oppressive structures of theologies. These three types of ecology flourished in complex interrelations in local regional settings. This can be seen as 'local distinctiveness', as Common Ground (a famous UK-based arts and environment NGO) termed it, or simply 'place'. Edward Casey (1998) asserts that modernity is hostile to the very idea of place.

All three ecologies are falling under the onslaught that is globalized consumer capitalism coupled with certain neoliberal ideologies about the human self as exceptional (and above nature). In terms of ecology type, it is clear that much of the loss in biodiversity has taken place in rural 'wilderness settings' as various forms of land use have devastated species-rich habitats and ecosystems. Indeed the city is the focus of the last main chapter of the WWF *Living Planet Report 2014*, which suggests how cities can be the engine of future sustainability by reducing their impacts. Urban biodiversity is another factor. I return to that shortly.

To consider how ecological biodiversity ecocide sits alongside cultural diversity ecocide, we need only to look at global hotspots of habitat loss and global hotspots of language loss. They echo each other and are playing in rural, wild areas. Other major challenges sit alongside biodiversity loss in rural/wildland space; as Yuval Harari points out:

> The disappearance of wildlife is a calamity of unprecedented magnitude, but the plight of the planet's majority population – the farm animals – is cause for equal concern. In recent years there is growing awareness of the conditions under which these animals live and die, and their fate may well turn out to be the greatest crime in human history. If you measure crimes by the sheer amount of pain and misery they inflict on sentient beings, this radical claim is not implausible.
>
> *(Harari, 2014: 159)*

The European Landscape Convention (Council of Europe, 2006) can be seen as a mirror image of ecocide, or a response to it, in so far as it wisely understood cultural and biological ecology to be interwoven and coproductive of each other across many rural areas of Europe. It is concerned with conserving the remaining remnants of rich, locally distinctive culture-natures where local forms of biodiversity go hand in hand with certain food cultures and other sociocultural formations. The conversion of wild lands to agricultural production and the spread of modern/industrial farming systems and methods across traditional production spaces mean that ecocide is playing out most powerfully in rural space.

Tuttle (2014), speaking in an educational/campaigning video about the impacts of human population growth since the dawn of the agrarian era and the rise of modern livestock farming methods, suggests that modern humans have 'stolen' the planet from wild species, and this is reflected in the fact that the fauna biomass of the planet has switched in the last 10,000 years from being dominated by what he calls 'free living animals' to being dominated by humans and their domestic livestock. Topographically this is driven in large part by the needs of urban areas in terms of inputs and outputs.

In a number of states in Europe and around the world, conservation bodies are seeking to counter ecocide through new 'integrated' and 'landscape-scale' approaches. They make the important step of seeing the ground for species and habitat conservation as being not based on separated, isolated spaces of special conversation (national parks, nature reserves, sites of special scientific interest). Such approaches seek to join up and make movement zones between areas of conservation and areas where important biodiversities still flourish or cling on. This is seen as especially important in relation to climate change and the possibilities for species and even habitat migration.

The forces of ecocide are systematic and will wash through these spaces and degrade them unless new practices are adopted. The countermeasures to ecocide *also need to be systemic* and to be applied to systems of energy, food, wastes, consumption and so on.

But the extent to which these approaches can 'deal with' and transverse densely built-up urban areas is still open to question. Perhaps, then, the city, as it is now 'in everything', is the key.

Conclusion: 'we love cities' (WWF): the city as rural and world future

It could be surmised that in the relatively (historically) new spaces and assemblages of urban space, new ecologies are forming such as urban green space, urban wild life and new forms of food production. As Webb (2010) points out:

> An ecological feedback loop is a natural extension of the idea that nature exists in the city, but it requires a change of thinking that is equally profound: There is no difference between urban nature and rural nature. It is all one ecology, adjusting and cross-pollinating in the face of change.

Bees in the UK are said to fare better in the city these days than they do in much of the countryside. This is because

> with their webs of non-human life, in mosaics of abandoned and planned spaces such as gardens, parks, allotments, derelict land, transport network verges, car parks, rooftops and underground systems, cities can offer much richer habitats than intensively farmed, but apparently green, rural landscapes. Maxeiner and Miersch (2006) point out that Berlin is in fact the biodiversity 'hotspot' of Germany, being home to 141 species of birds and more types of wild flowers per square kilometre than just about anywhere else in the country [. . .]. Norman (2006: 16) goes so far as to state that 'the city and not the countryside is the true home of nature' and that 'the bigger the city, the more ecological niches it offers to nature'.
>
> (Jones, 2009: 298)

Of course, this is not a simple and happy answer. Even if new forms of urban biodiversity are flourishing in some places, this is relative to the chronic decline in the space around them. The overall *bioproportionality* is inevitably drastically shifted to the human centre. Recognizing this and trying to ensure a more just and ecologically viable future for life on earth means rethinking biodiversity in relation to bioproportionality (Matthews, 2016). Of course, there are many progressive alternative assemblages in rural areas as well as in urban, but it is hard not to think that hard ecocide is harvesting many rural areas of their ecological and cultural diversities.

We need a deep shift towards understandings and practices of multispecies citizenship across space. Then in cities the hope might be that engaging in urban wildlife conservation helps city dwellers to understand the wider social-ecological systems they are a part of and hence to care more about their impact on urban and wild places. In rural space the illusion of 'nature' might still be a problem.

Acknowledgements

I am greatly indebted to the editors for their patience, support and guidance in the creation of this chapter; to Professor Kate Rigby for a number of insights; and to Penny Rogers for her skilled editing.

Bibliography

Amin, Ash, and Thrift, Nigel (2002), *Cities: Reimagining the Urban*, Cambridge, Polity.
Bate, Jonathan (1991), *Romantic Ecology: Wordsworth and the Environmental Tradition*, London and New York, Routledge.
Benton-Short, Lisa, and Short, John R. (2008), *Cities and Nature*, London and New York, Routledge.
Bouma, Jetske, and van Beukering, Pieter (eds.) (2015), *Ecosystem Services: From Concept to Practice*, Cambridge, Cambridge University Press.
Casey, Edward S. (1998), *The Fate of Place: A Philosophical History*, London, University of California Press.
Cloke, Paul, and Jones, Owain (2005), ' "Unclaimed Territory": Childhood and Disordered Spaces(s)', *Social and Cultural Geography*, 6 (3): 311–323.
Council of Europe (2006), *Landscape and Sustainable Development: Challenges of the European Landscape Convention*, Strasbourg, Council of Europe.
Cronon, William (ed.) (1996), *Uncommon Ground: Rethinking the Human Place in Nature*, New York, Norton.
Guattari, Félix (2000 [1989]), *The Three Ecologies*, London, Athlone Press.
Harari, Yuval (2014), *Sapiens: A Brief History of Humankind*, London, Harvill Secker.
Haraway, Donna (2015), 'Anthropocene, Capitalocene, Plantationocene, Chthulucene: Making Kin', *Environmental Humanities*, 6: 159–165.
Harrison, Robert P. (1992), *Forests: The Shadow of Civilisation*, Chicago, University of Chicago Press.
Hitchings, Russell (2010), 'Seasonal Climate Change and the Indoor City Worker', *Transactions of the Institute of British Geographers*, 35 (2): 282–298.
Ingold, Tim (2005), 'Epilogue: Towards a Politics of Dwelling', *Conservation and Society*, 3 (2): 501–508.
Ingold, Tim (2011), *Being Alive: Essays on Movement, Knowledge and Description*, London and New York, Routledge.
Jones, Owain (2002), ' "Naturally Not!" Childhood, the Urban and Romanticism', *Human Ecology Review*, 9 (2): 17–30.
Jones, Owain (2009), 'After Nature: Entangled Worlds', *in:* Castree, Noel, Demeritt, David, Liverman, Diana, and Rhoads, Bruce (eds.), *A Companion to Environmental Geography*, Oxford, Wiley-Blackwell: 294–312.
Jones, Owain (2013), 'The Animality of UK Rural Landscapes in Affective Registers', *Landscape Research Journal*, special edition on Animals and Landscape, 38 (4): 421–442.
Latour, Bruno (1993), *We Have Never Been Modern*, Hemel Hempstead, UK, Harvester Wheatsheaf.
McKibben, Bill (1990), *The End of Nature*, London, Penguin.
Mathews, Freya (2016), 'From Biodiversity-Based Conservation to an Ethic of Bio-Proportionality', *Biological Conservation*, 200: 140–148.
Maxeiner, Dirk, and Miersch, Michael (2006), 'The Urban Jungle', *in:* Norman, Jesse (ed.), *Living for the City: A New Agenda for Green Cities*, London, Policy Exchange: 52–67.
Mormont, Marc (1987), 'Rural Nature and Urban Natures', *Sociologia Ruralis*, 17: 3–20.
Murdoch, Jonathan, and Pratt, Andy C. (1993), 'Rural Studies: Modernism, Postmodernism and the "Post-Rural" ', *Journal of Rural Studies*, 9 (4): 411–427.
Norman, Jesse (2006), 'Introduction', *in:* Norman, Jesse (ed.), *Living for the City: A New Agenda for Green Cities*, London, Policy Exchange: 13–20.
Robin, Libby (2007), *How a Continent Created a Nation*, Sydney, UNSW Press.

Stengers, Isabelle (2015), *In Catastrophic Times Resisting the Coming Barbarism*, Paris, Open Humanities Press.
Tuttle, Will (2014), speaking in online video film *Impact Clips* by First Spark Media, available at: https://vimeo.com/93874570 (Accessed 27/10/2016).
Ward, Colin (1978), *The Child in the City*, London, Architectural Press.
Ward, Colin (1990), *The Child in the Country*, London, Bedford Square Press.
Webb, Sarah (2010), 'Urban versus Rural Nature', Sarah Webb Science Blog, available at: www.webbofscience.com/2010/09/14/urban-versus-rural-nature/ (Accessed 27/10/2016).
Williams, Raymond (1985), *The Country and the City*, London, Hogarth.
Williams, Rosalind (2008), *Notes on the Underground: An Essay on Technology, Society, and the Imagination*, Cambridge, MA, MIT Press.
Wilson, Edward O. (1984), *Biophilia*, Cambridge, MA, Harvard University Press.
Woods, Michael (2016), 'Family Farming in the Global Countryside', *Anthropological Notebooks*, 20 (3): 31–48.
WWF (World Wide Fund for Nature) (2014), 'Living Planet Report', available at: www.wwf.or.jp/activities/lib/lpr/WWF_LPR_2014.pdf (Accessed 27/10/2016).

13
URBAN ECOLOGY

Isabelle Hajek and Jean-Pierre Lévy

For most people, ecology and the urban are polar opposites, as are the city and nature. The less visible the presence of human beings, the more natural an environment is perceived to be, as if nature is necessarily to be found outside and in the areas most remote from the city. Far from being confined to the realm of ordinary ideas, this antinomy, until recently, characterized the thinking of researchers specializing in the study of the city or nature, in the same way as there was necessarily something fake about urban policy with an environmental goal, so the nature it produced would inevitably be artificial. For more than a century, the study of the city, as in essence a social organization, focused primarily on the forms of settlement and life, the use of urban space and systems of production and to a large extent ignored environmental factors; whereas conversely, scientific ecology remained little interested in the depletion of natural resources (Acot, 1988; Worster, 1994), seeing the city as an artificial milieu outside the scope of its study of the relations of plants and animals to their environment. City and nature were therefore generally conceived in a relation of mutual exclusion, with the city represented in a negative light. Since the 1980s, however, there has been a new rapprochement between city and ecology, under the combined influence of new social expectations and advances in an ecology of landscape, along with the manner in which sustainable development (see the chapter by Hamman in this volume) has prompted certain cities to reinterpret the question of nature (Langner and Endlicher, 2014).

In order to present this current rapprochement in all its originality, this chapter is structured in three parts. The first part shows how the very idea of urban ecology fits into a conceptual framework in which city and nature were long opposed, a framework that would subsequently come to include a concern with the ecological impact of cities and a first generation of research on urban ecology. The second part examines the adjustments made to this conceptual framework by a second generation of research, which led to considerable disciplinary diversification in the notion of urban ecology, part of a 'paradigm shift' (Coutard and Lévy, 2010), a new concept through which to think about the city and nature in their reciprocal relations. Finally, the last part explores how this new ecology is being transposed into urban policies that increasingly make space for modern and postmodern urbanistic ideas that emphasize 'nature in the city'.

A long-standing conceptual framework

Far from being radically new, urban ecology is, in reality, an old idea that first came on the scene during the eighteenth and nineteenth centuries, not so much in botany as amongst doctors and in urban chemistry, around an interest in the exchanges between milieus (air, earth, water) and 'trophic' cycles (or food chains) connected with the idea of 'unwholesomeness' (Guillerme, 1977; Barles, 1999).

Indeed, this era saw the birth of an interest in the matter entering and evacuated by the city, motivated by the magnitude of the sanitary and nutritional problems caused by the urban explosion (Barles, 2015). The emergence of a 'graveyard-city' in Europe gave rise to doctrines that sought the explanation for diseases in the polluted air and waste-strewn ground of the cities, reinforced by discoveries about oxygen production by plants and the respiratory mechanism and employed to advance a theory of the circulation/conduction of harmful elements. At the same time, growing urban populations and food requirements raised a problem of rural land fertility and agricultural output, occasioning a 'race for manure' of which the city would be the primary source. The fear of the putrid, linked with a medicalization of the perception of urban space, thus combined with the development of an emerging urban chemistry and the reigning utilitarianism in the interest applied to the 'circulation' of materials.[1]

These early forms of what was not yet called 'urban ecology', but was embodied in exchanges of materials between the city, industry and agriculture (Barles, 2005), were also part of a broader representation of the city, governed by the idea of building an urban order *over* nature. The Renaissance conception, in which the city was represented as the locus of 'culture', combined in the 1840s with the productions of an urbanism of regularization and sanitization (Agulhon, 1998) which sought to replace the stagnant city of the past with a 'city of flows' (Lévy, 2012): underground networks carrying clean water and wastewater were built to purify the city, green spaces introduced to oxygenate and embellish it, wide arteries to foster the flow of goods and people and fulfil the new ambitions of capitalism. The city, in which human activities break free of the ascendancy of tradition and the sacred and are defined by their own principles of efficiency and calculation (Weber, 2014), was to become the ultimate locus of the *distancing* of nature, a technical utopia where progress, whether in the sphere of health, work or technology, was to focus on the enhancement of human existence.

However, urban sprawl gradually led to a decline in attempts to achieve a circular urban ecology. It was not until the 1960s that the latter formally (re)appeared under the impetus of ecologists (Wolman, 1965; Duvigneaud, 1974; Odum, 1975) who joined forces with the protectors of nature to transpose ecosystem theory to the cities. Now it was not so much the city and its construction that were the focus of this new interest in urban ecology, as a rising awareness of the — pathological — effects of the city on nature: these approaches compared the city with a metabolism that 'absorbs nature, transforms it and then discharges it in materials and pollutants that are damaging to the planet, health and the quality of life of its inhabitants' (Coutard and Lévy, 2010: 4). Nonetheless, the conceptual framework was still that of the previous century, because not only was it necessary to be *distanced* from nature by an urban and civilizing order in order for a system of observing nature to emerge, but the emergence of a 'nature to be protected' was itself directly linked with the innovations of 'functionalist' thinking and urbanism through which natural parks were institutionalized as places built *against* man and his destructive power (Viard, 2012).

A paradigm shift

Under this rationale, therefore, it was sufficient to take technical action against urban dysfunctions in order to resolve them in a socially and economically acceptable manner, while social organizations continued to be perceived as largely irrelevant to the environmental sphere. This catastrophist conception, with its 'dehumanized' vision of the city, has nevertheless been changing in recent years, profoundly transforming a monolithic depiction of urban ecology in which the city is approached as a collection of dysfunctions, risks or problems that can only be resolved by the management of 'artificial systems'.

A new conception of ecology is emerging, in which urbanization is no longer apprehended solely in its negative aspects. In this perspective, the processes of urbanization and environmental production can either damage or contribute to biodiversity. Insofar as individual and group behaviours are increasingly seen as part of urban ecosystems, the scope of urban ecology — and more broadly of urban problems — is considerably enriched, both in the scientific field and in public action (Douglas *et al.*, 2015; Douglas and James, 2015).

The diversification of approaches to climate clearly illustrates this change. At the global scale, the city is often accused of being one of the main factors in global warming and the depletion of the world's energy resources. At a more fine-grained level, however, one current of climatology now emerging in relation to urban issues studies the role of the spatial concentration of human activities in the production of 'heat islands' at the scale of individual streets, neighbourhoods or even entire cities (Masson *et al.*, 2013). This shift is far from limited to climatology alone and now encompasses a large number of scientific problems relating to the urban environment. Examples include research on industrial ecology which argues that urban societies reproduce the metabolism of nature (Newel and Cousins, 2014; Clift and Druckman, 2016) or studies relating to urban services and networks (Coutard and Rutherford, 2011). One current of urban hydrology, for example, proposes ways of managing hydraulic networks that would make the city transparent to water (Chocat, 1997). In this perspective, global urban management would work through water cycles and the uses of water to avoid discharges by retaining water in the city. The same is true for approaches to energy consumption, which are no longer confined to the design or refurbishment of buildings, but seek to take into account the lifestyles and domestic practices of users (Lévy et al., 2014). Against this background, quite logically, architects and planners frequently legitimize the formal dimension of their projects by a concern for social and environmental equity. As a result, it is no longer unusual for suburban areas, so often disparaged, to be tackled as an 'ordinary' component of conurbations. There is a whole discussion under way about how they should be organized and planned so that their development is less damaging to ecosystems and the biosphere, but also respectful of the needs, lifestyles and practices of their residents.[2]

For urban ecology, the city is no longer synonymous with dysfunctions that need to be resolved 'artificially'. It is also important that the solutions should not restrict citizens by clashing with their way of life, while still protecting their residential environment. The preservation of the living environment, as much as the protection of the biosphere or biodiversity, is today an ecological issue (Moser and Weiss, 2003). Urban ecology is becoming a discipline, which includes historical, political and social dimensions, as well as the role of institutions, power relations and social organizations in environmental and urban questions. By fully recognizing the role of institutions in environmental issues, together with individual and collective behaviour and methods of global and local management, the study of urban functions ceases to be reduced to its disruptive effects. It becomes possible to consider urban organizations as an environmental resource, to draw on human activity, to mobilize lifestyles in an integrated approach, in order to contribute to knowledge about methods of urbanization, while broadening the spectrum of possible solutions for reducing their damaging effects.

Urban ecology: a conceptual framework for public action

Although this integrated approach, in which the natural, constructed and social components of the city are together taken into account, has a far from insignificant impact on the foundations of urban ecology, it also influences the norms of public action. For example, the links between the features of the urban environment and population health are becoming a societal issue. For this reason, all the places where individuals live out their lives (home, work, neighbourhood, school, leisure areas) need to be considered in terms of the health risks to which they may expose the people who use them (Dannenberg et al., 2011). The same is true of the social differences in exposure to natural and industrial risks, to pollution, to environmental nuisances of all kinds (noise, smells, visual discomfort), but also of access to all the resources the city is supposed to provide, be it water, energy, shops, transport or employment. In short, it applies to everything that has come to be called ecological inequalities, whether it is the right for all to live in a decent environment or the ability to access and move around the city (Faburel, 2012).

This shift is very clearly apparent in the forms of action that seek to incorporate nature into the city. In recognition of the way that certain wild animal species adapt to urbanized spaces, public parks and gardens are now created with the aim of producing spaces where fauna and flora can settle and reproduce. Periurban expansion to the boundaries of agricultural areas (see the chapter by Jones in this volume), or the introduction of farming areas within cities themselves (e.g. family allotments), promote forms of co-existence – which can be problematic – between human beings and nondomesticated animal and plant species. It is the human relationship to nature that has changed, generating new societal expectations. For example, most of the projects conducted in the guise of urban ecology now grant a growing role to modern and postmodern ideas of urban design that place value on 'nature in the city' (Hajek et al., 2015).

Nature is a way for urban action to include a vision of environmental quality, in which the city is idealized as a place of human well-being or planetary protection. It reflects the emergence of a demand for a sensitive city, where inhabitants can escape and find relief from an urban milieu perceived as threatening. In this way, nature is expected to enable city dwellers to perceive the city not only in terms of built space in the broad sense (buildings, materials, location, green spaces, etc.), but also through the urban ambiences conveyed by the natural elements that flow through it (light, noise, heat, smells and so on).

The inclusion of nature is also justified in urban action by the need to preserve or introduce 'biodiversity' and places able to accommodate fauna and flora. Development policies that seek to introduce nature into the city are everywhere in the form of green or blue corridors or public spaces set aside for nature (Clergeau and Blanc, 2013). Urban ecology offers a way for public action to vaunt itself as a *good practice* recognized by international standards, especially if it is accompanied by the emergence of a consensual 'citizen voice', provided that this voice agrees with the need to introduce an ecological turn into urban management.

So what this is about is the establishment of an urban order by a domesticated and aestheticized approach to natural spaces (Blanc, 2013). In a way, the political view of urban ecology helps to erase the opposition between city and country by naturalizing the city. So the relations between political action and nature reveal the existence of a homogenizing representation of the city, which seeks to domesticate urban nature for ecological, aesthetic and ultimately univocal purposes (Consalès et al., 2012). This political representation ignores the reality of an urban biodiversity that is also based on the existence of an untamed nature in the city; for a political perspective, nature in this form is wild, uncontrolled, dangerous and stigmatized. In other words, though the institutionalization of urban ecology forms a necessary bond between city and nature, it also entails a negation of unmanaged natural spaces, essential places of urban biodiversity which political action would nevertheless like to render invisible.

Situated between a domestication that underpins a sanitized urban order in which flows of urban materials are 'invisibilized' through incorporation into natural functions and the recognition of an 'uncontrollable' element within it, political action which claims to represent urban ecology remains a protean concept, difficult to pin down to a single definition, but one that is nevertheless undoubtedly reshaping the contemporary city. In a certain way, these actions are indistinguishable from the drive to sustainable development in its usual sense and its diversity. Although urban ecology is a way of claiming to defend quality of life or the development of social bonds, it is nonetheless the case that the spectrum of action can be very broad and does not reflect one single rationale. For example, what is the link between an ecology that sees the economy as something that serves individual well-being and one that supports the values of preserving the built and natural heritage or managing resources? One calls for a city that is a symbol of social equity, whereas the other is content to set a framework for urban intervention that complies with the imperatives of sustainable development.

Ultimately, for planners and politicians, urban ecology has become a tool for legitimizing their actions – contributing to the production of homogenized and standardized urban forms – and a single conceptual framework that is all the more radical in that it is universal and consensual. In light of this, its utility for research, as a significant new instrument for understanding the city, can only lie in the exploration of 'ordinary urban natures', experienced and shared on a day-to-day basis by a multiplicity of actors (inhabitants, artists, ecologists, scientists, etc.), and therefore arising less from the application of an ideological paradigm, a 'top-down' political order, than from the discovery of a mosaic of initiatives that combine ambiences, social practices and ordinary narratives.

Notes

1 Or what today we would call 'recycling' or 'reuse'.
2 At the same time, this new way of looking at periurban areas is helping to revive the debates in 'sustainable urbanism' on the 'compact city', where today it is readily acknowledged that compactness can be synonymous with a high degree of 'mineralization' (Clergeau and Blanc, 2013).

Bibliography

Acot, Pascal (1988), *Histoire de l'écologie*, Paris, Presses Universitaires de France.
Agulhon, Maurice (1998), *La ville de l'âge industriel. Le cycle haussmannien*, Paris, Seuil.
Barles, Sabine (1999), *La ville délétère. Médecins et ingénieurs dans l'espace urbain. XVIIIe–XIXe siècles*, Seyssel, Champ Vallon.
Barles, Sabine (2005), *L'invention des déchets urbains. France: 1790–1970*, Seyssel, Champ Vallon.
Barles, Sabine (2015), 'The Main Characteristics of Urban Socio-Ecological Trajectories: Paris (France) from the 18th to the 20th Century', *Ecological Economics*, 118: 177–185.
Blanc, Nathalie (2013), 'Aesthetic Engagement in the City', *Contemporary Aesthetics*, 11, available at: www.contempaesthetics.org/newvolume/pages/article.php?articleID=683&searchstr=blanc (Accessed 31/10/2016).
Chocat, Bernard (ed.) (1997), *Encyclopédie de l'hydrologie urbaine et de l'assainissement*, Paris, Tec et Doc and Lavoisier.

Clergeau, Philippe, and Blanc, Nathalie (eds.) (2013), *Trames vertes urbaines. De la recherche scientifique au projet urbain*, Paris, Éditions du Moniteur.
Clift, Roland, and Druckman, Angela (eds.) (2016), *Taking Stock of Industrial Ecology*, Heidelberg, Springer.
Consalès, Jean-Noël, Goiffon, Marie, and Barthélémy, Carole (2012), 'Entre aménagement du paysage et ménagement de la nature à Marseille: la trame verte à l'épreuve du local', *Développement durable et territoires*, 3 (2), available at: http://developpementdurable.revues.org/9268 (Accessed 31/10/2016).
Coutard, Olivier, and Lévy, Jean-Pierre (eds.) (2010), *Écologies urbaines*, Paris, Économica-Anthropos, series Villes.
Coutard, Olivier, and Rutherford, Jonathan (2011), 'The Rise of Post-Networked Cities in Europe? Recombining Infrastructural, Ecological and Urban Transformations in Low Carbon Transitions', *in:* Bulkeley, Harriet, Castan Broto, Vanesa, Hodson, Mike, and Marvin, Simon (eds.), *Cities and Low Carbon Transitions*, London and New York, Routledge: 107–125.
Dannenberg, Andrew L., Frumkin, Howard, and Jackson, Richard J. (eds.) (2011), *Making Healthy Places: Designing and Building for Health, Well-Being, and Sustainability*, Washington, DC, Covelo, CA, and London, Island Press.
Douglas, Ian, Goode, David, Houck, Mike, and Wang, Rusong (eds.) (2015), *The Routledge Handbook of Urban Ecology*, 2nd ed., London and New York, Routledge.
Douglas, Ian, and James, Philip (eds.) (2015), *Urban Ecology: An Introduction*, London and New York, Routledge.
Duvigneaud, Paul (1974), *La synthèse écologique. Populations, communautés, écosystèmes, biosphère, noosphère*, Paris, Doin Éditeurs.
Faburel, Guillaume (2012), 'The Environment as a Factor of Spatial Injustice: A New Challenge for the Sustainable Development of European Regions?', *in:* Ghenai, Chaouki (ed.), *Sustainable Development. Policy and Urban Development – Tourism, Life Science, Management and Environment*, Rijeka, Intech: 431–478.
Guillerme, Jacques (1977), 'Le malsain et l'économie de la nature', *Dix-huitième siècle*, 9: 61–72.
Hajek, Isabelle, Hamman, Philippe, and Lévy, Jean-Pierre (eds.) (2015), *De la ville durable à la nature en ville*, Villeneuve d'Ascq, Presses Universitaires du Septentrion, series Environnement et société.
Langner, Marcel, and Endlicher, Wilfried (eds.) (2014 [2008]), *Shrinking Cities: Effects on Urban Ecology and Challenges for Urban Development*, Frankfurt am Main, Peter Lang.
Lévy, Albert (ed.) (2012), *Ville, urbanisme et santé. Les trois révolutions*, Paris, Éditions Pascal.
Lévy, Jean-Pierre, Roudil, Nadine, Belaïd, Fateh, and Flamand, Amélie (2014), 'Les déterminants de la consommation énergétique domestique', *Flux*, 96: 40–54.
Masson, Valérie, Lion, Yves, Peter, Alfred, Pigeon, Grégoire, Buyck, Jennifer, and Brun, Éric (2012), ' "Grand Paris": Regional Landscape Change to Adapt City to Climate Warming', *Climatic Change*, 117 (4): 769–782, available at: www.cnrm-game-meteo.fr/IMG/pdf/masson_grand_paris_2013.pdf (Accessed 31/10/2016).
Moser, Gabriel, and Weiss, Karine (eds.) (2003), *Espaces de vie. Aspects de la relation homme-environnement*, Paris, Armand Colin.
Newell, Joshua, and Cousins, Joshua (2014), 'The Boundaries of Urban Metabolism: Toward a Political-Industrial Ecology', *Progress in Human Geography*: 1–27, available at: www.researchgate.net/profile/Joshua_Newell/publication/270891359_The_Boundaries_of_Urban_Metabolism_Towards_a_Political-Industrial_Ecology/links/54b7ff090cf269d8cbf645e2.pdf (Accessed 31/10/2016).

Odum, Eugène Pleasants (1975), *Ecology: The Link between the Natural and the Social Science*, New York, Holt, Rinehart and Winston.

Viard, Jean (2012), *Penser la nature. Tiers espace entre ville et campagne*, La Tour d'Aigues, Éditions de l'Aube.

Weber, Max (2014 [1921]), *La ville*, Paris, La Découverte, series Politique et sociétés, translated into English (1966) as *The City*, New York, Free Press.

Wolman, Abel (1965), 'The Metabolism of Cities', *Scientific American*, 213 (3): 179–190.

Worster, Donald (1994 [1977]), *Nature's Economy: A History of Ecological Ideas*, Cambridge, Cambridge University Press.

14
NATURE, ENVIRONMENT AND HEALTH

Lionel Charles

At the time of its creation in 1948, the World Health Organization (WHO) introduced in the preamble to its constitution a right to health which was later included in the Universal Declaration of Human Rights (article 25), adopted in December the same year. It also drafted a new and particularly broad definition of health: 'Health is a state of complete physical, mental and social well-being and not merely the absence of disease or infirmity'.[1] This definition, discussed and later completed, is a major reference for modern thought about health. As developed by Claudine Brelet (1995, 2002), the innovative and universal character of this definition must be seen in the light of the extensive preparatory work that, in the early 1940s under the aegis of Britain[2] and the United States, aimed to establish the foundations of a new and fully operating international organization replacing the League of Nations.[3] In elaborating this definition, the term 'health' was preferred to 'hygiene' because

> [h]ygiene conveys a rather negative attitude regarding disease, whereas the notion of health [. . .] calls for positive action mobilizing all the resources of preventive and curative medicine, and all the factors of physical and psychological improvements of individuals and peoples.[4]

Not limiting health to the absence of disease, freeing it from the overly exclusive hold of medicine, defining it as 'a state of complete physical, mental and social well-being' meant giving health a strong individual dimension through the subjective notion of well-being, as well as a relational one. This definition was also developed in a global perspective with the aim of embracing sanitary practices of Western modern states as well as those of more traditional societies.[5]

This definition questioned some of the most deeply rooted specificities of the Western medical tradition in terms of knowledge and practice. It greatly favoured the recognition of and an opening up to traditional medicine in many developing as well as developed countries (Brelet, 2002). This new orientation came to correct the ascendancy of a scientific and technical, strictly causal and reductionist approach to pathology that constitutes an obstacle to a more multidimensional and open vision of health and medical practice. Such a narrow approach can be a source of adverse effects (Illich, 1975) resulting in the development of limited and costly therapeutic strategies to the detriment of upstream interventions on potentially pathogenic social and environmental conditions in a widened vision of prevention. The massive development of noninfectious diseases, such as obesity, diabetes, cardiovascular diseases, cancers and degenerative diseases (such as Parkinson's and Alzheimer's), is a major contemporary health issue, related to both social (inequality, sedentary lifestyle, stress) and environmental (pollution, food) factors and very illustrative of that concern. The question is raised today of the obstacles urban planning can set up regarding regular physical activity, whose benefits for health are now widely acknowledged (Dannenberg et al., 2011; Sarkar et al., 2014).

This emphasizes that the general and polysemic term 'nature'[6] is of limited interest in establishing a relevant sanitary perspective as an operational reality; health is a complex and relative process, significantly affected by a wide range of social and environmental factors – especially at a time when human populations live more and more massively in vastly anthropized, in particular urban, settings. From that point of view, the term 'environment' seems better adapted to identifying the encompassing context in which individuals live and the multiplicity of factors that can affect their health, often in an indirect way and without the concerned individuals being clearly aware of this. One must emphasize the breadth of the perspective offered by the environment as a concept with both a heuristic and a pragmatico-contextual, reflexive dimension. As a heuristic concept, it confronts a reality that is only partly known but which it leads to investigate; as a pragmatico-contextual, reflexive concept, it expresses the fact that all living organisms can only exist through a relationship with a universe that surrounds them and with which they constantly interact in an exchange of matter and information on which they basically depend to exist as organisms. One can easily grasp the displacement introduced by the concept of environment regarding nature, replacing an ontology, always arbitrary, with a reflexive dynamic that responds to the massive and increasing action exerted by mankind on the physical and living world in a fundamentally temporal perspective. The interest of such a notion regarding traditional approaches of health must also be considered.

Traditional societies conceptualize health as the balance (or the imbalance) of a symbolic system, understood as an orderly view of the natural and human world, expressing a latent form of intentionality in an all-encompassing whole. The Chinese tradition, based on the interrelation of yin and yang, is very evocative in this respect. A similar, although distinct, concept of health is also present in the Hippocratic corpus, the oldest collection of works at the origin of the Western medical tradition, where it co-exists with another approach that sees itself as more specifically rational. This latter aspect was strongly developed and emphasized by Galen (second century CE) and has shaped Arabic and European medical ideas and practices until at least the seventeenth century,[7] certain of its features being still recognizable today.[8] In the Hippocratic treatise *Nature of Man*,[9] whose ideas would later be taken up and discussed by Galen, disease in man is due to the imbalance of humours 'which make the nature of his body, and through these he feels pain and enjoys health'. The humours are characterized by the combinations of four primary qualities: hot and cold, wet and dry. The four humours are phlegm, wet and cold; blood, wet and hot; yellow bile, dry and hot; and black bile, dry and cold. The four primary qualities, combined two by two, form the four elements of which the world is made: water, wet and cold; earth, dry and cold; air, wet and hot; and fire, dry and hot.

This theory reflects the relationship between diseases and characteristics or modifications of the environment, such as, for instance, seasonal changes and their variations in temperature and hygrometry (thus phlegm increases in winter, blood in spring, etc.). In another Hippocratic treatise, *Airs, Waters, Places*, the localization of cities and their exposure to the sun, wind and atmospheric conditions are subject to a systematized analysis in order to allow an itinerant physician to be aware of the diseases he will encounter in such cities. The same approach applies to waters, whether they are stagnant, from springs or from rain and snow ('from the sky'). The treatise ends with what we would consider today as a compared, ethnogeographic analysis of populations of Europe and Asia on the basis of environmental criterions, mostly climatic, which is striking in its attempt to provide a general explanation for the differences in the characteristics and lifestyles of populations. Another Hippocratic idea of disease, developed in the treatise *Winds*, states that diseases are transmitted by air loaded with miasma; that is, morbific elements which, depending on their nature, can affect either men or other living species.[10] These different ideas make it clear that there is no unified vision of the origin of diseases or of the action of the physician in the Hippocratic corpus; they also testify to the central place occupied by the environment, along with other aspects such as food or living habits, in the understanding of the origin of diseases. The elements of the Hippocratic anthropology have been summarized, in a simplified version, by Aristotle in *The Politics*, with the clearly asserted objective, as developed by Jean-François Staszak (1995), of demonstrating the superiority of the Greeks over the other peoples of Europe or Asia. Whereas Europeans are subject to a cold climate and Asian populations to a hot one, the Greeks enjoy an intermediate climate, which enables them to cumulate the qualities of the inhabitants of these two regions, and hence their superiority. Aristotelian ideas of climate determinism, and more widely environmental determinism, have influenced the thinking of geographers, as well as Montesquieu's climate theory, up until the anthropogeographical theories of Ritter and Ratzel of the nineteenth century.

The Hippocratic environmental approach with its penchant for empirical observation was not pursued by Galen's rationalization, which also ignored the collective, epidemic component of disease, but focused rather on the relationship between physician and patient. It was rediscovered in a very different context in seventeenth-century England and strongly developed during the following decades to form the first body of knowledge through which new sanitary instruments were set up in European countries. The English physician Thomas Sydenham (1624–1689) is the forerunner of this Hippocratic turn, initiating the European neo-Hippocratic movement. Sydenham's approach must be understood in the context of the powerful transformations English society had been undergoing during the course of the seventeenth century on the religious, political, philosophical, scientific and social levels. At the religious level, the diffusion of Calvinism after 1570 and the rise of the Puritan movement result in the rejection of the representations and values of Catholicism, of idolatry in all of its manifestations and of theology. It emphasizes the importance of faith, rooted in subjectivity, as the primary basis of one's involvement in the world and of the biblical text as a reference that should be regularly studied; the central place occupied by the individual; the major significance of education, learning and knowledge; but also the sense of an active relationship with the world created by God for humankind to act as its steward, to take care of it and improve it (Stoll, 2013). The influence of Puritanism in England in the first part of the seventeenth century is far reaching. Puritans play a major part in the process that leads, at the end of the English Civil War (1642–1651) and the Glorious Revolution (1689), to the confirmation of Protestantism as the religion of the Crown and to the vote of the Revolutionary Settlements, which institute a control of the monarchy by parliament, initiating the evolution towards a parliamentary democracy. This influence can also be felt in the great scientific effervescence of the time, particularly in the medical field with William Harvey's discoveries and Francis Bacon's work. Both advocate a new orientation for science, rooted in the rejection of scholasticism and vain discussion, with a leading role given to observation and experience within an empirical and operational perspective directed towards the improvement of the human condition through a coherent and sustained research dynamics. Bacon's ideas and vision are directly at the source of the Royal Society, the first modern major scientific institution, founded in 1660, after the restoration of the monarchy following Cromwell's Republic: its creation is inspired by and its activity associated with the most creative minds of the time, from Boyle and Hooke to Newton. The philosopher John Locke[11] is himself a physician for whom the right to health stands as one of the fundamental rights, together with the right to life, to freedom and to property (Locke, 1689). His psychology of an individual, whose cognitive processes are grounded in sensation, brings together the elements of a new vision of the human individual, as well as of politics rooted in empiricism, offering a wide basis for the environment.

Close to the chemist Robert Boyle and closely related to Locke, Sydenham is, above all, concerned with the efficiency of the physician's practice. He is deeply involved in bedside medicine, but also restores the epidemic approach to disease at a time when the work of John Graunt, followed by that of William Petty,[12] lays the foundations for a statistical approach to populations and pathologies at the origin of mortality. Sydenham stresses the Hippocratic notion of epidemic constitution in relation to air and seasons and renews the miasma theory, under the influence of the corpuscular air theory advocated by Boyle, involved at the time in experiments concerning air and void. This Hippocratic renewal is revived by the Italian physician Bernardino Ramazzini (1633–1714), by Friedrich Hoffman (1660–1742) in Halle and by Hermann Boerhave (1668–1738) in Leyden; they promote the diffusion of neo-Hippocratic ideas across all Europe. In 1733, the English physician John Arbuthnot publishes, in the perspective initiated by Sydenham, Boyle and Locke, *An Essay concerning the Effect of Air on Human Bodies*, in which he assembles the ideas developed by his predecessors and emphasizes the role of atmosphere, air and meteorology in epidemic studies. The book goes through numerous printings and translations and starts the vogue of 'aerism' which dominates the sanitary vision and practices throughout the eighteenth century, at a time when the collection of meteorological observations, initiated in particular by Robert Hooke (1635–1703), develops widely. James Clifford Riley has carefully analyzed the merging of arguments which give its full strength to the environmental explanation of the origin of disease (Riley, 1987). In a country pacified after the violence of the seventeenth century that has become considerably richer and widely urbanized with a fast-growing trade and economy, acknowledged today as the first consumption society, this sensibility to the environment, to meteorology, air, water as vectors of pathologies, generates a powerful movement in favour of sanitation, which develops spontaneously, without any preestablished programme. It arises from a variety of private, philanthropic and public initiatives on matters such as drainage and drying out of wetlands, washing of streets and removal of refuse and filth, ventilation and air circulation in collective spaces (hospitals, prisons, boats, military quarters), water supply and conveyance, paving of streets, building of numerous hospitals and free health centres and a widely shared concern of the population for personal cleanliness (washing, laundry). These initiatives result in a significant improvement of sanitary conditions to the extent that it is estimated that at the beginning of the nineteenth century, the city of London succeeds in reducing its excess of mortality over natality (Porter, 1991). According to James Clifford Riley (1987), this can be explained by the fact that the action on the environment, though ignorant of contagious mechanisms, had an indirect effect on many different potential vectors of disease such as mosquitoes, rodents and other visible organisms (flies, cockroaches, etc.).

In the nineteenth century, with the rise of industrialization and a powerful increase of the urban population due to the growth in the number of workers, the living conditions in cities strongly deteriorate once again. This situation sets Britain on the way to a renewed dynamic concerning public health, which results, despite numerous oppositions, in the 1875 Public Health Act. The act initiates a sanitary monitoring and engineering system at the local and national scale on an environmental basis, the first in the world, later strengthened by the work of Pasteur and Koch on the role of microbiological agents in the development of pathologies (Porter, 1999).

The evolution of public health and medical practice in France is noticeably different and, to a certain extent, the opposite of its British counterpart. The development of aerist medicine has a very significant echo in the 1740s and results in 1778 in the creation of the *Société royale de médecine*, which undertakes an ambitious programme of medical topographies of neo-Hippocratic inspiration, under the direction of Vicq d'Azir. The project aims to collect a vast amount of data concerning pathologies and numerous environmental factors – localization, meteorology, climate – that might influence them. But this very extensive project ends prematurely with the dissolution of the society by the French Revolution in 1793. It is not resumed in the postrevolutionary context, which highlights the importance of clinical medicine but also of liberal practice. As the British historian Matthew Ramsey (1994) or more recently Gérard Jorland (2010) have shown, France disposes at the beginning of the nineteenth century of all the elements that might enable it to build a public health system, but fails to develop it. As early as 1830, Villermé demonstrates that the environment is irrelevant in providing a precise account of the pathologies that plague Paris's population and replaces it with social inequalities (Barles, 2010). This rejection of the environment in relation to health dynamics is, of course, later strengthened by the work of Pasteur. Despite the Pastorian contribution, France experiences a strong difficulty in creating an efficient public health system (Murard and Zylberman, 1996; Jorland, 2010; Tabuteau, 2013). The 1902 Public Health Law, though not without weaknesses, represents a step forward, but the development of the health system after the Second World War – with the therapeutic successes that accompany it – leads to a minimization of the preventive dimension of medicine to the exclusive benefit of its curative role. This exemplifies the limits of health policies, particularly public health policies, today confronted with a massive drift in terms of cost but also of inequalities. The question of health inequalities (Wilkinson, 2005) has long remained in the shadows, becoming a serious research issue in France only at the end of the 1990s (Salem *et al.*, 1999; Leclerc *et al.*, 2000).

This parallel drawn between two evolutions which are not foreign to one another but which, on the contrary, have influenced each other in many ways, is interesting in several respects, particularly for the light it sheds on the long-term link between health and environment, but also for its meaning regarding the present situation. The historical relationship between environment and health of Hippocratic origin is reshaped by modernity, particularly with the development of Lockian psychology, into a much wider connection between empiricism and environment. In the Anglo-Saxon world, the environment carries great weight because it is inseparable from the constitution of subjectivity at the heart of a new relationship to the world linked with a renewed and powerful concern for health. The relationship between health and environment in the French world is widely dominated by a more restricted, impersonal and objective approach and by the rise of rationality springing from the Enlightenment, Rousseau, the Revolution and a rediscovery of Descartes.[13] This helps to better understand the contemporary French environmental approach, its emphasis on nature and the protection of nature,[14] both at the time of the creation of the Ministry of the Environment (1971) and later. It also sheds light on some of its flaws, as well as on its delay in considering environmental health, addressed institutionally only at the beginning of the 2000s, but without making much sense to the population because of the lack of an appropriate cultural background.[15] The contemporary situation shows an increasing but badly managed preoccupation with the role played by environmental factors in numerous pathologies but also with the improvement of the quality of life and the promotion of well-being. The last decades have seen rising anxieties concerning environmental sanitary risks, such as the diffusion of chemicals in air, water and soil able to affect many types of organisms, and eventually humans, directly but also indirectly through the concentration of pollutants along the food chain, without any proper background or guidance as to how one should deal with this situation on a personal or social level. The ubiquitous character of environmental exposures must be emphasized: indoor and outdoor air pollution is the most notorious of these environmental hazards. It mostly affects, particularly as far as indoor air is concerned, less advanced countries. After announcing in 2013 that air pollution is carcinogenic for humans, WHO reassessed a few months later the number of annual deaths for which it was responsible[16] to 7 million, twice its previous estimation. Research on environmental questions has increased recently, trying to show the benefits individuals and populations can draw from a favourable environment, the proximity with natural spaces and the presence of vegetation (Frumkin and Fox, 2011).[17] The concept of environmental health is not only relevant in providing the elements for a diagnosis: its operative power resides in its reflexive aim to act on the environment, not only in order to eliminate its potentially dangerous or harmful components, but also to promote favourable ones, opening a very broad field for collective action. It responds and gives full meaning to the notion of health as defined by the WHO.

But possibly the greatest contribution of environmental health is the light that it sheds on the meaning of 'the environment'. Its importance is in the way the concept emphasizes the relevance of a pragmatic, binding connection with the world, a connection that is subjective, active and not neutral or indifferent as valued by a tradition that draws on a purely objectifying and reductionist, scientistic and rationalist approach. What the environment reveals to investigation and to experience is basically the breadth and complexity of human relationship with the world at all levels, which is, of course, of particular importance and relevance in the field of health. This notion of involvement in the world drove action on the environment throughout the eighteenth century (Porter, 2000) and later, within a perspective that can retrospectively be seen as lacking scientific foundations; but this action turned out to be efficient in the generalized improvement of sanitary conditions it had initiated. A parallel with the present situation must be drawn, though the context is no longer that of a lack of knowledge but rather of its excess, and the indetermination it entails for human actions. So that, as illustrated by climate change, we are exposed today to risks capable of deeply altering our collective reality, noticeably in terms of potentially serious attacks upon health as well as on quality of life, a basic component of health in the definition proposed by the WHO in 1948. More than ever, it is now necessary to establish the logic and develop the institutions, the collective dynamics and the engineering, particularly with respect to sanitation, that support the idea of environmental health. This will enable us to get a hold of and manage in a more coherent way this new reality in which the environment, with its natural component, rooted in complexity, and society, with its mix of institutions and networks, do not oppose each other, but deeply interact.

Notes

1 Preamble to the Constitution of the World Health Organization as adopted by the International Health Conference, New York, 19–22 June 1946; signed on 22 July 1946 by the representatives of 61 states (Official Records of the World Health Organization, 1946, 2:100) and entered into force on 7 April 1948.
2 Claudine Brelet emphasizes the major role played by the ideas of the British anthropologist Bronislaw Malinowski and his functionalist and very wide vision of culture and cultural diversity in the elaboration of the United Nations international settlement.
3 The creation of the UN in 1945 is accompanied by the establishment of five specialized agencies aimed at the world coordination of specific fields: FAO (1945), for agriculture and food; UNICEF (1946), for childhood and childcare; UNESCO (1946), for science and culture; ILO (first created in 1919, attached to the UN in 1946), for work; and WHO, which became operational only in 1948, for health. Other agencies were created later, most prominently the United Nations Environment Program (UNEP) in 1972.
4 WHO, *WHO Chronicle*, 1 (14), cited in Brelet (1995).
5 Claudine Brelet points out the important part played by China, one of the Big Four, in the process of setting up the UN agencies, through its representative's direct implication and emphasis on the specificities of Chinese traditions, but also through the action of the Sino-British Science Cooperation, created in 1942 under the auspices of the Royal Society and directed by Joseph Needham. Author of a series published under the title *Science and Civilisation in China*, begun in 1954 and continued after his death in 1995 (a twenty-fourth volume has recently been published), Needham investigated and made known to the West the scope and depth of Chinese scientific and medical knowledge and its precedence in this last field, with its very early understanding of blood circulation (fourth century BCE), of the action of certain hormones and the subtle approach to health that it has developed.
6 The term 'nature' covers a wide range of meanings. Derived from the Latin *nascere* (to be born), it refers to the physical and biological world and all its components in their generic, native dimension.
7 Students kept studying Galen's works until well into the nineteenth century.
8 It has distinctively shaped the French medical tradition. One can recall its very critical evocation in Molière's play, *Le malade imaginaire* (*The Imaginary Invalid*, 1673), but it is still very present in the status and social representations of medicine and medical practice in French society today.
9 Attributed to Polybus. A complete edition of Hippocratic treatises has been published by Harvard University Press in their Loeb Classical Library series.
10 Jacques Jouanna (2001) notes a relationship between the concept of miasma as it is emphasized in the treatise *Winds* and its previous meaning in religious medicine, where it could be interpreted as disease related to the loss of blood.
11 Locke eventually joined the Royal Society.
12 A member of the Royal Society, John Graunt published in 1662 his *Natural and Political Observations Made upon the Bills of Mortality*, which lays the basis for modern demography

and social sciences. William Petty's *Essays in Political Arithmetick* were collected in a single volume and published in 1690. W. Petty is one of the founding members of the Royal Society.
13 One could add the weight of the medical tradition, deeply influenced by Galen's rationalism.
14 Which is, with the question of air pollution, the first field of action of the French Ministry of the Environment after its creation in 1971.
15 In Germany, the sanitary reference comes first in the understanding of the environment in a country deeply influenced by neo-Hippocratism (Riley, 1987).
16 International Agency for Research on Cancer (IARC), press release, 221, 17/10/2013. WHO, press release, 25/03/2014. *Cf.* WHO, *Burden of Disease from the Joint Effects of Household and Ambient Air Pollution for 2012, Summary of Results*, 2014.
17 There is an abundant literature on the subject. *Cf.* for instance: World Health Organization (WHO), *Ecosystems and Human Well-Being: Health Synthesis: A Report of the Millennium Ecosystem Assessment*, 2005. *Cf.* also the *UK National Ecosystem Assessment*, which draws an extensive picture of ecosystem services, including health in urban contexts.

Bibliography

Arbuthnot, John (1733), *An Essay concerning the Effect of Air on Human Bodies*, London, J. and R. Tonson, available at: https://archive.org/stream/essayconcerninge00arbu#page/n7/mode/2up (Accessed 05/10/2016).
Barles, Sabine (2010), 'De l'hygiénisme à la santé environnementale, regards sur la ville', *Pollution atmosphérique*: 11–21, special issue 'Environnement et santé, question de société'.
Brelet, Claudine (1995), *Anthropologie de l'ONU*, Paris, L'Harmattan.
Brelet, Claudine (2002), *Médecines du monde*, Paris, Robert Laffont.
Dannenberg, Andrew L., Frumkin, Howard, and Jackson, Richard J. (eds.) (2011), *Making Healthy Places: Designing and Building for Health, Well-Being, and Sustainability*, Washington, DC, Covelo, CA and London, Island Press.
Frumkin, Howard, and Fox, Jared (2011), 'Contact with Nature', *in:* Dannenberg, Andrew L., Frumkin, Howard, and Jackson, Richard J. (eds.), *Making Healthy Places: Designing and Building for Health, Well-Being, and Sustainability*, Washington, DC, Covelo, CA and London, Island Press: 229–243.
Graunt, John (1662), *Natural and Political Observations made upon the Bills of Mortality*, London, John Martyn, available at: www.neonatology.org/pdf/graunt.pdf (Accessed 05/10/2016).
Illich, Ivan (1975), *Medical Nemesis: The Expropriation of Health*, London, Marion Boyars.
Jorland, Gérard (2010), *Une société à soigner. Hygiène et salubrité publiques en France au XIXe siècle*, Paris, Gallimard.
Jouanna, Jacques (2001), 'Air, miasmes et contagion à l'époque d'Hippocrate, et survivance des miasmes dans la médecine posthippocratique', *in:* Bazin-Tacchella, Sylvie, Quéruel, Danielle, and Samama, Évelyne (eds.), *Air, miasmes et contagion. Les épidémies dans l'Antiquité et au Moyen-Âge*, Langres, Dominique Guéniot: 9–28.
Leclerc, Annette, Fassin, Didier, Grandjean, Hélène, Kaminski, Monique, and Lang, Thierry (eds.) (2000), *Les inégalités sociales de santé*, Paris, INSERM/La Découverte.
Locke, John (1988 [1689]), *Two Treatises of Government*, Cambridge, Cambridge University Press.
Murard, Lion, and Zylberman, Patrick (1996), *L'hygiène dans la République. La santé publique en France, ou l'utopie contrariée 1870–1918*, Paris, Fayard.
Porter, Dorothy (1999), *Health, Civilization and the State: A History of Public Health from Ancient to Modern Times*, London and New York, Routledge.

Porter, Roy (1991), 'Cleaning up the Great Wen: Public Health in Eighteenth Century London', *Medical History*, 11: 61–75.
Porter, Roy (2000), *Enlightenment: Britain and the Creation of the Modern World*, London, Allen Lane and Penguin.
Ramsey, Matthew (1994), 'Public Health in France', *in:* Porter, Dorothy (ed.), *The History of Public Health and the Modern State*, Amsterdam and Atlanta, GA, Rodopi BV: 45–117.
Riley, James Clifford (1987), *The Eighteenth Century Campaign to Avoid Disease*, London, Macmillan.
Salem, Gérard, Rican, Stéphane, and Jougla, Éric (eds.) (1999), *Atlas de la santé en France. Vol. 1: Les causes de décès*, Montrouge, John Libbey Eurotext.
Sarkar, Chinmoy, Webster, Chris, and Gallacher, John (eds.) (2014), *Healthy Cities: Public Health through Urban Planning*, Cheltenham, Edward Elgar.
Staszak, Jean-François (1995), *La géographie d'avant la géographie. Le climat chez Aristote et Hippocrate*, Paris, L'Harmattan.
Stoll, Mark (2013), 'Les influences religieuses sur le mouvement écologiste français', *in:* Mathis, Charles-François, and Mouhot, Jean-François (eds.), *Une protection de l'environnement à la française (XIXe–XXe siècle)*, Seyssel, Champ Vallon: 313–326.
Tabuteau, Dominique (2013), *Démocratie sanitaire. Les nouveaux défis de la politique de santé*, Paris, Odile Jacob.
Villermé, Louis-René (2008 [1830]), *La mortalité dans les divers quartiers de Paris*, Paris, La Fabrique.
Wilkinson, Richard G. (2005), *The Impact of Inequality: How to Make Sick Societies Healthier*, London and New York, Routledge.

15

SUSTAINABLE URBANISM

Philippe Hamman

(Re)thinking urbanism in the era of sustainability

The concept of sustainable development was initially devised on the global stage in institutions such as the United Nations, at the intersection of economic, environmental and social concerns (Du Pisani, 2006). Although originally the main impetus was to preserve the planet without explicit reference to the urban sphere, cities now play an important role in this movement (Baker and Eckerberg, 2008). Urban professionals (experts, urban planners, architects, etc.) exchange references across national boundaries that contribute to making urban development increasingly 'green', while its principles, policies and technologies are also more and more 'globalized'. This chapter focuses on the impact of these new trends in Europe in the wake of the 'European Sustainable Cities and Towns' campaign that paved the ground for the 1994 Aalborg Charter, by way of which signatory municipalities committed to setting up local Agendas 21,[1] on a European scale, which requires policy planning and establishing priorities.

This chapter investigates how and to what extent the repertoire of sustainable development is applied to the urban environment using a knowledge-based approach and looks at sustainability as both a rhetorical corpus and a principle of action in order to better understand how sustainability has brought about transformations in urban development. It shows how the overarching incentive to take into account 'sustainability' now informs what has become both a field of knowledge and a field of practices and how this has found an echo in urban theories (Keitsch, 2012). The impact of sustainability on conceptions of the forms and functions of European cities has been extensively debated: although it has led to innovations, it has also had normative effects in terms of 'good practices' in which technical and economic rationales prevail over ecological and social concerns, as with the concept of 'green growth' (Viitanen and Kingston, 2014). This is illustrated by the controversies surrounding 'smart cities':

> On the one hand, smart city policies support new ways of imagining, organising and managing the city and its flows; on the other, they impress a new moral order on the city by introducing specific technical parameters in order to distinguish between the 'good' and 'bad' city.
>
> *(Vanolo, 2014: 883)*

First, sustainable development can be read as a public policy category translated into an object of knowledge. It is ingrained in all the practices and representations involved in the manufacture of regulation of social relationships, through their political legitimization and the recognition of that legitimization in interactions between policymakers and citizens. Second, this concept, initially deeply rooted in sociopolitical arenas (United Nations, networks of political representatives and activists, etc.) has now percolated into scientific circles to the extent that it can no longer be ignored, even by critical urban theorists, who are mostly concerned with the intellectual and political debates surrounding urban climate change (Whitehead, 2013). Nicole Mathieu has evidenced four types of attitudes in the research community: reasoned rejection (for those who see sustainable development as a disguised extension of a neoliberal model of growth and globalization), indifference (towards those who stick to established divides and disciplinary framings, such as the city, work or public policy), opportunism (feigning interest to secure contract funding while conducting the same type of research as previously) and utopianism (sustainable development as a cognitive and practical rupture) (Mathieu, 2006: 378).

The presence of these two dimensions explains the coexistence of a literature with operational purposes – concerned with *what to do*, particularly regarding urban public policy, about global warming and environmental change (Dryzek et al., 2011) – and research applying the register of sustainable development to urban planning with cognitive or critical purposes. The latter approach allows us to reconsider hasty associations. In particular, where urban policy in the so-called 'sensitive' neighbourhoods chiefly addresses the interaction between economic and social development, sustainable urban development primarily means a wider environmental repertoire, starting with 'nature in the city' and revegetation (see the chapter by Hajek and Lévy in this volume), through local participatory initiatives (as reflected in many handbooks; for instance, Douglas et al., 2015).

This calls for two remarks. First, there is no consensus. Admittedly, the greening of public spaces has become a mainstay of urban sustainable development, particularly in brownfield areas, pursuing 'a broad array of aesthetic, infrastructure, recreational, ecological, and economic development objectives at various scales' (De Sousa, 2014: 1049). Yet, for instance, grassing over tramway lines, a common practice in large cities, consumes a lot of water; does it deserve to be called an environmental measure? Additionally, the past few years have witnessed the emergence of categories of intervention in the evaluation of the 'quality of urban life' entailing the recognition of professional skills – much as urban sustainable development has become a cornerstone of local policies. This suggests more generally questioning the approach taken by the proponents of postpolitical consensus, focused on participatory methods for engaging local citizens into the 'New Urbanist' model of place-making, but which in practice benefits policymakers and the interests of consultants and experts (MacLeod, 2013).

What are we talking about when we discuss the relations between the city and nature in the light of sustainability, considering that so-called sustainable urban development recycles older repertoires – nature, ecology and the environment (Douglas *et al.*, 2015)? Theoretically speaking, 'one way of viewing the relationship between sustainable development and nature is to explore the extent to which human-made capital can be substituted for nature ("natural capital")', knowing that 'this replacement exposes societies to different risks and uncertainties' (Redclift and Woodgate, 2013: 92). By extension, there is not a simple opposition between the city and nature – by definition, nonbuilt nature – or an artificial complementarity – by which green spaces materialize everyday 'quality of life' for residents living in a mineral- if not concrete-filled environment. In a more complex way, nature only exists in the city insofar as it is politically and socially addressed. Although spontaneous flora and fauna – and therefore biodiversity – are of little interest to urban dwellers and decision-makers alike, this is not the case for deliberately aestheticized, gardened forms of nature (like botanical gardens) often devised to be efficient (for instance, when trees are planted to reduce heat). Such uses of nature are part and parcel of urban planning and influenced by distinct forms of knowledge (on ecosystems, micro-climatization, etc.). Urban forests, trees and green spaces are critical in contemporary planning and have social, cultural and psychological dimensions. In line with the plurality of possible references to 'green spaces', benchmarks of 'green performance' in European cities have been developed in urban economics; depending on the variables under consideration – accessibility or planning performance – respectively, Southern and Northern European cities are ahead according to a multicriteria approach including indicators such as 'quantity and availability of urban green spaces', 'changes in green spaces', 'planning of urban green spaces', 'financing of urban green spaces', etc. (Baycan-Levent *et al.*, 2009).

We may thus question sustainable urban development in terms of its ability to connect the relation to nature with the social, economic and political dimensions of the city:

- First, because the nature in question is largely hand-picked and domesticated – like lawns – whereas biodiversity conservation areas remain often perceived by residents as unkempt areas, mismanaged by public authorities.
- Then, because the city concentrates many activities and a large population on a limited territory that passes externalities onto neighbouring ecosystems (this

is the urban/rural interdependence and the fact that 'nature in the city' also means the extension of urban spaces on 'natural' spaces, particularly in the case of the construction of eco-districts in the periphery of cities) and affects global socioeconomic and ecologic systems (production of heat, waste, etc.). Overall, the city consumes most of the resources produced by human society and remains strongly dependent on nature despite apparent evolutions in lifestyles.
- Also, because this nature is socially appropriated by some groups who are better off than others (about 'ecological gentrification', see Dooling, 2009), which attests to the lingering effects of ordinary socioecological injustice in urban space.
- Lastly, because the recourse to the repertoire of sustainability reflects a change of direction since the 1990s towards a more global approach breaking away from the more 'operational' representations forged during the 1960s and 1970s: social and symbolic dimensions were seldom considered in urban metabolism approaches, for instance, and even political ecology in the 1980s remained rather technical in vision. Sustainable development now serves as a lever for the transformation of local policies, with an effort of coherence between various actors, institutions and action levels. This fits within the dialectics of adaptation and rupture that characterized dynamics of socio-ecological change at the time of the Anthropocene, i.e., a biosphere shaped by human action.

(Lockie et al., 2014: 95–105)

Theorizing sustainable urban development? Epistemological and practical controversies

Sustainable urban development has become a key issue for electoral representatives, technicians, industrials and associative actors. This also goes for academic studies, even though as a social and political construct, it poses a challenge for sociological analysis. There has been much criticism of the concept, including of its 'catch-all' character. Yet the fuzziness of the term makes it possible to develop practical convergences between actors and groups with different interests and values, including through discursive uses of identical terms pertaining to sustainability with changing contents. Research institutions have themselves contributed to the institutionalization of the 'sustainable city' with their ongoing programmes and their calls for proposals, both national and international. Worth mentioning are, for instance, 'Transformations to Sustainability', a new global research funding programme launched in 2014 by the International Social Science Council[2]; and in France, the Interdisciplinary Programme on Sustainable Urban Development (PIDUD) of the National Centre for Scientific Research (CNRS) between 2003 and 2007, or the Interdisciplinary Research Programme on Cities and the Environment (PIRVE) launched by the National Research Agency (ANR) in 2008; another example in Switzerland, the project 'Living with Hard Times. How Citizens React to Economic Crises', lays emphasis on the context of the economic crisis in Europe since 2007.[3]

Sustainable development has now seeped into so many different levels that it has become a feature of common discourse. Some publications are turned towards the promotion of sustainable urban development without necessarily providing any analytical insights; their output tends to resemble project sheets or to emphasize innovations. Occupational publishers put out sizeable amounts of applied and prescriptive literature – for instance, in France, the publishing houses of the Scientific and Technical Centre for Housing (CSTB) and of the Union of Developers (*Union des constructeurs immobiliers*). The book *Sustainable Urbanism: Urban Design with Nature* by Douglas Farr (2008), the chair of the LEED-Neighbourhood Development initiative, displays a similar mix of calls for action and ready-made and reproducible operational solutions, explaining how to implement sustainable urbanism through leadership and communication in cities, communities and neighbourhoods. These books reflect the routinization of the issue in the city's decision-making, institutional and expert (urban planners, architects) spheres. Many 'experts' champion sustainability as applied to organizations, like communication specialist Alan AtKisson (2010) who promoted his ISIS Method (Indicators, Systems, Innovation, Strategy) as a 'positive' aid to decision-making in a successful book.

Embodied through action *and* reflection on action, sustainable development belongs both to the realm of the ideal and of the real, to the practical and scientific worlds. Theorization essays produced in social science and urbanism refer to it either as a (performative) *utopia* or as a *narrative*. Proponents of the two approaches concur in addressing sustainability as a new paradigm.

Some see the repertoire of sustainable development as the political form of a utopia, consisting of the three principles of solidarity, precaution and participation, all challenges inherent to the very formulation of the tension/connection between development and sustainability. This echoes the 'utopic realism' of Anthony Giddens (1990) – whose vocation is both analytical and normative – as well as research on 'ecological modernization' (Hajer, 1995), which evidence a trend towards the similarly double-edged technicization and economicization of ecology. On the one hand, ecological modernization constitutes an analytical framework to grasp the transformations of the management of environmental issues. On the other, in normative terms it encourages the shift from ecology considered as activist and radical resistance to ecology as a source of technological solutions to the environmental crisis, ready to compromise with the rise of market-oriented rationales in the regulation of urban environment and planning (Lockie *et al.*, 2014).

For others, the 'sustainable city' reads as a new meta-narrative in the era of postmodernity – which is precisely characterized by increasingly scattered and delegitimized great narratives – based on a 'global' ecological argument emphasizing the need to preserve biodiversity, the threats of technological disasters for mankind, etc. This 'global' approach to sustainable development offers no ready-made model to be applied universally. This has two consequences. First, such projects are not only managed by urban professionals (architects, technicians, etc.); they involve different groups of actors whose positions must be reconciled (including environmental organizations or neighbourhood groups). Additionally, even though the repertoire of sustainable development gained currency by asserting its universal dimension (with emphasis on global threats), nonuniversalism has become a new urban utopia consisting of finding meaning in the local level in the era of globalization.

In terms of urban theory, how does sustainable development fit between continuity and change – between the promotion of a renewed or hybridized set of references and of the emergence of a brand-new paradigm? This question, which remains open, is of particular importance today as public debate is often characterized by blind spots concealed by 'consensus politics', as a result of which no one is allowed to claim to be against urban sustainability (Swyngedouw, 2009).

Sustainable development, sustainable city, sustainable urbanism

The concept of 'sustainable city' can be considered both as an offshoot of urban sustainable development and as a way to frame policies within that perspective, surrounding at least four major models (Hamman *et al.*, 2016):

- the 'recyclable city', whose inspiration is primarily economic (i.e. the idea of a city that is able to renew itself without requiring growing investments);
- the 'compact city', a response to the expansion and fragmentation areas (and, by extension, to space consumption);
- the 'mixed city', an attempt at addressing sociospatial segregation;
- the 'participatory city', built around local democracy arenas (public meetings, forums, popular juries, etc.) meant to promote proactive citizens and increase the efficiency of decision-making processes.

These four registers are in no way complementary; on the contrary, they tend to be conflicting, and each of them is subject to debate. The 'recyclable city' raises the question of anticipation: Does the incentive to cut costs in the management of urban space mean that cities should save on resources or pursue investments in infrastructure encouraging more sustainable practices? This dilemma is exemplified by the construction of tramway lines: developing a new district in a city and connecting it to the city centre with a tramway line immediately can be seen either as expanding urban sprawl or as anticipating the need for an alternative to car traffic.

The 'compact city' is likewise not a self-evident concept: densification is generally not welcomed by residents; the attention to 'nature in the city' leads to greener but more sprawling urban areas (with biodiversity conversation spaces, etc.), and the very combination of sustainability and compactness has been called into question (Burton, 2000).

'Social mixing' has also attracted criticism. Policymakers are often accused of using social housing for the benefit of the solvent middle class instead of addressing precariousness and ghettoization in underprivileged areas. Sustainable urbanism is also involved in strategies of positioning devised by cities in regional, national and international competitions, which requires the maintenance or promotion of segmented, gentrified areas, particularly for the upper classes (Dooling, 2009).

Lastly, the 'participation' of local residents in urban policies in some cases merely amounts to the fact that elected representatives and technicians pass on information to them after the decisions have already been taken, or reflects the normative promotion of 'reasonable environmental citizenship' (Hailwood, 2005).

Additionally, a number of areas of action have tended to be neglected. These include social housing renovation programmes, which have spurred debates on social sustainability at the metropolitan scale (Davidson, 2009) and support to employment and the local economy through urban farming and short food supply chains. In a similar perspective, the actions promoting sustainable development aimed at reducing environmental injustice used in urbanism (Schlosberg, 2013) may also create new social dividing lines, for instance, between the eco-districts and the others and, at a time of energy transition, the energy-efficient buildings and those that fail to meet similar standards.

The so-called 'new sustainable urbanism' crucially relates to the production of value attached to a place, that is, in practice, a piece of the city – for instance, an ecodistrict and its urban services – not an entire urban area. It can also be read as a product of a neomanagerial influence (Viitanen and Kingston, 2014), resulting in an increasing concern for the attractiveness of territories and growing competition between cities. In this sense, sustainable development is more and more considered by local policymakers as a way to boost economic development, at the service of growth rather than of social interests.

Indeed, sustainable cities became perceived engines of economic growth in the 2000s. In terms of the ecological domain, mostly technical innovations have been achieved; there is a sense that we can still grow, but grow 'greener' – especially dealing with local energy transition 'because the upsurge of local climate policies results from the alliance between transnational municipal networks, international institutions and cities, with cross-influences between these levels' (Emelianoff, 2014: 1378). Sustainable development today often creates social injustices resulting from a neoliberalization of 'best practices'.

Controversy has also surrounded the hypothesis of continuity or discontinuity of sustainable development in the different ways cities are built. Some researchers question the idea that the 'sustainable city' is a new register. They defend two main positions: either they see it as a smokescreen in light of the continued progress of economic globalization – an approach defended by the proponents of degrowth (Georgescu-Roegen, 1971); or they look at sustainable development as a recycled version of the usual calls in urban planning to improve 'quality of life' in cities in the face of urban sprawl, pollution and other nuisances. Some have pointed out that many of the objectives of sustainable urbanism echo past conceptions of the city; for instance, the functional urbanism of the 1950s may have been called 'Fordist', but it was somewhat similarly aimed at improving living conditions in cities marred by 'slums'.

Other scholars argue that references to the 'sustainable cities' have introduced discontinuity in European knowledge systems, pointing to a reversal in approach from Le Corbusier's Athens Charter (1942) and the Charter of European Sustainable Cities of Aalborg (1994): the first charter introduces a *generic* model to be implemented – architectural functionalism[4] – whereas the second calls for case-by-case *local* solutions. In that sense, sustainable urbanism is primarily of a procedural (rather than substantial) nature, much like 'public debate' for the experts of deliberative democracy (Holden, 2011); it has affected the legitimization mechanisms of public policy in that way and eventually became inescapable, resulting in a renewal of principles of action in urbanism (for a critical assessment, see MacLeod, 2013).

Conclusion

Sustainable urbanism is a *recent* and *evolutive* reference in Europe, diverging partly from sustainable development in its conceptual and historical dimensions: more than simply serving as a global or alternative motto, it is embodied by interacting networks of cities and professional interests (Emelianoff, 2014). Close scrutiny of its uses suggests reassessing the association sometimes made by policymakers between the three registers of local economic development, the 'sustainable city' and 'creative urbanism' (Krueger and Buckingham, 2012), by raising the question of the production of a form of 'consensual' urban politics between often competing groups of actors. Likewise we should not overestimate the ubiquitous eco-city model, which tends to be based on international transfers involving partnerships between the private and public sector (Joss *et al.*, 2013), and make sure to properly contextualize these concepts that are being constantly redefined.

Sustainable urbanism leaves at least two key questions open. The first one is the decategorization of urban public policy principles, as there is no longer a single, overarching type of legitimacy, which by compensation may result in the development of a language that is either quickly adopted as such or remains deliberately vague (as evidenced by the numerous meanings of the 'sustainable city' and the rise of the discourse on 'nature in the city'). The second question is that of the transformations of the venues and forms of the city and of urban politics (Swyngedouw, 2009). Although some are content with the procedural interpretation of 'participatory' sustainable urbanism, how are we to rethink urban planning in venues and arenas that are no longer solely those of public policy, but also those of citizenship?

This also invites examination of the sociospatial dynamics at work: sustainable urbanism has shifted a number of urban frames and representations as far as their relationships to the environment and nature are concerned (functionalism, mixing, compactness, etc.). In this respect, it can be considered a contingent (i.e. transitional) concept, whose practical relevance was at least shown in the 1990s and early 2000s by its influence on the references of public policy in European countries. It now faces competition from other concepts and other relationships to knowledge on nature.

On the one hand, as we witness the limitations of the sustainability paradigm faced with the realities of the Anthropocene, there has been growing discussion about local and urban 'resilience'. Derived from the ecology works of Crawford S. Holling (1973), this term makes a direct analogy with nature regarding its ability to return to a former (but not necessarily original) state, for instance, following a natural disaster or pollution. Yet it may be argued that this posture overlooks the suffering involved in these processes and neglects the unequal abilities of various actors and groups to adjust, that is, social and environmental inequalities (Schlosberg, 2013). Can everything be overcome by nature and human societies?

On the other hand, the past few years have witnessed the emergence of 'transition', for instance, with the movement of *transition towns*. It can be seen as semantically opposed to resilience, as it calls for 'migrating towards' rather than 'going back to'. Crucially, it emphasizes that in the current economic context one cannot simply call for 'revolutions' to move on or fuel catastrophism without inciting severe counterproductive reactions. Public policymakers are thus left with sociotechnical transition, which has become a new buzzword in the field of energy (Emelianoff, 2014). This has created categorization and normativity effects similar to those observed with sustainability, as resilience and transition selectively point to a few aspects, among others, of what sustainable urbanism can mean. These issues indicate the relevance of lesser emphasis on technology as a solution to sustainability problems and more emphasis on social relationships, especially in urban areas.

Notes

1 The 1992 Rio Earth Summit resulted in the adoption of the 'Agenda 21' by 173 countries. The principles of the Agenda 21 are implemented through 'local Agendas 21' at national, regional and municipal levels.
2 www.worldsocialscience.org/activities/transformations/ (Accessed 31/10/2016).
3 www.livewhat.unige.ch/ (Accessed 31/10/2016).
4 Architectural functionalism is a theory according to which the forms and organization of urban spaces must be suited to their purposes, with four main functions: housing, work, play and transport – each embodied in its own space.

Bibliography

AtKisson, Alan (2010), *The Sustainability Transformation: How to Accelerate Positive Change in Challenging Times*, London and New York, Routledge.
Baker, Susan, and Eckerberg, Katarina (eds.) (2008), *In Pursuit of Sustainable Development: New Governance Practices at the Sub-National Level in Europe*, London and New York, Routledge.
Baycan-Levent, Tüzin, Vreeker, Ron, and Nijkamp, Peter (2009), 'A Multi-Criteria Evaluation of Green Spaces in European Cities', *European Urban and Regional Studies*, 16 (2): 193–213.
Burton, Elizabeth (2000), 'The Compact City: Just or Just Compact? A Preliminary Analysis', *Urban Studies*, 37 (11): 1969–2006.
Davidson, Mark (2009), 'Social Sustainability: A Potential for Politics?', *Local Environment*, 14 (7): 607–619.

De Sousa, Christopher (2014), 'The Greening of Urban Post-Industrial Landscapes: Past Practices and Emerging Trends', *Local Environment*, 19 (10): 1049–1067.

Dooling, Sarah (2009), 'Ecological Gentrification: A Research Agenda Exploring Justice in the City', *International Journal of Urban and Regional Research*, 33 (3): 621–639.

Douglas, Ian, Goode, David, Houck, Mike, and Wang, Rusong (eds.) (2015 [2010]), *The Routledge Handbook of Urban Ecology*, 2nd ed., London and New York, Routledge.

Dryzek, John S., Norgaard, Richard B., and Schlosberg, David (eds.) (2011), *The Oxford Handbook of Climate Change and Society*, Oxford, Oxford University Press.

Du Pisani, Jacobus A. (2006), 'Sustainable Development – Historical Roots of the Concept', *Environmental Sciences*, 3 (2): 83–96.

Emelianoff, Cyria (2014), 'Urban Energy Transitions: Places, Processes and Politics of Socio-technical Change', *Urban Studies*, 51 (7): 1378–1393.

Farr, Douglas (2008), *Sustainable Urbanism: Urban Design with Nature*, Hoboken, NJ, Wiley.

Georgescu-Roegen, Nicholas (1971), *The Entropy Law and the Economic Process*, Cambridge, MA, Harvard University Press.

Giddens, Anthony (1990), *The Consequences of Modernity*, Cambridge, Polity Press.

Hailwood, Simon (2005), 'Environmental Citizenship as Reasonable Citizenship', *Environmental Politics*, 14 (2): 195–210.

Hajer, Maarten (1995), *The Politics of Environmental Discourse: Ecological Modernisation and the Policy Process*, Oxford, Oxford University Press.

Hamman, Philippe, Anquetin, Virginie, and Monicolle, Céline (2016), 'Contemporary Meanings of the "Sustainable City"', *Sustainable Development*, 24, doi:10.1002/sd.1660.

Holden, Meg (2011), 'Public Participation and Local Sustainability: Questioning a Common Agenda in Urban Governance', *International Journal of Urban and Regional Research*, 35 (2): 312–329.

Holling, Crawford Stanley (1973), 'Resilience and Stability of Ecological Systems', *Annual Review of Ecology and Systematics*, 4: 1–23.

Joss, Simon, Cowley, Robert, and Tomozeiu, Daniel (2013), 'Towards the "Ubiquitous Eco-City": An Analysis of the Internationalisation of Eco-City Policy and Practice', *Urban Research and Practice*, 6 (1): 54–74.

Keitsch, Martina Maria (2012), 'Sustainable Architecture, Design and Housing', *Sustainable Development*, 20 (3): 141–145.

Krueger, Rob, and Buckingham, Susan (2012), 'Towards a "Consensual" Urban Politics? Creative Planning, Urban Sustainability and Regional Development', *International Journal of Urban and Regional Research*, 36 (3): 486–503.

Lockie, Stewart, Sonnenfeld, David A., and Fisher, Dana R. (eds.) (2014), *The Routledge International Handbook of Social and Environmental Change*, London and New York, Routledge.

MacLeod, Gordon (2013), 'New Urbanism/Smart Growth in the Scottish Highlands: Mobile Policies and Post-Politics in Local Development Planning', *Urban Studies*, 50 (11): 2196–2221.

Mathieu, Nicole (2006), 'Pour une construction interdisciplinaire du concept de milieu urbain durable', *Natures Sciences Sociétés*, 14 (4): 376–382.

Redclift, Michael, and Woodgate, Graham (2013), 'Sustainable Development and Nature: The Social and the Material', *Sustainable Development*, 21 (2): 92–100.

Schlosberg, David (2013), 'Theorising Environmental Justice: The Expanding Sphere of a Discourse', *Environmental Politics*, 22 (1): 37–55.

Swyngedouw, Erik (2009), 'The Antinomies of the Postpolitical Cities: In Search of a Democratic Politics of Environmental Protection', *International Journal of Urban and Regional Research*, 33 (3): 601–620.

Vanolo, Alberto (2014), 'Smartmentality: The Smart City as Disciplinary Strategy', *Urban Studies*, 51 (5): 883–898.
Viitanen, Jenni, and Kingston, Richard (2014), 'Smart Cities and Green Growth: Outsourcing Democratic and Environmental Resilience to the Global Technology Sector', *Environment and Planning A*, 46 (4): 803–819.
Whitehead, Mark (2013), 'Neoliberal Urban Environmentalism and the Adaptive City: Towards a Critical Urban Theory and Climate Change', *Urban Studies*, 50 (7): 1348–1367.

16

INDUSTRIAL ECOLOGY

Between model and metaphor: visions of nature in industrial ecology

Nicolas Buclet

The initial idea of industrial ecology can be traced back to the nineteenth century and the publication of the first studies of biogeochemical cycles by Justus von Liebig. Likewise, the roots of the concept of metabolism of human activities have been dated back to the 1860s, according to Marina Fischer-Kowalski (2003). Taking into consideration the metabolism of human activities – especially economic ones – alongside the metabolism of human organisms in order to account for the interactions between the economy and its environment reflects an attempt to reconcile man and nature. Addressing contemporary sustainable development challenges today requires rethinking industrial society, with a view towards achieving a loop of material and energy flows. Humankind should no longer be looked at as an exception for whom the constraints of the biosphere do not apply; an exceptional being whose essence is intrinsic and not connected to the environment, in a vision of the Western world as 'a set of discrete and independent entities, each of which constitutes an essence in itself' (Schaeffer, 2007: 39). After outlining the principles of industrial ecology, this chapter will investigate the superficial ties between ecology and industrial ecology and go on in the third section to evidence their contradictions based on the case of Kalundborg (Denmark). The conclusion will discuss the perspectives of a genuine interchange between these two disciplinary fields.

Industrial ecology and its principles

The discipline's founding act was penned in 1989 by two General Motors engineers: vice president for research Robert Frosch and head of the engine research department Nicholas Gallopoulos (Graedel and Lifset, 2016). In their paper, they outlined the necessity of moving from a linear economy model – in which resources are extracted from the ecosystem, developed for human activities, and brought back in degraded (or nondegradable) form – to a cyclical economy model that is dematerialized as it consumes few natural resources for the purposes of producing and meeting human needs (Frosch and Gallopoulos, 1989). The ultimate utopia of industrial ecology is to achieve a closed loop of material and energy flows. Brad R. Allenby and Deanna J. Richards (1994) thus considered that all industrial systems must function in an entirely cyclical manner; solar energy would make up for the inevitable losses. This vision, which prevailed within the international community of industrial ecology, strove towards the systemic optimization of industrial society based on two prerequisites that influenced the orientations to follow: the embedding of industrial society within a dominant market economy and the rise of a society based on the development of environmental technologies. The dominant trend in industrial ecology hinges on the basic strategic principle of the substitution of natural resources by the rise of technology. With respect to sustainable development, this unquestionably means favouring a weak sustainability model over a strong one; it is considered possible to replace 'natural capital' with 'technological capital' or any other capital of anthropogenic origin.

Under this approach, industrial ecology supports the necessity of moving on from the current 'juvenile' industrial systems towards 'mature' ones, the only ones enabling a closed loop of material and energy flows – a condition considered by these authors as inherent to the sustainability of natural ecosystems. According to Suren Erkman (1998), this includes:

- reusing waste as resources;
- closing material cycles and reducing dissipative releases;
- dematerializing products and economic activities;
- decarbonizing energy.

The authors who support this view added the caveat that these four guidelines have limitations. Operations induced by industrial ecology have impacts in terms of energy; although it is possible to substantially reduce the waste of resources through recycling or dematerialization, the overall results remain mixed if in parallel the increase in the quantity of products leads to greater resource consumption flows.

In light of these limitations, other authors have reflected on the need to introduce other principles. James J. Kay (2001), for instance, identified the causes of the lack of practical implementations of industrial ecology. He attributed its mixed results to the fact that society does not see the need for it, but also to inadequate knowledge on how ecological systems work. From this he deduced four new principles:

- The principle of the interface between man and ecosystems in order to limit human interference in the functioning of the latter and maintain their potential for ecological services. The goal is not to disrupt ecosystems whose usefulness has been proven (natural capacity for sewage treatment, natural capacity for CO_2 absorption in some milieus), as well as those whose usefulness has

not (yet?) been evidenced, considering how little knowledge is available about how ecosystems work.
- The principle of bionics or biomimicry, according to which human society must follow the model of ecosystems in their behaviours and structures.
- The principle of biotechnologies: when possible, functions necessary to human societies must be fulfilled by the biosphere's ecosystems.
- The principle of using nonrenewable resources only in cases where it is conducive to subsequent widespread use of renewable resources; additionally, the use of renewable resources must be quantitatively and qualitatively lower than their renewal rate.

Adopting these principles requires much finer knowledge of how natural ecosystems work. This means achieving a better sense of man's position in relation to the biosphere and how to change human behaviours in light of this new position in a logic of symbiosis whereby humanity is one of the components of living organisms within the biosphere.

Ecology and industrial ecology

The twentieth century has witnessed the apex of a major trend in Western societies, resulting from the scientific and industrial revolutions – a conception based on an ontic rupture between humankind and nature. Initially intellectual, affecting conceptions of humanity's place in its surroundings, this rupture progressively extended to human activities in practice. The approach that consisted in drawing fossil and mineral resources from the environment to meet the needs of a growing population in search of better living conditions reinforced the sense that nature had such a vast pool of resources that it could be tapped without moderation. As the consequences of the massive release of materials processed and artificialized by humans into the environment were not immediately perceptible, it was believed that this linear approach was viable. This approach was called into question by the promoters of industrial ecology, who were concerned both with the depletion of resources and the damage to the environment. Thus, simple ideas such as using discharges from one living organism as a resource for another living organism were turned into powerful catchphrases for this disciplinary field, such as turning the waste of one species into resources for another. As they formulated these ideas, the promoters of industrial ecology were attempting to revive a way of thinking that was still current in many areas of the world and had only been abandoned about one century before in the Western world, as Sabine Barles (2005) shows in her book about household waste management in Paris between 1830 and 1930. Systematic recycling is ultimately a return to principles already known in societies that have conceptualized the scarcity of resources, thanks to authors such as Thomas Malthus and Karl Marx, but it was legitimized in the name of an analogy with the functioning of natural ecosystems. Authors like Brad Allenby (1999) even claim that this is the key to sustainability.

The concept of metabolism, central for industrial ecology, is considered a biological concept. It is one of the main analogies that are mobilized by the field and yet has been surprisingly seldom analyzed (Wassenaar, 2015). Metabolism is used by industrial ecology simply as 'a biological concept which refers to the internal process of a living organism' (Fischer-Kowalski and Haberl, 1998: 573), with no deeper insight in the way a biological metabolism works. Baccini and Brunner stated that applications of the term 'metabolism' to organisms larger than physiological entities is anyway a metaphor, be it for natural ecosystems or for industrial ones (Baccini and Brunner, 2012). Following another point of view, Wassenaar (2015) claims that historically the use Marx made of the concept of metabolism in the fields of economy and sociology during the nineteenth century and the use industrial ecology is now making of it are no less legitimate than in physiology. In that sense, the ways in which different fields have made use of the concept have run in parallel developments.

More problematic is the theme of the optimization of the closed loop system, which is the guiding principle of industrial ecology, and is directly inspired by the functioning of natural ecosystems, where any release from an organism (except heat dissipation) is sooner or later assimilated by another organism. According to this approach, organizing industrial societies as natural ecosystems would 'suffice' to create the conditions of their sustainability. Yet this raises a crucial issue: Are we certain that the promoters of industrial ecology know and understand what makes natural ecosystems sustainable, beyond the simplistic emphasis on closing the loop? Several authors (including Gérald Hess) have evidenced this problem, pointing to the confusion between references to the ecosystem as a model or as a mere metaphor. Indeed, it is not the same thing to apply the 'natural' ecology pattern to industrial ecosystems or to refer to a simplified representation of how ecosystems work as a source of inspiration. According to Gérald Hess (2010), due to this confusion it is difficult to establish whether reference is made to the reality of natural ecosystems or to a biased vision of them. In the former case, studies in the field of ecology are essential and knowledge of the properties of natural ecosystems must be used as a basis for the definition of the practical orientations of industrial ecology – the reference to natural ecosystems becomes a heuristic of action. In the latter case, the heuristics of action are inspired by a representation that ultimately has little to do with the effectively observable and analyzable functioning of natural ecosystems.

Dominant discourses and most of all the implementation of industrial ecology suggest that what we are dealing with is a metaphoric use of *nature*. As a result of this, instead of being strengthened by scientific advances shedding light on how natural ecosystems effectively work, the theory of industrial ecology is systematically weakened by them. The concepts of industrial ecology are not those of ecology; they were progressively developed by their promoters. Researchers in industrial ecology work on concepts that feed on insights from multiple disciplines that structure the scientific community's vision in the field. Hess (2010) describes this as an epistemological error. The industrial ecology scientific community is uncomfortable with this metaphoric positioning and supports a rapprochement between ecology and industrial ecology, even though industrial ecology, which grew from the intuition of the necessity of drawing inspiration from natural ecosystems, has strayed from ecology in conception and practice. In particular, these authors seem to view Darwin's idea of evolutionism as an idea of progress – that of a nature that works according to a plan of continuous improvement towards an optimal equilibrium. As in the case of the conception of sustainable ecosystems (i.e. mature ecosystems that would no longer produce waste that isn't fully recycled internally), the dominant current in industrial ecology overlooks that in nature, ecosystems of various types coexist, and less mature ecosystems, that is, those which produce waste (for instance, oxygen or plant nutrients) that is then used as resources for other living organisms or other ecosystems are just as indispensable to the development of life. Not only do these authors neglect the reversal of perspective between objective knowledge and metaphoric construction, but they also even consider it pertinent to apply the principles of industrial ecology to the 'Earth system' (Allenby, 1999). It is no longer the multiple interactions of natural ecosystems that come to the rescue of industrial society in a dead end, but technology that saves the Earth (injections of CO_2 into the depth of the oceans or of NO_2 into the stratosphere), thanks to the development of geoengineering.

Lessons from Kalundborg

Kalundborg, a small Danish town that is home to around 20,000 people (now part of a larger municipality of 50,000 inhabitants) and a major port between the North Sea and the Baltic Sea, has been considered since the 1990s (see, for instance, Gertler, 1995) as the archetype of a successful industrial symbiosis following the precepts of industrial ecology. The port grew around a power plant and an oil refinery. In the 1960s, the municipality, which was concerned with the quality and availability of water, asked the management of the power plant and of the refinery to address this worrying situation. It was thus under pressure from the municipality that the power plant began collecting cooling water from the oil refinery for its own use. Similarly, the regulation on polluted waters encouraged the refinery to invest in its own sewage treatment facility in order to provide sufficiently clean water to fulfil the needs of the power plant. Thanks to demanding regulation that still gave industrial actors some leeway in devising their own solutions to address these demands, industrial ecology principles were subsequently followed routinely. In the following fifty years, many other synergies allowed industries on the site and the city to reduce the global energy and hydric impact of this industrial ecosystem.

Due to its results, Kalundborg has become a model to follow for those seeking to implement industrial ecology approaches. In the 1990s, many initiatives inspired by Kalundborg emerged across the world; yet their results have always failed to reflect their ambitions. Ultimately, few studies have investigated Kalundborg's similarities with natural ecosystems. Suren Erkman (1998) did point out the absence of redundancy of supply (for instance, the Asnaes power plant is the only supplier of gypsum for the plasterboard manufacturer Gyproc): in this respect Kalundborg's symbiosis differs from natural ecosystems, which are characterized by significant redundancies aimed at making up for the failings of one organism with other organisms fulfilling the same functions. Yet such observations are not based on an ecological analysis of Kalundborg. Still it is quite striking that Kalundborg's success story was never convincingly replicated elsewhere, even though the actors who promoted these initiatives had the objective of creating eco-industrial synergies, which was not at all the intention behind Kalundborg, which was developed at a time when the very concept of industrial ecology did not exist yet! Few have noted that what distinguishes Kalundborg from other experiments pertains to the capacity of maturation, the time allowed for the evolution of a human ecosystem in which actors have developed an awareness of the value of adopting cooperative behaviours to meet regulatory requirements. Unlike this progressive research of new cooperations, other projects have often sought to plan synergies between actors that are expected to yield concrete results within a relatively short time span (a few years); if this is not achieved the projects are often stopped or at least deprived of financial and organizational support. This is quite far removed from the usual functioning and constraints faced by a natural ecosystem left to evolve at its own pace. This forcing is evident in the case of projects openly aimed at achieving industrial symbioses, which, for instance, neglect the importance of ecological succession (i.e. the natural evolution process of an ecosystem from an initial or 'pioneer' state to a mature state); that is, of going through a series of stages involving functional constraints in their succession to support the slow, but balanced and consistent, evolution of a living environment. Thanks to technology, humankind is thought to be able to plan and achieve a systemic equilibrium, whereas nature leaves time for evolution and room for chance.

What should we copy from nature?

From a scientific standpoint, the connection between ecology and industrial ecology is fairly distended, if not malleable. Yet the question remains of what we should copy from nature if we treat it as a model and not as a metaphoric object. The first principle is that energy and/or matter produced by a living species is consumed by another, even though excess heat from industrial processes is dissipated into the atmosphere and potentially recyclable products are released into nature (Gibbs and Deutz, 2007: 1684). This is where the principle of synergies comes from; industrial ecosystems are thought to have a vocation to adopt this principle entirely. Yet, finer observation of natural ecosystems would enable us to call into question the progressive and linear vision of the human ecosystem. Among other authors, Thomas Graedel (1994) conceptualized three types of type I ecosystems consume resources in a way that produces waste; type II includes both cyclicality and waste production; type III ecosystems work in a fully cyclical manner. Based on this typology Graedel argues that all ecosystems should aim to become type III.

As they move towards type III, anthropogenic production systems are thought to become part of a sustainable economic system. Yet, in ecology, nothing supports the claim that type I ecosystems are less evolved than the others or that there is a clear path to follow between type I and type III. Crucially, the ecological balance requires the coexistence of these different types of ecosystems, as their functioning is complementary. Type I ecosystems are fundamental for the other ecosystems, if only because of the 'waste' they produce – sediments or oxygen.

Without going into too much detail on the implications of in-depth reflection on possible parallels between natural and human ecosystems, researchers in industrial ecology would gain considerable conceptual insights from in-depth study of how 'nature' actually functions. This would in particular also feed into the reflection on what can be expected from the concepts of progress and development and provide input into a serious consideration of what sustainability represents for a human society taken as a special case of ecosystem. In other words, by way of a conclusion, an approach drawing on research in ecology can undoubtedly contribute to thinking differently of society and move beyond one-track thinking.

Bibliography

Allenby, Brad (1999), 'Earth Systems Engineering: The Role of Industrial Ecology in an Engineered World', *Journal of Industrial Ecology*, 2 (3): 73–93.
Allenby, Brad, and Richards, Deanna (1994), *The Greening of Industrial Ecosystems*, Washington, DC, National Academy Press.
Baccini, Peter, and Brunner, Paul (2012), *Metabolism of the Anthroposphere: Analysis, Evaluation, Design*, Cambridge, MA, MIT Press.
Barles, Sabine (2005), *L'invention des déchets urbains. France. 1790–1990*, Seyssel, Champ Vallon.
Erkman, Suren (1998), *Vers une écologie industrielle: comment mettre en pratique le développement durable dans une société hyper-industrielle*, Paris, Charles Léopold Mayer.
Fischer-Kowalski, Marina (2003), 'On the History of Industrial Metabolism', *in:* Bourg, Dominique, and Erkman, Suren (eds.), *Perspectives on Industrial Ecology*, Sheffield, Greenleaf: 35–45.
Fischer-Kowalski, Marina, and Haberl, Helmut (1998), 'Sustainable Development: Socio-Economic Metabolism and Colonization of Nature', *International Social Science Journal*, 50 (158): 573–587.
Frosch, Robert, and Gallopoulos, Nicholas (1989), 'Strategies for Manufacturing', *Scientific American*, 261: 144–152.
Gertler, Nicholas (1995), 'Industrial Ecosystems: Developing Sustainable Industrial Structures', MIT Thesis, available at: https://dspace.mit.edu/handle/1721.1/11556 (Accessed 05/10/2016).
Gibbs, David, and Deutz, Pauline (2007), 'Reflections on Implementing Industrial Ecology through Eco-Industrial Park Development', *Journal of Cleaner Production*, 15 (17): 1683–1695.
Graedel, Thomas (1994), 'Industrial Ecology: Definition and Implementation', *in:* Socolow, Robert, Andrews, Clinton, Berkhout, Frans, and Thomas, Valerie (eds.), *Industrial Ecology and Global Change*, Cambridge, Cambridge University Press: 23–26.

Graedel, Thomas, and Lifset, Reid (2016), 'Industrial Ecology's First Decade', *in:* Clift, Roland, and Druckman, Angela (eds.), *Taking Stock of Industrial Ecology*, Heidelberg, Springer: 3–20.

Hess, Gérald (2010), 'The Ecosystem: Model or Metaphor? Epistemological Difficulties in Industrial Ecology', *Journal of Industrial Ecology*, 14 (2): 270–285.

Kay, James (2001), 'Ecosystems, Science and Sustainability', *in:* Ulgiati, Sergio, Brown, Mark, Giampietro, Mario, Herendeen, Robert, and Mayumi, Kozo (eds.), Proceedings of the International Workshop *Advances in Energy Studies: Exploring Supplies, Constraints and Strategies* (Porto Venere, Italy, 23–27 May 2000): 319–328.

Schaeffer, Jean-Marie (2007), *La fin de l'exception humaine*, Paris, Gallimard.

Wassenaar, Tom (2015), 'Reconsidering Industrial Metabolism: From Analogy to Denoting Actuality', *Journal of Industrial Ecology*, 19 (5): 715–727.

17

THE ECOSYSTEM SERVICES PARADIGM

Rise, scope and limits

Roldan Muradian

The ecosystem services (ES) framework is one of the most successful conceptual innovations in sustainability science, probably only comparable with the concept of sustainable development in terms of widespread adoption and rapid dissemination. The notion of ecosystem services started as a metaphor created by ecologists to stress society's dependence on natural ecosystems, and the framework was consolidated in the Millennium Ecosystem Assessment (MEA) (2005). Since then, it has been rapidly adopted in policy and academic circles as a guiding approach to conceive the relationship between human societies (and in particular economic processes) and the natural environment (Chaudary et al., 2015). There are several definitions of ecosystem services, and some recent publications have reviewed them (Danley and Widmark, 2016). For the sake of this discussion, however, I refer to the original definition adopted by the MEA, namely '[e]cosystem services are the benefits people obtain from ecosystems'. The key point from this perspective is that most of these services have traditionally been 'free of charge'. That is, they have not been incorporated into markets, and therefore – the argument follows – they have usually been neglected in economic decisions and tend to be 'invisible' in strategic decision-making. The main goal of the concept of ecosystem services is to acknowledge such benefits and make them visible, and in so doing to favour the conservation of ecosystems.

There are two core components in this framework: (1) a classification of ecosystem services, which divides them into four categories: supporting, provisioning, regulating and cultural; and (2) an explicit connection between those services and human well-being. The ES framework has been very appealing, in part due to its simplicity. After a decade of dissemination at an impressive rate, we can confidently say that it has become the mainstream approach for understanding human–nature relations. Given the significant influence that it has acquired in both academia and policy design, it is necessary to review it critically. After the consolidation of the ES framework, it is time to ask questions such as: Has it actually enhanced our capacity to understand human interactions with ecosystems and to stop the global drivers of massive biodiversity loss and environmental degradation? This chapter aims to recapitulate the contributions of the ES framework and to assess to what extent this particular way of looking at human–nature relations provides appropriate analytical tools that can indeed advance our understanding of the drivers of socioenvironmental transformations. I discuss the rise of the ES paradigm, its analytical background and contributions, as well as its main limitations. I devote special attention to what I consider to be its main inconsistencies. The chapter also briefly discusses an alternative foundation for understanding human–nature relations in a more comprehensive way, aiming to address some of the limitations of the ES framework.

The impressive rise of the ecosystem services concept in both academic and policy arenas probably can be explained by a specific combination of factors: (1) the decline of the previous dominant paradigm (integrated conservation and development projects) in the 1990s, which opened a window of opportunities for new discourses; (2) that the ES discourse is based on anthropocentric and utilitarian values and conveys a simple message (to pay attention to the importance of human reliance on nature) created new opportunities of dialogue between social groups, and more particularly, between academics from different fields, policymakers and the business sector; and (3) the paradigm's compatibility both with the premises of neoclassical economics (seeing the degradation of ecosystems as the result of market failures) and the methods for economic valuation of the environment that created political and analytical synergies that mutually strengthened market environmentalism and the ES paradigm. The ES paradigm comes with a specific academic/policy agenda (Braat and de Groot, 2012), based on the following basic steps: first, identify ES; second assess and estimate them; and third, capture and manage values (incorporate them into decision-making).

Despite the widespread adoption of ES in academic and policy circles, some controversies have also emerged. In the policy domain, the concept has been contested by some governments (particularly from Latin America) on the grounds that it is associated with a neoliberal agenda and undermines indigenous visions of the relationship between humans and nature. Such controversies have been reflected in the development of the conceptual framework of the Intergovernmental Platform on Biodiversity and Ecosystem Services (Borie and Hulme, 2015). Some practitioners are also concerned about the fact that the utilitarian and anthropocentric values of the ES concept might mark a departure from the core values of the community of environmentalists, traditionally associated with nonutilitarian and eco-centric stands (Fisher and Brown, 2014).

In the academic domain, criticisms of the ES paradigm have revolved mainly around the issues of the implications of utilitarian values and the analytical usefulness of its categories (Schröter et al., 2014). Some scholars argue that due to the anthropocentric and utilitarian values driving ES management, engineering ecosystems aiming to maximize the provision of ES would be detrimental to the long-term survival of the nonhuman parts of ecosystems (Pröpper and Haupts, 2014). For some conservation ecologists, the fixed categories of ES seem to be ill suited to incorporating the interlinked and dynamic phenomena involved in human–environment interactions, where uncertainties and irreversible effects are common (Chee, 2004; Barnaud and Antona, 2014). For example, though depicted in a simplistic way in the ES framework, the relationship between ES and biodiversity is very complex (Lele *et al.*, 2013). In addition, as ecosystems services reflect changing consumer preferences, willingness (and ability) to pay and available technologies, they might tend to be unstable categories for long-term decision-making – the proper scale for taking decisions for the conservation of ecosystems (Vira and Adams, 2009). Due to complexities and nonlinear effects, how different ecosystems services relate to each other is not self-evident (Hauck *et al.*, 2013). How to deal with trade-offs between ecosystems services has not been satisfactorily addressed in the ES framework (Howe *et al.*, 2014). Due to these shortcomings, for some authors, the ES concept might actually hinder communication, and it may also strengthen the position of those who hold the power to reduce complexity and define ecosystem services (Menzel and Teng, 2009). Silvertown (2015) also argues that the mainstreaming of the ES framework entails the risk of constraining thought and the emergence of alternative visions.

Background and analytical contribution of the ES framework

The ES framework is essentially a discursive tool. Its analytical contribution is basically the proposition of ES classification (which we will discuss later). The framework has been undeniably successful in reinvigorating the environmental agenda at the global level, particularly after the relative failure of integrated conservation and development projects for biodiversity protection and the progressive decline of the concept of 'sustainable development', whose meaning (due in part to its widespread and indiscriminate use) had been considerably eroded when the notion of ecosystem services gained momentum. The ES framework constituted a discursive renovation whose facilitation of a number of developments can partly explain its rapid rise: a new research agenda has been set up around the demand, supply and governance of ES, linked to this rising interest in policy interventions based on the notion of ES; new communication bridges have been built with the private sector (facilitated by the monetary valuation of ES); additional public and private financial resources have been channelled to the environmental agenda; and new policy instruments (such as payments for ecosystem services) and governance platforms (such as the Intergovernmental Platform on Biodiversity and Ecosystem Services) have emerged associated with the framework.

One of the reasons why the dissemination of the ES framework was so rapid is that it is a good fit with theoretical and methodological developments previously elaborated by environmental economists. First of all, the notion of services rendered to human societies by ecosystems is compatible with the concept of natural capital. Ecosystems can be conceived of as a stock of natural capital that provides services (either through markets or outside of them). In principle, as far as methods for assessing nonmarketed services are available (whether through their contribution to economic processes, the evaluation of stated preferences or the cost of replacing them), the economic value of such a stock can be estimated. Second, the classification of ES (into supporting, provisioning, regulating and cultural) has its conceptual roots in the classification of environmental values for the cost–benefit analysis of ecosystems developed in environmental economics. The classic classification used in social cost–benefit analysis of environmental assets divides values into two broad categories: use and nonuse; and subsequently the former is subdivided into direct, indirect and option values, and the latter into existence and bequest values. This classification is intrinsically linked to the notion of total economic value (TEV). This concept assumes that the 'total' value of an environmental asset (e.g. ecosystem) can be calculated by adding up the estimations of independent values (Turner *et al.*, 2003). For such estimations, both stated and revealed preference methods can be used (Christie *et al.*, 2012). The value classification on which social cost–benefit analysis relies and the ES framework share a key assumption: (a) each of the categories into which both values and ES are classified are considered independent, and hence, with a proper classification, it is possible to avoid double-counting; and (b) the values derived from these categories can be added up in order to reach a 'total' value. These values are therefore assumed to be commensurable and additive. Both social cost–benefit analysis and ES assessment use the same types of methods, and both frameworks correspond to accounting systems. In order to be consistent, such systems have to comply with a set of criteria, including the independent, additive and commensurable character of the categories of classification.

It could be argued that the ES framework is essentially a reinterpretation of the TEV approach, using a new discourse. The similarities in the assumptions and methodological tools of both approaches are evident (de Groot *et al.*, 2010). The discursive shift that took place with the adoption of the ES concept constituted a renewal that did not enable the development of new methods for the economic valuation of ecosystems, but new applications of the existing methods. Even though the economic valuation of ES is not inherent in the ES framework, a key goal of the framework is to incorporate benefits humans derive from ecosystems in economic decision-making. Within the framework, ES are basically seen as positive environmental externalities. One of its assumptions is that the fact that ES are often 'free of charge' (i.e. with a market value equal to zero), which is the main reason for the massive destruction and degradation of ecosystems worldwide, leading to considerable losses in economic efficiency. From this perspective, the devastation of ecosystems is seen as the consequence of market failures (basically due to lack of information on the nonmarketed economic benefits that human societies obtain from the natural environment). A key proposition is that in order to stop this decline in the condition and land cover of ecosystems, ES should gain an explicit economic value. Though the framework acknowledges a plurality of values and different dimensions of human well-being (beyond monetary ones), its main role, at its inception and thereafter, has been to facilitate the incorporation of the economic benefits from ecosystems in decision-making. Essentially, it assumes that the best strategy to make ecosystem services 'visible' in strategic decision-making is to allocate an economic value to them. This vision has eased the dialogue between environmentalists and the private sector. The acknowledgement of the economic contributions of ES is expected to lessen the trade-off between economic development and environmental conservation. From this viewpoint, incorporating ES into decision-making should be beneficial to both, ending a long-term divide between environmentalists and capitalists. Such 'conciliatory' discourse can be appealing for both parties.

The valuation of ES requires a number of assumptions about the nature of ES. First, the services need to be commensurable using a common measurement unit, or at least liable to be integrated into a common decision-making framework, which usually requires the use of units or dimensions that can be compared (inter-dimensional comparison). Second, ES has to be discrete in order to be added; that is, ES needs to comprise categories that can be differentiated and compartmentalized. Third, it has to form a coherent structure in terms of giving a comprehensive and consistent account of the benefits human societies derive from ecosystems. In order to be useful for valuation purposes, the ES framework needs to have the consistency of an accounting system. The following paragraphs critically discuss the consistency of the ES framework and, more specifically the ES classification, as an accounting system. My argument refers to the latest available version (4.3) of the Common International Classification of Ecosystem Services (CICES: see www.cices.eu, accessed 29/10/2016) developed by the European Environment Agency (EEA) as the reference for the classification of ES. I argue that the framework suffers from significant inconsistencies, which call into question its analytical contribution. I have divided what I consider to be accounting inconsistencies into three categories: relational, scope and ontological.

Relational inconsistencies

This type of inconsistency pertains to the classifications of ES and the relations between the classification categories. As discussed earlier, in order to be part of a consistent accounting system, these categories have to meet a series of criteria: they have to be discrete (with clear boundaries) and comparable (if not commensurable in the same units, at least they need to be integrated into the same decision-making structure). In this section, I will focus on the nature of what have been initially coined 'supporting services' and their relations with other categories of services. The MEA defines supporting services as 'those that are necessary for the production of all other ecosystem services'. Initial examples (in the MEA report) of supporting services included production of atmospheric oxygen, soil formation and retention, nutrient cycling, water cycling and provisioning of habitat. Even though this category is still widely used in the literature, it has been dropped from the CICES. However, in this classification system, these types of services have been regrouped under the category 'regulation and maintenance', which has also replaced the initial 'regulating services' MEA label. The 'regulation and maintenance' category includes a broad range of services, such as bioremediation, filtration and sequestration of sediments and toxic elements, dilution of waste, mass stabilization and control of erosion rates, maintenance of nursery populations and habitat, soil formation and composition, maintenance of chemical condition of water sources, micro and regional climate regulation, pest and disease control, pollination, etc. The main accounting problem with these services is that they constitute critical processes influencing other services within other categories of classification, such as 'provisioning' or 'cultural', but also the maintenance of the ecosystems themselves. For example, micro and regional climate regulation affect the structure and functioning of ecosystems and therefore most of its 'services'. The fact that ecosystems are self-regulated (creating the conditions for their own existence) makes double-counting in ecosystem services accounting unavoidable. Part of the problem is that the ES framework mixes up 'benefits' and 'processes'. The former are understood as 'values' associated with a particular human endeavour, and the latter as a series of relations and operations, some of them resulting in regulation and maintenance of parameters defining the system itself (which is characteristic of life systems). A particular structure (composition of species and populations and their interrelations) and functioning (flow of nutrients and energy) of ecosystems is what gives economic value to human societies. The regulation and maintenance of this structure and functioning, however, depend on a series of 'internal processes', as well as on historical human agency. Using the metaphor of natural capital, the ES framework mixes up the services rendered by natural capital with the internal processes required for its maintenance (the very existence and utility of the capital). Counting both nonetheless will likely lead to double-counting.

Scope inconsistencies

The ES framework, at least as it has been developed so far, only considers benefits human derive from nature. That is, it exclusively takes into consideration ecosystem services, disregarding 'ecosystem disservices'. However, ecosystem disservices (negative effects and costs on human societies induced by ecosystems) are as pervasive as the services. Despite this, very few publications have discussed or estimated them (Escobedo *et al.*, 2011; Lele *et al.*, 2013; Lyytimäki, 2014), and they are not part of the classifications commonly used in academic or policy-oriented publications adopting the ES framework. This blind spot is difficult to explain, because any accounting system based on a utilitarian vision of ecosystems also needs to consider the negative impacts of nature on humans. The decision to exclude ecosystem disservices from the ES framework is probably the consequence of a justifiable ideological bias that assumes that the historical denial of the benefits from nature has led to the current environmental crisis (Shapiro and Báldi, 2014) and a particular policy agenda (promoting environmental conservation).

TABLE 17.1 Tentative classification of ecosystem disservices

Categories	Subcategories	Examples
Body integrity/ health	Pathogens	Bacteria
		Viruses
		Fungi
	Allergies	Pollen
	Predation or attacks	Attacks of wild animals
	Nuisances	Mosquitoes/ants/spiders
Production	Crop destruction	Pests/crop damages by wild animals
	Forgone productive land use opportunities	Ecosystems versus agriculture/ urbanization
	Forgone services	Reluctance of tourists to visit malaria-prone areas
Infrastructure	Direct damage	Termites
	Indirect damage	Forest fires
		Ecosystem-induced rains
	Obstacles	Barriers to infrastructure development
Cultural	Aesthetic dislike	Social aversion for forested areas or wetlands
Security and illegal activities	Enabling of conflicts	Hiding places for armed groups
	Enabling of illegal activities	Illegal crops

However, this choice is analytically flawed, because there is no consistent case to be made for leaving ecosystem disservices out of the ES framework. The same utilitarian arguments used for the conceptualization and estimation of ES should be applied to justify the systematization, assessment and incorporation of ecosystem disservices into decision-making. Table 17.1 shows a tentative classification of ecosystem disservices. It is not comprehensive, but it contains what I consider to be the main categories. The magnitude of ecosystem disservices is very far from being negligible. Pathogens alone are responsible for about 50 per cent of years of life lost globally, and the incidence of pathogens is strongly related to the local level of biodiversity (Dunn et al., 2010). The magnitude of these ecosystem disservices is therefore significantly higher in tropical regions, which host most of the world's biodiversity. The inclusion of ecosystem disservices will likely significantly change the calculations of the economic value of ecosystems and make more explicit the implications (scope and limitations) of a utilitarian approach for conceiving human–nature relations.

Ontological inconsistencies

The MEA defines cultural ecosystem services as 'benefits people obtain from ecosystems through spiritual enrichment, cognitive development, reflection, recreation, and aesthetic experiences'. These include a wide range of dimensions, such as cultural diversity, spiritual and religious values, knowledge systems, educational values, inspiration, aesthetic values, social relations, sense of place, cultural heritage and recreation. A variety of indicators have been developed to assess cultural ES (Hernández-Morcillo *et al.*, 2013). Nonetheless, the main problem with this classification category is that it implicitly assumes that the great diversity of dimensions characterizing human culture and their interactions with ecosystems can be somehow reduced to the notion of 'services' and therefore fit within a utilitarian interpretation of human–nature relations. I think this entails an 'ontological' inconsistency because not all these domains of human culture are compatible with such an interpretation. The argument that the entire complexity of the cultural aspects of human–nature interactions can be encapsulated into the notion of 'services' is simply preposterous. The category of 'cultural ecosystem services' seems to be particularly problematic, because it calls for understanding culture as a special type of commodity: a 'form of consumption, subject to trade-off between benefits and costs' (Winthrop, 2014). This conceptualization sharply contrasts with the notion of culture as a meaning-giving endeavour. The latter conception would render meaningless, or at least extremely problematic, the standardization of the dimensions incorporated into cultural ES and their comparison with other utilitarian uses of ecosystems, meaningless or at least extremely problematic because they belong to different relational domains (see later). Even in contemporary Western culture, where the scope of markets and commoditization is very broad, reaching many aspects of social life, it would be absurd to try to reduce 'culture' to a particular form of consumption. If 'cultural ES' do not share the same ontological (utilitarian) foundations with the other categories of ES, they cannot be comparable. Some authors have already pointed out that the ontological differences between the MEA categories of ES create problems of aggregation and comparison across categories (Kull *et al.*, 2015).

Following Fiske (1992), I argue that human relations (including relations with nature) can be explained by a combination of certain universal elements. He has classified these elements into four fundamental forms (or structures) of social relations: communal sharing, authority ranking, equality marching and market pricing. These elements can be found in all cultures. Variations between cultures concern the social contexts (social relations) with which they are associated. Communal sharing refers to equivalence relations, in which symmetry and the existence of common bonding elements are dominant features. Authority ranking refers to relations characterized by linear ordering. They are characterized by asymmetry. Equality matching refers to a mode of interaction based on even balance and one-for-one correspondence, dominated by a notion of egalitarian distributive justice. Market pricing refers to a model stressing proportionality in social relations, driven by considerations about ratios and rates. Which of these forms dominates a particular social interaction is culturally determined (it is a social convention), and therefore what type of moral judgements and ideological positions are formed in relation to them in a particular situation can vary greatly between cultural contexts. The proposition is that the elements are universal, but the ways in which they are used to frame social relations are contextual. Each of these fundamental forms represents a distinct type of representation, used for interpreting experience and guiding action in a particular social context. Each of them has its own expectations, customs and normative conventions; that is, its own grammar, which is not transferable to any other model. A further proposition is that even though trade-offs of values within one relational model usually do not represent a major problem, trade-offs *between* relational models are often are seen as impermissible (because there is no relational metric for comparison), resulting in moral dilemmas or taboos. Trade-offs between distinct relational models usually threaten social relationships and society. The breach of boundaries between models is typically considered bizarre, offensive or insane (Fiske and Tetlock, 1997).

Even though this theory was developed for social relations, its basic principles can also be applied to human–nature relations. From this perspective, 'utilitarian' relations between humans and ecosystems (mediated by 'services') correspond to the 'market pricing' mode. Within this form, people organize their relations with reference to cost–benefit ratios, rational calculation of utility or expected utility. The ES framework, including its conceptualization of cultural ES, is based on this relational model. The market-pricing model of interaction is, however, just one of the possible structures conditioning human–nature relations. The three other categories developed by Fiske (communal sharing, authority ranking, equality marching) nevertheless do not necessarily work for describing such relations. Table 17.2 summarizes an attempt to develop a more comprehensive approach to the understanding of human–nature relations. To build such an approach, I do not assume the common distinction made between intrinsic, instrumental and relational values (Chan et al., 2016). I assume that all the values underlying human

TABLE 17.2 Relational models between humans and ecosystems

Relational model	Core element	Key dimension for decision-making	Main driver of change	Mode of interaction
Utility	Calculative interaction	Cost/benefit ratio	Price/economic values	Market/nonmarket economic benefits
Affinity	Care-habitat Faith	Affective connection (belonging) May include sacredness	Livelihoods Identity Spiritual connection	Responsibility/stewardship/worship (unity)
Beauty	Aesthetic experience	Preservation (differentiated treatment)	Aesthetic preferences	Contemplation
Threat	Fear	Risk reduction	Risk perception	Hostility
Domination	Entitlement (human superiority)	Occupation	Territorial expansion	Indifference/blindness

relationships (either with nature or with humans) are relational values. What have been called 'intrinsic' and 'instrumental' values are forms of relational values (incorporated into the relational models elaborated next).

The 'utility' category basically corresponds to the 'market pricing' form. It refers to a utilitarian and calculative vision of ecosystems (based upon cost–benefit ratios). In this model ecosystems are essentially seen as 'natural capital', from which services can be derived (either through or outside markets). The 'affinity' relational model shares many elements with the 'communal sharing' form. Its core element is the sense of belonging and emotions related to care, identity and livelihood, and it may also incorporate the notion of sacredness. The main mode of interaction characterizing relationships dominated by this model is stewardship (based on feelings of responsibility and identity) towards ecosystems.

The 'beauty' model refers to relations founded on an aesthetic experience. Aesthetic values may result in the enactment of a special status for ecosystems (similar to art pieces considered especially valuable), which may be kept out of the market spheres (such as natural parks). This model devotes special importance to the preservation of 'pristine' ecosystems. In relations dominated by this mode, ecosystems can be 'contemplated', but under restricted land uses and practices, aiming to keep ecosystems as free as possible from human intervention. Ecosystem preservation and economic activities are seen as essentially antagonistic. Neither the 'affinity' nor the 'beauty' models respond to sheer cost–benefit calculations. The latter, in particular, holds an opposite vision: valuable ecosystems should be left out of such calculations and preserved as public goods with a special status (similar to the justification used for the existence of museums). The fourth model (threat) refers to negative feelings towards ecosystems, based on fear. In this model ecosystems are seen mainly as a source of hazards and therefore perceived with hostility. The last category (domination) has as a core element the notion of human superiority and the entitlement of human societies to occupy the (land or marine) space. This model is not necessarily driven by utilitarian calculations, but rather by a strong preference for intervened spaces and an obsession for 'occupation'. It is very common in remote 'frontiers' (between human occupations and ecosystems), like the agricultural frontiers in the Amazon. This vision is rather indifferent or blind to ecosystems, which are mostly just seen as 'empty' space to occupy.

The ES framework is built on the utility model. Its discourse and internal grammar therefore reflect the precepts of this relational form. It would not, however, be appropriate to apply it to relations based on other models. As stated earlier, the application of the precepts of a relational model to another often results in intractable problems and taboo trade-offs. I argue that such intractable problems are the result of 'ontological inconsistencies'. They are particularly evident in the case of cultural ES. For instance, within the ES framework, relations between human societies and ecosystems based on the notions of identity and belonging are considered part of cultural ES. However, to apply the grammar of the utility relational model to situations characterized by the norms of belonging and identity feelings is likely to lead to mismatches and intractable situations. Emotional attachments to ecosystems based on identity feelings are hardly negotiable. In such situations, people often do not accept trade-offs with other 'services', because relations dealing with identity issues have to do with some key constituents of people's existence and psyche, namely with who they are and where they 'belong'. Many human–nature relations considered part of the ES cultural services are actually hardly comparable with services allocated to other categories (provisioning, regulating) in terms of trade-offs, which breaks the principle of additivity (one of the prerequisites for consistency in an accounting system).

The ES framework can be useful in promoting a policy agenda for favouring the protection of ecosystems. However, with regard to the incidence on social decision-making, its scope of action should be restricted to those dimensions that are compatible with the 'utility' relational model. The framework can be particularly useful in situations where the acknowledgement and valuation of economic benefits derived from ecosystems can become a key input for decision-making. For influencing decisions dealing with human–nature relations based on other models, the use of such grammar is nonetheless simply inappropriate. Table 17.3 aims to systematize the different models for influencing social decision-making (in favour of ecosystems conservation) along the five categories of relational models described earlier. Each of these models is associated with a particular discursive strategy, which is not necessarily applicable to the other models. A discursive strategy based on the notion of rights (affinity model), for example, usually does not incorporate cost–benefit considerations (utility model), and can even be antagonistic to it. Accordingly, acknowledging the appropriate scope of action of the ES framework could actually enhance its capacity to influence social decision-making. Nonetheless, trying to make it a comprehensive approach to interpret all types of human–nature relations is both analytically misleading and inappropriate to influence policy design.

TABLE 17.3 Mode of influencing social decision-making

Relational model	Strategy to influence policy design (in favour of ecosystems conservation)	Discourse	Main fields of action
Utility	Valuation and acknowledgement of economic benefits	Economic values	Technocratic
Affinity	Rights enhancement/ resistance	Rights	Social movements Communities
Beauty	Delimitation and enactment of special status regimes	Differentiation	Technocratic
Threat	Communication and education	Risk management	Public campaign
Domination	External control	Setting of boundaries	State interventions

The mainstreaming of the ES concept may entail discursive mismatches that also reflect conflicts surrounding the underlying values and motivations driving the environmentalist movement (Fisher and Brown, 2014). Chan *et al.* (2012) propose that the incorporation of cultural dimensions into ES land planning and management would require an overhaul of the ES framework. Indeed, these dimensions tend to be neglected in decision-making because they are ill suited to economic valuation. Following Daniel *et al.* (2012), the authors contend that the ES framework should be revised in order to adequately define and incorporate cultural ES. I argue, however, that to incorporate all cultural dimensions within the ES framework would be misleading, because such a framework is only able to deal with the 'utility' relational model, and most cultural aspects fall in other relational categories (with their own grammars). The scope of the ES should be rather restricted to human–nature relations that fall within the utility category. The framework should be then revised, but rather to restrict its scope to utilitarian relations, instead of trying to make it an all-comprehensive approach.

In this chapter I have argued that the discursive innovations associated with the notion of ecosystem services have opened new opportunities of dialogue between sectors and disciplines, as well as reinvigorated the environmental agenda at the global level. However, the analytical contributions of the ES framework seem rather disappointing, which likely will undermine its influence and usefulness in the long term. The framework suffers from a number of inconsistencies pertaining to (1) the definition of the categories of ecosystem services, (2) the relations between these categories and (3) the scope of its accounting system. Instead of revising the ES framework, I believe that we should develop more comprehensive models for conceiving human–nature relations, capable of acknowledging the diversity of 'grammars' framing these relations. The utilitarian relational model, on which the notion of ES is based, is only one of the different models that shape the complex interactions between humans and ecosystems. The chapter proposes the adoption of five relational models. Each of these models has its own discourse, core elements and 'set of rules', and they cannot be easily comparable through a single measurement unit or reduced to a single accounting system. Each of these models is also associated with particular fields of action and ways to influence policy design (in favour of ecosystems conservation). A framework that acknowledges a diversity of relational models is expected to be more internally consistent, as well as better suited to integrating different disciplinary and social perspectives, not through a single analytical lens, but by considering a multiplicity of visions. Such an approach will hopefully better reflect the array of ways in which we interact with ecosystems.

Bibliography

Barnaud, Cécile, and Antona, Martine (2014), 'Deconstructing Ecosystem Services: Uncertainties and Controversies around a Socially Constructed Concept', *Geoforum*, 56: 113–123.
Borie, Maud, and Hulme, Mike (2015), 'Framing Global Biodiversity: IPBES between Mother Earth and Ecosystem Services', *Environmental Science and Policy*, 54: 487–496.

Braat, Leon, and de Groot, Rudolf (2015), 'The Ecosystem Services Agenda: Bridging the Worlds of Natural Science and Economics, Conservation and Development, and Public and Private Policy', *Ecosystem Services*, 1 (1): 4–15.

Chan, Kai, Balvanera, Patricia, Benessaiah, Karina, Chapman, Mollie, Díaz, Sandra, Gómez-Baggethune, Erik, Gould, Rachelle, Hannahs, Neil, Jax, Kurt, Klain, Sarah, Luck, Gary, Martín-López, Berta, Muraca, Barbara, Norton, Bryan, Ott, Konrad, Pascual, Unai, Satterfield, Terre, Tadaki, Marc, Taggart, Jonathan, and Turner, Nancy (2016), 'Why Protect Nature? Rethinking Values and the Environment', *Proceedings of the National Academy of Sciences*, 113 (6): 1462–1465.

Chan, Kai, Satterfield, Terre, and Goldstein, Joshua (2012), 'Rethinking Ecosystem Services to Better Address and Navigate Cultural Values', *Ecological Economics*, 74: 8–18.

Chaudary, Sunita, McGregor, Andrew, Houston, Donna, and Chettry, Nakul (2015), 'The Evolution of Ecosystem Services: A Time-Series and Discourse-Centered Analysis', *Environmental Science and Policy*, 54: 25–34.

Chee, Yung (2004), 'An Ecological Perspective on the Valuation of Ecosystem Services', *Biological Conservation*, 120: 549–565.

Christie, Mike, Fazey, Ioan, Cooper, Rob, Hyde, Tony, and Kenter, Jasper (2012), 'An Evaluation of Monetary and Non-Monetary Techniques for Assessing the Importance of Biodiversity and Ecosystem Services to People in Countries with Developing Economies', *Ecological Economics*, 83: 67–78.

Daniel, Terry, Muhar, Andreas, Arnberger, Arne, Aznar, Olivier, Boyd, James, Chan, Kai, Costanza, Robert, Elmqvist, Thomas, Flint, Courtney, Gobster, Paul, Grêt-Regamey, Adrienne, Lavek, Rebecca, Muhar, Susanne, Penker, Marianne, Ribe, Robert, Schauppenlehner, Thomas, Sikor, Thomas, Soloviy, Ihor, Spierenburg, Marja, Taczanowska, Karolina, Tam, Jordan, and Dunk, Andreas (von der) (2012), 'Contributions of Cultural Services to the Ecosystem Services Agenda', *Proceedings of the National Academy of Sciences*, 109 (23): 8812–8819.

Danley, Brian, and Widmark, Camilla (2016), 'Evaluating Conceptual Definitions of Ecosystem Services and their Implications', *Ecological Economics*, 126: 132–138.

Dunn, Robert, Davies, Jonathan, Harris, Nyeema, and Gavin, Michael (2010), 'Global Drivers of Human Pathogens Richness and Prevalence', *Proceedings of the Royal Society*, available at: http://rspb.royalsocietypublishing.org/content/277/1694/2587 (Accessed 29/10/2016).

Escobedo, Francisco, Kroeger, Timm, and Wagner, John (2011), 'Urban Forests and Pollution Mitigation: Analyzing Ecosystem Services and Disservices', *Environmental Pollution*, 159: 2076–2087.

Fisher, Janet, and Brown, Katrina (2014), 'Ecosystem Services Concepts and Approaches in Conservation: Just a Rhetorical Tool?', *Ecological Economics*, 108: 257–265.

Fiske, Alan (1992), 'The Four Elementary Forms of Sociality: Framework for a Unified Theory of Social Relations', *Psychological Review*, 99 (4): 689–723.

Fiske, Alan, and Tetlock, Philip (1997), 'Taboo Trade-Offs: Reactions to Transactions that Transgress the Sphere of Justice', *Political Psychology*, 18 (2): 255–297.

Groot, Rudolf (de), Alkemade, Rob, Braat, Leon, Hein, Lars, and Willemen, Louise (2010), 'Challenges in Integrating the Concept of Ecosystem Services and Values in Landscape Planning, Management and Decision-Making', *Biological Complexity*, 7: 260–272.

Hauck, Jennifer, Görg, Christoph, Varjopuro, Riku, Ratamäki, Outi, and Jax, Kurt (2013), 'Benefits and Limitations of the Ecosystem Services Concept in Environmental Policy and Decision Making: Some Stakeholder Perspective', *Environmental Science and Policy*, 25: 13–21.

Hernández-Morcillo, Monica, Plieninger, Tobias, and Bieling, Claudia (2013), 'An Empirical Review of Cultural Ecosystem Service Indicators', *Ecological Indicators*, 29: 434–444.

Howe, Caroline, Suich, Helen, Vira, Bhaskar, and Mace, Georgina (2014), 'Creating Win-Wins from Trade-Offs? Ecosystem Services for Human Well-Being: A Meta-Analysis of Ecosystem Service Trade-Offs and Synergies in the Real World', *Global Environmental Chance*, 28: 263–275.

Kull, Christian, Arnauld de Sartre, Xavier, and Castro-Larrañaga, Monica (2015), 'The Political Ecology of Ecosystem Services', *Geoforum*, 61: 122–134.

Lele, Sharachchandra, Springate-Baginski, Oliver, Lakerveld, Roan, Deb, Debal, and Dash, Prasad (2013), 'Ecosystem Services: Origins, Contributions, Pitfalls, and Alternatives', *Conservation and Society*, 11 (4): 343–358.

Lyytimäki, Jari (2014), 'Bad Nature: Newspaper Representations of Ecosystem Disservices', *Urban Forestry and Urban Greening*, 13: 418–424.

Menzel, Susanne, and Teng, Jack (2009), 'Ecosystem Services as a Stakeholder-Driven Concept for Conservation Science', *Conservation Biology*, 24 (3): 907–909.

Millenium Ecosystem Assessment (2005), *Ecosystems and Human Well-Being: Synthesis*, Washington, DC, Island Press.

Pröpper, Michael, and Haupts, Felix (2014), 'The Culturality of Ecosystem Services: Emphasizing Process and Transformation', *Ecological Economics*, 108: 28–35.

Schröter, Matthias, Zanden, Emma (van der), Oudenhoven, Alexander (van), Remme, Roy, Serna-Chavez, Hector, Groot, Rudolf (de), and Opdam, Paul (2014), 'Ecosystem Services as a Contested Concept: A Synthesis of Critique and Counter-Arguments', *Conservation Letters*, 7 (6): 514–523.

Shapiro, Julie, and Báldi, András (2014), 'Accurate Accounting: How to Balance Ecosystem Services and Disservices', *Ecosystem Services*, 7: 201–202.

Silvertown, Jonathan (2015), 'Have Ecosystem Services Been Oversold?', *Trends in Ecology and Evolution*, 30 (11): 641–648.

Turner, Kerry, Paavola, Jouni, Cooper, Philip, Farber, Stephen, Jessamy, Valma, and Georgiou, Stavros (2003), 'Valuing Nature: Lessons Learned and Future Research Directions', *Ecological Economics*, 46: 493–510.

Vira, Bhaskar, and Adams, William (2009), 'Ecosystem Services and Conservation Strategy: Beware the Silver Bullet', *Conservation Letters*, 2 (4): 158–162.

Winthrop, Robert (2014), 'The Strange Case of Cultural Services: Limits of the Ecosystem Services Paradigm', *Ecological Economics*, 108: 208–214.

PART V
Human–animal

The culture–nature divide establishes a profound discontinuity between human and animal worlds. This socially instituted division only masks reality and the plurality of the relationships between men, animals, plants and minerals. It is, moreover, based on the culturally shaped preconception stating that it is possible to dissociate the kinds of relationships human beings have with each other from those they have with other living beings, thus totally eschewing the important issue of the several modes of being, thinking and acting. Challenging this divide has opened up new fields of inquiry that go beyond the traditional oppositions used to think about the meaning of 'culture', 'civilization' and what constitutes society in its links with 'nature'. It has also led to important new cross-disciplinary studies about the relationships between men and animals.

Thus in Chapter 18, Éric Navet, after showing that ecocide and ethnocide are the two faces of the same desire to negate (in thought) and eradicate (in action) what is considered 'natural', substantiates and adopts the perspective of the 'savage' (in the noble meaning of the term). According to him, in striving to preserve in multiple ways another mode of being, thinking and acting based not on the opposition but on the complementarity between all the elements (human and nonhuman, individual and collective, past and present) constituting the living world and on the balance of their relationships with each other, the so-called 'traditional' peoples are defending interconnected human, ecological and spiritual values. The chapter shows that the many studies of ecocide should lead us to try to defend both the environments and the peoples who live in symbiosis with these environments.

The man–animal divide is originally founded on the idea of the division between mind and body which was defended by René Descartes – see his theory of the 'animal machine' (Descartes, 1996 [1646]) – and Nicolas Malebranche (1994 [1688]) and which has been fiercely challenged ever since, up to the most recent studies in biology, palaeoanthropology and ethology (see, for example,

Chapouthier, 2009), which have demonstrated that animals are also endowed with thought, technology and culture. Questioning this divide has led to very fruitful cross-disciplinary investigations, in line with the debunking of the opposition between nature and culture. This is exemplified by the rise of human–animal studies and of cultural and literary animal studies (Haraway, 2003; Bodenburg, 2012; Borgards, 2015). This new field was born in the United States in the 1980s and has been developing in Germany and France since the 2000s, aiming at rethinking the relationship between men and animals. Roland Borgards (Chapter 19) thus explains that over the last ten years a method for the investigation of animals has been established which offers an alternative to the traditional natural sciences. The main idea underlying animal studies is the realization that it is in no way self-evident what an animal is and who may know this. Such questionings have also profoundly reshaped specific disciplines. We will dwell more particularly on history: the history of animals has only been written from a human point of view. Éric Baratay (Chapter 20) therefore pleads for the creation of an *animal history*, one that would discard Western anthropocentric views of the world and consider animals as real subjects. The construction of such an animal history and the reconstitution of animals' experiences may be achieved through the association of historical methods and ethological knowledge.

Bibliography

Bodenburg, Julia (2012), *Tier und Mensch. Zur Disposition des Humanen und Animalischen in Literatur, Philosophie und Kultur um 2000*, Freiburg, Rombach.

Borgards, Roland (2015), 'Introduction: Cultural and Literary Animal Studies', *Journal of Literary Theory*, 9 (2): 155–160.

Chapouthier, Georges (2009), *Kant et le chimpanzé. Essai sur l'être humain, la morale et l'art*, Paris, Belin.

Descartes, René (1996 [1896]), 'Lettre au marquis de Newcastel (23 novembre 1646)', *in:* Descartes, René, *Œuvres*, vol. 4, Paris, Vrin: 568–576 [after the edition by Adam and Paul Tanney].

Haraway, Donna (2003), *The Companion Species Manifesto: Dogs, People, and Significant Otherness*, Chicago, Prickly Paradigm.

Malebranche, Nicolas (1994), 'Premier entretien sur la mort (1688)', *Conversations chrétiennes*, Paris, Gallimard, series Folio essais: 534–538 [edition established by Geneviève Rodis-Lewis].

18

ECOCIDE, ETHNOCIDE AND CIVILIZATIONS

Multiple ways of destroying life

Éric Navet

In *Anthropologie de la mort* (1980), Louis-Vincent Thomas described ecocide, without calling it by that name, in the following terms:

> The destruction of the ecosystem by man is both that of our planet Earth (terricide) and of some of the animals populating it (animalcide). [. . .] This is the outcome of a single implacable logic that has many faces, the thanatocratic logic. It sees the pursuit of profit as the driving force of development, the accumulation of capital as the means of growth, the myth of happiness (or opulence) as an incentive to produce/consume, and the arms race as a factor of dissuasion.
>
> *(Thomas, 1980: 104)*

A merit of Louis-Vincent Thomas's approach lies in considering the destruction of human beings and environments as related[1]: the 'thanatocratic logic' of industrial society works on human and ecological levels alike. The history imposed by certain civilizations shows that ethnocide and ecocide are part of a joint effort that has been largely motivated and spurred, more or less consciously, by religious ideologies that created and justified industrial and liberal systems.

The wide array of the world's cultures fall under two main modes of being, thinking and acting: the first belongs to traditionally hegemonic civilizations (essentially Christianity and Islam). They are fundamentally ecocidal and ethnocidal, characterized by a clearly asserted drive to dominate, exploit and subjugate – and thus ultimately to destroy – human beings, species and natural spaces by submitting them to a single model under the pretence of disalienating from a 'hostile' nature. The second belongs to traditional civilizations and is based on ecological, social and spiritual values.[2]

Think, for instance, of the founding texts of Christianity: Yahweh – God – created man after all the other creatures, and before woman, to be the master of a kingdom placed at his disposal: 'And God created man in His own image [. . .] God said to them: "Be fruitful and multiply, and fill the earth, and subdue it; and rule over the fish of the sea and over the birds of the sky, and over every living thing that moves on the earth"' (*Holy Bible*, 1980, Genesis 1). This was arguably the cornerstone for the development of Western history (See also the chapter on Ecospirituality by Choné in this volume) which, through the colonization of bodies, souls and spaces, became the history of the world itself – an ideology that combats the 'natural' within and outside of human beings and the wilderness in man and spaces.

The Christian man thus started out by suppressing his own nature, denying his kinship with the animal world and other living creatures. He glorified and sanctified (through beatification and canonization) those who used discipline to tame the wild beast within them, seen as the devil's share. He turned an unlikely virgin mother and asexual angels into models.

As they ate the 'forbidden fruit', Adam and Eve – the ancestors of humanity according to Christian tradition – discovered their sexual natures, and as they were cast out from the Garden of Eden, they turned their backs on their nature and on nature in the wider sense once and for all. This pivotal event transformed a relationship of intimacy and identity – safeguarded and promoted by traditional societies[3] as a moral rule – into one of domination and enslavement, following the Bible, of anyone failing to submit to this illusory desire for power and, by doing so, undermining the entire undertaking.

The duty of evangelism is none other than a destructive and suicidal manifestation of a desperate attempt to do away with nature and the 'naturals'. This makes every Christian a potential missionary, as the Bible puts it: 'Go into all the world and preach the gospel to all creation. He who has believed and has been baptized shall be saved; but he who has disbelieved shall be condemned' (*Holy Bible*, 1980, Mark 16:16). Natural peoples and societies, also called 'savages',[4] who believe in a different ideal, which consists of preserving the 'order, harmony and beauty' of a world dreamed by the Creator,[5] have no choice but to convert or perish.

In addition to this duty of conquering souls, the Bible promotes the conquest of bodies by advocating the total destruction of nonbelievers in certain situations. In biblical tradition, anathema (*herem* in Hebrew) 'includes renouncing all spoils and handing them over to God: man and animals are put to death; precious objects are given to the sanctuary. This is a religious act, a rule of holy war, which follows a divine order' (Bugnon, 2007).

Under this ideology, Earth is only valuable for what it offers human beings. Animals are not parents or totems as they are to Amerindians. They do not deserve respect, first because they are devoid of souls, and second because their only reason to exist is what they can offer men. It ensues that animals, like plants, fall into two categories – 'pests' and 'useful' animals. Thus horses are 'man's noblest conquest' and dogs his 'most faithful servant'. Because they are independent and only submit if fed and stroked, cats were, until recently, tortured and slaughtered in large numbers during Christian celebrations of the renewal of life. Animals are first and foremost game, inferior creatures that can be killed and consumed without second thoughts.

This fundamentally ecocidal attitude is the same that led Jesus to curse a fig tree that bore no fruit to satisfy his hunger[6] and dismiss nonedible plants as 'weeds'. While evangelization aims at subjecting all of humanity to the Christian model, the 'implacable' thanatocratic logic described by Louis-Vincent Thomas in the introduction to this chapter is also at work in colonization in the broader sense.

Jacques Cartier, as all the other great discoverers of new worlds, justified his request for ships by his duty to go and evangelize the 'savages' believed to be awaiting the Good News on the other side of the Atlantic. He was, in fact, just like the others, looking for new sources of material wealth and was greatly disappointed when he learned that the rocks he brought back, believing they were gold, were actually just pyrites. In Canada, which was unimaginatively named New France, the first American land reached by the navigator in 1534 was the '*Isle aux ouaiseaulx*' (Funk Island) off the coast of Newfoundland. Exhausted and plagued by scurvy, the sailors found an island that was literally covered by great auks (*Alca impennis*). They slaughtered them in vast numbers, foreshadowing one of the first noted zoocides in history: a few centuries later, the overhunted species went completely extinct. The last great auks, such as the Mauritian dodo (*Raphus cucullatus*) and the passenger pigeon (*Ectopistes migratorius*), are now showcased in natural history museums.

The first inhabitants of Newfoundland, the second American land where Cartier set foot, would suffer the same fate as the great auks: the Beothuk Indians were systematically and savagely murdered[7] by Christians bearing the Good News. The last living Beothuk, known by her Christian name Nancy, died of tuberculosis a Christian and the maid of a British settler in 1829.

The conquest of the West was based on the Western legal principle of *terra nullius*[8]: a land was considered 'virgin' as long as it was not used for cultivation. Many Native Americans did not cultivate the land, and they, too, were *terra nullius*, like a wild land to be domesticated and civilized because they were not Christians.

In North America, the history of the conquest of the East, of the West and of the North (still ongoing) has followed a dual movement of eradication of the natural (ecocide) and of the 'naturals' (ethnocide). George Washington, a founder of the American democracy and nation and a national hero, cynically advocated treating Indians as wolves, animals who were considered pests and ferociously hunted in the Old World and in the New:

> [. . .] policy and economy point very strongly to the expediency of being upon good terms with the Indians, and the propriety of purchasing their Lands in preference to attempting to drive them by force of arms out of their Country; which [. . .] is like driving the Wild Beasts of the Forest which will return as soon as the pursuit is at an end and fall perhaps on those that are left there; when the gradual extension of our Settlements will as certainly cause

the Savage as the Wolf to retire; both being beasts of prey tho' they differ in shape. In a word there is nothing to be obtained by an Indian War but the Soil they live on and this can be had by purchase at less expense, and without that bloodshed, and those distresses which helpless Women and Children are made partakers of in all kinds of disputes with them.

(in: Utter, 2001: 387–388)

The Pequot, the Natchez, the famous Mohicans and many Eastern American tribes were decimated or exterminated before the Plains Indians were themselves victims of a genocide at the hands of traders and the American cavalry, and of an ethnocide by a wide range of missions and religious boarding schools, as well as more recently and perniciously by Westerns and comics. In accordance with the biblical rule of anathema, during the massacre of Washita River (1864) – called 'battle' in the official history – in which Colonel George Chivington, a Presbyterian preacher, raided a peaceful Cheyenne village, human beings (men, women and children) were not the only ones killed. The same fate befell all the horses. In the late nineteenth century, General Phil Sheridan considered exterminating the bison, the main source of subsistence for Plains Indians, as the best way to finally solve the 'Indian problem'. The bison did almost disappear, like the great auk, the passenger pigeon, the ivory-billed woodpecker, the Carolina parakeet and other North American species.

The nearly 30,000 natives that populated Guiana in the seventeenth century were down to 2,000 in the late nineteenth century, decimated by diseases brought by the whites, particularly in the Jesuit missions established on the coast and along the Oiapoque River in the first half of the eighteenth century. Thanks to discrete and effective medical aid, they have overcome this demographic slump, but they now face the challenge of surviving culturally as their social and natural environments suffer multiple degradations. Numerous schools opened on native lands after part of Guiana (the most populated on the coast) was turned into a French department in 1946. They were given a secular mandate[9] to assimilate the 'primitives'[10] and make them adopt the French lifestyle.

The unabashed policy of *francization* accelerated in the 1960s and ultimately resulted in the departmentalization of the entire Guiana territory and the creation of new municipalities in a space that was until then known as the 'Territory of Inini'.[11] Bringing populations and spaces into the French administrative framework meant implementing 'development' policies, creating infrastructure designed to 'make local populations benefit from the advantages of progress',[12] organized around three institutions thus defined by the first prefect of Guiana, Robert Vignon: 'By order of importance, there needs to be a priest, a doctor and a schoolteacher' (Vignon, 1985: 91). Again, these assimilation policies targeted not only men, but also spaces, and they had both ethnocidal and ecocidal dimensions.

The forced displacement[13] of communities towards large villages such as Camopi, along the Oiapoque (at the Brazilian border), and the introduction of new practices and more 'efficient' technologies had social and ecological consequences.

Populations were forced to live in places they had not chosen (in flood-prone areas or, on the contrary, far from bodies of water), with other people they did not necessarily want to have as neighbours; chiefs given the title of 'captain' who had been appointed by the colonial authorities were in some cases not recognized by the population. One of the most egregious 'developments' took place in Camopi, a place almost entirely populated by Wayampi and Teko natives: in the 1990s, as part of a 'housing improvement' programme, a village was built with 'French-style' houses (separate rooms, no kitchen hut, no place for collective gatherings), covered with corrugated iron roofs – a modern material, granted, but one that, unlike the traditional leaf roofs, caused the houses to be unbearably hot.

Various forms of noise pollution (outboard engines, all sorts of music machines, lawn mowers, etc.) accompanied the multiple causes of pollution that went with 'progress' and 'development'. Waste processing was now a problem for municipal authorities, as 'civilized' objects and products are not – or not readily – biodegradable. Wild animals, still a major source of food for these populations despite the rise of wage labour, obviously flee large human gatherings, and hunting them requires travelling much greater distances. Likewise, there is increasingly less room for the *abattis* where manioc, a core product in Amerindian food, is planted.

In 2007, after long and protracted years of debates, the Guiana Amazonian Park was opened. It was aimed at protecting a vast swathe of tropical forest that still covers (but for how long?) most of the department. This was admittedly a commendable initiative, considering that Guiana has the only part of the tropical forest that depends on a 'rich' northern country – France – and that these forests and their biodiversity are vital to the survival of humanity and the maintenance of ecological balances in general. The Amerindian peoples (the three peoples from the interior: Wayana, Wayampi and Teko) living within the proposed park's bounds only supported the project in the hope that it would put an end to illegal and legal placer mining, which is currently the greatest threat to the environment and to the lives of the populations who still depend on it directly. Their hopes have been dashed: despite grand statements by the highest government officials (and the president of the republic) and largely publicized high-profile police raids, placer mining has spread, inflicting 'open wounds'[14] on the forest, as well as causing pollution (particularly mercury related) that makes the continuation of traditional activities that singlehandedly guarantee ecological balances extremely problematic.[15] The Native Americans also fear that the park will lead to limitations on their rights to fish, hunt and access natural resources in a forest they have themselves never endangered.

Resistance to ethnoecocide is now visibly expressed by attention to the preservation of traditional culture and techniques that are being threatened and by the construction of new smaller villages, more conducive to social life and to the conservation of flora and fauna. Yet half a century of 'development' in Camopi has led to the degradation of living spaces and of the moral and physical health of residents. The intended beneficiaries of this development have been culturally impoverished.[16]

Obviously, what is happening and has happened in America has also occurred in all places where civilization has imposed its standards through a colonization process that has taken the successive guises of Christianization, civilization, progress, development and, more recently, globalization. As a result the current state of our planet is catastrophic, and ecocide has assumed endless forms: chemical pollution of water, land and air; nuclear accidents and radioactive contamination; destruction of the ozone layer and climate warming; deforestation and extension of road networks; overexploitation of mining and mineral resources; excessive urbanization[17]; absurd technological inflation; junk food; etc.

The promotion of monocultures, the widespread use of pesticides, the transformations of biotopes (for instance, with the removal of hedges in Western France) are degradations that lead to the extinction of numerous zoological and botanical species and varieties. In addition to zoocide, phytocide is another prevalent form of ecocide.

The physical, mental and intellectual consequences on human beings and on all other living beings are considerable, ranging from new diseases to innumerable and bloody wars and conflicts between the largest totalitarian ideologies.

If we consider that human beings are not free agents but links in the ecological chains, then the distinction between ecocide and ethnocide has little relevance – except to simplify discourse – cultural diversity is just as crucial as biological diversity and it is fully part of it. Traditional peoples have understood this and do not treat human issues as separate from environmental issues. Ecology is a core component of indigenous claims, as Ernest Tootoosis, a Cree aboriginal medicine man (shaman) from Saskatchewan[18] explained to me in a 1977 interview:

> God did not want Man to kill his mother, the Earth, by draining out all its blood and flaying it to death; this cannot go on! Luxury is not worth the price it costs if we deprive the next generation from vital resources such as drinking water, heat and energy. This world's natural environment must be preserved.

Evidently human populations also expand to the detriment of other animal and vegetal species, though it is difficult to accurately measure the consequences of this zoocide and phytocide – two major aspects of ecocide. Franz Broswimmer, a researcher from the University of Hawaii, imagined what news broadcasts 'informed by ecological realism' might sound like. He wrote this thirteen years ago, but things have kept getting worse since:

> Also today as many as 100 animal and plant species have become extinct, some further 50,000 hectares of tropical rainforests have disappeared; the deserts have expanded worldwide by another 20,000 hectares; the global economy has consumed today the equivalent of 22 million tons of oil and we will consequently have collectively released during the same 24 hours another 100 million tons of greenhouse gasses into the atmosphere.

(Broswimmer, 2002: 5)

The destruction of environments and grand projects such as the Northern Gateway in the Canadian North or the Belo Monte dam in the Brazilian Amazon primarily affect the habitats of traditional peoples – 'first peoples' or 'natural peoples' as they call themselves today – who are fully part of these natural worlds:

> In the daily battle between a growing, always ravenous civilization and an ancient ecosystem, the ecosystem is losing badly. So are the indigenous cultures who depend on the forest. Disappearing along with the trees and the living species are [. . .] an estimated 50 million tribal people who still live in the tropical rain forests.
>
> *(Gore, 1992: 114–115)*

When the geographer and anthropologist Jean Malaurie said of the West '[u]ltimately, whether or not we are believers, we all remain deeply Christian',[19] he meant that industrial societies are only applying the founding principles of the civilizations they have built or from which they have expanded. Even more than the current outcome of this process, ongoing trends are worrying: the destruction of human and nonhuman environments is global – and it is accelerating instead of slowing down. The demographic explosion and the planet's growing anthropization occur necessarily at the expense of other living species. Considering that the population growth rate is higher in poor countries than in rich ones, the solution to the planet's destruction and the genuine improvement of living conditions for all species – if this is our ultimate goal, which does not seem to be the case now – necessarily entails the better distribution of wealth, as well as arguably a redefinition of what we mean by 'wealth'.

The issue of ecocide requires an interdisciplinary approach, which is the only one suited to a thoughtful assessment of the stakes of adapting or interrupting 'development' policies for humanity and the living world as a whole.

This will first involve compiling a comprehensive overview of the state of the planet, questioning concepts such as 'progress' and 'development', the religious and/or economic hegemony of certain modes of being, thinking and acting. Then, suggestions will have to be made to change the course of these policies. Adam D. C. Cherson (2009, 2010), a man of many talents who presents himself as a socioecologist, lawyer, historian, musician, inventor, actor, etc., best embodies the need to call upon all resources and sources of knowledge. The legal approaches of authors like Jennifer Huseman and Damien Short (2012) and Damien Short (2016), who have examined the case of subarctic indigenous peoples threatened by shale gas extraction; Polly Higgins (2010, 2011); or Laurent Neyret (2015), may usefully complement the sociological, anthropological, economical and philosophical approaches developed by such thinkers as Donald A. Grinde and Bruce Johansen (1991, 1995), Serge Latouche (2004, 2005), Christian Godin (2012) and Kevin Bales (2016).

Although all living beings, and human beings in particular, are affected by ecocide, traditional peoples (Amerindians, Australian Aborigines, etc.) suffer most from the blows struck against their environments due to their greater physical and spiritual proximity to them – tropical and temperate forests, deserts, arctic regions, coastal areas, etc. Authors such as Ward Churchill (2002) and the journalist Carlita Shaw (2015), who represent and defend these populations' interests, emphasize the link between ethnocide and ecocide and define a mode of being, thinking and acting that would be more mindful of natural balances and laws. Traditional peoples, who may be called 'native peoples', 'first nations', 'natural peoples', etc., also have their say and use every opportunity they have to express themselves in national and international forums (on the environment), online media, social networks, newspapers, the arts, etc.

We must also probably become aware that 'we too, civilizations, are mortal'. This remark was made by writer Paul Valéry in 1924, in the aftermath of the First World War, which made millions of casualties and washed out the cultures of huge, relentlessly bombed lands – as was the case half a century later in Vietnam. We must realize that the loss of our real sources of wealth – the ability to create, the power to dream, the diversity of languages, cultures and thoughts – concerns everything that lives on this water planet. All the forces that work to weaken biodiversity and ethnodiversity, all forms of ecocide and ethnocide, pose a threat that may be even greater than the mushroom clouds of atomic bombs.

We are thus now left to rethink our relationship to the world, to others and probably to ourselves, by inventing ways of living together and an ethic based on recognizing the principles of interdependence and exchange that govern the living world. We must also acknowledge that there are multiple paths to knowledge in this world. Insights from ethnoecology and socioecology (particularly the current represented by the Canadian Jean-Guy Vaillancourt: see Vaillancourt and Gendron, 2007, also the chapter on ecosociologies by Woodgate in this volume) might inspire us to invent human frameworks in rural and urban areas that meet the real needs of human and nonhuman beings. As gardens start to bloom on the roofs of skyscrapers, the hope formulated by the writer Alphonse Allais ('building cities in the countryside') might not be as absurd as it once seemed. It could be that the mode of being, thinking and acting of traditional peoples is not at all obsolete or retrograde, but actually a source from which we could draw to at least partially resolve problems relating to 'modernity'. This view has been expressed by authors like Jerry Mander:

> What is romantic is to believe that technological evolution will ever live up to its own advertising, or that technology itself can liberate us from the problems it has created. So far, the only people who, as a group, are clear-minded on this point are the native peoples, simply because they have kept alive their roots in an older, alternative, nature-based philosophy that has proved effective for tens of thousands of years, and that has nurtured dimensions of knowledge and perception that have become opaque to us. It is the native societies, not our own, that hold the key to future survival.
>
> *(Mander, 1991: 384)*

Notes

1 Likewise, one cannot dissociate relationships between human beings from their relationships with other living beings.
2 Here I obviously do not mean to rehabilitate the idea of a *mentalité primitive* (primitive mentality) – in the words of Lucien Lévy-Bruhl (1922) – seen only in 'traditional peoples'; I refer instead to a potential shared by our entire species. To various extents all human societies partake in both modes, with more or less emphasis on death and life-oriented tendencies.
3 See the example of the indigenous Ojibwa of Canada (Navet, 2007).
4 Savage means 'of the forest' and relates to the untamed world of nature and its qualities.
5 See my chapter 'From Anthropogeography to Ethnoecology' in this volume.
6 Holy Bible (1980), Matthew 21:19.
7 A man named Rodgers boasted of having alone killed at least sixty Beothuk and claimed to be the 'greatest Indian killer on the entire island'.
8 This Latin phrase refers to a political doctrine and means 'land without a master'.
9 It was not entirely secular, as many native children were taken away from their villages – in some cases abducted – to be raised by missionaries from the coast.
10 The authorities routinely used the term until the 1960s.
11 This status effectively recognized the existence of two different forms of society in Guiana: the coastal people (Creoles, mainland French, etc.), who had been inculcated with the Western ideals of the market-based economy, and the tribal populations (Amerindians and Bushinengues), who still practised a subsistence economy based on hunting, fishing, gathering and slash-and-burn agriculture.
12 The phrase was used in a personal conversation by a departmental councillor during a visit to Camopi.
13 Amerindians are increasingly dependent on European products and especially on money, the main cause of the negative changes that have affected social relations. Mandatory schooling also requires being close to the schools, which are concentrated in a few localities.
14 I borrow this phrase from Camopi's former mayor, René Monerville.
15 The phrase 'guardians of the forest' is often used to refer to Amerindians.
16 On the situation of Amerindians in Guiana, see Navet (1991) and Navet and Panapuy (2005).
17 In France, there have been talks of rezoning spaces to turn rural areas into periurban areas, in a move reminiscent of some science fiction movies.
18 The Cree Indians form the most numerous aboriginal people in Canada. Saskatchewan is a Canadian province.
19 Note taken from a class given by Jean Malaurie at the EHESS in the 1980s.

Bibliography

Bales, Kevin (2016), *Blood and Earth: Modern Slavery Intersects with Climate Change*, New York, Spiegel and Grau.
Broswimmer, Franz J. (2002), *Ecocide: A Short History of the Mass Extinction of Species*, London, UK, and Sterling, VA, Pluto Press.
Bugnon, Roland (2007), 'L'anathème ou l'interdit dans l'Ancien Testament', 16th March, available at: www.interbible.org/interBible/decouverte/comprendre/2007/clb_070316.html (Accessed 31/10/2016).
Cherson, Adam D. C. (2009), *Ecocide: Humanity's Environmental Demons*, New York, Greencore.
Cherson, Adam D. C. (2010), *Political Ecologies: Essays in Environmental Science and Policy*, New York, Greencore.

Churchill, Ward (2002), *Struggle for the Land: Native North American Resistance to Genocide, Ecocide and Colonization*, San Francisco, City Lights.
Godin, Christian (2012), *La haine de la nature*, Seyssel, Champ Vallon.
Gore, Al (1992), *Earth in the Balance: Ecology and the Human Spirit*, Boston, MA, Houghton Mifflin.
Grinde, Donald A., and Johansen, Bruce (1991), *Exemplar of Liberty: Native America and the Evolution of Democracy*, Oakland, CA and Los Angeles, University of California Press, series UCLA American Indian Studies.
Grinde, Donald A., and Johansen, Bruce (1995), *Ecocide of Native America*, Santa Fe, NM, Clearlight.
Higgins, Polly (2010), *Eradicating Ecocide: Laws and Governance to Prevent the Destruction of Our Planet: Exposing the Corporate and Political Practices Destroying the Planet and Proposing the Laws Needed to Eradicate Ecocide*, London, Shepheard-Walwyn.
Higgins, Polly (2011), *Earth Is our Business: Changing the Rules of the Game*, London, Shepheard-Walwyn.
Holy Bible, New American Standard Bible (1980), Guelph, The Gideons International in Canada.
Huseman, Jennifer, and Short, Damien (2012), 'A Slow Industrial Genocide: Tar Sands and the Indigenous Peoples of Northern Alberta', *International Journal of Human Rights*, 16 (1): 216–237.
Latouche, Serge (2004), *Survivre au développement: de la décolonisation de l'imaginaire économique à la construction d'une société alternative*, Paris, Mille et une nuits.
Latouche, Serge (2005), *L'occidentalisation du monde: essai sur la signification, la portée et les limites de l'uniformisation planétaire*, Paris, La Découverte.
Lévy-Bruhl, Lucien (1922), *La mentalité primitive*, Paris, Presses Universitaires de France.
Mander, Jerry (1991), *In the Absence of the Sacred: The Failure of Technology and the Survival of the Indian Nations*, San Francisco, Sierra Club.
Navet, Éric (1991), *Ike min anam. Il était une fois: 'la dernière frontière' pour les peuples indiens de Guyane française*, Épinal, Nitassinan.
Navet, Éric (2007), *L'Occident barbare et la philosophie sauvage. Essai sur le mode d'être et de penser des indiens Ojibwé*, Paris, Homnisphères.
Navet, Éric, and Panapuy, Jammes (2005), 'La forêt tropicale de Guyane française et les projets de développement: problèmes écologiques et humains', *in:* Mohamed Taabni (ed.), *La forêt: enjeux comparés des formes d'appropriation, de gestion et d'exploitation dans les politiques environnementales et le contexte d'urbanisation généralisé*, Poitiers, Maison des Sciences de l'Homme et de la Société, Laboratoire ICoTEM: 283–294.
Neyret, Laurent (2015), *Des écocrimes à l'écocide: le droit pénal au secours de l'environnement*, Brussels, Bruylant.
Shaw, Carlita (2015), *The Silent Ecocide: The Environmental Crisis is a Crisis of Human Consciousness*, CreateSpace Independent Publishing Platform.
Short, Damien (2016), *Redefining Genocide: Settler Colonialism, Social Death and Ecocide*, Chicago, University of Chicago Press.
Thomas, Louis-Vincent (1980), *Anthropologie de la mort*, Paris, Payot.
Utter, Jack (2001 [1993]), *American Indians. Answers to Today's Questions*, Norman, OK, University of Oklahoma Press.
Vaillancourt, Jean-Guy, and Gendron, Corinne (eds.) (2007), *Environnement et sciences sociales, les défis de l'interdisciplinarité*, Québec, Presses de l'Université Laval.
Vignon, Robert (1985), *Gran Man Baka*, Paris, Davol.

19
ANIMAL STUDIES

Roland Borgards

Definitions: animal studies, human–animal studies, critical animal studies, cultural animal studies

Since the positivist turn of the sciences in the nineteenth century, and until the end of the twentieth century, which was dominated by the life sciences, the academic investigation of animals was reserved almost exclusively for the natural sciences. The physiology, ethology and ecology of animals were the provinces of zoologists; in addition, veterinarians and agronomists mainly concerned themselves with the efficient utilization of animal resources. Within the humanities, however, animals played a minor part at best. This was systematically grounded in the humanities' claim to address – in deliberate distinction from the natural sciences – the specific achievements of the *human* species, particularly its linguistic, artistic and cultural accomplishments. Under these conditions, a systematic and methodically conceived investigation of animals could not take place.

Over the past thirty years, this division of tasks has become less stringent. The natural sciences may still be seen as intrinsically authorized and competent, especially where public awareness is concerned. Yet with the advent of animal studies, a new branch of scholarship has established itself, offering an alternative to the traditional natural sciences that is well grounded in theory and committed to 'rethinking animals'. The autonomy of this approach is currently showing itself in its incipient institutionalization, for example, in networks such as 'Minding Animals', operating worldwide with a broad interdisciplinary range and having a political agenda, or the 'Australasian Animal Studies Association', founded in 2005 and publishing their *Animal Studies Journal* since 2012; in research centres like the Institute for Critical Animal Studies, located in New York and focusing on questions of animal justice and animal politics, or the 'British Animal Studies Network', concentrating on the humanities and the social sciences; in study programmes such as the Interdisciplinary Master in Human-Animal Interactions at the Vienna Messerli Institute; and in a number of pertinent handbooks (for instance, Marvin and McHugh, 2014; Borgards, 2015) and journals like *Humanimalia* (since 2009), which assembles contributions especially from the humanities (history, literature, philosophy, etc.), or the *Journal of Critical Animal Studies* (since 2003), which mostly shares the strand of arguments of the animal liberation movement.

An important historical starting point for animal studies can be found in the ecological movements of the 1970s. In this respect, they build up – even today – on a critique of technological rationality, a mindframe that might be useful to humanity at times, yet often perilous to Planet Earth with its flora and fauna. Proceeding from this insight, it became necessary to develop a new attitude towards Nature in general and the animals in particular – both on a practical and political and on a theoretical and scientific level, not keeping theory and practice separate, but mutually reflecting them.

An important theoretical point of departure for animal studies is the insight that it is not a given what an animal is; which, in turn, begs the question 'Who can even know what an animal is?' Animal studies do not see this twofold uncertainty as a problem, but as a useful challenge, responding with a far-reaching disciplinary pluralism. Naturally, the traditional animal sciences are not excluded; they do, however, lose their guiding function. Hence, animal studies are not only interdisciplinary, but also transfaculty, integrating the humanities and cultural studies, the natural and social sciences, jurisprudence and agronomics. Almost any and all disciplines are assembled in animal studies, including philosophy, sociology, political science, ethnology, theology, psychology, zoology, ethology, ecology, archaeology, geography, climatology, botany, jurisprudence, history, classical and literary studies, musicology, theatre and dance science, media and film studies and art history.

Accordingly, animal studies do not work with a homogeneous but with a multiply differentiated research design. As this approach sometimes leads towards the limits of the practically feasible, several varieties have established themselves by now, pursuing their particular focal interests under the general heading of animal studies. First and foremost, they are critical animal studies, human–animal studies and cultural animal studies.

Critical animal studies (Taylor and Twine, 2014) operate on three levels. First, they provide a philosophical analysis of the implicit and explicit animal cruelty of the Western tradition of thought, from Aristotle's anthropocentrism via Descartes' dualism to Heidegger's humanism. Second, they aim at a historical and sociological analysis of the wrongs and the injustice done to animals in the past and today, from the hunt in protohistoric times to current methods of factory farming. And third and last, they demand practical acts of resistance to any form of animal abuse and the shift towards alternative, animal-friendly lifestyles (e.g. vegetarianism or veganism).

Human–animal studies (Marvin and McHugh, 2014) concentrate on the relationship between animals and humans, not on the animals themselves. This is based on an epistemological rationale: in their uniqueness and otherness, animals remain fundamentally inaccessible to humans, but what is accessible is the relationship that humans enter into with animals. The object of human–animal studies therefore is not simply the butterfly, but its taxonomical classification by the zoologist; not the rat, but its experimentalization in the laboratories of the pharmaceutical companies; not the bonobos, but their study by ethologists or their breeding in zoos, etc. Like critical animal studies, human–animal studies also derive practical consequences from their fundamental epistemological considerations: what may be changed is the relationship that humans take up with animals.

Cultural animal studies share the fundamental epistemological assumptions of all disciplines in cultural studies, namely that all forms of knowledge are connected to cultural practices and that every object humans relate to becomes a cultural object through this very relationship alone. In this sense, 'culture' refers to the manner in which humans make the world accessible to themselves, practically and scientifically. 'Cultural animals', then, are not only farm animals and pets, as distinct from wild animals, but rather all animals in their respective relationship to human culture. This relationship can be very close, as in the case of the dog as the accompanying animal of human culture; but it can also be quite distant, as with the eyeless species of spider, *Sinopoda scurion*, which was only discovered in the Laotian province of Khammuan in 2012. From the perspective of cultural animal studies, this is a quantitative but not a qualitative difference, because friendship and undiscoveredness are relationship determiners of equal value.

Although belonging among the general cultural studies, those working in cultural animal studies nevertheless also see themselves as making a methodological challenge to the fundamental assumptions of cultural studies. For looking at animals makes discernible the implicit anthropocentrism that influences cultural studies in many ways. In classic cultural studies analyses, animals frequently appear as mere objects and projection screens for human action, but rarely as entities in their own right. This creates a remarkable tension between the implicit anthropocentrism of cultural studies, on the one hand, and the explicit decentring of the human being in animal studies, on the other hand. This tension may be made methodologically profitable by differentiating between an epistemological anthropocentrism that perceives the human being as the inevitable origin of knowledge and an ontological anthropocentrism which untenably sets up the human being as the destination point of the universe (Tyler, 2012).

Between critical animal studies, human–animal studies and cultural animal studies, there are many and varied overlaps, both in terms of their proponents and in the methods they use. In their research history, a vague sequence may be traced: a beginning was made with critical animal studies with centres in New Zealand and Canada; then human–animal studies established themselves, particularly in America and the UK; and finally, cultural animal studies appeared on the scene, proceeding from the European theory formations of poststructuralism and new materialism. Yet despite their shared basic views, there are considerable differences as well. Critical animal studies, for instance, sometimes accuse cultural animal studies of only being interested in coldly rational analysis, but not in warm-hearted interrelation with animals, which, as a last consequence, leads to an affirmation of their inferior social status quo (Best, 2009). In turn, cultural animal studies sometimes accuse critical animal studies of being blind to the implicit anthropocentrism of their own position, which, as a last consequence, leads to an affirmation of the very power relationships they are trying to combat (Plumwood, 2012).

Theories of cultural animal studies: Foucault, Agamben, Deleuze/Guattari, Derrida, Haraway, Latour

Cultural animal studies work with a great variety of animal-theoretical positions. In recent years, six theories in particular have proven inspirational and fruitful: the historical discourse analysis of Michel Foucault, the concept of the anthropological machine of Giorgio Agamben, the becoming-animal paradigm of Gilles Deleuze and Félix Guattari, Jacques Derrida's *animot*/animalword, Donna Haraway's companion species and the political ecology of Bruno Latour.

For Foucault, animals are, first of all, only one possible object among many that historical discourse analysis might look at. As such, Foucault does not formulate an explicit animal theory. And yet, Foucault's approach has been received intensely in cultural animal studies. The reasons for this are methodological. For insofar as Foucault's central interest is in the productive correlations between power, knowledge and subject, he addresses three important issues of animal studies: the power that determines the relations between humans and animals, the knowledge of the animals that is always permeated and shaped historically and culturally and the human subject trying to constitute itself by investigating the animal. So, for instance, an analysis of the history of animal experimentation, which is based on the writings of Foucault, can show the historically changing discourses and practices and their impact on the history of the subject and the scientific truth (Guerrini, 2003).

Foucault's concept of biopower, and respectively biopolitics, is highly compatible with cultural animal studies as well. Essentially, it revolves around the historical transformation of classic natural history into modern biology that dates back to the decades around the 1800s (Foucault, 1966), and its paradoxical effect that humans become the objects of political actions precisely because they are animal entities (Foucault, 1976). Proceeding from Foucault's analyses, a distinct research context has emerged by now, primarily investigating animals in the history of the sciences and the history of political theory. This provides new insights, for example, into the history of animal welfare, into the changing concepts of farming and breeding and into the transformations of political animal metaphors like the wolf-like man, as conceptualized in the political theory of Thomas Hobbes.

With his concept of the 'anthropological machine', Agamben picks up on Foucault's thesis of biopolitics, expanding and generalizing it. For Agamben, biopolitics is no specifically modern phenomenon; rather, every type of politics since antiquity has always been biopolitics (Agamben, 2004). At the heart of biopolitics as understood in this way lies the act of differentiating between human and animal: wherever this differentiation is performed, the anthropological machine is set in motion and the space of the political is opened up. Cultural animal studies have, above all, profited from Agamben's observation that the boundary between human and animal is neither given nor natural, but must always be laboriously produced and artificially maintained. Therefore, not only the human–animal boundary must be subjected to examination, but also the practical and theoretical procedures of its production. Wherever this occurs, it will become visible that between human and animal, there only *seems* to be a clear boundary; in reality, it is an indeterminate 'threshold' or 'zone', in which the human and the animal intermingle.

From an animal-theory perspective, Agamben may be criticized for his critical analysis of the anthropological machine, only focusing on the effects of this machine on humans. The impact that animals have to bear hardly interests him. Yet he – as opposed to Foucault – proposes an explicit animal theory. He has been widely received in animal studies, especially in work on the historically different versions of the anthropological machine. The aim of studies orientated by Agamben is almost always to prove the culturally 'made' character and the systematic uncertainty of the human–animal boundary. Especially in literary scholarship, Agamben's arguments have been used to point out the specific predispositions of literary texts to unsettle the anthropological difference, for example, by performing queer hybridizations between the human and the animal, as in Franz Kafka's famous novella *The Metamorphosis* (German *Die Verwandlung*, 1915), where a man awakes as an insect.

A particularly efficacious theory metaphor has been provided by Deleuze and Guattari (1993): becoming-animal. Becoming-animal may be seen as the opposite of the anthropological machine: whereas the anthropological machine produces and stabilizes the difference between human and animal, in becoming-animal an uncertainty enters into the anthropological difference. Deleuze and Guattari do not mean this in any concrete mimetic sense. Becoming-animal is not about a human being becoming similar to an animal, and it is even less about emphasizing the animal in oneself; and finally, it has nothing to do with taking up a compassionate or merely friendly relationship to an animal. All of this makes becoming-animal a model that is largely unsuitable to critical animal studies.

Deleuze and Guattari use the term 'animal' in an obviously metaphorical and strategic way: by talking about 'human becoming animal' they disturb the traditional concept of the anthropological difference. In this sense, 'becoming-animal' means to cease being a subject as conceptualized by the metaphysical tradition from Aristotle to Kant and Heidegger. In the process of 'becoming-animal', the human being is no longer autonomous, self-sufficient, self-aware and self-identical, but fundamentally heteronomous: it is constitutively influenced by other living and nonliving entities; it is dependent on these conditions; it is driven by nonrational corporeal motivations, and it is split into a diversity of different aspects. Above all, becoming-animal is a way to philosophically deconstruct the concept of the subject.

Deleuze and Guattari may actually speak of the significance of becoming-animal for humans; what this might mean for the animals is of no interest to them. With Deleuze and Guattari, becoming-animal is an element of a poststructuralist subject theory; it is not part of a thoroughly formulated animal theory. And yet, insofar as becoming-animal is to be understood as a subversion of the Western (in particular modern age) subject, cultural animal studies can do much with it. The reception of the concept in cultural animal studies becomes questionable when it is used to describe the rapprochement processes of humans towards animals. Nevertheless, it can still be helpful here, even if it is only to make the aporias and impossibilities of such a rapprochement stand out more sharply.

Foucault, Agamben and Deleuze and Guattari ask the question of what humans do with animals and what this means for humans. Derrida, however, does not begin with the actions of humans, but with the action of an animal: with the gaze of his cat, coming upon him as he is standing naked in his bathroom (Derrida, 2006). If one wants to have philosophy begin in this way, not with humans but with animals, then, according to Derrida, one must first of all succeed in recognizing and accepting the animal gaze. For Derrida, this decides all philosophy. If it denies and rejects the animal gaze, then it will remain within the conventional framework of classical metaphysics. If it recognizes the animal gaze, then it can lead to a revision of the entire conceptual field that has formed around an assumed opposition of human and animal that is as firmly established as it is questionable. It is of decisive importance for this ethical and political redefinition of the human–animal relation to understand animals as plural. There is nothing like the *one* animal, there are only *the* animals. And if there are only *the* animals but not the *one* animal, then between humans (plural) and animals (plural) there may be found not only the *one* single boundary, but *many* boundary lines (plural). This pluralization of the boundaries between humans and animals leads Derrida to introduce the efficacious term 'limitrophy', the proliferation of boundaries.

Derrida's insistence on the plural and the attention consequently given to limitrophical dynamics have been received in cultural animal studies especially widely. The reason for this is that Derrida's theory allows two different but related elements of the human–animal relation. On the one hand, Derrida pinpoints the philosophical and discursive foundation of the cruelty against animals which is common in Western culture: if you want to understand how humans deal with animals, you have to analyse first how they think about animals and how they understand themselves in and through their relations to animals. On the other hand, Derrida reveals the underlying contradictions in the Western conception of the animal as a passive, speechless being: if you look closely at how philosophers from Aristotle to Levinas talk about animals, you can see that animals have been always and everywhere at the core of philosophy itself. Acknowledging the fact that an animal may look at you – in the full sense of the term 'looking': that's where philosophy begins.

As justified as the deconstruction of the metaphysical human–animal schematics may be, from the perspective of Haraway, Derrida arrives at the wrong conclusions (Haraway, 2008). Whereas Derrida understands the animal gaze merely as a prompt to move his body back to his desk and to direct his mind towards Western philosophy with its forgetfulness of animals, Haraway voices a demand to understand such animal gazes as an invitation to joint action. Haraway perceives this human–animal action as a 'becoming-with', in which animals are no longer the passive objects of human action, but active companions of humanity, 'companion species'.

On the one hand, the concept of the companion species is a descriptive category: the lives of humans and animals are, in fact, interlinked in many ways. On the other hand, Haraway also formulates utopia: the intermingling of humans and animals constitutes a model of a future, better life. Cultural animal studies have taken up both elements, the descriptive and the utopian one. In both cases, the materiality of the human–animal relation plays an important role, especially where a critical distancing from the text-oriented approaches of discourse analysis and of deconstruction is involved. Whereas discourse analysis and deconstruction primarily perceive animals as semiotic entities, as sign animals, Haraway's approach makes it possible to integrate their physical materiality into the analysis. Animals are neither mere signs, nor pure matter. They are 'material-semiotic nodes or knots in which diverse bodies and meanings coshape one another' (Haraway, 2008: 4). A real dog is always an animal with a material body; but at the same time, it is always shaped by and linked with a whole set of meanings, concepts and conventions. A literary dog is always an animal with a semiotic meaning; but at the same time, it is always shaped by and linked with the corporeal and material dogs, which lived as companions with humans. In this sense, animals are paradigmatic objects of study for new materialism.

As with the broader field of environmental humanities, new materialism is currently emerging as a guiding theory in the more closely circumscribed area of cultural animal studies. Most influential in this process is actor-network theory (ANT), cofounded by Latour (2007). In ANT, animals at first have no special position. They are, as in Foucault, one possible object of study among many others. This also has methodological reasons. For ANT is not interested in inverting the old hierarchies (human/animal, culture/nature) and, in doing so, unintentionally affirming them. Instead, its goal is to not let them become effective in the first place. It is not the attempt to overcome the old hierarchies and oppositions, but the attempt to sketch an analysis without them.

Nevertheless, ANT is intensively used as a methodological and theoretical basis in cultural animal studies. For in networks, animals are effective as agents, in quite the same way as humans, devices, concepts or texts. With Latour, animals are agents of a politics of Nature. Like Haraway's 'companion species', Latour's concept of 'political ecology' (Latour, 1999) also is both a critical descriptive category and a utopian project: this is the factual constitution of the world – and this constitution should also be recognized as such. So in fact, animals, too, are agents, and only if you are willing to recognize them as agents, you can – on a theoretical level – give a suitable interpretation of their place on Earth and – on a practical level – render them the justice they deserve.

In their reception of Latour, cultural animal studies have integrated both tendencies as well. Certain cultural animal practices (e.g. zoos, laboratories, breeding) may be grasped descriptively as networks that are unthinkable without animal agents. And the recognition of this agent status for animals could lead to a future political ecology.

Cultural animal studies distinguish themselves by connecting these theoretical propositions in many and varied ways, also drawing on other theoretical options, such as critical theory understanding the animal as one possible paradigm of the oppressed and the powerless (Horkheimer and Adorno, 1984), alterity theory taking the animal as opportunity to theorizing otherness (Levinas, 1963), ethnography dealing with the extreme cultural differences in the conceptions of animals (Descola, 2005) or Berger's canonical essay 'Why Look at Animals?' sketching the changing attitudes to animals in European history from its beginnings to the present times (Berger, 1980).

Work fields: philosophy, history, the arts

The claim to knowledge which drives cultural animal studies is universalist: animals are in play everywhere, and therefore everything can be investigated from a cultural animal studies perspective. In a first approach, animals often have a diagnostic value in this. For their way of dealing with animals characterizes individual institutions (e.g. the entertainment industry or the sciences), specific forms of society (e.g. the capitalism of Europeans or the totemism of the aborigines) or certain worldviews (e.g. Western or Eastern thought). At the same time, it must be examined what this does to the animals in each case: the entertainment industry, capitalism, Eastern thought. Cultural animal studies thus have a double aim: starting from the animals, they want to say something about the cultures; and starting from the cultures, they want to say something about the animals.

Given their universalist claim to knowledge, cultural animal studies have the same importance for all disciplines of the humanities and of cultural studies, and thus for film, media and image studies as well (Lippit, 2000; Parikka, 2010; Aloi, 2011). Yet in particular, there are three work fields in which research has intensified over the past years: philosophy, history and the arts. Philosophy, ever since its historical beginnings in antiquity, has always dealt with questions regarding animals. Three problem areas can be identified here: animal ethics (what are we allowed to do to animals?), anthropological difference (how are humans and animals different?) and animal mind (how do animals think?). Today, these problem areas are being discussed anew within the new theory spectrum of animal studies (Palmer, 2006; Calarco, 2007; Wild, 2010).

In contrast to philosophy, historical scholarship has only begun a systematic investigation of the animals of history in the course of what has been called the 'animal turn' (Weil, 2010). Thematically obvious research areas initially were classic institutions such as the hunt, the zoological sciences, animal experimentation and animal protection, zoos and circuses, etc. Yet what is more important for historical scholarship than this thematic discovery of animals is that in the process of the animal turn, it also revised its methodology. As a consequence, the question of which animals had their appearances at which moment in history has been expanded into the question of how familiar historical processes (epoch-changing events, revolutions, mentalities, etc.) may be described from an animal-history perspective. One instance of an area described from this fresh perspective is the history of European imperialism and colonialism.

Similarly to this shift in historical scholarship, in literary studies animals have only advanced to become a research area in their own right, often under the headings of 'literary animal studies' or 'cultural literary animal studies' (CLAS), in the course of the animal turn. Objects of study are, on the one hand, canonical animal texts like E.T.A. Hoffmann's *Kater Murr* or Herman Melville's *Moby-Dick* and, on the other hand, the work of authors who treat animals with a particular intensity, for example, Franz Kafka or J. M. Coetzee, or authors who, next to their literary works, also conducted zoological or scientific research, for example, Johann Wolfgang Goethe or Georg Büchner. Yet cultural literary animal studies only offer a truly new approach when they inherently question the status of animals in literature. What does it mean for the established categories of literary criticism (author, period, narrator, genre, fable, novella, etc.) when they are examined with the animals as a starting point? In what way do literary texts appear as media of the representation and reflection of historical and present-day animal situations? And to what extent is literature itself a part of the animal lifeworld, or, as Latour has it, an element of the political ecology in which animals live?

These recent tendencies in historical scholarship and literary studies show that animals are more than just a new field of study. They steer us into a fundamental reflection on our own academic methods and theories. Only when this happens can we justly and truthfully speak of an 'animal turn': as a turning towards the animals that previously were neglected as objects of research, and as a turning back from the animals to our own positions, which must be rethought from the direction of the animals (Weil, 2010). 'Rethinking animals', then, not only means 'rethinking the human', but simultaneously 'rethinking the humanities'.

Because of this, animal studies belong to the field of environmental humanities and their project of 'rethinking Nature'. Insofar as animals always live in specific environments, animal studies are obliged to include the perspectives and methods of the environmental humanities. And insofar as environments are always populated by specific animals, the environmental humanities have to be complemented by the insights of animal studies. And yet, there also exists a specific tension between animal studies and environmental humanities, in that animal studies mostly concentrate on individual species or even individual animals, whereas environmental humanities tend to operate more within the overall ecological context (Plumwood, 2012). This tension gets obvious, for example, in the different aims of animal ethics and environmental ethics. Animal ethics tends to protect the individual animal: you may not kill, torture or abuse this chicken or that bonobo. Environmental ethics, in contrast, tends to protect not the individual living being, but broader ecological systems: to save a specific ecosystem (e.g. the ecosystem of the island of Juan Fernandez), it can be necessary to kill a lot of animals (e.g. masses of hares and goats). Not to dissolve this confliction between these both methodological perspectives, between animal studies and environmental humanities, but to make it grow productive in concrete analyses, must be the goal of future research.

Bibliography

Agamben, Giorgio (2004 [2002]), *The Open: Man and Animal*, Stanford, CA, Stanford University Press.
Aloi, Giovanni (2011), *Art and Animals*, London, Tauris.
Berger, John (1980), 'Why Look at Animals', *in:* Berger, John (ed.), *About Looking*, New York, Pantheon Books: 1–26.
Best, Steven (2009), 'The Rise of Critical Animal Studies: Putting Theory into Action and Animal Liberation into Higher Education', *Journal for Critical Animal Studies*, 7 (1): 9–52.
Borgards, Roland (ed.) (2015), *Tiere. Ein kulturwissenschaftliches Handbuch*, Stuttgart, Metzler.
Calarco, Matthew (2007), 'Animals in Continental Philosophy', *H-animal*, available at: https://networks.h-net.org/node/16560/pages/32233/animals-continental-philosophy-matthew-calarco (Accessed 31/10/2016).
Deleuze, Gilles, and Guattari, Félix (1980), *Mille plateaux*, Paris, Minuit, translated into English (1993) as *A Thousand Plateaus*, Minneapolis, University of Minnesota Press.
Derrida, Jacques (2006), *L'animal que donc je suis*, Paris, Gallimard.
Descola, Philippe (2005), *Par-delà nature et culture*, Paris, Gallimard, translated into English by Janet Lloyd (2013) as *Beyond Nature and Culture*, Chicago, University of Chicago Press.
Foucault, Michel (1966), *Les mots et les choses. Une archéologie des sciences humaines*, Paris, Gallimard, translated into English (1970) as *The Order of Things: An Archaeology of the Human Sciences*, New York, Pantheon Books.
Foucault, Michel (1976), *La volonté de savoir*, vol. 1 in the series *Histoire de la sexualité*, Paris, Gallimard.
Guerrini, Anita (2003), *Experimenting with Humans and Animals: From Galen to Animal Rights*, Baltimore and London, Johns Hopkins University Press.
Haraway, Donna (2008), *When Species Meet: Posthumanities*, Minneapolis, University of Minnesota Press.
Horkheimer, Max, and Adorno, Theodor W. (1984 [1947]), *Dialektik der Aufklärung. Philosophische Fragmente. Gesammelte Schriften*, vol. 3, Frankfurt am Main, Suhrkamp, edited by Rolf Tiedemann.
Latour, Bruno (1999), *Politiques de la nature. Comment faire entrer les sciences en démocratie*, Paris, Gallimard, translated into English (2004) as *Politics of Nature: How to Bring the Sciences into Democracy*, Cambridge, MA, Harvard University Press.
Latour, Bruno (2007), *Reassembling the Social: An Introduction to Actor-Network-Theory*, Oxford, Oxford University Press.
Levinas, Emmanuel (1963), 'Nom d'un chien ou le droit naturel', *in:* Levinas, Emmanuel (ed.), *Difficile liberté. Essais sur le judaïsme*, Paris, Albin Michel: 199–202.

Lippit, Akira Mizuta (2000), *Electric Animal: Toward a Rhetoric of Wildlife*, Minneapolis, University of Minnesota Press.
Marvin, Gary, and McHugh, Susan (2014), *Routledge Handbook of Human–Animal Studies*, London and New York, Routledge.
Palmer, Clare (2006), 'Animals in Anglo-American Philosophy', *H-animal*, 18 December, available at: https://networks.h-net.org/node/16560/pages/32232/animals-anglo-american-philosophy-clare-palmer (Accessed 31/10/2016).
Parikka, Jussi (2010), *Insect Media: An Archeology of Animals and Technology*, Minneapolis, University of Minnesota Press.
Plumwood, Val (2012), 'Animals and Ecology. Towards a Better Integration', *in:* Plumwood, Val (ed.), *The Eye of the Crocodile*, Canberra, ANU Press: 77–90.
Taylor, Nuk, and Twine, Richard (eds.) (2014), *The Rise of Critical Animal Studies: From the Margins to the Centre*, London and New York, Routledge.
Tyler, Tom (2012), *Ciferae: A Bestiary in Five Fingers*, Minneapolis, University of Minnesota Press.
Weil, Kari (2010), 'A Report on the Animal Turn', *Differences*, 2: 1–23.
Wild, Markus (2010), *Tierphilosophie zur Einführung*, Hamburg, Junius.

20
CONSTRUCTING AN *ANIMAL* HISTORY

Éric Baratay

Since social sciences, from America to Europe, have become interested in animals, their focus has been almost exclusively directed on the human side of the question, dealing with human uses, actions and especially representations, in line with the ever-growing popularity of cultural readings since the 1980s. After years of such practice, as a historian working on the history of the relationships between humans and animals, I have been led to think that these approaches are often too limited because they have established and maintained a gaping black hole at the centre of their discourse: animals are never considered beings endowed with feelings or the capacity to act and react. Studies say much about humans but very little about animals, which are simply absent or transformed into mere pretexts, mere objects on which humans' representations, knowledge and practice come to bear.

Looking at real animals

It is necessary to discard this approach, which is largely reliant on Western cultural conceptions, and which offers a sadly reductive view of the dialectical interaction between humans and animals, limiting it to a one-way relationship (from humans to animals) and overlooking or pushing aside a great deal of its reality and complexity. It is essential to investigate the influence of animals in their relationship to humans, their active role, at a time when ethology is increasingly insisting on the behaviour of animals as active beings, individuals or even persons (even if only certain species are considered, their number is steadily rising), on their cognitive capacities, on their group behaviour and culture, so that purely human approaches are now found wanting. Moreover, source material shows if one does not reject this aspect as anecdotal, that humans have seen, guessed and appraised the actions of animals and that they have responded, acted and thought accordingly.

Social sciences started to conceive of animals as active beings in the late 1980s, in the wake of a general positive reappraisal of the notion of action (Ingold, 1988; Haraway, 1991). Yet one has to admit that, other than such reflexions, truly innovative work is still scant (Shapiro, 1990; Sanders, 1999; Goode, 2007; Vicart, 2014). The last authors mentioned also chose to position themselves at an equal distance from animals and humans to evaluate their interactions.

In my work, I have tried to view things exclusively from the side of animals to gain a *greater* understanding (saying a better one would depreciate existing studies) of situations which are always more complex than one initially thinks. My aim is first to gain a *greater* understanding of these active beings who deserve to be studied for themselves, for their lived experience (their physiological, psychological and behavioural ways of experiencing conditions, circumstances and events), by positing that they – at least the species under study – are complete and complex active beings, who even act as specific individuals. As a result, I hope to gain a *greater* understanding of their relationships with humans.

Recently, philosophy has started to tackle this 'animal side' of the question (Bailly, 2011), and ethologists have raised the question of point of view (Bräuer, 2014; Udell *et al.*, 2014), but effective studies are scarce (Kohler, 2012). Taking the side of animals means standing next to them and trying to adopt their geographical perspective, to understand what they experience and undergo, the way they act and react; it also means trying to project oneself into their minds in order to grasp their psychological point of view, what they see and feel. It can, of course, only be an intention, an attempt at self-projection, a method, as used by naturalists, hunters, taxidermists or ethologists, but it leads to a decentring of the self and may yield many positive returns, as ethnologists have for a long time experienced.

All this means that it is necessary to expand our current definition of history – 'the science of men in time' – still favoured by many historians, where there is nothing sacred about it, as it is a historical construct. The definition of history must now once again be broadened, becoming the science of living beings in time and directing its attention to their evolutions, at least where there is a historical record enabling the historians to do their job and make use of their skills.

At the same time, it is necessary to go beyond, if not to discard, the cultural approach which tends to reduce social sciences to the task of deconstructing discourses in order to bring out underlying representations, as if they were the only reality that could be studied. This is a necessary task, but the triumph of cultural interpretations has transformed this indispensable preliminary investigation into the ultimate goal. We must go back to the study of reality, using the concept of 'situated knowledges' (Haraway, 1991) which helps to construct knowledge without ignoring the context of its elaboration; we must apply it to the various people who use, approach and watch animals and describe them through a combination of observations and representations, which means that we must take into account the conditions of production of their texts, working with partial and biased information that will have been 'situated', criticized, connected together, and thus controlled, revised and completed, allowing us to gain access to the reality of things.

We must also leave aside the Western, historically constructed conception of animals as passive and replace it with the idea that animals are endowed with the capacity to feel, to react, to adapt, or even posit that animals are not only able to influence humans through their actions or that animal agency enables them to construct relationships with humans, to use the current fashionable Anglo-Saxon concept of 'agency' (*History and Theory*, 2013), but that animals are individuals, with specific characteristics, persons even, with distinctive behaviour, or even subjects. Such ideas are no longer taboo (Miklosi *et al.*, 2014) and must be tested in the field, leaving definitions open enough. It is indeed dangerous to start with (too) well-defined concepts and try to verify their relevance, because the risk is then to adopt a familiar, human-centred or even European-centred and time-specific version of them, and thus to run into the pitfalls of ethnocentrism and anthropocentrism. We must keep in mind that our concepts are situated: in time, as historians show; in space, as ethnologists demonstrate (Descola, 2005); and in the world of living beings, as ethologists are starting to point out.

Testing strong concepts does not mean falling into the trap of anthropomorphism, just as leaving some openness and variability to these investigative tools does not mean indulging in some kind of blurry impressionism. This open, wondering, questioning form of anthropomorphism allows us to look at things with open-minded curiosity and to raise strong questions, to test strong concepts, without necessarily imposing human-derived notions on animals and denying their specificities. It also grants more potentialities to animals, which are still so little known. It allows us to see in what diverse ways some faculties can be actualized, and thus to adopt extended definitions of these faculties. Whereas physical capacities have already been admitted such latitude of definition (we know that many species do not see the world as we do, but we do not deduce from this that they cannot see), there is greater reluctance concerning mental capacities because they are usually considered proof of our superiority.

The goal is not to confuse all living beings together, but to get a sense of their diversity and richness, which means that we have to give up the vain, artificial, puerile and wrong dualistic opposition of humans/animals that philosophy and religion have been forcing upon us for 2,500 years. It is vain, because it opposes a concrete species, humankind, to a concept, animals, which does not exist in the exterior world, which is only a category masking the reality of multiple species, all very different from each other. Puerile, because enhancing the difference between a reality and a concept has never enabled humans to know animals better, but only to take pride in their own superiority. Wrong, because animals are still very little known (and often there is little desire to get to know them and a temptation to prefer convenient stereotypes over real knowledge) and differences are predicted on mere preconceptions. Anthropocentrism must also be discarded, because it leads to human-derived definitions and to a refusal to look at things from the side of animals, thus foreclosing all investigation.

Still, in order to build an *animal* history, other sciences must be marshalled next to history: ecology, which can study the environment and its influence on behaviour, and ethology, which can interpret animal behaviour. This dialogue with the sciences of nature should not seem any more distasteful than that initiated by historians with economy, demography or sociology from the mid-twentieth century on; it merely represents a new stage in history's opening to other sciences and cannot be repudiated or considered illegitimate because it concerns other sciences than social sciences. Such a position would boil down to clinging to a restrictive, human-centred definition of history and to imitating those early twentieth-century historians who rejected the alliance between history and social science because they believed history could only be political.

It is necessary to link together history and ethology when working on the available documents. It may seem paradoxical to use such human-created documents to reconstruct the actions of animals, all the more so as they may seem unreliable, biased and incomplete, because these documents only focus on a few species, races or individuals and only on a few aspects, whose reality was not entirely recorded either at the time, the authors only recording what they could and what they desired to see, reading and distorting reality through the prism of their imagination, self-interest and preconceptions specific to a particular species, time and place. Still, such problems also abound in human history, and historians often have to resort to intermediaries: for instance, most records about peasantry were elaborated by members of the social elite, but they can still be used to write rural history. In our case, the problem is indeed greater, but not radically different. And, even today, animals can only speak through humans, their writings, photographs or films.

All available sources must be studied. Which does not mean that there should be no sorting. The people who did the recording must have been interested in animals' real actions, must have watched and transcribed them without their subjectivity totally obliterating their meaning. The texts may, of course, vary in their degree of observation or precision, and they should be confronted with today's most fruitful ethological hypotheses. The goal is not to use ethological theories as validation, because this could lead to repudiating or to distorting the texts to make them fit the theories, but to read together different situated observations and knowledge: those of contemporary observers, who may have missed certain aspects but just as well have seen what today's observers cannot see or do not want to see, and those of today's naturalists, who may know more and in a better way than in the past, but may just as well neglect certain sides of the question. Past observations should not be rejected or considered useless anecdotes, as laboratory ethology assumed for a long time, but treated as data collected on a field of observation situated in the past, in the same way as psychologists and cognitive ethologists are now dealing with contemporary stories and anecdotes (Bates and Byrnes, 2007).

Finally, placing oneself on the side of animals means standing next to them, showing empathy so as not to deny them anything prematurely but in order to adopt their geographical point of view, to understand what they experience, undergo, how they act and react; it also means trying to project oneself into them in order to detect their psychological point of view, what they see and feel. Once all these goals have been set – knowing that they will be more or less difficult to reach depending on the animals under study – what kind of *animal* history can we try to build?

History as lived by animals

The simplest kind of history records animals' enlistment in great human historical phenomena, because documents are aplenty and it is possible to understand the way animals experienced these phenomena in their mind and in their flesh. Let me refer to what I tried to do (Baratay, 2012a) concerning the period of the nineteenth to the twenty-first centuries, when animals were widely used, rather well observed and listened to in order to be made more productive and widely written about. It is thus possible to gain access to the experience of pit horses, placed at the heart of the Industrial 'Revolution'. The same is true of dairy cows, who found themselves at the heart of the agricultural 'revolution'.

Let us also mention the case of the animals that participated in the First World War that I studied in depth and expanded to an international scale in another book (Baratay, 2013) in order to present the role played by ethology when it engages in dialogue with history and what history can contribute to the dialogue. Thanks to ethological knowledge, it is possible to better understand and interpret historical accounts, for instance, to conclude, when reading vets' records of requisitions in Europe or sales in America, that horses suffered indeed from stress, and so to better analyze and use witness accounts. Ethology can also reveal things that were still unknown at the time and led to misinterpretations or neglect on the part of the soldiers, and so help grasp the causes of the misunderstanding between horses and soldiers: for instance, horses refused to get into railroad cars, so much so that several men, up to seven or eight, had to force them into them, but this refusal was only due to their high degree of panoramic vision, leading them to believe that they were being rushed forward towards an obstacle, their optical field remaining empty otherwise. Or again, the high death rate of horses in the summer of 1914 was due to quick dehydration caused by hard labour and heat, but this form of dehydration did not provoke a thirst strong enough to serve as a warning and so did not lead horses to express this need to human beings.

Conversely, history provides ethology with data which can help it distance itself from present-day animal situations: for instance, it can point to the differences in the behaviour of the still wild horses of the American or Argentinian plains and domesticated European horses, or show how difficult it was to train dogs taken from kennels, which had not been abandoned by their masters but were wandering dogs, reluctant to cooperate, contrary to what today's ethologists state when studying present-day pet dogs, which they transform into universal, ahistorical, 'natural' dogs. Or it can reveal that travelling pigeons were not able to fly by night because they had not been trained to use their magnetic compass in that way, which seems to show that this is not an innate but an acquired skill, contrary to what today's ethologists maintain.

These approaches and methods make it indeed possible to build a new form of history, far removed from human versions of events, which does not emphasize the same points, helps to better see and understand animals' interactions with humans, grasp them in their complexity and historical context and get a sense of the important role of individual and group factors in the animal world.

Animal biographies

The importance of individual factors must encourage us to build a second type of history, centred on individuals, through the composition of animal biographies. Writers have long entertained the desire to tell the story of an animal from its own point of view, as the Comtesse de Ségur experimented in *Mr Cadichon, Memoirs of a Donkey*, but this endeavour has often reached an anthropomorphic dead end. Aware of the danger, the few professional or amateur historians who have recently attempted to deal with the life of famous animals have preferred to tackle the subject from the human angle, by focusing on the intellectual, political, social or artistic upheaval these animals caused. Historians should, however, come to grips with the problem and try to account for the experience and feelings of an animal at a specific moment or during its whole life.

Because the question of the available records is of prime importance in history, famous animals provide the easiest cases to study as they were the object of many accounts, whereas there are none at all about anonymous animals. I am thus working on a few animal biographies, one of which, for example, will focus on the journey of a giraffe in France in 1827. The journey was documented through the judicious accounts of naturalists, recording the arrival of the giraffe in Marseilles and its walk to Paris. It drew crowds because it was the first time a living giraffe had come to France, and it raised as much curiosity, imagination and passions as would an alien landing on earth today. Yet it was no stuffed animal that people came to see, but a living being whose actions and reactions played a crucial part in shaping the event – the encounter between a European population and an exotic animal, in which both parties discovered each other and reacted in their own way, forming an interacting couple which must be analyzed from the point of view of each of the parties.

Let me here only mention the main aspects concerning the animal. First, the animal was in great stress, as can be deduced from its stereotyped movements in successive stables, the absence of deep sleep, which giraffes normally reach when lying in a particular position, which would have been recorded by the naturalists if the giraffe had adopted it and from the fact that, while awake, it was afflicted by fragmented bouts of somnolence. This stress varied according to time and place. It reached its peak when the giraffe arrived by night in Marseilles and refused to walk through the dark gate and the narrow streets, when it reached Aix and heard people yelling at the windows of their houses, when it was scared off by the crowds in Lyons and ran away and when it was presented to the king in Saint-Cloud and to thousands of Parisians in the Jardin des Plantes. The giraffe also felt stress when in Marseilles it was handled by naturalists, who wanted to study its anatomy, when it had to learn to walk while being attached by tethers, to endure the frenzy of crowds rushing to see it pass along, when it was forced to open its hind legs and bend down its neck to be able to eat the leaves that were placed on the ground and that it loved – a position that giraffes adopt as rarely as possible when free and only use to drink from time to time, so as not to prove vulnerable to predators, and that, therefore, caused a certain anxiety to our giraffe.

It did survive. It may have been due to the fact that it had been captured when it was about six months old, young enough to accept substitute mothers and old enough to have learned to remain alone when adults went grazing. It was also female, destined to collective life in a group, and thus more liable to endure crowds than nomadizing males. But it was, above all, thanks to its individual character traits, which had already been noticed by the Arabian mahouts who were used to comparing their catches, that the giraffe was able to overcome all these trials, thus showing that animals are not passive objects, but that they invest a great deal of themselves in the parts they are being made to play: calm and submissive, the giraffe did not try to run away after being captured, unlike others; adaptable and obliging, it got used to walking, free, side by side with its captors; its delight in having fun, in jumping and rearing up, proved stronger than the stress and depression which caused many others to waste away.

In France, it progressively got used to the demands of the people and of the journey. It first accustomed itself to living in a narrow stable in Marseilles; it learned, while restrained by tethers, to jump up and down in the yard in order to relax and to enjoy the daily outings in the streets, even getting impatient as the time approached; it got calmer in the presence of the audience, so much so that it was only held by two drivers after a while instead of the four or even six that were needed at first. It also learned to alleviate stress by focusing on the foliage of the trees planted along the avenues and in the squares, in the roads around Marseilles and along the journey. It then slowly accepted being fed in front of the crowds, which it had refused in Marseilles, and to eat the hay given to European domestic herbivores, which it had refused during the first months. It also adapted itself to walking 25 to 35 kilometres a day, in about eight hours, and got into the habit, after a few days, of setting out on its own, progressively acquiring physical endurance, especially after Lyons, and familiarizing itself with the crew, men and especially animals.

Herein lies the main reason for the giraffe's survival. When it arrived in Marseilles, it was encouraged to enter the city by a horse that had been conveniently placed before her, a reassuring sight because the giraffe had been living with members of that species since its capture. In its stable, it lived with three cows, two draft horses and two antelopes which had been imported at the same time. The official reason for their presence was that they provided milk, kept each other warm and needed to familiarize themselves with Europe before being sent to Paris, but they were mainly useful in reassuring the giraffe, because it could look at them, smell them, listen to the sounds they made. These animals helped it to adapt, to endure, while establishing a link with its previous experience in the savannah, where, due to the instability of giraffes' groupings and to the peaceful cohabitation with herbivores, other animals were well accepted, and even sought out. The giraffe soon learned to walk in the streets and paths as, having learnt from the initial experience in Marseilles, men now placed the dairy cows in front: it followed them quietly, feeling a strong affinity for those placid ruminants, which belonged to the family Bovidae like the antelopes it had encountered in the savannah. It was not only interested in those cows but in all those it met during the journey, and the cows in turn did not feel any fear, unlike the horses or mules which pricked up their ears in anxiety, pawed the ground when they were made to wait and rushed away whenever they could as the giraffe observed them, tried to follow them and watched them go. This fundamental link with other animals was reinforced by the fact that the cows played a crucial part when the crew entered a city or walked through it, walking in front, keeping the giraffe from bolting, showing it the peaceful attitude to adopt. It is certainly no coincidence that the giraffe's panic in Lyons occurred in their absence.

All of these elements resulted in a behaviour that did not smoothly go from stress to adaptation, but that was characterized by a series of ups and downs, the giraffe being strongly disturbed on arriving in Marseilles, progressively adapting to its new conditions during its stay in the city, being again affected by stress and fatigue on resuming the journey along the crowded Rhone corridor, experiencing a new period of peace after Lyons, especially when going through the quieter Morvan region, before undergoing new bouts of stress in Paris and finally adapting itself to life in the Jardin des Plantes, a period that is little known because of the lack of adequate documents. Our giraffe died in 1846.

This animal vision of the journey is far remote from the human vision of a festive exhibition: it rather presents us with the difficult encounter between two worlds and its attendant fears, anxieties, misunderstandings, trials and adaptations undergone by the animal but also by the humans, who sometimes took fright, were also puzzled but tried less hard to understand.

Two points must be emphasized to distinguish this scientifically aimed biographical project from the aforementioned literary experiments. First, the method used is radically different, because it rejects forced anthropomorphism and strives for a more modest result by only working on the elements mentioned by the witnesses of the events and refusing to add anything to them, so that the biographies rather read like slices of life, leaving aside (for instance) the life of the giraffe in Africa because the texts are too vague or incomplete. Still, there is some similarity in the writer's necessary resort to imagination, though it is here severely controlled, in order to project himself out of his condition and by the side of the animal, or even into its mind, in order to try to understand and to reconstruct its experience, as field ethologists are now increasingly trying to do through observation and participation. All of them are striving toward asymptotic goals, trying to break the walls and to push toward the other, all the while knowing that the two worlds will never perfectly meet but will only at best move closer to each other, and that their reconstructions are human works and always contain hints of anthropomorphism, even if this danger is known and controlled, just as ethnologists use a form of controlled ethnomorphism when studying non-Western populations.

This biographical work should make it clear that in every species, each individual has its own personal trajectory and its own apprehension of the world, that these ways of seeing the world may change through time, as can be seen when working on a series of dog biographies, and that each individual experiences a unique type of encounter with humans, which also evolves through time, as shown by the biographies of great apes (Herzfeld, 2016).

An ethological history

That is why these histories must be subsumed within an ethological history (Baratay, 2012b), centred on animals and on their transformations and working on the fundamental assumption that species, groups and individuals experience a continual process of adaptation to their ecological and human conditions, and so that there is a fluctuation in animals' behaviour, collective life and culture. This idea is discarded by the behaviourist and classical schools of ethology, the latter arguing that what defines a species are specific types of behaviour, which are therefore conceived of as unchanging. And yet, field ethologists have been struck by changes in individual behaviour within a species, resulting, by a process of imitation, in changes in group behaviour, from the spreading practice among Japanese macaques of dipping sweet potatoes into salt water, to the changes in humpback whale song. Some now even speak of animal cultures, though only adopting a geographical perspective and forgetting the temporal dimension which is necessarily linked to it because individuals and then groups adopt new social behaviours at a specific time. Besides, this approach is much closer to the Darwinian theory of evolution, which first affects marginal individuals before spreading to the whole species, an intuition dismissed by classical ethology and rediscovered by cognitive ethologists who are increasingly interested in animal inventions and their modes of transmission. Some ethologists point in the direction of a history of animal behaviour by resorting to the notion of evolutionary social competence, without yet perceiving the necessity of historical research on the subject (Miklosi and Topal, 2013). And those who advocate a social and cultural history of animals that would illuminate the conditions of emergence of new practices, inventions, blendings and transformations only do so in the future tense, compiling a sum of observations without any ancient documents or tools with which to read them (McGrew, 2010; Whiten, 2010). Nineteenth-century species monographs, indeed, did not pay any attention to behaviour or to its history until the last third of the century. The historian therefore has a crucial role to play in order to show that animal societies are not ahistorical, as was still thought not so long ago of 'traditional' human societies – which, by the way, suggests that granting or not granting a history to Others is not an innocent act, but a truly political one.

Herein lies the cross-disciplinary interest of an ethological history, that would insist on fluctuations, and of a historical ethology, that would study animals at a given time and measure the differences with other times, ethology being now revisited and cross-pollinated with concepts derived from the social sciences. A few studies, recent or ongoing, by French-speaking scholars show that such a task is perfectly feasible: Corinne Beck, Éric Fabre and Julien Alleau link history and ecology in order to define the areas appreciated by wolves, better understand their actions and inquire into the causes of their extinction in the nineteenth century (Beck and Fabre, 2010). Such an ethological history would link up with the attempts of various biologists to write a history of the species from the perspective of animals – for instance, the studies on domestication, showing that it not only results from a forced imposition on animals by humans, but also from animals' acceptance of humans' offers, the studies on the diversification of the members of a species after domestication (Coppinger, 2002); or on the evolution of the species to adapt to the human environment (Miklosi and Topal, 2013; Miklosi, 2014). All those studies, though, tend to consider that there has been no further transformation since, which is contradicted by history, or they neglect to delineate the different historical stages. Combining approaches and results must help establish truly cross-disciplinary modes of inquiry in order to develop a history of animal behaviour, of its modes of construction and transmission, of its different time strata – in a word, a history of animal cultures.

Bibliography

Bailly, Jean-Christophe (2011), *The Animal Side*, New York, Fordham University Press.
Baratay, Éric (2012a), *Le point de vue animal, une autre version de l'histoire*, Paris, Seuil.
Baratay, Éric (2012b), 'Pour une histoire éthologique et une éthologie historique', *Études rurales*, 189 (1): 91–106.
Baratay, Éric (2013), *Bêtes des tranchées, des vécus oubliés*, Paris, CNRS Éditions.
Bates, Lucy, and Byrnes, Richard (2007), 'Creative or Created: Using Anecdotes to Investigate Animal Cognition', *Methods*, 42: 12–21.
Beck, Corinne, and Fabre, Éric (2010), 'Interroger le loup historique? Entre la biologie et l'histoire: un dialogue interdisciplinaire', *in:* Moriceau, Jean-Marc, and Madeline, Philippe (eds.), *Repenser le sauvage grâce au retour du loup*, Caen, Maison des Sciences Humaines: 13–21.
Bräuer, Julius (2014), 'What Dogs Understand about Humans', *in:* Kaminski, Juliane, and Marshall-Pescini, Sarah (eds.), *The Social Dog, Behaviour and Cognition*, London, Academic Press: 295–317.
Coppinger, Raymond, and Coppinger, Lorna (2002), *Dogs: A New Understanding of Canine Origin, Behavior and Evolution*, Chicago, University of Chicago Press.
Danto, Arthur (ed.) (2013), special issue 'Does History Need Animals?', *History and Theory*, 52 (4): 1–167.
Descola, Philippe (2005), *Par-delà nature et culture*, Paris, Gallimard, translated into English by Janet Lloyd (2013) as *Beyond Nature and Culture*, Chicago, University of Chicago Press.
Goode, David (2007), *Playing with My Dog Katie: An Ethnomethodological Study of Dog–Human Interaction*, West Lafayette, IN, Purdue University Press.

Haraway, Donna (1991), *Simians, Cyborgs and Women: The Reinvention of Nature*, London and New York, Routledge.
Herzfeld, Chris (2016), *Wattana: An Orangutan in Paris*, Chicago, University of Chicago Press.
Ingold, Tim (1988), *What Is an Animal?*, London, Unwin Hyman.
Kohler, Florent (ed.) (2012), 'Sociabilités animales', *Études rurales*, 189 (1): 11–31.
McGrew, William Clement (2010), 'New Theaters of Conflict in the Animal Culture Wars', *in:* Lonsdorf, Elisabeth (ed.), *The Mind of the Chimpanzee*, Chicago, University of Chicago Press: 173–175.
Miklosi, Adam (2014), *Dog, Behaviour, Evolution, and Cognition*, Oxford, Oxford University Press.
Miklosi, Adam, and Topal, Jozsef (2013), 'What Does it Take to Become Best Friends? Evolutionary Changes in Canine Social Competence', *Trends in Cognitive Sciences*, 17: 287–294.
Miklosi, Adam, Turcsán, Borbála, and Kubinyi, Eniko (2014), 'The Personality of Dogs', *in:* Kaminski, Juliane, and Marshall-Pescini, Sarah (eds.), *The Social Dog, Behaviour and Cognition*, London, Academic Press: 191–222.
Sanders, Clinton (1999), *Understanding Dogs: Living and Working with Canine Companions*, Philadelphia, PA, Temple University Press.
Shapiro, Kennet (1990), 'Understanding Dogs through Kinesthetic Empathy, Social Construction and History', *Anthrozoös*, 3: 184–195.
Udell, Monique A. R., Lord, Kathryn, Feuerbacher Erica N., and Wynne Clive D. L. (2014), 'A Dog's-Eye View of Canine Cognition', *in:* Horowitz, Alexandra (ed.), *Domestic Dog Cognition and Behavior*, New York, Springer: 221–240.
Vicart, Marion (2014), *Des chiens auprès des hommes. Quand l'anthropologue observe aussi l'animal*, Paris, Petra.
Whiten, Andrew (2010), 'A Coming Age for Cultural Panthropology', *in:* Lonsdorf, Elisabeth (ed.), *The Mind of the Chimpanzee*, Chicago, University of Chicago Press: 96–98.

21
OUTLOOK
Environmental humanities

Sabine Wilke

Rethinking the idea of nature is at the core of the project of the environmental humanities. Not only for that reason is it fitting that a volume with chapters on new ways of thinking about the relationship between nature and culture from a variety of different angles concludes with a reflection on this newly emerging field of inquiry. The environmental humanities as a concept is an umbrella term for a transdisciplinary approach to environmental issues that builds on and, at the same time, transcends traditional humanistic forms of scholarship, linking methods of hermeneutic interpretation to scientific, even technical, approaches to nature and the environment in an effort to address an ever greater complexity of issues with a new set of interconnected questions, ideas, values and approaches. As this volume demonstrates, this newly emerging form of inquiry comes as a response to a crisis of the idea of nature that lies at the heart of Western civilization, an idea that also informs the theoretical frameworks of the academic disciplines that are preoccupied with the study of nature, from philosophy to history, culture, the arts and the environmental sciences. Mankind's mastery of nature is, on the one hand, alluded to in the concept of the Anthropocene, the age in which human activity is of such scale that it is leaving a geological record on the surface of the Earth. Yet this mastery has evidently resulted in a very problematic record of disentanglements between humankind and nature that can only be addressed from a perspective that embraces a complex network of interconnections. The environmental humanities represent the latest and most ambitious attempt to approach such interrelated complexities with respect to environmental issues from a perspective that includes language, culture, history and values while, at the same time, encouraging a dialogue with the sciences and technological approaches (Revkin, 2014).

Institutionally speaking, the environmental humanities follow in the footsteps of interdisciplinary research groups and programmes such as the environmental sciences. These clusters typically include the full spectrum of humanities disciplines such as history, philosophy, language, literature, culture, art history and the study of religion, but also reach out to scholars and practitioners in the arts and social science disciplines such as anthropology or communications in so far as they are interested in addressing environmental issues from a perspective that includes questions of meaning and value. As opposed to environmental approaches within single disciplines such as environmental history, environmental ethics, ecocriticism or the environmental sciences, the environmental humanities bring a different outlook to our understanding of environmental problems as they question the nature and value of disciplinary boundaries and introduce a horizon of expectations that is oriented around problems and questions, thus adopting a language and mode of thought that is modelled after the sciences. Although this new language and mode of thought facilitates interaction with scientists and data-driven research, it also introduces an unprecedented level of reflection and self-reflection into research collaborations that insists on including the cultural, historical and ethical dimension of environmental issues in every problem-oriented research design. This is a radical departure for both sides, as it challenges humanists, who are usually trained to work alone in applying interpretive hermeneutic questions to their material, to work in teams and translate their research into problem-oriented 'findings', and scientists, who often work in teams encompassing members from a variety of different science disciplines, to include cultural issues and questions of history, representation and value into their research.

Institutional frameworks for the environmental humanities

Several universities and research centres in North America, Australia, the UK and in Europe have embraced the environmental humanities at various levels. With respect to scholarly publications, several venues are specifically targeted to publish research on environmental humanities topics such as the journals *Environmental Humanities*, now published with Duke University Press, and *Resilience: A Journal of the Environmental Humanities* based at the University of Nebraska Press. With respect to Anthropocene studies there are already a number of publishing venues that invite scholars from all kinds of backgrounds to share their research, such as *The Anthropocene Review*. All of these scholarly journals combine rigorous peer review with the need for transdisciplinary discussions of environmental issues at the highest critical level (Rose *et al.*, 2012; Robin, 2013). Although many other journals address specific research in subdisciplines such as environmental communications, environmental ethics, environmental history and literary ecocriticism, or in subareas such as animal studies, the establishment of a specifically European journal for research in the environmental humanities, *Ecozon@*, is a welcome departure from the monolingual English-only culture in which many of these cross-disciplinary conversations take place. As a multilingual and multicultural space, Europe can set a trend in the environmental humanities that demands greater inclusiveness of different linguistic traditions and a more rigorous international angle on the field. A robust multilingual and multicultural articulation of the environmental humanities has the potential to enrich and deepen these conversations, especially because the cultural dimension of environmental problems is so central to its *modus operandi*.

Aside from scholarly publication venues, a number of centres, programmes and initiatives are dedicated specifically to advancing the environmental humanities on an institutional level. In North America and the Anglophone context, Stanford was one of the first universities to build an institutional forum for transdisciplinary discussions of environmental issues with its 'Environmental Humanities Project' that not only advances scholarly discussions but also seeks to engage with the public on ecological debates (https://ehp.stanford.edu).[1] Princeton has embraced an 'Environmental Humanities Initiative' within the Princeton Environmental Institute and is actively recruiting environmental humanities scholars to serve on its faculty (www.princeton.edu/pei/ehp). The University of Wisconsin, Madison, established a Center for Culture, History, and Environment (http://nelson.wise.edu/che). UCLA organized a Sawyer seminar on 'What Is the Environmental Humanities?' in which many of the questions posed in the introduction of this chapter were discussed (http://environmental.humanities.ucla.edu).

The University of California, Santa Barbara, is host to an Environmental Humanities Initiative (http://ehc.english.ucsb.edu). The University of California, Davis, has organized an Environmental Humanities supercluster (http://environmental humanities.ucdavis.edu). Oregon State University has an 'Environmental Arts and Humanities Initiative' (http://environmentalhumanities.ucdavis.edu) and Arizona State University and the Mellon Foundation run a digital website called 'Humanities for the Environment' with a number of observatories through which people all over the world interact and address global environmental challenges (http://hfe-oberservatories.org). This is just a small selection of institutional initiatives that speak to the attractiveness of providing institutional support for this newly emerging research in the Anglophone world. Some of these institutional initiatives have also translated into programmatic initiatives. Students can now earn undergraduate or graduate degrees in the environmental humanities at Arizona State University, the University of Pennsylvania, the University of Utah and Bath Spa University (UK), with many more in the making as this volume goes to press. This is, by any measure, not an exhaustive list of all environmental humanities initiatives in the English-speaking world, but just a sample of programmes that demonstrates how fast the environmental humanities is catching on and the wide variety of institutions, public and private, that is lending its support to this effort.

Just as Europe was able to make an important contribution to the world of publishing in the environmental humanities with the multilingual and multicultural approach taken by its signature journal, it is showing exceptional leadership with respect to providing the funds for environmental humanities centres, networks and study programmes, particularly in the Scandinavian countries and Germany due to federal initiatives and the central role that green ideas have played in their politics, in the case of Germany going back to an old and established tradition of thinking about nature and the environment in Romanticism, nature philosophy and phenomenology. The Rachel Carson Center for Environment and Society at the University of Munich (LMU) in cooperation with the Deutsches Museum, now in its second funding round, is providing institutional support for environmental humanities scholarship in the form of fellowships, affiliations, workshops, lectures and publication venues (www.carsoncenter.uni-muenchen.de/index.html). It is also host to an interdisciplinary PhD programme. The Transatlantic Research Network in the Environmental Humanities that was kick-started with funds from the Alexander von Humboldt Foundation (https://environmental-humanities-network.org) organized workshops and conferences, published special theme issues on environmental topics, and is now preparing a concluding volume of essays titled *Readings in the Anthropocene: The Environmental Humanities, German Studies, and Beyond* for Bloomsbury Press (Wilke and Johnstone, 2017). The French website 'Humanités environnementales' (http://humanitesenvironmentales.fr) serves as a site for new articulations of environmental awareness across disciplines. Switzerland is home to the digital platform 'Seeing the Environment through the Humanities' (http://environmentalhumanities.ch). Italy hosts an Environmental Humanities International Research group at the University of Turin (www.dipartimentolingue.unito.it). Stockholm is the location for the KTH Environmental Humanities Laboratory with a dynamic set of programmes that address an increasing demand for knowledge production to meet global challenges (www.kth.se/en/abe/inst/philhist/historia/ehl). The Nordic Network for Interdisciplinary Environmental Studies provides support (www.miun.se/nies). The recently launched ECOHUM laboratory at Mid Sweden University links research projects and provides connections to institutional and organizational partners (www.miun.se/ecohum). It is also a charter member in the European Environmental Humanities Alliance connecting humanities research in Europe with the challenges of global environmental change (http://europeanenvironmentalhumanities.wordpress.com). The key idea is that the 'emerging field of the environmental humanities represents an under-utilized resource of knowledge, activity and practice that can and must be activated and integrated with the other sciences to guide a more humane transformation of environment and society' (europeanenvironmentalhumanities.wordpress.com). This is an interesting mission statement as it emphasizes the benefits gained from including the humanities in environmental discussions by highlighting the idea that research outcomes will benefit as they reflect the complexity of the problems, that knowledge of environment and society will be qualitatively enhanced, and that society will gain from a more successful integration of scientific and humanistic study. In a declaration presented initially at the 'Horizons for Social Sciences and Humanities' conference in Vilnius, Lithuania, in 2013, the alliance asserts the need to rethink the idea of nature and the relationship between nature, humans, and culture, especially in the new era of the Anthropocene. In other words, the European landscape with respect to the environmental humanities is in part coordinated through this alliance, a development that will hopefully be strengthened in the near future, but for the most part different countries and universities have their own articulations at various stages of development that are largely due to the initiative of individual scholars and research groups.

I only have time to discuss one example of a fully articulated institutional agenda, and I will take it from the context that I am most familiar with, that is, the platform at the University of Augsburg where the environmental humanities serve as a major research focus for the entire university (www.wzu.uni-augsburg. de/Environmental-Humanities.html). Perhaps a closer look at what they are doing in Augsburg can give us a better idea about the basic research questions and their applications. First of all, the environmental humanities are described as 'one of the most important and innovative paradigms of the contemporary humanities' of today. What is important and innovative in this new field are two things: the bringing together of formerly more or less strictly separated disciplines within the humanities themselves and the dialogue with the natural sciences. Another factor of innovation is global collaboration, starting with European partnerships and extending all over the world on a fast scale. Why is this innovative? It represents thinking outside the box, promotes creativity in research design, a global outlook on issues, and it promotes a holistic approach to environmental issues that integrates scientifically informed knowledge with an awareness of the centrality of language, culture, history, and meaning. What is more, the environmental humanities at Augsburg University provide a critique of the current science-based environmental discourse from a novel standpoint that includes historical analysis of the evolution of the prominent issues within modern environmental discourses. Environmental issues are not addressed from the perspective of individual disciplines and then put together in an overarching framework, but the questions, methods, and concerns are co-produced and codesigned from the start. This is definitely new, and it seems to have worked productively for the scholars at Augsburg University who have been working on individual case histories for a number of years: these are material histories in which political and social conflicts and their cultural dimensions are connected with the production, synthesis, use, and dissipation of these substances and the question of literature as cultural ecology, that is, a concept that recognizes the ecological force in culture that can serve as a vital sensorium of critical diagnosis and creative renewal (Müller and Sauter, 2012; Zapf, 2016), to mention only two of the many projects sponsored under the umbrella of the environmental humanities at this university.

Research agendas and emerging paradigms

The environmental humanities are evolving from research begun in individual disciplines such as environmental history (Cronon, 1995), ecocriticism (Garrard, 2014; Clark, 2015), environmental ethics (Zylinska, 2014), ecosociology (Bell and Ashwood, 2015), ecopsychology (Kahn and Hasbach, 2012), and cross-disciplinary research agendas such as ecofeminism (Plumwood, 2009). Because individual chapters in this volume are devoted to these subdisciplines and research agendas,

I can be brief here and focus on the most important ideas and impulses that have shaped the environmental humanities into an emerging scholarly paradigm. One important development was the increasing commitment to rethinking the relationship between the local and the global. Some of the earlier thinkers of ecocriticism, for example, made the transition from interpreting literary and cultural texts from specifically local and national frameworks to highlighting more global international concerns, thus linking the significance of the literary text to broader concerns about the meaning of culture in an environmental context (Buell, 2005). This trend is not to be confused with the death of national literature or the rise of comparative literature or, more recently, the newly emerging concept of world literature. On the contrary, literary texts and cultural artefacts produced in certain historical, linguistic and aesthetic settings still need to be studied and understood in these environments. But the environmental humanities add an analysis of how these contexts and settings relate to larger environmental concerns. Robust multilingualism as the precondition for understanding multiculturalism is an important ideal that preserves the necessity of understanding specific national traditions, especially in research contexts that highlight global environmental questions. This is what scholars of French, German, Italian, Japanese, etc., can bring to the environmental humanities and where a multilingual and multicultural framework is more inclusive and better equipped for tackling complex environmental problems. To provide just one example, I am currently working on a virtual exhibit on German literature and culture in the Anthropocene to broaden and enrich existing discussions that focus exclusively on English-language sources. I decided to prepare a fully bilingual German–English edition of the exhibit that gives visitors the chance of engaging with the materials and my explanatory narrative in the original as well as in translation. Although the sources are all taken from the German tradition, my narrative merges specific cultural and historical context with broader concerns such as transformations of landscape, deforestation, cultures of waste and glacial environments that connect these specific sources to greater environmental challenges.

Another shift in research that prepared the transition from these more compartmentalized environmental subdisciplines to the greater line of questioning that is typical for the environmental humanities is precisely what is thematized in this volume (i.e. a greater and more critical reflection on the idea of nature and the role of narrative). In fact, the environmental historian William Cronon pioneered this new reflection in 1994 when he asked a group of scholars to spend some time at the University of California, Irvine, Humanities Research Institute to reflect on the topic of 'Reinventing Nature', a discussion that was documented in a collection of essays in 1995 (Cronon, 1995). At issue was the concept of wilderness that is so crucial for understanding American attitudes toward nature and a new emphasis on narrative and attention to structures of representation. Without a keen awareness of the power of narrative, nature cannot be understood fully. Rethinking the idea of nature has to reflect critically on older notions of wilderness as areas without human impact and focus instead on the relationship between nature and culture.

A third impulse that was formative for the broadening of the research agenda of the environmental humanities was a more sustained reflection on the relationship between colonial and postcolonial studies and environmental concerns (DeLoughrey and Handley, 2011; Nixon, 2011), and in tandem with that a greater emphasis on species thinking and the question of posthumanism (Wolfe, 2013). Environmental problems transcend national borders and breach cultural divides, but they also tend to affect the less privileged on a greater scale. As such, they need to be addressed with greater attention to our shared futures without losing sight of power, the question of justice and the unequal distribution of resources (Malm and Hornborg, 2014). This is where the social sciences and their long-standing experience with the critical analysis of power at all levels of society can inform the analysis of environmental issues within the greater concept of the environmental humanities. At the same time, it is important to note that the traditional modes of analysis of power must also undergo severe scrutiny if they want to continue to be relevant for our age. In the Anthropocene, it is no longer sufficient to point to winners and losers in a worldwide power struggle over the process of gaining access to resources and globalized processes of modernization. In fact, it was the historian Dipesh Chakrabarty, himself an experienced historian and critic of colonial and postcolonial issues, who challenged his own discipline to include deep time and species thinking into the project of specific and local historical analysis in the face of the enormous challenges posed by climate change, extinction, and the Anthropocene (Chakrabarty, 2009). According to Chakrabarty, the global dimension of geological time and the common history of humankind force us to rethink the agency of humanity on a species level. History as a discipline needs to take that level into account while, at the same time, not losing sight of the legacy of imperialism, colonialism, and the continued need for a critique of power structures (Emmet and Lekan, 2016).

Open questions and future horizons for the environmental humanities

What are the central questions raised in the newly emerging research agenda of the environmental humanities that may account for the need of environmental criticism that does not lose sight of power imbalances (Biro, 2011)? And what role do literary texts, artistic documents, cultural artefacts, and visual records play in this context (Miles, 2010)? What are the issue items that are emerging as the most pressing problems that lie ahead for us as we approach a radically globalized world defined by complex networks of interconnections? We might start by identifying the need to analyze the category of the human and humanity to the necessity of rethinking the idea of nature and the relationship between nature and culture, or nature and humans. In a specific way, the critical analysis of the category of the human is developed in the cross-disciplinary fields of critical animal studies (Heise, 2013; Borgards, 2015), multispecies studies, and radical articulations of new materialisms (Phillips and Sullivan, 2012). What constitutes humanity and what is the relationship between humans and nonhumans, be that the animal world, other biological agents (Morton, 2007), or machines for that matter (Haraway, 2003)? What constitutes agency, and how do we rethink the framework of construction and deconstruction that has informed critical thinking in the humanities and social sciences for decades? A posthuman perspective sheds critical light on the legacy of humanism and situates the category of humanity as part of an ecological system defined by the idea that all life forms are interconnected. The environmental humanities are better equipped to address such questions because of the transdisciplinary make-up of its research agenda where specific issue items such as the meaning of humanity are refracted through a variety of lenses. The question of the human and the posthuman is also an excellent example for an issue item where the formation of elective affinities between certain disciplinary traditions can be observed, in this case, perhaps between philosophy, the study of culture and science that all share a common interest in the subject, and a willingness to engage in the articulation of communal research questions.

Beyond the question of the human and the posthuman, it is the insistence on the cultural dimension of environmental issues and problems ranging from climate change, extinction, and the Anthropocene that informs research in the environmental humanities (Kolbert, 2014). From this perspective, all cultural documents are radically interconnected with nature and the environment and vice versa and cannot be studied in isolation. This has significant consequences for humanistic scholarship, as it can no longer focus exclusively on questions of form, structure, rhetoric, style, and theme in the interpretation of its sources but also needs to consider how these modes of aesthetic expression relate to environments in a physical as well as metaphoric way. What forms of aesthetic expression support carbon cultures, for example, where the availability of a certain form of energy facilitates a mode of excess also characteristic of certain cultural forms and genres and, vice versa, what forms of aesthetic expression shape cultures of extraction, a question the German filmmaker Werner Herzog posed so pointedly in his 1992 documentary of the burning oil wells in Kuwait after the first Gulf War, *Lessons in Darkness*? New forms of cultural expression that have not made it into the standard repertoire of classical genres might come into focus, standard literary histories may need to be rewritten just like standard historical narratives, and philosophical arguments need to be retooled if they want to link their sources to these new issue items in a newly emerging field of inquiry.

The awareness of radical interconnections between forms of cultural expression and natural life forms and the need for an analytical framework that reflects the hybridity and plurality of that plenitude urges scholarship in the environmental humanities to embrace collaborative models in which larger issue items are studied in teams or scholarly networks with broad representation from a variety of different backgrounds, including the sciences and the broader public. This is easier said than done, as there are huge differences in academic cultures and deep-seated epistemological divides about questions such as what constitutes facts, truths, and evidence. What a scientist considers a fact of nature may not be what a historian believes to be a fact of nature, if indeed there is one. The humanist emphasis on value, meaning, and the importance of structures of representation may not be what a scientist considers important in designing a research study. The team approach that is needed to address complex questions in an ever more complex network of interconnectivities requires a radical openness of the researchers towards different perspectives, a culture of respect that values diversity and inclusiveness, and the skill of translating specific research outcomes into 'findings' that can be understood and appreciated by other team members. Humanists do not commonly think about their research in terms of 'findings'. We interpret cultural documents from a historical, aesthetic, linguistic, or philosophical perspective in a holistic and hermeneutic process that has nothing in common with problem-solving in the narrow sense of the word. But we have to learn how to translate our interpretations into a language that can be understood by nonspecialists and that addresses an important aspect of the issue item we are studying. How do we make our interpretations relevant for a larger public that may not care about the specific intricacies of the poetic form we are analyzing? By the same token, scientists have to learn to respect and appreciate humanistic scholarship for its genuine contribution to understanding the cultural dimension of the phenomena they are studying in a much more goal-oriented format.

Several recent trends within humanistic scholarship have the potential for propelling the environmental humanities toward greater affinities with larger research questions shared by other fields, such as the analysis of space and the so-called spatial turn in cultural studies which links questions of humanistic interpretation to cultural geography, for example, or the digital humanities that can bringing together a broad array of scholars from various backgrounds, including nontraditional collaborators such as librarians in the production of complex research tools, editions, and research websites. One fascinating issue that would greatly propel environmental humanities scholarship into the centre is the need for a deep and critical analysis of the process of visualizing data. Every cross-disciplinary research team that wants to communicate its findings, in fact, everyone who presents their research to any type of audience, specialized or not, needs to present their data in a narrative or visual image. These stories and visualizations are not neutral and free of value, but are derived from a specific set of values. Disciplines like art history and cultural visual studies are able to dissect these visualizations critically, as Birgit Schneider and Thomas Nocke (2014) have done so recently on the example of images of climate change. When Al Gore performs the 'hockey stick' in his 2006 documentary of his slide show on global warming, *An Inconvenient Truth*, this is not an arbitrary or neutral action on stage but an effective tool of mobilizing his audience into action that provides a particularly compelling example of visualizing a select set of scientific data and models them into a streamlined curve that conveniently underemphasizes significant variation in data and scientific uncertainty.

A related area of application is the emphasis on the need for new narratives relating to environmental concerns. All narratives have cultural dimensions. The environmental humanities, especially the strands that address an international and comparative perspective, have a unique edge in understanding the world from a perspective that balances local with global issues and that allows for the richness in nuances that we encounter in the world of human experience. Languages and the knowledge of different cultures is a core skill set that will play a central role in envisioning complex solutions to complex problems. If we wish to succeed in addressing the most crucial problems of today and tomorrow, the environmental humanities, with their unique profile, will be an indispensable asset in any scientific and scholarly effort that aims for success on a wider scale.

Note

1 All cited websites were accessed 31/10/2016.

Bibliography

Bell, Michael Mayerfeld, and Ashwood, Loka L. (2015), *An Invitation to Environmental Sociology*, London, Sage.

Biro, Andrew (ed.) (2011), *Critical Ecologies: The Frankfurt School and Contemporary Environmental Crises*, Toronto, University of Toronto Press.

Borgards, Roland (ed.) (2015), special issue 'Cultural and Literary Animal Studies', *Journal for Literary Theory*, 9 (2): 155–292.

Buell, Lawrence (2005), *The Future of Environmental Criticism: Environmental Crisis and Literary Criticism*, Hoboken, NJ, Wiley.

Chakrabarty, Dipesh (2009), 'The Climate of History: Four Theses', *Critical Inquiry*, 35: 197–222.

Clark, Timothy (2015), *Ecocriticism on the Edge: The Anthropocene as a Threshold Concept*, London, Bloomsbury.

Cronon, William (ed.) (1995), *Uncommon Ground: Rethinking the Human Place in Nature*, New York, Norton.

DeLoughrey, Elizabeth M., and Handley, George B. (2011), *Postcolonial Ecologies: Literatures of the Environment*, Oxford, Oxford University Press.

Emmet, Rob, and Lekan, Thomas (eds.) (2016), special issue 'Whose Anthropocene: Revisiting Dipesh Chakrabarty's "Four Theses"', *Rachel Carson Center Perspectives*, 2.

Garrard, Greg (ed.) (2014), *The Oxford Handbook of Ecocriticism*, Oxford, Oxford University Press.

Haraway, Donna (2003), *The Common Species Manifesto*, Chicago, University of Chicago Press.

Heise, Ursula (2013), 'Encounters with the Thing Formerly Known as Nature', *Public Books*: 1–8, available at: www.publicbooks.org (Accessed 31/10/2016).

Kahn, Peter, and Hasbach, Patricia (2012), *Ecopsychology: Science, Totems, and the Technological Species*, Cambridge, MA, MIT Press.

Kolbert, Elizabeth (2014), *The Sixth Extinction: An Unnatural History*, New York, Holt.

Malm, Andreas, and Hornborg, Alf (2014), 'The Geology of Mankind? A Critique of the Anthropocene Narrative', *The Anthropocene Review*, 1 (1): 62–69.

Miles, Malcom (2010), 'Representing Nature, Art and Climate Change', *Cultural Geographies*, 17: 19–35.

Morton, Timothy (2007), *Ecology without Nature: Rethinking Environmental Aesthetics*, Cambridge, MA, Harvard University Press.
Müller, Timo, and Sauter, Michael (eds.) (2012), *Literature, Ecology, Ethics: New Trends in European Ecocriticism*, Heidelberg, Winter.
Nixon, Rob (2011), *Slow Violence and the Environmentalism of the Poor*, Cambridge, Cambridge University Press.
Phillips, Dana, and Sullivan, Heather (2012), 'Introduction', *in:* Phillips, Dana, and Sullivan, Heather (eds.), special issue 'Material Ecocriticism: Dirt, Waste, Bodies, Food, and Other Matter', *ISLE*, 19 (3): 445–447.
Plumwood, Val (2009), 'Nature in the Active Voice', *Australian Humanities Review*, 46: 113–129.
Revkin, Andrew C. (2014), 'Does the Anthropocene, the Age of Humans, Deserve a Golden Spike?', *The New York Times*, October 14, available at: dotearth.blogs.nytimes.com (Accessed 31/10/2016).
Robin, Libby (2013), 'Histories for Changing Times: Entering the Anthropocene?', *Australian Historical Studies*, 44 (3): 329–340.
Rose, Deborah, Dooren, Thom (van), Chrulew, Matthew, Cooke, Stuart, Kearnes, Matthew, and O'Gorman, Emily (2012), 'Thinking through the Environment, Unsettling the Humanities', *Environmental Humanities*, 1 (1): 1–5.
Schneider, Birgit, and Nocke, Thomas (eds.) (2014), *Image Politics of Climate Change: Visualizations, Imaginations, Documentations*, Bielefeld, Transcript.
Wilke, Sabine, and Johnstone, Japhet (eds.) (2017), *Readings in the Anthropocene: The Environmental Humanities, German Studies, and Beyond*, London, Bloomsbury.
Wolfe, Cary (2013), 'Human, All Too Human: "Animal Studies" and the Humanities', *Publications of the Modern Language Association*, 124: 564–575.
Zapf, Hubert (2016), *Literature as Cultural Ecology: Sustainable Texts*, London, Bloomsbury.
Zylinska, Joanna (2014), *Minimal Ethics for the Anthropocene*, Michigan Publishing, University of Michigan Library, available at: www.openhumanitiespress.org (Accessed 31/10/2016).

CONCLUSION

How nature matters

Aurélie Choné, Isabelle Hajek and Philippe Hamman

Redefining the concept of nature in three ways

This textbook focuses on the concept of nature, which encompasses the processes defining the conditions under which societies and human actions are deployed, with a great capacity for transformation. In this respect, it connects with a long-standing European tradition inspired by the humanities. Its first originality lies in its emphasis on tracking down genealogies of thinking about nature, rather than pursuing an exhaustive account. By referring to nature instead of environment – today a more frequently used notion – we underline the importance of history and its deconstruction for a better understanding and response to contemporary challenges. As Bruno Latour noted during his 2013 Gifford Lectures in Edinburgh,[1] there is no escaping the fact that we have to face 'Gaia'. Of course, this also goes for researchers, who should not consider themselves above this but must recognize their 'fully political authority'. 'Gaia' is not in the position of the arbiter that the Moderns ascribed to nature when they described 'laws of nature' inspired by the principle of causality. Without a sovereign force, there is no longer a (deanimated) object or an (overanimated) subject, and humans are left to face a situation of 'war', requiring them to stop being negligent and to acknowledge the finiteness of the world and its resources (Latour, 2015: 325–327, 366).

Although our contributors are primarily concerned with how knowledge circulates across disciplines and scientific fields, they are also eager to remain connected to the social world and to help build a new framework for understanding nature and its role in a constant process of redesign through culture. Ideological and epistemological biases are necessarily taken into account, not only for critical purposes, but also to shed light on the historical and cultural production of knowledge about nature. Hence, the second main concern of our authors is the deconstruction and ongoing reconfiguration of academic fields, which cannot ignore the current global and local problems of our world.

This approach is particularly relevant at a time of far-reaching theoretical reconfiguration following the spread – including in Western countries – of postcolonial critiques and of critical deconstructions of Eurocentric/Western visions and of the traditional nature/culture divide. In this respect, the third original contribution of this textbook is that it results from collaboration between French- and English-speaking European and American scholars who are particularly aware of these issues. Thus these developments are addressed in light of their complementary research traditions, with approaches from areas of study that have been nourished by such interactions as environmental ethics (Catherine Larrère), ecofeminism (Margot Lauwers) or the environmental humanities (Sabine Wilke). This volume offers an introduction to debates that have been broached in some recent dictionaries published either in the United States or in France (e.g. Adamson *et al.*, 2016, in English; Bourg and Papaux, 2015, in French), but have received little cross-national attention. This productive dialogue enables us to rethink nature and the environment on both theoretical and practical levels. As such this textbook provides important input into international debates on the current and future states of environmental studies and environmental humanities, as well as on the status of social science, literary and cultural studies.

Reflexive insights and pathways towards better-informed action

Our textbook highlights the epistemic and practical efficacy of these cross-disciplinary forms of knowledge about 'nature'. In doing so it proposes two main responses to the basic question underlying each of the entries: How can we define today the relations between nature and society?

First, far from calling into question the very idea of nature, the book challenges the exclusively scientific and technical conceptions of nature derived from the natural sciences and their ontological foundations. We move from a substantialized definition of nature towards a reflexive dynamic (clearly identified in Lionel Charles's chapter). Several contributors highlight the emergence of badly identified new risks and of 'socionatural' artefacts – combining 'facts' and 'values' (as, for instance, shown by ecospirituality and ecopsychology: see Aurélie Choné and Dennis Merritt). They challenge the traditional split between social and natural sciences underpinning Western societies' ambition to 'master nature' (see, among others, Éric Navet, Roland Borgards and Éric Baratay). Rethinking the concept of nature now requires a highly *relational* approach conducive to addressing the many ways in which human and nonhuman beings live together (Descola, 2013 [2005]). We must be mindful of countless connections, within different spaces in interaction (such as rural/natural and urban spaces: see Owain Jones, Philippe Hamman, Isabelle Hajek and Jean-Pierre Lévy) and between animals, plants, human beings, living beings, etc. Here we did not partake in the mythology of the nature/culture duality; our concern has been to consider the intricacies of nature and culture. This leads us to challenge, first, discourses revolving around concepts of evolutionism and progress and, second, the split between natural sciences versus literary and cultural studies, humanities and social science. This position brings together areas of inquiry that have too often neglected each other. Most importantly, it entails attention to the diversity of ways of being – be it biodiversity or cultural diversity.

Second, many contributions to this book evidence two connected dynamics at the heart of the renewal of studies on nature, one reflexive, and the other action oriented.

There is first a *reflexive dynamic* at work, in the sense that new frameworks for thought need to be invented to reflect the relational dimension of nature. One of the key features of deep ecology, for instance, consists of approaching nature as a 'milieu', understood as a 'relational field' (see Stéphane-Hicham Afeissa). The writings (ecocriticism, epistemocriticism) and aesthetics of nature are particularly important in this respect (Nathalie Blanc, Emmanuelle Peraldo, Laurence Dahan). This reflexive dynamic shifts the emancipatory aims of the 'human subject' from the modern project of objectivizing and ruling nature towards emancipation through the attention to other living beings. Questioning the place of nature in these new forms of knowledge therefore also means investigating the humanities and their reconfigurations, including canonical social science disciplines (ecosociologies and ethnoecology: Graham Woodgate, Éric Navet) and the 'ecology' movements (political ecology: Catherine Repussard; ecofeminism: Margot Lauwers). We must also look at the environmental humanities (Sabine Wilke), a field designed to bring together studies on the environment defined as a material condition for the existence of human and social activities.

These changing fields and areas of knowledge are also characterized by a *pragmatic dynamic*, relating to our engagement in the world, in the sense that they are also concerned with inventing new ways of living together and changing our relationship to nature. Particularly practice-oriented disciplines include sustainable urbanism (Philippe Hamman), urban ecology (Isabelle Hajek and Jean-Pierre Lévy), environmental health (Lionel Charles), ecosystem services (Roldan Muradian), industrial ecology (Nicolas Buclet) and human/animal studies. The new relationship to nature also implies a new relationship of humanity to itself and to its inner nature, as humans are fully a part of nature (as is evidenced in the chapters on ecosophy, ecospirituality and ecopsychology). This raises the question of sense at physical, metaphysical, individual and social levels: What sense do we ascribe (or want to ascribe) to nature? This ties in with the central question of *Making Sense of Nature* (Castree, 2014): what is called 'nature' is not only part of the construction of a shared or conflicting social sense (social order or social change); it also involves the development of a sense of nature for ourselves, so that we may individually and collectively take part in key decisions about the future of life on Earth. In the words of Castree (2014: i), 'We need to be more alert to how, why and with what effects ideas about "nature" get fashioned and deployed in specific situations', including to rethink the role and relevance of citizens as well as institutions, both formal and informal, to address the fundamental challenges of governance and politics in the Anthropocene (Pattberg and Zelli, 2016).

Ultimately the main lesson to be drawn from this textbook as we consider the next steps in research is that the production of renewed forms of nature-knowledge is not an end in itself. The question of how they relate to the real world is key: to retain their humanity, humans have no choice but to reconsider the living, refashion their relationship to the world, to others and to themselves. This means inventing new ways of living together that are mindful of our dependence on a relational nature, and correspondingly repoliticizing the present, far from the ready-made solutions of predictive models such as sustainable development or green economy (Kenis and Lievens, 2015). We believe that the variety of academic, local and practical approaches on display here amply demonstrates that thinking about nature and living with nature are two intimately connected endeavours.

Note

1 Available at: https://knowledge-ecology.com/2013/03/05/bruno-latours-gifford-lectures-1-6/ (Accessed 31/10/2016).

Bibliography

Adamson, Joni, Gleason, William A., and Pellow, David N. (eds.) (2016), *Keywords for Environmental Studies*, New York, New York University Press.
Bourg, Dominique, and Papaux, Alain (eds.) (2015), *Dictionnaire de la pensée écologique*, Paris, Presses Universitaires de France.
Castree, Noel (2014), *Making Sense of Nature*, London and New York, Routledge.
Descola, Philippe (2005), *Par-delà nature et culture*, Paris, Gallimard, translated into English by Janet Lloyd (2013) as *Beyond Nature and Culture*, Chicago, University of Chicago Press.
Kenis, Anneleen, and Lievens, Matthias (2015), *The Limits of the Green Economy: From Re-Inventing Capitalism to Re-Politicising the Present*, London and New York, Routledge.
Latour, Bruno (2015), *Face à Gaïa. Huit conférences sur le nouveau régime climatique*, Paris, La Découverte/Les Empêcheurs de penser en rond.
Pattberg, Philipp, and Zelli, Fariborz (eds.) (2016), *Environmental Politics and Governance in the Anthropocene: Institutions and Legitimacy in a Complex World*, London and New York, Routledge.

INDEX

Abbey, E. 80
Acot, P. 158
Acott, T. G. 34
actor-network theory (ANT) 227–8
Adams, C. 108
Adamson, J. 255
aesthetics of nature: distinguishing between environment and nature 68–9; ecological emergency 70; emergence and main ideas of 67; environmental aesthetics 70, 72–3; forms and environments 69–70; greenways and blueways 70–2; urban ecology and 161–3
Afeissa, H. S. 12, 29, 43, 256
Agamben, G. 224–5
Agulhon, M. 159
Alaimo, S. 89
Alexander the Great 129
Alexander von Humboldt Foundation 246
Allais, A. 218
Alleau, J. 241
Allenby, B. R. 188–9, 191
Alliance Sud 41
Aloi, G. 228
Amin, A. 151
animal biographies 237–40
animal gaze 226–7
animal studies: actor-network theory 227–8; anthropological machine 224–5; becoming-animal theory 225–6; companion species 226–8; constructing animal history 232–41; critical animal studies 222–3; cultural animal studies 223–8; definition of 221–4; historical scholarship 228–9; human–animal studies 222–3; literary studies 229; philosophy 228; work fields 228–30
Animal Studies Journal 221
Anthropocene 24, 68, 95, 100, 109, 125, 147, 179, 184, 243
Anthropocene, Readings in the (Wilke and Johnstone) 246
Anthropocene Review, The 244
anthropocentrism 17–18, 22, 24, 35, 41, 76, 114, 129, 222–4, 234
anthropogeography 128–9
anthropological machine 224–5
Anthropologie de la mort (Thomas) 211
anthroposophy 42
Arbuthnot, J. 170
Arendt, H. 141
Ariès, P. 102
Aristotle 31, 168, 222, 226
Arizona State University 245
Armbruster, K. 89
artialization 72
Ashwood, L. I. 247
Association for the Study of Literature and Environment (ASLE) 78
AtKisson, A. 180
Austin, M. 78
Australasian Animal Studies Association 221

Baccini, P. 190
Bacon, F. 169
Bahuchet, S. 136

Bailly, J. C. 233
Baker, S. 176
Bal, P. 101
Báldi, A. 200
Bales, K. 217
Baratay, É. 210, 236, 255
Barbadoro, G. 42
Barles, S. 159, 170, 189
Bate, J. 79, 146
Bates, L. 235
Bath Spa University (UK) 245
Battista, C. 81
Baudelaire, C. 63
Baycan-Levent, T. 178
Bayer, G. 76–7
Beck, C. 241
Beck, U. 19
becoming-animal theory 225–6
Bell, D. 114
Bell, M. M. 247
Benedict XVI, Pope 40, 45
Bennett, M. 76
Benton-Short, L. 146, 148
Berger, J. 228
Bergman, T. 85
Berkes, F. 136
Berleant, A. 69
Berque, A. 72
Berry, T. 41, 56
Besnier, J. M. 89–91
Best, S. 224
Beyond Nature and Culture (Descola) 135
Biehl, J. 46
biocentrism 17–18
biodynamic agriculture 42, 44
biopolitics 224–5
biopower 224–5
Blanc, N. 64, 72, 75, 162, 256
blueways 70–2
Boas, F. 135
Bodenburg, J. 210
Boerhave, H. 170
Bonneuil, C. 100
Bookchin, M. 102
Borgards, R. 210, 222, 249
Borie, M. 196
Botkin, D. 89
Bouma, J. 145
Bourg, D. 255
Bouvard and Pécuchet (Flaubert) 87–8
Boyle, R. 169–70
Braat, L. 196
Brady, E. 72
Brelet, C. 166–7
Brereton, P. 111

Broswimmer, F. 216
Brower, D. 101
Brown, K. 196
Brown, M. 51, 56
Browner, C. 101
Brunner, P. 190
Buckingham, S. 183
Buclet, N. 143–4, 256
Buell, L. 75–7, 88, 248
Bugnon, R. 212
Burton, E. 181
Butler, W. 34
Buttel, F. H. 116
Buzinde, C. N. 121
Byrnes, R. 235

Calarco, M. 228
Caldecott, L. 107
Callicott, J. B. 22–3, 30, 32–3
Carius, A. 101
Carlassare, E. 109
Carolan, M. S. 121–2
Carson, R. 79, 94, 99–100
Cartier, J. 129, 213
Casey, E. 153
Castree, N. 93, 256
Catholic Church 45
Catton, W. R., Jr. 114–15, 118
Chakrabarty, D. 249
Chalquist, C. 50
Chan, K. 203
Chapouthier, G. 210
Charbonneau, B. 102
Charbonnier, P. 141
Charles, L. 143, 255–6
Chaudary, S. 195
Cherson, A.D.C. 217
Chichilnisky, G. 101
Chivington, G. 214
Chocat, B. 161
Choné, A. 12, 255
Christie, M. 198
Chu, S. 101
Churchill, W. 218
cities: as everywhere and in everything 151–2; as human invention in opposition to nature 148–50; as rural and world future 155; rural/urban dimensions of ecocide 152–4; shape and feel of history in rural/urban space 150–1; sustainable city models 181–3; sustainable urbanism 176–84; urban ecology 158–63
civilization 130–1
Clare, J. 151
Clark, T. 247

Claval, P. 131
Clergeau, P. 162
Clift, R. 160
Cloke, P. 151
Cluet, M. 98
Coetzee, J. M. 229
cognitive psychology 52–3
Colibris 44
Collapse: How Societies Choose to Fail or Succeed (Diamond) 100, 137
collective unconscious 54–5
Common International Classification of Ecosystem Services (CICES) 199
compact city 181
companion species 226–8
complexity theory 50
Comte-Sponville, A. 44
Conklin, H. C. 135
Consalès, J. N. 162
Convention on Biological Diversity 17, 34
Coppinger, R. 241
Country and the City, The (Williams) 75, 147, 151
Cousins, J. 160
Coutard, O. 159–60
creative urbanism 183
critical animal studies 222–3
Critique of the Power of Judgement (Kant) 67
Cronon, W. 147, 247–8
Cruikshank, J. 136
Crutzen, P. 68
cultural animal studies 223–8
culture/nature divide 145–7, 150

Dahan, L. 256
Daniel, T. 206
Danley, B. 195
Dannenberg, A. L. 161, 167
Dantec, M. 89
Davidson, M. 182
Death of Nature, The (Merchant) 77, 106–7
D'Eaubonne, F. 106–7
De Champlain, S. 129
deep ecology 27–36, 43–5, 53
Defoe, D. 80
De Groot, R. 196, 198
degrowth 102–3, 182
Deleuze, G. 224–6
Delort, R. 19
DeLoughrey, E. M. 249
Del Vasto, L. 39, 44
Derrida, J. 226–8
Descartes, R. 209
Descola, P. 69, 90–1, 95, 135–6, 228, 234, 255

De Sousa, C. 177
Deutz, P. 192
Devall, B. 53
Dewey, J. 70
Diamond, J. 95, 100, 137
Dietz, T. 115, 117
Dillard, A. 80
disease 170
Ditfurth, J. 46
diversity 21–4
Diversity of Life, The (Wilson) 33
Division of Labour in Society, The (Durkheim) 119
Dolphijn, R. 70
Dooling, S. 182
Douglas, I. 160, 177–8
Drew, E. 76, 79
Druckman, A. 160
Duflo, C. 84–5
Dumont, R. 100
Dunlap, R. E. 114–15, 118
Dunn, R. 200
Du Pisani, J. A. 176
Dupuy, J. P. 44
Durkheim, É. 118–19
Duvigneaud, P. 159

Earth and Its Inhabitants, The (Reclus) 98
Earth Service, Inc. 41
Earth summits 101
Eckerberg, K. 176
ecocide 147, 152–4, 211–18
ecocriticism: definition of 76–8; diachronic perspective on objects of study 78–81; goals and ambitions of 78; limits of 80–1; origins and meanings of 75–8
Ecocriticism and Geocriticism (Tally & Battista) 81
Ecocriticism Reader, The (Glotfelty) 77
ecofeminism: beyond essentialism and eurocentrism 108–10; challenges 111–12; intersectionality of power relations and 107; overview 106–7; rhizomatic developments 110–11
ECOHUM laboratory 246
Ecological and Postcolonial Study of Literature, An (Marzec) 76
ecological modernization as a social theory (EMT) 116–17, 124
Ecological Psychology (Winter) 49
ecological reform theories 115–18
ecologic-religious mysticism 45–6
Ecology as Politics (Gorz) 102
ecopsychology: challenges 57–9; collective unconscious and our (dis-)connection

with nature 54–5; ecology of psyche 50–2; ecology of psychological approaches 51–4; emergence of 49; importance of establishing sense of sacred in humans and in nature 55–6; mathematics of the organism and 49–50; role of science 56–7, 59; self as archetype of God 49–50
Ecopsychology (Roszak) 49
ecosociology 114, 121–5
ecospirituality: critical views on 45–6; ecologization of religion 40–2; emergence and main ideas of 38–40; spiritualization of ecology 43–4
Ecospirituality Foundation 42
ecosystem services (ES) framework: background and analytical contribution of 197–9; classification categories 199–201; core components in 195; development and adoption of 195–7; influencing social decision-making 205–6; ontological inconsistencies 201–6; relational inconsistencies 199–200; relational models between humans and ecosystems 202–5; scope inconsistencies 200–1
Ecuador 23
Egger, M. M. 41
Eichendorff, J. von 45
Eighteenth-Century Background Studies on the Idea of Nature in the Thought of the Period, The (Willey) 79
Elective Affinities (Goethe) 85–7
Ellul, J. 19, 102
embeddedness 54
Emelianoff, C. 182–4
Émerillons 133
Emerson, R. W. 16, 78
Emmet, R. 249
Endlicher, W. 158
Energy and Equity (Illich) 102
environmental aesthetics: aesthetics of nature and 72–3; distinguishing between environment and nature 68–9; overview 70
environmental degradation theories 115–18
environmental health 171–3
environmental humanities: institutional frameworks for 244–7; open questions and future horizons for 249–52; research agendas and emerging paradigms 247–9
Environmental Humanities journal 244
Environmental Imagination, The (Buell) 76
environmental policies 28–9
environmental pragmatism 34

environmental sociology: revisiting sociology's foundational works 118–21; theories of environmental degradation and ecological reform 115–18; towards an integrating framework for ecosociologies 121–5
environments: forms and 69–70; greenways and blueways 70–2
epistemocriticism: naturalization of social relations 84–6; beyond nature and culture 88–91; nature humanized 86–7; overview 83–4
Erkman, S. 188
Escobedo, F. 200
esotericism 41–2
Essay Concerning the Effect of Air on Human Bodies, An (Arbuthnot) 170
Essentially Speaking: Feminism, Nature and Difference (Fuss) 109
Estes, C. P. 109
ethics: animal ethics 230; of conservation 24; Earth ethic 22; ecocentric 18–19; environmental ethics 230; environmental pragmatism 34; of globality and diversity 21–4; instrumental value 30–3; intrinsic value 17–18, 30–4; land ethic 16, 22, 33, 53; of respect 15–19; of responsibility 16, 19–21, 29, 44
ethnoecocide 213–18
ethnoecology 128
ethnology 132–3
ethological history 240–1
eurocentrism 108–10
European Environmental Humanities Alliance 246–7
European Landscape Convention 154
evolution 130–1

Fabre, É. 241
Faburel, G. 161
Faivre, A. 41–2
Farr, D. 180
Feminism or Death (*Le féminisme ou la mort*) (d'Eaubonne) 106
Ferry, L. 44–6
Fischer-Kowalski, M. 122–4, 187, 190
Fisher, J. 196
Fiske, A. 202–3
Flannery, T. 57
Flaubert, G. 87–8
Foerster, N. 75
Foster, J. B. 117, 119, 124
Foucault, M. 224–7
Fox, J. 172

Fox, M. 56
France 237–9
Francis of Assisi, Saint 41
Freud, S. 51–2
Freudenberg, W. R. 121
Frosch, R. 187–8
Frumkin, H. 172
Fulton, H. 78
Fuss, D. 109

Gaard, G. 107, 109–11
Gaia hypothesis 22, 43, 46, 254
Galen of Pergamon 168
Gallopoulos, N. 187–8
Gandhi, M. K. 39, 44
gardens 86–7
Garrard, G. 76–7, 79, 247
Generosity (Powers) 90
geocriticism 80–1
geography 128–33
Georgescu-Roegen, N. 142, 182
Gersdorf, C. 89
Gertler, N. 191
gestalt psychology 53
Gibbs, D. 192
Giddens, A. 180
giraffe 237–9
globality 21–4
Glotfelty, C. 77
Godin, C. 217
Goethe, J. W. von 63, 85–7
Goodboy, A. 84
Goode, D. 233
Gore, A. 217, 251
Gorz, A. 102
Gottlieb, R. S. 43
Graedel, T. 187, 192
grafting 86–7
Graunt, J. 169
Green Letters 78
Greenpeace 23
green political parties 103
greenways 70–2
Grenard, P. 136
Griffin, S. 106–7
Grinde, D. A. 217
Grubacic, A. 102
Guattari, F. 146, 152–3, 224–6
Guiana 214–15
Guillerme, J. 159

Haberl, H. 86–8, 190
Hadot, P. 63
Haeckel, E. 99
Hailwood, S. 182

Hajek, I. 142, 162, 255–6
Hajer, M. 180
Hamilton, C. 100
Hamman, P. 143, 181, 255–6
Handley, G. B. 249
Hannon the Great 129
Harari, Y. 154
Haraway, D. 89, 152, 210, 224, 227, 233, 250
Hardy, T. 79
Harrison, R. P. 150
Harvey, W. 169
Hasbach, P. 54, 58, 247
Hauck, J. 197
Haupts, F. 197
Hayden, T. 41
health 166–73
Heidegger, M. 19, 222
Heise, U. 249
Hepburn, R. 67
Hermitte, M. A. 23
Hernández-Morcillo, M. 202
Herodotus 129
Herzfeld, C. 240
Herzog, W. 250
Hess, G. 190
Higgins, P. 217
Hillman, J. 57, 59
Hippocratic anthropology 167–70
Hirsch, R. E. 100
history: animal studies 228–9; constructing animal history 232–41; ethological history 240–1; as lived by animals 236–7; looking at real animals 232–6
Hitchings, R. 151
Hitt, C. 79
Ho, M. W. 50
Hobbes, T. 224
Hoffman, F. 170
Hoffmann, E.T.A. 229
Holden, J. 101
Holden, M. 183
Holleman, H. 119
Holling, C. S. 184
Holloway, J. 102
Hooke, R. 170
Hopkins, R. 52
Hornborg, A. 249
Houellebecq, M. 90
Howe, C. 197
Hulme, M. 196
human–animal studies 222–3
human exceptionalist paradigm (HEP) 114, 118
Humanimalia 222

264 Index

humanistic psychology 53
Humanities for the Environment (website) 245
Humboldt, A. von 129
Huseman, J. 217
hygiene 166

Illich, I. 102, 167
Imperative of Responsibility, The (Jonas) 20, 97
Inconvenient Truth, An (Gore) 251
industrial ecology: copying from nature and 192–3; ecology and 189–91; lessons from Kalundborg 191–2; principles 187–9
industrial growth society 58
Ingold, T. 69, 95, 134, 136–7, 145, 147, 150, 233
inner nature 256
Institute for Critical Animal Studies 221
instrumental value 30–3
Intergovernmental Panel on Climate Change (IPCC) 101
International Perspectives in Feminist Ecocriticism (Gaard) 111
International Union for Conservation of Nature (IUCN) 23
intrinsic value 17–18, 32–4
Iovino, S. 111
ISLE: Interdisciplinary Studies in Literature and Environment 78
ISLE Reader, The 8, 76

James, P. 160
Jamieson, D. 23, 30
Jean-Brunhes Delamarre, M. 132–3
Jenness, D. 134–5
Johansen, B. 217
John Paul II, Pope 45
Johnstone, J. 246
Jonas, H. 20–1, 23, 39, 94, 97
Jones, O. 142, 150–1, 155, 255
Jorland, G. 170–1
Joss, S. 183
Journal of Critical Animal Studies 222
Jung, C. G. 39, 49–52, 58–9
Juris, J. S. 102

Kaeppelin, P. 130–1
Kafka, F. 225, 229
Kagan, S. 63
Kahn, P., Jr. 54, 58, 247
Kalundborg, Denmark 191–2
Kant, I. 17, 21, 67
Kater Murr (Hoffmann) 229
Kay, J. J. 188

Kenis, A. 257
Kerridge, R. 77, 80
Kheel, M. 108
Ki-moon, B. 101
King, M. L., Jr. 44
Kingston, R. 177, 182
Klein, N. 57
Koffka, K. 53
Kohler, F. 233
Kohler, W. 53
Kolbert, E. 250
Kreitler, P. 41
Krueger, R. 183
Kull, C. 202

Lamb Lash, J. 44
Landis Barnhill, D. 43
Land of Little Rain, The (Austin) 78
Langner, M. 158
Larrère, C. 12, 24, 255
Larrère, R. 24
Latouche, S. 102, 217
Latour, B. 23, 147, 224, 227–8, 254
Lauwers, M. 94, 255–6
Leclerc, A. 171
Lekan, T. M. 45, 249
Leland, S. 107
Lele, S. 200
Leopold, A. 16, 18–19, 22, 31, 33, 53–4, 99
Lessons in Darkness? (Herzog) 250
Levinas, E. 226, 228
Lévi-Strauss, C. 136
Lévy, J. P. 142, 159–161, 255–6
Lewin, K. 52
Lidskog, R. 118
Lievens, M. 257
Lifset, R. 187
Light, A. 16
Lindzen, R. 100
Linnaeus, C. 88
Lippit, A. M. 228
Littérature et environnement. Pour une écocritique comparée (Suberchicot) 80
Locke, J. 169–70
Lockie, S. 179–80
Lomborg, B. 100
Love, G. 77
Lovelock, J. 39
Lubchenco, J. 101
L'utopie ou la mort! [Utopia or Death!] (Dumont) 100

McCright, A. 118
McGrew, W. C. 240
McHugh, S. 222

McKibben, B. 147
MacLeod, G. 179, 183
McMichael, P. 124–5
Macnaghten, P. 117
Macy, J. 51, 56
Making Sense of Nature (Castree) 256
Malaurie, J. 136, 217
Malebranche, N. 209
Malm, A. 249
Man and Nature or Physical Geography as Modified by Human Action (Marsh) 67, 98
Mander, J. 218
Manuel-Navarrete, D. 121
Marsh, G. P. 39, 67, 98
Martinez-Alier, J. 93
Marvin, G. 222
Marx, K. 119, 124, 141–2
Marzec, R. P. 76
Maslow, A. 53
Mathews, F. 155
Mathieu, N. 141, 177
Mauch, C. 87
Mauss, M. 136
Mayer, S. 89
Meadows, D. H. 102
Mellon Foundation 245
Melville, H. 229
Memoirs of a Donkey (Ségur) 237
Menzel, S. 197
Merchant, C. 77, 106–7
Merleau-Ponty, M. 22, 54, 68–9
Merritt, D. 13, 50, 52, 56–7, 59
metabolism 119–20, 144, 160, 179, 187, 190
Metamorphosis, The (Kafka) 225
metaphysical anthropocentrism 24
Michaud, Y. 89
Mid Sweden University 246
Mies, M. 107, 109
Miklosi, A. 234, 240–1
Millennium Ecosystem Assessment (MEA) 195, 199–202
mixed city 181
Moby-Dick (Melville) 229
Mohanty, C. 109–10
Mohawks 137
Mohicans 214
Mol, A.P.J. 116–17
moral anthropocentrism 24
Morgan, L. H. 131
Mormont, M. 149
Morton, T. 250
Moser, G. 161
Muir, J. 16, 67
Müller, T. 247
Muradian, R. 144, 256

Murard, L. 171
Murdoch, J. 149
Murphy, P. D. 111–12

Naess, A. 12, 34–6, 39, 43, 53, 99
Nash, R. 17
Natchez 214
National Religious Partnership for the Environment 41
Native Americans 133–4, 213–15
native knowledge 135–7
Nattero, R. 42
natural evolutionism 131
nature: aesthetics of 67–73, 161–3; collective unconscious and our (dis-)connection with 54–5; copying from 192–3; culture/nature divide 145–7, 150; distinguishing between environment and 68–9; ecospirituality and 40–2; epistemocritical perspectives on 83–91; health and 166–73; humanized 86–8; importance of establishing sense of sacred in humans and in 55–6; as legal subject 44; losing 147–8; rurality and 148–50; urban ecology and 161–3; value of 16–19
Nature (Emerson) 67, 78
Nature in American Literature (Foerster) 75
Nature of Man (Polybus) 168
Naturphilosophie 39, 41, 87
Navet, É. 95, 133, 209, 255–6
Nazarea, V. 136
Near View of the High Sierra, A (Muir) 67
New Age movement 42, 46
new ecological paradigm (NEP) 114
Newell, J. 160
Neyret, L. 217
Nicomachean Ethics (Aristotle) 31
Nixon, R. 249
Nocke, T. 251
Norgaard, R. B. 121
Norton, B. G. 18, 34

Obama, B. 101
Observations on the Feeling of the Beautiful and Sublime (Kant) 67
Odum, E. P. 159
Ojibwa 133
Oppermann, S. 111
Oregon State University 245

pagan cults 42
Pagden, A. 19
Palmer, C. 228
Papaux, A. 255

Parikka, J. 228
Parsons, T. 114
participatory city 181–2
particules élementaires, Les (*Atomised*) (Houellebecq) 90
Pasteur, L. 171
Pattberg, P. 256
Pequot 214
Peraldo, E. 64, 256
Perception of the Environment, The (Ingold) 134
Perls, F. 53
Perrot, N. 129
Petty, W. 169
Pfeiffer, E. 42
Phillips, D. 249
philosophy 15, 27, 228, 233
phytocide 216
Piaget, J. 52
Pister, E. P. 30
Pitte, J. R. 72
Plains Indians 214
Plato 31
Plumwood, V. 107, 224, 229, 247
Polanyi, K. 141
political ecology: development of 97; early centres and thinkers of 'ecologism' 98–9; heuristics of fear and 97, 99–101; from *Lebensreform* to 97–103; market ecology *vs*. growth objectors 102–3
Politics, The (Aristotle) 168
Polo, Marco 129
Porter, R. 170, 172
postcolonial ecocriticism 5
postcolonialism 76, 248
posthuman paradigm 88–91, 248
Powers, R. 90
Practical Ecocriticism (Love) 77
pragmatic dynamic 256
Pratt, A. C. 149
Prelude (Wordsworth) 79
Primavesi, A. 43
Princeton Environmental Institute 245
Pröpper, M. 197
psyche 50–2, 57
psychoanalysis 51–2
psychology 49, 51–4
public health 170–1
Public Health Act of 1875 170
Public Health Law of 1902 170
Pye, L. 59

Rachel Carson Center for Environment and Society 246
Ramazzini, B. 170

Ramsey, M. 170
Randers, J. 102
rationalism 45, 109
Ratzel, F. 128
Recht, R. 88
Reclus, É. 98
recyclable city 181
Redclift, M. 118, 121, 178
reflexive dynamic 256
Relation of the Hanunoo Culture to the Plant World, The (Conklin) 135
religion 38–47, 49–59, 128–37, 169, 234
Republic (Plato) 31
Repussard, C. 94, 98, 256
Research Foundation for Science Technology and Ecology 102
Resilience: A Journal of the Environmental Humanities 244
respect 16–19
responsibility 19–21, 29, 44
Revkin, A. C. 243
Richards, D. J. 188
Richter, L. 118
Rigby, K. 84
Riley, J. C. 170
Robbe, P. 136
Robin, L. 146, 244
Robinson, R. 55–6
Robinson Crusoe (Defoe) 80
Roger, A. 72
Rolston, H., III 16, 32–3, 43
Romantic Ecology (Bate) 79
Romanticism 46
Roncayolo, M. 141
Roosevelt, T. 16
Rosa, E. A. 115, 117–18
Rose, D. 244
Roszak, T. 49, 58
Routley, R. 16, 31
Routley, V. 31
Rozzi, R. 43
Rueckert, W. 75
rurality: nature and 148–50; rural/urban dimensions of ecocide 152–4; shape and feel of history in rural/urban space 150–1
Ruse, M. 43
Rutherford, J. 160
Ryley, N. 56

Sachs, J. D. 101
sacred 55–6
Safir, M. A. 83
Sagan, C. 55
Sahlins, M. 136

Salem, G. 171
Salleh, A. 107, 110
Sammells, N. 77, 80
Sampson, S. 58
Sand County Almanac, A (Leopold) 16, 18, 22, 31, 33, 99
Sanders, C. 233
Sarkar, C. 167
Sauter, M. 247
Scarce, R. 101
Schaeffer, J. M. 187
Scheffer, M. 88
Schnaiberg, A. 116–17
Schneider, B. 251
Schneider, M. 124–5
Schröter, M. 196
science 56–7, 59
science fiction 77
Scott, B. 55, 57–8
Seasons, The (Thomson) 79–80
Ségur, S., comtesse de 237
Self 50
Serres, M. 44
Sessions, G. 53
Shackley, S. 117
Shamdasani, S. 49
Shapiro, J. 200
Shapiro, K. 233
Shaw, C. 218
Sheridan, P. 214
Shiva, V. 102, 107, 109
Short, D. 217
Short, J. R. 146, 148
Silent Spring (Carson) 79, 100
Silvertown, J. 197
simplicité volontaire contre le mythe de l'abondance, La (Ariès) 102
Sitter, J. 76, 79
Skeptical Environmentalist, The (Lomborg) 100
Skinner, B. F. 52
social evolutionism 131
social metabolism 122–5
social mixing 181–2
social psychology 52
Société royale de médecine 171
Spinoza, B. 39
Staszak, J. F. 168
Staudenmaier, P. 46
Steedman, I. 103
Steiner, R. 39, 42
Stengers, I. 86, 152–3
Steward, J. H. 135
STIRPAT model 116–17
Stoll, M. 169

Suberchicot, A. 80
Sullivan, H. 249
supporting services 199–200
sustainable urbanism: challenges 183–4; epistemological and practical controversies 179–81; major models 181; (re)thinking urbanism in era of sustainability 176–9; sustainable city and 179–83; sustainable development and 179–83
Sustainable Urbanism: Urban Design with Nature (Farr) 180
Swyngedouw, E. 181, 183
Sydenham, T. 169–70

Tabuteau, D. 171
Tally, R. T., Jr. 80–1
Tarnas, R. 59
Taylor, N. 222
Taylor, P. 17, 32
technology 19–20
Teilhard de Chardin, P. 39, 56
Teko 133, 215
Teng, J. 197
terra nullius 213
Testart, A. 136
Tetlock, P. 203
Thomas, L. V. 211
Thomson, J. 79
Thoreau, H. D. 16, 44, 78, 99
Thrift, N. 151
Tootoosis, E. 216
Topal, J. 240–1
total economic value (TEV) approach 198
Tour Thro' the Whole Island of Great Britain, A (Defoe) 80
Toward an Ecological Society (Bookchin) 102
traditional ecological knowledge (TEK) 135–6
traditional societies: ethnoecocide 213–18; health and 167–8; native knowledge 135–7; origin of the world for 133–5
Transatlantic Research Network in the Environmental Humanities 246
transition towns 184
transpersonal psychology 53
Tuin, I. 70
Tupi-Guarani 133
Turner, K. 198
Tuttle, W. 154
Twine, R. 111, 222
Tyler, N. 223

Udell, M. 233
United Nations Environment Programme (UNEP) 23

University of California, Davis 245
University of California, Irvine 248
University of California, Los Angeles 245
University of California, Santa Barbara 245
University of Munich (LMU) 246
University of Pennsylvania 245
University of Utah 245
University of Wisconsin-Madison 245
urban ecology: conceptual framework for public action 161–3; long-standing conceptual framework 159–60; paradigm shift 160–1
urban public policy 183–4
Urry, J. 117
Utter, J. 213–14

Vaillancourt, J. G. 218
Valéry, P. 218
value 17–18, 30
Vanolo, A. 177
Viard, J. 160
Vicart, M. 233
Vignon, R. 214
Viitanen, J. 177, 182
Vilkka, L. 30
Viridis Graduate Institute of Ecopsychology and Environmental Humanities 59
Voice of the Earth, The (Roszak) 49
voluntary simplicity 44, 102–3

Walden (Thoreau) 16, 67, 78, 99
Wallace, K. 89
Walter, F. 19
Ward, C. 151
Warleniusa, R. 124
Warren, K. 107
Washington, G. 213
Wassenaar, T. 190
Watt, J. 68
Wayampi 215
Wayana 215
Webb, S. 155
Weber, A. G. 88
Weber, M. 119, 159
Weil, K. 229

Weintrobe, S. 51, 54
Weiss, K. 161
Welzer, H. 100
Wertheimer, M. 53
Westphal, B. 80
White, L. Jr. 12, 15, 19, 31, 40
White, L. A. 135
Whitehead, M. 177
Whiten, A. 240
Widmark, C. 195
Wild, M. 228
wilderness 17–18
Wilderness Act of 1964 17
Wilke, S. 246, 255–6
Wilkinson, R. G. 171
Willey, B. 79
Williams, R. 75, 147, 151
Williams, R. H. 150
Wilson, E. O. 33, 58
Winter, D.D.N. 49, 52–4, 58
Winthrop, R. 202
Wolfe, C. 249
Wolman, A. 159
Woman and Nature: The Roaring Inside Her (Griffin) 106
Women Who Run with Wolves (Estes) 109
Woodgate, G. 95, 118, 121, 178, 256
Woods, M. 149
Wordsworth, W. 79
world climate summits 101
World Health Organization (WHO) 166, 173
World until Yesterday: What We Can Learn from Traditional Societies, The (Diamond) 137
World Wide Fund for Nature (WWF) 23, 147, 153
Worster, D. 158
Writing for an Endangered World (Buell) 76
Wynne, B. 117–18

Zapf, H. 247
Zavalloni, M. 103
Zelli, F. 256
zoocide 216
Zylberman, P. 171